The Gospel of J. Edgar Hoover

The Gospel of
J. Edgar
Hoover

HOW THE FBI AIDED AND ABETTED THE RISE OF WHITE CHRISTIAN NATIONALISM

Lerone A. Martin

PRINCETON UNIVERSITY PRESS

PRINCETON AND OXFORD

Published by Princeton University Press
41 William Street, Princeton, New Jersey 08540
99 Banbury Road, Oxford OX2 6JX

press.princeton.edu

All Rights Reserved
First paperback printing 2025
Paperback ISBN 9780691259659
Cloth ISBN 9780691175119
ISBN (e-book) 9780691244983
LCCN: 2022010826

British Library Cataloging-in-Publication Data is available

Editorial: Fred Appel and James Collier
Production Editorial: Sara Lerner
Text and Jacket/Cover Design: Heather Hansen
Production: Erin Suydam
Publicity: Kare Hensley and Kathryn Stevens
Copyeditor: Karen Verde

Frontis: FBI Director J. Edgar Hoover shaking hands with noted religious broadcaster and revivalist Billy Graham at FBI Headquarters, May 1, 1969. Source: Record Group 065, Photos of FBI Personnel and Activities, 1935–1972, Still Pictures, Photo HN-9005, Box 17, National Archives and Records Administration, II, College Park, MD

This book has been composed in Arno Pro with Clarendon URW

For my parents—

Larry & Rose Martin

Who raised their children according to Matthew 7:12,
"In everything, therefore, treat people the same way you
want them to treat you, for this is the Law and the Prophets."

Contents

Prologue: Suing the FBI

I sued the FBI to write this book. On August 12, 2018, I filed suit against the US Department of Justice (DOJ) for FBI records on Billy Graham (*Martin v. United States Department of Justice, 2018*, Case Number 18-1885). I was convinced the preacher had an FBI file. No American in the mid-twentieth century could reach his level of fame, notoriety, and influence, yet manage to escape the vigilant, prying eyes of Hoover's FBI. And no civilian was permitted into Hoover's inner sanctum for a staged photograph without knowingly or unknowingly enduring a thorough background check. In one way or another, Graham was involved with the FBI, and I thought the Freedom of Information Act (FOIA) was the key to find out how. But I was wrong. The FBI played hardball, so I sued. It was my only recourse, a desperate attempt to force the FBI to abide by the FOIA.

Revelation is the purpose of the modern FOIA. President Lyndon Johnson signed it into law on Independence Day, 1966. LBJ publicly praised the bill, which gave Americans the opportunity to petition for records of US executive branch agencies. "This legislation springs from one of our most essential principles: a democracy works best when the people have all the information that the security of the Nation permits," he proudly announced. Privately, however, the president despised the bill, allowing it to languish on his desk. Johnson finally signed "the fucking thing," as he scornfully referred to it, after much persuasion, narrowly ducking its pocket veto. His reluctant attitude foreshadowed how executive branch agencies would execute the law.[1]

My ordeal with Graham gave me firsthand experience with their approach. I made my original FOIA request on February 21, 2018. It was the day Graham died, and his legal privacy rights, at least in textual materials, went to the grave with him. The FBI acknowledged my FOIA request, yet failed to make a determination within the twenty-day statutory deadline mandated by Congress. The FBI did not bother to claim "unusual" or "exceptional" circumstances to excuse their malfeasance. They just ignored me. I heard from the Bureau almost two months later. The April letter was as bold as the typeface in which it was set. The Bureau did not concede breaking the law. They simply informed me they would not disclose or even acknowledge the existence of any records concerning Billy Graham and his relationship to law enforcement or national security. These were significant and ironic exclusions for Graham. The preacher had advised US presidents for more than half a century, advocating evangelical Christianity as the key to national security, yet there would be no disclosures. If the FBI determined there were files that resided outside of this broad purview, they pledged to make them public via their FOIA website at some undisclosed date in the future. Then, and only then, would I be informed. The Trump DOJ dug in their heels. This should not have been surprising. President Donald Trump's attorney general, William Barr, was constantly lambasting the FOIA as a dangerous nuisance, that amounted to "constant harassment" of the DOJ. I decided to join the torrent of disturbance, filing suit in the US District Court for the District of Columbia.[2]

The civil litigation produced a saga of hide and seek, lost and found. The FBI admitted a number of records on Graham had been destroyed in accordance with a 1986 court order. The ruling created the FBI Records Retention Plan, a rubric that assigns preservation schedules for FBI files based on their potential research value. More than three decades later, the same court informed me that records pertaining to the nation's most famous evangelist had been legally destroyed by the FBI. What was valuable to me was deemed legally disposable by the FBI. Worse, the FBI testified that other files had been lost or were "unable to be located." Judge Christopher R. Cooper, an Obama appointee, supervised the FBI as it located and turned over files on a rolling basis. The FBI produced a deluge of documents detailing investigations of deranged death threats targeting Graham, as well as an obsessive amount of

newspaper clippings covering the preacher's whereabouts and statements. However, there was nothing detailing Graham's relationship to
Hoover, the FBI, or any other executive agency.

The promised transparency of President Biden's administration pro-
vided false hope. In July 2021, Kathleene Molen, Assistant United States
Attorney (AUSA) for the US Attorney's Office for the District of Columbia, brought good tidings. AUSA Molen informed my counsel, Tuan
Samahon, "the FBI has located a file that it had previously been unable
to locate. The FBI indicates that the file is related to Billy Graham."[3]
With no explanation, the FBI miraculously "found" a thirty-page file on
Billy Graham. I did not care if it was the result of an actual miracle, political timing, or just the correction of incompetence: I counted it a
godsend. But my joy was short-lived. The once lost, now found file was
largely more of what I had already received.

But I refused to stop. The case was settled, with the DOJ agreeing to
pay "for attorney fees and other litigation costs." Upon turning my
attention to Graham's official archives, I quickly learned the FBI had a
co-conspirator in its archival cover-up. Shortly after my public lawsuit,
Billy Graham's son Franklin Graham, a staunch right-wing evangelist,
announced Billy Graham's archival holdings would be moved from their
original longtime home of Wheaton College to North Carolina. This
may not have been a coincidence. The FBI has a practice of releasing
"High Visibility Memoranda," warning various government and civic
entities of a proposed release of high-profile files and the possible
fallout.[4] The Bureau denied the existence of such a memo in my case.
However, the result was the same. Billy Graham's family took cover,
protecting Billy Graham's legacy as the figurehead and proxy of modern
white evangelicalism at all costs. Now Graham's archival holdings, dating back to 1940, are under the complete control and supervision of the
Graham family, specifically Franklin Graham, and cannot be accessed
without his blessing.

The younger Graham is the latest in a long line of white evangelicals
vying to protect and police the legacy of modern white evangelicalism
and its complicated relationship with white Christian nationalism. Pioneering white evangelical institutions such as *Christianity Today*, the

National Association of Evangelicals, and the National Religious Broadcasters have scrubbed detailed references to J. Edgar Hoover and the FBI from their respective archives. The deafening silence led me to seek FBI files on the white evangelical world that surrounded Billy Graham—the clergy, churches, magazines, and organizations the evangelist helped to establish—the foundational entities of modern white evangelicalism.

My labor was not in vain. The pages that follow draw upon thousands of newly declassified and released FBI files. The revelations therein are enhanced by my interviews with FBI special agents who worked for Hoover. Together, they show that J. Edgar Hoover and his FBI were central to postwar religion and politics. Hoover's FBI joined forces with the founding architects of white evangelicalism to aid and abet the rise of white Christian nationalism as a legitimate force in American politics. *The Gospel of J. Edgar Hoover* moves this partnership out of the shadows and into the light.

This discovery illuminates the past, helping to explain twenty-first century US religion and politics. Following a string of white Christian nationalist violence, most notably the January 6, 2021, attack on the nation's Capitol, the FBI announced renewed efforts to squarely deal with the domestic security threat of white Christian nationalism. The Bureau's mission will be hampered if it does not trace the multiple origins, dwelling places, and institutional expressions of the threat—even if that trail leads all the way back to FBI headquarters and field offices. Likewise, many prominent white evangelicals have stated a desire to better understand when and how white nationalism came to possess a large portion of the movement. They believe this quest will help exorcise the demons. This book calls them to reconsider the very foundations of modern white evangelicalism, to reckon with the fact that the groundwork was laid, in part, by J. Edgar Hoover and his FBI.

J. Edgar Hoover's Stained Glass Window

On Sunday morning, June 26, 1966, the Capitol Hill Methodist Church dedicated a magnificent thirty-three-foot-tall stained glass window to FBI Director J. Edgar Hoover. It was the congregation's second worship service in their new million-dollar church (an expenditure of about $17 million today). The prominent 1,200-member all-white congregation, located just five blocks from the US Capitol, purposely built the new church "precisely on the spot of the birthplace of Mr. Hoover." The church was erected as an evangelical shrine to J. Edgar Hoover, and the glorious window was consecrated: "THE J. EDGAR HOOVER WINDOW."[1]

With J. Edgar Hoover seated in the front pew, Protestants of all stripes praised him as a Christian champion. Hoover's pastor, Reverend Dr. Edward L. R. Elson, spoke for the masses of white evangelicals. The Presbyterian clergyman was a founding contributor to *Christianity Today*—the literary mouthpiece of modern white evangelicalism. He told the congregation that naming the window after Hoover "was eminently merited and highly appropriate." The pastor of the Methodist church, Reverend Edward Lewis, preached the sermon. The shepherd of the largest white Protestant church in Washington, DC, chose the divine calling of Samuel as his biblical text. His sermon drew a parallel between Samuel and Hoover. Samuel answered God's call to turn Israel away from sin and idolatry, and toward God. J. Edgar Hoover had done likewise: he heeded God's call to turn America away from subversion and back to

FIGURE 1. A view from the pulpit. *Source*: Photographic History of the J. Edgar Hoover Window—J. Edgar Hoover Estate Collection of the National Law Enforcement Museum, Accession number 2010.11.

God. The congregation received the sermon by offering thanks for Hoover's service, followed by a plea that he would be the first among many white male Christian defenders. "We honor today . . . a man of Christian stature and national leadership," they prayed, "we offer our thanks to thee for such men as J. Edgar Hoover and pray that more like men will be forthcoming in our nation."[2]

Methodist Bishop Wilbur E. Hammaker offered the prayer of dedication. After he confessed to being "an unashamed hero worshipper" of Hoover, the virulent anti-communist elder blessed the window. "In the name of the Father, Almighty God, I dedicate the 'J. Edgar Hoover Window' at the Capitol Hill Methodist Church in the shadow of the nation's capitol proclaiming to the throngs that will see it that Christian virtues produce great statesmanship." A large tablet was blessed and fixed on the interior and exterior of the window for all to see: "THE J. EDGAR

FIGURE 2. A view from outside. *Source*: Photographic History of the J. Edgar Hoover Window—J. Edgar Hoover Estate Collection of the National Law Enforcement Museum, Accession number 2010.11.

HOOVER WINDOW: Statesmanship Through the Christian Virtues. Dedicated on June 26, 1966 to J. Edgar Hoover Director of the Federal Bureau of Investigation who was born on this site January 1, 1895."[3]

The service culminated with a congregational prayer of nationalism. The faithful beseeched God for salvation not by supernatural means, but through Hoover and his federal agency. "We are grateful for the consistent work of the Federal Bureau of Investigation under his leadership," they prayed in unison, "through their direction, make of us citizens who honor God."[4]

Why did white evangelicals look to J. Edgar Hoover to lead them to salvation when the FBI director was not a "born-again" Christian? Why did they crown him their political champion when court cases such as *Coplon v. United States, 1950*, revealed the FBI director regularly ordered his agents to conduct unlawful break-ins and unconstitutional surveillance, and to lie about it under oath? Why was Hoover deemed the aspirational model of white Christian manhood and the foremost protector of family values when he never married, but for more than three decades enjoyed a domestic partnership with the FBI's second in charge, Special Agent Clyde Tolson? And, perhaps most important, what does this glorification of J. Edgar Hoover tell us about the FBI and modern white evangelicalism?

The Gospel of J. Edgar Hoover answers these questions. It explains why white evangelicals—from the pulpit to the pew, from the local church to the international parachurch—honored FBI Director J. Edgar Hoover as an anointed leader. Specifically, the book chronicles how Hoover built up the FBI as a white Christian force that partnered with white evangelicals to aid and abet the rise of white Christian nationalism.

This story is not a rumination of an evangelical outsider. I was saved in the evangelical tradition and educated in its white institutions. This is not a narrative of decline, in which a once pure faith was hijacked by disingenuous political operatives beginning in the 1970s. Rather, it is a history of the modern origins of white evangelical moral and political norms. What follows, then, is not a history of the white evangelical fringe, nor an accounting of white evangelical exceptions. It is a story that details how foundational figures and entities of mainstream white evangelicalism and the everyday faithful willingly partnered with J. Edgar Hoover and the extralegal practices of his FBI to bring America back to their God.

White Christian nationalism—the impulse to make whiteness and conservative Christianity the foundation and guidepost of American governance and culture—has received renewed attention in public discourse of late. Histories of its development in postwar America have rightly centered on the influence of white evangelical Christianity. Studies have identified clergy, politicians, captains of industry, Hollywood, the military, and suburbanization as driving forces of white Christian nationalism. White evangelicals confronted the New Deal, the Cold War, and the Civil Rights Movement by merging their Jesus with American notions of whiteness, virulent anti-communism, capitalism, hypermasculinity, and political conservatism.[5]

The FBI was a major part of this landscape, yet it has been overlooked. President Franklin Roosevelt issued a series of presidential directives in the 1930s which morphed Hoover's FBI from a small outfit investigating interstate crimes, to the nation's largest domestic intelligence agency. As the bulwark of national security, the bureau was conspicuous in American anti-communism. Hoover and his all-white male Christian force of special agents served as the producers, directors, and stars of the ideological drama that was the Cold War. Hoover and his FBI set the table upon which white evangelicals feasted. The FBI also served as the clearinghouse of national belonging, defending the status quo, and regulating who should participate in the democratic process. Hoover's white Christian nationalist worldview determined legitimate statecraft from subversion, and godliness from atheism.

Narrow definitions of evangelicalism have hindered us from perceiving Hoover's evangelical significance. Scholars and journalists have largely relied on professionally defined theological commitments— ultimate biblical authority, Christ atonement, conversion, prayer, evangelism, social reform, and church membership—to determine who is in the white evangelical camp.[6] However, salvation is a cosmic matter for white evangelicals, far too important to leave exclusively in the hands of theological and professional elites. White evangelical faith has never lived by theology alone, but by the very practices of the faithful. It is a lived faith, a religious identity that is constructed and maintained in daily practices—consumption habits, voting, political affiliations—that take place outside of official evangelical institutions. And the lived experience of postwar white evangelicalism has been marked by steadfast commitments to white Christian nationalism: a worldview and cultural framework centered on the fusion of American civic life and a particular Christian identity. This all-encompassing faith assumes the naturalness and righteousness of nativism, white supremacy, patriarchal authority, heteronormativity, gender difference, and militarism.[7] These evangelical commitments made J. Edgar Hoover a white evangelical not by virtue of being born-again, nor by church membership or name, but by something far more important: his fight for a white Christian nationalist nation. As the editors of *Christianity Today* joyfully announced in 1962, J. Edgar Hoover was not only a part of the message of white evangelicalism, he was also part of its "mission."[8]

Hoover was an important part of the evangelical errand. He did not simply ride the wave of Cold War evangelicalism; he helped to create it. He fused together virulent anti-communism with what would become the other political hallmarks of the movement: anti-statist statism, Christian traditionalism, subplot epistemology, and individual liberty. Hoover's career embodied anti-statist statism. He bemoaned the rise of the New Deal liberal state, yet he owed his increasing power to the very same enlarged federal apparatus. He welcomed government involvement in American life when it enforced his traditional Christian notions of sexuality, gender, and race, yet he decried the tentacles of "big government" when state reforms ran counter to his beliefs (i.e., racial integration, school busing, voting protections). His subplot epistemology saw an existential crisis behind every political difference. Hoover did not view actions, ideas, or policies that countered his Christian worldview as simply differing opinions. Rather, Hoover saw such differences as subplots to a grand cosmic conspiracy to destroy the nation. Therefore, his commitment to individual liberty hinged upon virtue. Liberty was not licentiousness, but an ordered freedom in which government helped to cultivate virtuous individual souls. Virtue stood guard, protecting liberty. Statecraft had to be soulcraft. Hoover's faith served as the foundation of it all: a white Christian nationalism that wedded conservative Christianity and American statecraft. The nation, he once told an NBC audience, had to have "faith to be free." When postwar white evangelical conservatives heard the gospel of Hoover, they believed they heard the gospel truth.[9]

Studies of the FBI have also been slow to pinpoint this gospel. Scholars of the Bureau rarely consider the director's faith, let alone its influence upon the Bureau and the nation. Yet, during Hoover's lifetime, his faith and storied religious partnerships were central to how Americans understood him and his Bureau. Histories of the FBI have chronicled the FBI's surveillance of clergy and its antagonism toward faith communities. This book narrates the Bureau's embrace and promotion of faith. Previous histories have identified which religious folk Hoover deemed subversive—Dorothy Day, Father Berrigan, Fannie Lou Hamer, Malcolm X. Now it is time to focus on which clergy the FBI Boss branded as partners. The Bureau had many enemies, but it also had plenty of friends. History has shown us how the Bureau attempted to silence its enemies, hindering democratic debate, and ultimately push American politics toward an authoritarian far right. *The Gospel of J. Edgar Hoover* offers a new story, detailing how the religious commitments of Hoover and his FBI also ushered our nation's politics toward the *religious* right.[10]

The following pages tell the story. Part 1, "Proselytizing Faith," displays how Hoover—the longest-standing high-level appointee in US government history—made white Christian nationalism the bedrock of the modern national security state. US presidents came and went, as did ruling political paradigms, and crises, but Hoover remained. As FBI director from 1924 until his death in 1972, Hoover was a political constant, paying lip service to the Constitution, but establishing white Christian nationalism as the actual foundation of his FBI. It mattered little who was in office or which party was in control of Congress. Faith helped him determine the nation's enemies and how they should be attacked and defeated. He saw national security in cosmic terms. Nothing was more existential than national security, the very salvation of the nation's soul.[11]

Hoover remade the FBI—the federal agency in charge of the nation's domestic security—in his own image: a squadron of white men who viewed themselves as white Christian soldiers and ministers. They were spiritually and morally formed by the FBI's religious culture, a suite of religious practices that took on both Catholic and Protestant forms. Hoover's white Christian nationalism eschewed the rampant anti-Catholicism of the day in favor of a unified white Christian order. Maintaining a white Christian nation required that all respectable white Christian men join the struggle, regardless of ecclesiastical commitments or theological differences. As part of their training, FBI special agents pledged to be Christian soldiers and ministers, while also attending FBI spiritual retreats and special worship services run by leading white Catholic and Protestant clergy. The FBI made it very clear: a secure and safe America was a Christian America, one in which white evangelicals and conservative white Catholics worked together to maintain the levers of cultural and political power. The FBI was the nation's defense against the enemy within. And the Bureau's religious culture fashioned the G-men accordingly, shaping them into an army of white male Christian nationalists commissioned to protect, serve, and maintain Christian America. The FBI had a "Christian purpose," Hoover told his troops. Their federal duty was to "*defend* and *perpetuate* the dignity of the Nation's Christian endowment."[12]

Part 2, "Promoting Faith," explains how Hoover and white evangelicals partnered to authenticate and materially support white Christian nationalism. Both shared the same claims upon the nation-state. They firmly believed America was founded as a Christian nation, and the country would be destroyed the moment it ceased to be. Hoover called it "Americanism," while Billy Graham and other white evangelicals called it "Christian America." It was the same belief: a cultural framework that venerated and advocated for the fusion of white conservative Christianity with American civic life.[13] They viewed one another as valuable partners for their shared crusade. As the majority of mainline white Protestants turned toward liberalism and the social gospel, Hoover saw white evangelicals as a vital means to save the nation and keep the country on the path of Americanism. White evangelicals, in turn, saw Hoover as a warrior, fighting to preserve Christian America. They were soldiers in the same army.

Every war has its propaganda. The FBI and white evangelicals teamed up to promote their shared nationalism through the pages of *Christianity*

Today, all at the expense of taxpayers. The messages were a hit. White evangelicals lauded Hoover's words as sacred gospel. In lieu of their own sermons, preachers preached Hoover's epistles verbatim from the pulpit, making Hoover the ghostwriter of countless white evangelical sermons. Other clergy, such as Billy Graham, peppered their sermons with quotes from Hoover. The faithful in the pews loved it. Grassroots religious activists wrote Hoover for copies of his homilies to use in their Bible studies, political action groups, and evangelism efforts.

The strength of his writings and popularity led Hoover to become a lauded evangelical leader. The FBI Boss helped white evangelicals establish social and political authority. The Protestant Establishment—the network of white mainline churches, prominent personages, and elite organizations—exercised considerable social and political authority in the nation's halls of power, and had for hundreds of years. However, as the leader of the FBI, Hoover's presence in the white evangelical world helped to authenticate the newly established religious movement as the rightful custodian of national morality and security. The association with J. Edgar Hoover and his FBI put white evangelicals on the fast track to significant political standing, a status that is alive and well to this day.

If Billy Graham was America's pastor, then J. Edgar Hoover was its bishop, adjudicating the faith and shepherding white evangelicals toward white Christian nationalism. Part 3, "Policing Faith," examines how Hoover and his FBI took jurisdiction over white evangelical identity. White evangelicals overlooked Hoover's very public lawbreaking, lies, and eschewing of evangelical theology and embraced his power and Christian nationalist commitments. They publicly honored the FBI chief as their political and religious standard-bearer, looking to Hoover to police evangelical politics, piety, and belonging. Evangelical churchgoers inundated the FBI with letters seeking Hoover's religious guidance, advice, and blessing on matters of faith and politics. Beseeching a higher authority than their pastor, they asked Hoover to shepherd them toward which Bible they should read, which preacher they should listen to, what church they should attend, and even how to remain faithful. A small, vocal remnant of white evangelicals protested the movement's glorification of Hoover, but their cries were ignored. The majority remained faithful to the FBI Boss to the very end. They feared for their country. They saw the future through the dark skies of Hoover's tempestuous reign. The white faithful lauded him and his federal agency as the crusaders and adjudicators of the faith.

Clergy followed suit, writing to Hoover to request *his* pastoral guidance on all things religion and politics. These clergy, what I call "Bureau Clergymen," gelled into an evangelical syndicate. They privately and publicly worked with the FBI to create the Christian America in which they jointly believed. Leading white evangelical clerics partnered with the FBI to hire white evangelical college graduates to get them within the halls of power, while also working in the streets and media to discredit and destroy the Civil Rights Movement and one of its most prominent figures: Reverend Martin Luther King Jr. White evangelicals put their trust in Hoover and his FBI to shepherd the nation into the Promised Land, by any means necessary.

The story of J. Edgar Hoover's FBI and white evangelicals has consequences for our present and future. Bringing the gospel of J. Edgar Hoover to the fore is central to understanding the current state of white Christian nationalism and its relationship to white evangelicalism specifically and to the nation more broadly. *The Gospel of J. Edgar Hoover* details how the mutually beneficial merger between a federal agency focused on national security and a conservative white Christian religious movement helped to transform the landscape of contemporary American religion and politics.

Going through the FBI is the only way to fully grasp the historic relationship between white evangelicals and state power. Without this historical treatment, we lack a full historical explanation of why white evangelicals have readily blessed extralegal practices and embraced political figures that fall far short of the movement's professed theology and morality. The general narratives fall short, charting a downfall from the "respectable" and moral foundation laid by Reverends Billy Graham and Carl F. H. Henry and *Christianity Today*. The decline, they argue, is marked by evangelical endorsements of politicians such as Donald Trump and the embrace of white supremacist organizations such as the Oath Keepers and the Proud Boys, as well as conspiracy theories such as QAnon, and Christian nationalist violence. The cause, they reason, can be found in the nation's demography. A shrinking white population, a decrease in Christian hegemony and church attendance, along with the political gains of racial and ethnic minorities provoked a white backlash. Economic shifts—the decrease in the white middle class and the loss of manufacturing jobs—also shoulder the blame in these narratives. Accordingly, these cultural changes have forced white evangelicals to suddenly loosen their moral and theological standards. The fog of war clouded their moral and theological vision, giving way to the politics of pragmatism in order to bring America back to their God. White evangelicalism, they argue, essentially jumped the tracks.[14]

If we look at white evangelicalism through J. Edgar Hoover's stained glass window, however, the train appears to be running right on time. *The Gospel of J. Edgar Hoover* shows us that white evangelicals are who they have always been. From the beginning, the founders of modern white evangelicalism preached that American politics needed Christian piety and traditional morality while their political practice was marked by the gospel of amoral pragmatism and abusive power in the name of Jesus. Their gospel labors went beyond partnerships with famous white Protestant clergy or bona fide evangelical elected officials, activists, and businessmen. If we draw back the curtain on the white evangelical attempt to take America "back" for God, we find a partnership with the infamous J. Edgar Hoover, who worked diligently behind the scenes and at the forefront for nearly five decades. Hoover deployed the sophisticated federal war chest, the notorious activities of his FBI, and white evangelicals in the battle for a white Christian America. White evangelicals sanctified his immoral, illegal, unconstitutional, and violent labor as the work of God. And they have followed his lead ever since.

The whole process began on the site of J. Edgar Hoover's stained glass window, back when it was simply the boyhood home of a young Sunday school teacher by the name of John Edgar Hoover.

CHAPTER 1

Hoover's Faith

There is . . . a deep spirituality and sense of justice in the essence of [Hoover's] being, which informs his ideas and directs his actions. What you see in the man and feel in the whole structure and operation of the FBI began in the boy.

—HOOVER'S PASTOR, REVEREND EDWARD L. R. ELSON[1]

The picture of a young Hoover says it all (figure 3). By the age of seventeen, John Edgar Hoover was the man he would always be. He stood at his physical apex, approximately five foot eight inches tall. His eyes were ever vigilant, watchful. His posture, stiff as the starched navy blue jacket and confederate grey slacks of his Central High School Brigade of Cadets uniform. His grip on the saber was as unforgiving as his opinions. The gold epaulets that gleamed from his square shoulders signified his leadership rank of captain. He was a soldier on guard, ready to do battle against anything and anyone at odds with his worldview.

But this man-child was no ordinary soldier—he was a soldier in the army of the Lord. The earnest teen wore his cadet uniform to bark orders at his fellow cadets, and to teach his Sunday school class at Old First Presbyterian Church. His peers thought it an extreme gesture, but Hoover believed it to be holy and appropriate. Sunday school was boot camp, the training ground in the battle for the soul of the nation, and Hoover dressed the part. It was 1912, and J. Edgar Hoover was his own

FIGURE 3. John Edgar Hoover at seventeen years old in Central High Cadet uniform, 1912. *Source*: J. Edgar Hoover Personal Estate, Photographs Box 3, Folder 9. Collection of the National Law Enforcement Museum, Accession number 2010.11.

man: a soldier and a minister fighting the good fight with military precision. It was a lifelong commitment, an unceasing crusade to keep America a white Christian republic. Hoover pledged to be its soldier and
minister—its defender and custodian—until his dying day.[2]

—

J. Edgar Hoover was a white Christian nationalist. He believed America
had divine origins. Throughout his career, Hoover reminded the public
that "The American ideal has its roots in religion."[3] The nation was conceived by God and thus chosen for a special purpose. God revealed the
sacred plan to the white Founding Fathers. "Those men who laid the
foundations . . . of the American Republic," Hoover consistently noted,
"had a vigorous, indomitable, all-encompassing faith . . . They believed
in God . . . And they sought to create a government in harmony with
those immutable laws by which He rules His universe." These faithful
men sketched out this vision in America's founding documents. The
Declaration of Independence and the US Constitution were more than
just political statements and blueprints of governance, they were holy
writ, principles and ideas that were supernatural in origin and authority.
They established America not just as a nation-state with physical boundaries, but as a sacred concept and calling. America's covenant with God
necessitated that conservative Christianity and narrow biblical literal-
ism be the foundation of American governance, civil law, and societal
arrangements. Failure to recognize and protect this fact, Hoover warned,
would cause the nation to "wither to extinction."[4]

Hoover's white Christian nationalism was not concerned with theological purity or conformity. Nor did Hoover advocate establishing
Christianity as the official state religion. He recognized the United
States was comprised of many faiths. However, Hoover was convinced
that the nation's origins, as well as its natural customs, morals, and culture,
made one thing clear: "The United States is fundamentally a Christian
nation." This Christianity was an all-encompassing worldview. It was
built upon a set of American myths, traditions, symbols, and narratives
that were interpreted through a particular reading of the Bible in which

America's natural order was white supremacist, patriarchal, heteronor-
mative, and authoritarian. Hoover's Christianity was as religious as it
was racial, gendered, and political.[5]

Hoover dubbed his conflation of nationhood, citizenship, religion,
and political identity: *Americanism*. To obey American law and observe
dominant social customs was to serve God, and to serve God was to
obey the law and observe dominant social customs.[6] Those who expressed dissatisfaction with traditional American values and customs
were guilty of blasphemy and subversion. At best, their yearnings for
change were the ramblings of misguided souls; at worse, plots by sinners to deliberately destroy America. There was no in between.

Hoover proudly admitted that his upbringing—his "home, Sunday
School, and church"—nurtured him in Americanism. This trinity helped
him to heed and accept his divine calling as a soldier and minister of his
white Christian America.[7]

The Home

J. Edgar Hoover was born at home on New Year's Day in 1895. The
family's modest two-story stucco home was whitewashed, just like
the neighborhood. The house, 413 Seward Square SE, was located in
Washington, DC's Capitol Hill neighborhood, a racially segregated and
exclusively white community, just five minutes from the Capitol. The
call to federal service was the prevailing ethos of the neighborhood, it
was the social oxygen he breathed. The rows of identical houses were all
occupied by white Protestant civil servants, including Hoover's dad.
Dickerson N. Hoover was a Presbyterian and a civil servant for the US
Coast and Geodetic Survey office, the oldest scientific agency in the
federal government. He was a loving and doting father, as caring as he
was anxious. Severe depression and hallucinations stalked him until his
death in 1921.[8]

Hoover's mother, Presbyterian Annie M. (Scheitlin) Hoover, was the
head of the house. She was short in stature, but casted a large discipli-
narian shadow over Edgar. Her bloodline was full of Swiss mercenaries,
and she believed it was her job to ensure J. Edgar Hoover continued the

legacy of decorated government men. Her disciplinary regime was administered with military precision: perpetual rewards for obedience, and punishment for insubordination.[9]

Protestant faith was the bedrock. "Faith was a living thing in our home," Hoover remembered. Edgar's Christian commitments were nurtured by the Bible, the *Westminster Shorter Catechism*—the chief staple of instruction within Presbyterianism—and the importance of disciplined, orderly worship.[10] The idea of conversion or being "born-again" was foreign to Hoover. Unlike many modern evangelicals who point to a singular moment of Christian conversion, Hoover recalled, "No such exploding suns blaze on the horizons of my memory."[11] Hoover was nurtured in the faith. The idea of Christian nurture was popularized by Horace Bushnell (1802–1876). The "Father of Progressive Orthodoxy" believed that a baptized soul that was nurtured in a Christian home and the church had no need to experience a singular conversion moment. In fact, Bushnell argued, a soul that was properly cultivated in Christian institutions would not recall being anything other than a child of God.[12] Hoover held fast to this faith for his entire life. In adulthood, white evangelicals such as the Billy Graham Evangelistic Association tried to push their understanding of conversion upon Hoover, inquiring about the moment when he "made a commitment to Christ." Hoover, borrowing a page from Bushnell, responded, "Because I grew up in a Christian home, I feel that Christ has always been a part of my life."[13]

Bible study was central. "I recall vividly the Sunday evenings when we sat in a family circle listening to the Word of God," he reminisced. The structure of the family's Bible study provided Hoover with his earliest lessons in the propriety of patriarchy and white supremacy. Annie Hoover was the established parental authority, yet she ceded religious authority to men. Hoover's great-uncle John Hitz, the top-ranking Swiss consul, always led the Sunday evening ritual. The white-bearded diplomat vigorously expounded upon the Bible with graphic tales of fire and brimstone. The family revivalist damned the fate of those who consumed alcohol and other similar heathens. Such characteristics, he preached, came natural to "colored folk." For this reason, the family's revolving cast of Black maids were excluded from the sacred table, while everyone else in the Hoover house gathered around the "lamplit" table for the family ritual. Hoover was encouraged to see segregation as righteous and white supremacy as natural. Indeed, the family practiced the racial exclusion that flowed from their local church and the nearby halls of federal power. In 1904, when Edgar was nine, bathrooms and locker rooms in federal government buildings were legally segregated, giving way to segregated public accommodations, parachurch organizations, and neighborhoods. From the family's sacred table, to their church, community, and on to the White House, Hoover's America was constructed on the braided elevation of white male superiority, Protestant faith, and government service.[14]

Family devotions also shaped Hoover's enduring view of holy writ. The youngster was required to study the Bible and be quizzed on each lesson during family worship. The Bible drills led him to a lifelong commitment to extolling the Bible, particularly the King James Version, as a divinely inspired text that held the key for the salvation of souls, morality, and American governance. The Bible was not just a historical document; it was the Word of God. He described it as "the sacred writings of the divinely-inspired prophets of old and the apostles who shared in the life and teachings of Jesus Christ and preserved for us the wonderful lessons of His redemption." The Bible was the only place one could find "the guidance, the inspiration, the consolation and the hope that is ever man's need in realizing his goal of everlasting salvation." The Bible was also the guide book for personal morality. Hoover viewed the Bible as "the Word of God—handed down for all generations to come—as a guidepost for living." It was "the source of spiritual food, [and] the solution to life's problems," and "the inspiration for Christian living." There was no morality apart from the Bible. "It is quite impossible," he noted, "to believe that progress along the road to righteous living may be accomplished without the guidance of the Bible." Finally, he believed that the Bible was the basis of American democracy. "The essential elements of democracy," Hoover once wrote, "are very vividly summed up for us in the Ten Commandments."[15] The Bible was the source of all things; holding the keys to salvation, morality, and governance. As Hoover told the *New York Times*, "The goal of life [was] defined [in] the sixth chapter, eighth verse of Micah: 'And what doth the Lord require of thee, but to do justly, and to love mercy, and to walk humbly with thy God?'"[16]

The School

Loving thy neighbor as thyself was easy for young Hoover. His neighbors were just like him. The public school system—in faith and practice—was an extension of Hoover's home. Hoover's schools were legally segregated and they preached that success, academic or otherwise, was predicated upon Christian piety. The belief was built on the myth and illusion that such accomplishments relied solely on individual merit and not the reality of government preferences for whites.[17] Hoover heard this message from his earliest school days. He began matriculation at Brent Elementary School. Each day began with prayer and a Bible lesson. One of Hoover's teachers said it best, telling the class "'In order to receive passing grades and qualify for graduation each of [you will] have to master the three R's of reading, writing and arithmetic. But," she added, "you will also find that there is a fourth R. . . . It is Religion.'"[18]

Hoover's high school offered more of the same. In 1909, he enrolled at the prestigious Central High School, three miles away, instead of his neighborhood school Eastern High, which was just a block away. His older siblings attended Eastern, but Hoover charted his own path. Founded in 1882, Central was the first and the most academically decorated white public high school in the nation's capital. It was the cradle of Washington's future white elite, a prerequisite for white upward mobility and respectability. One of Hoover's classmates recalled that graduates departed to become "distinguished citizens—doctors, lawyers, diplomats." This factory of white upward mobility proudly practiced segregation and anti-Black racism. Graduation speakers routinely cracked jokes about innate Black inferiority, while the school's assortment of publications were littered with homages to white superiority. White Protestant faith underscored it all. Ministers performed the invocation prior to important school assemblies and graduations. And any time one of the school's teams earned a victory, the student body sang the Doxology, "Praise God from whom all blessings flow."[19]

Hoover fully embraced the culture of white Protestant middle-class striving. He embodied Central's Latin motto: "tenax propositi," meaning "steadfast to your purpose," or "tenacious to your calling." Unlike other teenagers, he dismissed leisure and embraced a disciplined and ordered life. He kept a full academic schedule, while filling his free time with school activities. When his frail frame got him cut from the junior varsity football team on sight, he threw himself into track and choir, and eventually became head of the school's cadets. Hoover led Company A, comprised of the most popular and gifted white male students. The men wore their uniforms to school twice a week for practice. J. Edgar Hoover added Sunday to his routine. He took the mantle, pledging to his classmates to "work all the time." He was a man of his word. He spent hours drilling his elite squadron of sixty some men, hosting weekly meetings, convening early in the evening and lasting until early in the morning. His peers marveled at his staccato voice "rattling good military aggregation." Hoover's time spent commanding the cadets—barking orders and demanding uniformity and cohesion—was dress rehearsal for his life to come.[20]

Hoover also learned valuable life lessons on the debate team. In the midst of battle, Hoover, the team's lead speaker, often based his arguments on conservative notions of Protestant faith. He referred to God's natural order when he affirmed "The Fallacies of Women's Suffrage." His spirited opposition, one classmate commented, was like a "tornado." In a debate brief on the question of capital punishment, Hoover argued, "The Bible stands for Capital Punishment. All Christian nations uphold it."[21] It was simple: either you were Christian nation or you were not. Hoover was very deliberate in his verbal jousting. He told his high school newspaper that debate was "a practical and beneficial example of life, which is nothing more or less than the matching of one man's wit against another." Hoover's experiences on the debate team taught him to become a student of others' weaknesses; lurking, waiting, and training himself to know when and how to pounce. When he did strike, he learned that it was best to present his ideas and positions not as personal beliefs and opinions, but as natural enduring truths set in motion by a higher authority.[22]

Hoover was the embodiment of all the high school held dear. The 1913 high school year book called him an "old school" Centralite, "a gentleman of dauntless courage and stainless honor, one of the best Captains and Captain of one of the best [cadet] companies that have ever been seen at Central." Central immortalized his legacy as a standard-bearer, concluding, "Indeed, it would be well for us did we have many others like Hoover." Hoover graduated with ease in 1913, ranking fourth in his class. Nevertheless, he was selected class valedictorian because of the combination of his "academic achievement and moral character." J. Edgar arrived at the high school a scrawny, unknown student with a slight stutter, but departed an admired student, military commander, debater, and established member of the rising white middle class.[23]

Church

Hoover's home and school planted the seeds of faith, and the church watered them. Hoover believed that humankind was the only creature that was endowed with a spiritual nature. Like the physical body, the spiritual side required "nourishment, discipline and cultivation," he argued. Church was the place where men and women satisfied these needs. When asked why he attended church, he responded, "Because I have found that man is incomplete in himself. His need of God is overwhelming. Each of us needs a reservoir of strength which springs only from the cultivation of the spiritual resources within."[24] Hoover tapped into these resources from an early age.

He began worshipping at Eastern Presbyterian Church, followed by Metropolitan Presbyterian Church, until he finally settled at Old First Presbyterian Church, where he remained for the rest of his life. Old First possessed everything to satisfy Hoover's professional ambitions. It was an esteemed and historic church, founded in 1811. Prior to erecting its own church building, the congregation worshiped in the Supreme Court chambers in the Capitol Building, boasting presidents, Supreme Court justices, and congressmen among its members. Young

Hoover made himself known to the city's professional elite. When he greeted church members, especially those employed by the federal government, he pressed one of his mimeographed business cards in their hand, announcing: "John Edgar Hoover, Student, Central High School, Washington, D.C."[25]

Young Hoover adored church. At ten years old he led the scriptural recitations. By age twelve, the pious pre-teen sang soprano in the choir and was a featured soloist. One year, he attended Sunday school fifty-two consecutive Sundays. His unrivaled devotion was awarded with a branded New Testament Bible. His zeal for the Lord vaulted him to the distinguished position of secretary of his Sunday school class. The position was prescribed for a "young man of quiet, gentlemanly habits, accustomed to business . . . perhaps a clerk or accountant . . . [who] takes pleasure . . . [in] contribut[ing] to the promotion of the cause." Hoover was ideal. The vigilant teen kept a systematic account of the minutes, attendance, proceedings, and the spiritual growth of his Sunday school class. He never relinquished these skills, overseeing the same for his special agents during his tenure as director of the FBI.[26]

Hoover became even more involved with the church during his teenage years. While his peers looked to push the limits of propriety, Hoover strengthened the bonds of piety. At age thirteen, he was baptized, joyously documenting the sacred ritual in his diary, pinpointing the moment of his purification: "Sunday December 27, 1908 at 5pm." A few days later, on January 3, 1909, the now baptized fourteen-year-old was elected by his admiring peers to the post of corresponding secretary of the entire Sunday school. He took stock and reported on the congregation's entire Sunday school, relaying the record to the national body.[27]

In his service to the church, Hoover tried his best to mimic the pastor. He idealized Reverend MacLeod as the embodiment of Christian manhood. The Canadian-born preacher was pious, yet still played baseball with Hoover and his neighborhood peers. The preacher espoused a muscular Christianity; preaching and practicing the gospel via the performance of fitness and athleticism. Hoover affectionately remembered MacLeod as a "vigorous, forthright Calvinist, whose rigorous sense of duty and clear-cut view of right and wrong did nothing to suppress his sense of humor or his joy in life." Reverend MacLeod was male, white, devout, legalistic, fit, and a racial segregationist. He was, Hoover reflected, "my ideal of manhood." It was because of Reverend MacLeod, he confessed, "I wanted to become a minister."[28]

Reverend MacLeod encouraged Hoover to explore his call, appointing the youth a Sunday school teacher. Sunday school teachers were to be persons "of general information and culture" who "have a good address and pleasant manners, which come much more from care and painstaking than from nature." In additional to possessing cultivated gifts, Sunday school teachers were expected to invest in the "preparation of the heart which comes from earnest, devoted piety," enabling them to develop a "burning love for the salvation of souls." Hoover's gifts, his determination to hobnob with the congregation's finest, and his previous experience made teaching Sunday school the perfect place for young Hoover to explore his call.[29]

Hoover took his ministry very seriously, and was forever shaped by it. It was "Sunday school," he recalled, that gave him "a firm faith in God." It continued to nurture the assurance of his militant spirituality, even in adulthood. He called Sunday school "a citadel of real spiritual influences." Donning his cadet uniform for class was no empty performance. It was a reflection of the martial faith in which he believed. Sunday school, he surmised, "instilled within me a spirit of 'no compromise' when dealing with persons and situations opposed to the ideal of a good Christian life."[30]

He was an earnest and orderly teenage soldier for the Lord. The Sunday school faithful promoted the popular teacher to assistant superintendent of Old First's Junior Department.[31] The uniformed cadet was charged with overseeing all the youth in the department, while also preparing his own weekly lesson for a class of boys slightly younger than himself. Each lesson was based on a biblical text assigned by the national American Sunday School Union (ASSU). Hoover began preparing his lessons early in the week, usually on Monday, always careful to document his progress in his diary. His crisp, pressed uniform matched the militaristic sharpness of his lesson plans, replete with drills to help his students memorize the Bible, the Ten Commandments, and the

Sermon on the Mount. Sunday school, he reflected, helped to "impress upon receptive youth the principles of Christianity," which he concluded "are foundational in a democracy."[32]

The future lawyer's lessons were laid out like a legal brief, aimed to wrestle a verdict for Jesus. The lessons were geared toward leading souls to salvation, not the transformation of society. The first aim of the Sunday school teacher, wrote the editor of the *Sunday School Times*, "is to bring the scholars to a saving knowledge of Jesus Christ—to secure their salvation." Teachers were to be single-minded. "Aim at the conversion of your scholars. Until this is accomplished the work is incomplete . . . everything, is subordinate to this," the editor argued.[33] The lesson plans avoided historical criticism of the Bible. The Bible, the ASSU noted, was for the common man, not the ruminations of elites.[34] On September 4, 1910, Hoover taught his class from Matthew 21:23–46. The lesson was anchored by verse 43: "Therefore I say to you, the kingdom of God will be taken from you and given to a nation bearing the fruits of it." The emphasis of the lesson was the importance of preserving a Christian America. If America rejected Christ, it would lose its birthright as a chosen nation and suffer the consequences. As one Sunday school commentary surmised the lesson's central thought, "To reject Christ is to perish."[35]

Two weeks later, on September 18, 1910, Hoover taught his class how the nation could remain steadfast, a lesson he would later spend his entire career trying to instill in America. He used Matthew 22:15–22, 34–46 for the text.[36] The gospel story depicts Jesus telling the Pharisees, in part, to "Render therefore to Caesar the things that are Caesar's, and to God the things that are God's." Christ then tells his audience that the first and greatest commandment is to "love the Lord your God with all your heart, with all your soul, and with all your mind," and to "love your neighbor as yourself." It was one of Hoover's favorite Bible verses. The ASSU directed Hoover to teach his class that "Jesus was the ideal citizen." Jesus combined "civic duty with moral and religious duty." Politics, the lesson continued, was best understood as a "vehicle of a Divine force, by which the world is divinely governed. This is the exclusive way in which the religious man sees politics." Hoover was instructed to drill into his students that real white Christians wanted "saints in politics as well as theology; we want them even more in the political arena than the theological," because godly men elevated politics out of the "realm of personal egotism, personal ambition, and party advantage" into a much higher, divine purpose.[37] Hoover took this lesson to heart.

Federal Government

Hoover's heart was set on attending seminary and then ministry. However, his father's illness changed everything. "I intended to enter the ministry . . ." he privately admitted, but life made it "necessary for me to seek employment and contribute to the support of my home rather than enter the seminary." Still intending to serve his God, he decided to work during the day, and study God's law at night. After graduating from high school in 1913, he enrolled in George Washington University's novel, evening Masters of Law program. While taking evening classes, he worked as a junior messenger in the Order Division of the Library of Congress during the day, rising from cataloguer to clerk for a salary of $840 a year. After he graduated in 1917 and passed the bar, he used his mother's familial connections to avoid the military draft. He was gifted a job in the Department of Justice (DOJ) on July 26, 1917. As a clerk in the files division, he made $990 per year (the US Attorney General earned $15,000).[38]

Hoover's humble beginnings were short-lived. As America's brightest young men fought in the Great War in Europe, Hoover's relentless drive and discipline made him a standout at the DOJ. He pursued the job with the tenacity of a Sunday school teacher seeking to save souls. He even dressed the part, resembling a flashy evangelist more than a lawyer. He worked twelve-hour days, seven days a week. "I discovered he worked Sundays and nights," special assistant to the attorney general John Lord O'Brian noted. Like his experience in church, Hoover was quickly promoted. O'Brian, who was good friends with Hoover's uncle, recalled, "I promoted him several times, simply on merits." In less than a year, Hoover was promoted to the rank of "attorney," doubling his salary. By the age of twenty-two, he was put in charge of a unit in the Alien Enemy Registration Section. He became a hunter of wayward, disloyal souls.[39]

Hoover approached the job as a divinely commissioned soldier and moral custodian. He assessed all social, economic, and civic issues according to one standard: Did they reaffirm the righteousness of the dominant "Christian" social order? "Our democracy cannot survive," he persisted, "without the constant influence of the Christian faith."[40] For a year and a half, he reviewed cases of German "aliens" and decided their fate. The "alien" status of the "enemies" under Hoover's supervision placed them outside the norms of constitutional protections. The drudgery of the legal process was too cumbersome and too slow for Hoover's quick-witted inquisition. He preferred the righteousness and speed of his moral purview and pen, allowing his judgment to replace the Constitution. He possessed the power to determine Christian patriots or traitors; freedom or internment. The Sunday school teacher probed alien beliefs and moral commitments. He excused lawbreaking by those he deemed good "aliens," but was vicious toward those whose opinions and political ideology he found unchristian and therefore un-American. The process whetted Hoover's appetite for authority in the midst of war—hot or cold—circumstances that would enable him to exalt his judgment above constitutional restraints.[41] It was a power he relished and craved for the remainder of his life.

J. Edgar showcased this hunger during the Palmer Raids. In the early months of 1919, a series of homemade bombs exploded across the country, targeting the "capitalist class." The home of US Attorney General Mitchell A. Palmer was one of the targets. He turned to J. Edgar Hoover, the newly appointed head of the Radical Division of the DOJ, to help unleash a holy war against the purported atheists and communists who were responsible. He placed "all necessary manpower" at Hoover's disposal. Hoover identified every communist he could, and pursued them. The holy warfare was not sanctioned by search warrants, court orders, or evidence of wrongdoing. These people were guilty because J. Edgar Hoover said so. On January 2, 1920, Hoover's men illegally entered houses, meeting places, and other private venues across thirty-three cities. The raids resulted in the mass arrest of six thousand supposed Reds and subversives. In twenty-four hours, men and women who were suspected of being atheists, disloyal, and hell-bent on revolution were rounded up on blank arrest warrants and placed in holding. It was an authoritarian dream, but a constitutional nightmare. The majority of the unconstitutional arrests were dismissed, while the bulk of the deportation cases were overturned. It was a public relations disaster. The nation's newspapers condemned the raids as "anti-American." It was the coldest criticism in the all-American eyes of J. Edgar Hoover.[42]

Hoover learned his lesson. He saw his failure as tactical, not ideological. While the FBI would largely concentrate on interstate crime, Hoover still believed Americanism was the answer to whatever ailed the nation. Instead of wanton public lawbreaking, Hoover decided to employ another strategy: convincing the public of the threat, and then fighting it with a crusade of Americanism, by any means necessary. If he could convince the DOJ, the nation would follow. Attorney General Harlan Stone was the first domino to fall. On May 10, 1924, he appointed J. Edgar Hoover the head of the Bureau of Investigation, what would later be called the Federal Bureau of Investigation. The former Sunday school teacher happily accepted the position, not just as a federal employee, but like the Jesus he taught in Sunday school: as a man with a religious duty to invade politics with "divine force." That force was unleashed, once again, in the realm of national security and counterespionage when FDR passed a series of presidential directives, most notably in September 1939 following the German invasion of Poland, making the FBI the chief domestic intelligence agency in the nation. Hoover picked up right where he left off. Atheism and communism were still the enemy. Nothing, not even the Constitution or facts, could change that. As one of his Bureau executives noted, "as far as Communism is concerned, Hoover's view was the same on the day he died as it was back in the days of Palmer's Red menace."[43]

Hoover made the FBI his ministry. His pastor marveled that Hoover approached the job with "a motivation not unlike one has when one volunteers to be a missionary or evangelist, or a pastor in the church." "As soon as Mr. Hoover became Director of the FBI," his pastor noted, "he began applying his high Christian principles to the Bureau." Hoover, his pastor insisted, took over the FBI and started a "reformation."[44] Hoover's goal was to make his men soldiers and ministers who were prepared for the battle to come. Hoover wanted his Bureau to be just like his seventeen-year-old self. Instead of the Company A Cadets, Hoover would divide the FBI into divisions and squads and order a battalion of white men to march in uniformity. All the women and men of color were removed from the ranks of special agents, and the majority of Jewish agents suffered the same fate. Hoover began to exclusively recruit white Protestant and Catholic college-educated men. And, like the uniformed Sunday school teacher he was, Hoover compelled his men to undergo spiritual exercises. The Protestant, Catholic, and Jewish prayers in the FBI Academy dining hall were insufficient. Hoover wanted his men to experience regimented spiritual formation; to be trained to be pious soldiers who followed Hoover as Hoover followed God. Hoover's pastor said it best. The FBI director expected his special agents to approach "the business of law enforcement with the sacrificial consecration befitting a missionary or minister."[45] Hoover recreated the FBI in his image, establishing an internal religious culture that fashioned the FBI into a battalion of dedicated soldiers and ministers for white Christian America.

Proselytizing Faith: Soldiers and Ministers— The Religious Foundations of Hoover's FBI

The Bureau was my seminary.

—ASSEMBLIES OF GOD PASTOR AND FORMER FBI SPECIAL
AGENT, REVEREND OLIVER COLLIER, 1971[1]

J. Edgar Hoover required FBI special agents to take a vow. The FBI
Pledge for Law Enforcement Officers asked FBI special agents to swear,
in part, "I shall, *as a minister*, seek to supply comfort, advice and aid to
those who may be in need of such benefits; *as a soldier*, I shall wage
vigorous warfare against the enemies of my country, of its laws, and of
its principles." Hoover promised, "Just as those entering the medical
profession take the oath of Hippocrates . . . so are all the Special Agents
of the Federal Bureau of Investigation executing the FBI Pledge for Law
Enforcement Officers."[2] In Hoover's FBI, being a special agent was a
sacred vocation, one that was authenticated and standardized not simply by man-made boards or federal agencies, but also by a divine call to
be a minister of, and soldier for, God's chosen nation. Hoover's FBI law
enforcement pledge made it clear: men of the FBI would be employed
by the DOJ, but they would work for God; a mission that was synonymous with white Christian nationalism.

J. Edgar Hoover created the modern FBI according to his own worldview.
Under his watch, white Christian nationalism became the foundation of
national security. The Boss viewed this job through the Protestant Reformed

tradition. Working in federal law enforcement was not simply a federal appointment; it was a divine vocation, one he considered a "high calling." Hoover saw himself as a co-laborer with God, sanctified for an errand. He restructured the FBI accordingly. Under Hoover's religious zeal, FBI investigators were more than just workers, they were set apart. They were "Special" agents of the FBI. It was not just a salaried federal job in the DOJ, it was a vocation for white men to be crusaders for religious nationalism, traditional morality, and white male supremacy. The message was clear, a retired special agent reminisced. "The purpose of the Bureau was to create a kind of world that Hoover thought should exist."[3]

Detective Inspector H. A. Leslie of the Metropolitan Police in London, UK, took note of the centrality of Hoover's law enforcement pledge and all that it represented. During a law enforcement exchange program, the Englishman visited the Bureau, examining the FBI's training procedures and courses. He noted that all the members of the class signed Hoover's pledge. They were like new converts, joining the faith, armed with their pledge cards and a renewed worldview and mission. Amazed, Leslie sent a copy of the pledge across the Atlantic to his superiors at New Scotland Yard. Hoover, the Detective Inspector told his superiors, was in the midst of "conducting a crusade."[4]

It was a national crusade; one in which the words of Hoover's pledge became flesh in the form of the religious culture of the FBI. The Bureau instituted Jesuit spiritual retreats as well as Catholic Communion Breakfasts and Protestant Vesper Services. These Bureau-sanctioned religious practices created a religious culture that borrowed from white Catholic and Protestant forms, but was wholly other. The FBI had its own religious culture, a sacred ethos that ensured special agents understood and ritualized their formation and labor as America's "soldiers" and "ministers" who did God's work. The "G-men," as one clergyman noted in 1943, were not just federal investigators, they were "Apostles of JUSTICE."[5]

CHAPTER 2

Soldiers

J. Edgar Hoover employed the spiritual practices of St. Ignatius of Loyola to cultivate his special agents into soldiers for Christ. The spirituality of the sixteenth-century saint was ideal for warring men. Ignatius was a soldier who dedicated his sword and life to the Lord while recovering from a battle wound. Following his conversion, the man who would become known as the "soldier-saint" and the foremost patron saint of soldiers founded and became the first superior general of the Society of Jesus, the religious order popularly known as the Jesuits. The order became the first fully worldly religious community, called to a mission to engage secular society while maintaining stringent obedience to superiors. The faith they carried with them was masculine and virile, saturated in martial language to take on the world for Christ. One American Jesuit priest proclaimed, "Ignatius did not envision a Society of companionable pussycats. He wanted a band of tigers." Another noted, "The Church is an army, the 'Ecclesia Christi militans . . .' St. Ignatius seeks to rouse all and aid all in fighting valiantly beneath the Banner of Christ."[1] Hoover saw the spirituality of the soldier-saint as commensurate with his law enforcement pledge and its aim to chisel his men into godly soldiers. He told a group of Jesuit college students that their "sound, time honored and proven principles" of Ignatian spirituality prepared men for work in the Bureau. In fact, he assured them, their spiritual practices were "analogous to the FBI's approach to training and everyday relations between Special Agents."[2]

The FBI Boss was not exaggerating. Beginning in the 1930s, Hoover instituted an annual Jesuit spiritual retreat for all his FBI agents: Protestant, Catholic, Jew, and Mormon alike. The yearly Jesuit retreats, which lasted until Hoover's death, taught the men of the FBI that the only way to be a good special agent was to surrender their body, mind, and spirit to Christ. As Father Michael McPhelin, SJ, told retreatants, the aim of an Ignatian retreat is "to help you gain mastery over yourself."[3] Special agents of the FBI had to win the battle for their own soul before they could win the battle for the soul of America.

Hoover and the Jesuits

Hoover embraced the American Catholic Church. The Boss was not Catholic, he was a committed Presbyterian. However, he cherished the Catholic Church's strong belief in hierarchal norms and feverish anti-communism, while the emphasis on Christianity as the foundation of education appealed to Hoover's religious nationalism. The FBI director was one of the countless American Protestants of the early twentieth century who adamantly expressed admiration for Roman Catholic figures and their gospel labors.[4]

The American Catholic Church, in turn, embraced Hoover and his FBI. Lauding Hoover and his FBI aided the efforts of white-ethnic Catholics to become "white" and "American." The Church made concerted efforts to show that Catholicism could be adapted to American racial ideals as well as modernity, democracy, human rights, and anti-communism.[5] The Church's connection with Hoover and his G-men provided a very public opportunity for the Church to display the compatibility of Catholicism and American patriotism. Hoover, his FBI, and the American Catholic Church shared a mutual attraction. It was a match made in heaven.

The Jesuits were Hoover's preferred Catholics. He found the masculine spirituality of the religious order to be ideal. And his personal life made him even more attracted to the Jesuits. One Jesuit priest was particularly close to Hoover. Reverend Robert S. Lloyd, SJ, the spiritual director of the Jesuit retreat house in Annapolis, Maryland, became acquainted with Hoover in 1932. The priest served as a liaison for the Bureau during the Lindbergh kidnapping case. He became a frequent visitor to FBI headquarters, supplying the director with intel and advice on various Catholic groups. Moreover, at Hoover's direct invitation, Father Lloyd offered the invocation and benediction for forty consecutive graduations of the FBI National Academy—the periodic training sessions in which local police were schooled in the Bureau's "modern" tactical and spiritual practices of law enforcement. Hoover labeled Father Lloyd "a friend" of the Bureau. In 1936, Reverend Lloyd was placed on the FBI "special correspondents list," a catalogue of journalists, corporate executives, politicians, and ministers who supported and collaborated with the Bureau. It was a sign of the Bureau's favor and trust.[6]

The admiration was reciprocal. Father Lloyd described the FBI director as "fearless, unselfish, absolutely honest," and "a God-fearing man who believes in the spiritual formation of all his men." Hoover's single-minded dedication, Lloyd believed, bore fruit in the form of an FBI full of men who mirrored Hoover, "the very cream of American manhood." He told the director, "[I] feel your presence in your wonderful men. They reflect you."[7] Father Lloyd remained loyal to Hoover at all costs, even in the face of his Jesuit peers. When *America*, the Jesuit national weekly magazine, accused Hoover of resurrecting old fears of subversion and manufacturing more, Father Lloyd rebuked his colleagues, telling them that Hoover was "a great American," and "dearly loved by those who really knew him and worked for him."[8] Nothing, not even his own religious order, could separate Father Lloyd from his love of Hoover and the FBI.

The two men shared a personal affection as well. "It is a distinct honor and privilege for me to be so close to you and at your service," Father Lloyd once confessed to Hoover. The Jesuit priest expressed his closeness to the FBI Boss by bringing him personal gifts, including items for Hoover's beloved home garden. He also relentlessly expressed personal concern for Hoover, urging him to eat and rest properly, and even invited the director to visit the Jesuit retreat house for a period of relaxation: "I do hope that you and I can get together for a quiet and restful visit somewhere, sometime," he wrote. In one telegram he entreated Hoover, "Would like to see you very much and on Sunday if convenient to you. Kindly determine place and hour and let me know."[9] Hoover repaid the favors, with interest. The FBI director told his subordinates that Lloyd was not only his "close personal friend," but also "an inseparable member of our family." He checked on the priest, making sure he was taking care of himself and minding his "hyper-tension." He arranged for Lloyd to have VIP access to the Presidential Inaugural Parade, and when Lloyd traveled to national Jesuit conferences in Saint Louis and the like, Hoover made sure the Jesuit priest had a local FBI contact charged with "extending every possible courtesy" to Father Lloyd.[10]

The Jesuit priest cemented his place in Hoover's life when he shepherded Hoover through a personal crisis: the death of his mother. Mrs. Anna Hoover succumbed to illness on February 22, 1938. Father Lloyd accompanied Hoover to the burial at the Congressional Cemetery. Hoover left Washington, DC, to grieve in Florida, but he never left Father Lloyd's care. On March 2, the FBI director sent a heartfelt handwritten letter to the Jesuit priest. "I just had to write you a few lines to let you know the thanks and gratitude which is in my heart for you." The death of his mother forever changed him. "There will always be a void," he confessed to Lloyd. But Lloyd was there. "You will never know how much you have served as a sustaining factor for me not only during Mother's long illness but more particularly during these long days which have followed her passing onto peace and comfort which I pray is now hers." Hoover then assured Father Lloyd he was maintaining his belief in the Christian reformed notion of Sovereignty. "I am trying hard to absorb some of the power of God's will which I see on all sides exemplified in the beauties of nature. Certainly, there must be some of it for us poor humans." He confessed, it was "a hard struggle and I of course know the hardest is yet to come when I return to take up again the broken ends of life." Broken in spirit, Hoover concluded his grief-stricken letter with determination. "But one has to carry on and I believe it is as Mother would have it. I am trying hard to remember your many helpful words to strengthen me. With deep appreciation I am your sincere friend."[11]

Hoover made the friendship and admiration known in a 1939 public address. The occasion marked the twenty-fifth anniversary of the layman's retreat movement in the Archdiocese.[12] Father Lloyd invited Hoover to attend the celebratory dinner at the Washington, DC, Mayflower Hotel, Hoover's favorite place to dine. The FBI director graciously accepted the august opportunity to dine with the "largest and most distinguished audience of clergy and laity ever to attend" the banquet, including several Catholic bishops, priests, the president of Georgetown University, several US Senators, and prominent Catholic laymen such as US Attorney General Frank Murphy. The festive crowd included some eight hundred Catholics and Protestants, at a hefty cost of $2.50 per person (contemporary income value of approximately $200).[13]

Hoover was unexpectedly called to the podium to address the group. The Boss accepted. Hoover spoke, as he put it, "extemporaneously" and without "notes or even a mental outline." He spoke from the heart.[14] His heart overflowed with praise for Father Lloyd, the American Catholic Church, and its fight against the cosmic forces of atheism and subversion. He did so while meticulously maintaining his Protestant bona fides. He told the overflow ballroom that Reverend Lloyd was the epitome of all that was right with Christianity in America. He praised the Jesuit priest for his faithfulness and pastoral care following the death of his mother. "In the past year I have had my trials and sorrows, deep sorrows," he confessed. "And I can say from my heart tonight that if it had not been for the steadfast friendship of Father Lloyd and the consolation he gave to me, I do not know how I would have stood them."[15] Next, Hoover turned to the clear and present danger of godlessness. "The American people need to be told that the thing we have to fear most in this country are the godless and the subversive groups which are endangering our very existence." Thankfully, men like Archbishop Michael J. Curley and Father Robert Lloyd were leading the triumphant army of Catholic men in "the fight in this country against things un-American and subversive." For Hoover, this commitment to Americanness and the fight against godlessness made the Catholic Church, not Protestants, the leading force in saving the nation. "I am a Protestant," he reminded the crowd sandwiched between ice sculptures of a Jesuit retreat center and the Capitol Building. "And as a Protestant, I say sincerely and from experience, that the Catholic Church is the greatest protective influence in our nation today."[16] The praise was due, in part, because the Church emphasized religious nationalism in education. "I, as a Protestant pay tribute to the Catholic Church. I pay tribute to your Catholic educational institutions in which the love of God and love of country are taught and practiced. I wish that more of our universities and colleges were teaching love of God and country."[17]

The Boss's speech was a hit in the Catholic press. Admirers noted that Hoover "caught the vast group present by his sincerity and by his recognition that this country needs above all things else, Religion, if it is to be saved." The Catholic Review crowned him "one of the best speakers ever heard at a meeting in the Archdiocese," adding "his English was that of a scholar. He has a punch to his sentences." The Manresan observed, "the ten-minute address, absolutely extemporaneous, was a prefect gem and merited the most sincere and prolonged applause of the evening."[18]

Hoover was a Protestant—he left no doubt about that. Yet, he endorsed the "Americanness" of Catholicism. He saw it embodied in men like Father Lloyd, who he reckoned as a leader "in our common movement" against godlessness and subversion. These vocational, spiritual, and personal affinities led Hoover to declare at the Mayflower Hotel, "The Federal Bureau of Investigation has no chaplain, but if it could have one, it would like to have Father Lloyd." Father Lloyd, Hoover persisted, was "at least" the FBI's "honorary chaplain." Eventually, Hoover dropped the "honorary" prefix, and publicly referred to Father Lloyd as "Chaplain of the FBI," an honor Hoover continually bestowed upon the Jesuit priest until his death in 1960.[19]

Father Lloyd's title may have been titular and unofficial, but his impact on the Bureau was real and official. Following the event, Hoover began the process of institutionalizing Jesuit spirituality in the Bureau. The Boss sent his white male special agents at FBI headquarters as well as those at the Washington, DC, and Baltimore field offices to Father Lloyd's Jesuit retreat house for a time of prayer, worship, and spiritual revival. Other field offices across the country followed suit. African Americans, who joined the ranks of trained special agents in 1962, were excluded. These private closed religious gatherings were exclusively for white G-men. They were officially voluntary; however, the cultivation of the godly soldier was not. The hierarchal paramilitary structure of the Bureau gave the annual retreats a mandatory quality. Father Lloyd's chaplaincy and his retreats were not established in the official written regulations of the Bureau; but they were a mainstay in the Bureau's unwritten rules and ethos.[20]

Organizing the Retreats

The FBI spiritual retreats took place every year during a strategically orchestrated Spring weekend around the Easter holiday. Each year a high-ranking FBI special agent, often from the Domestic Intelligence Division, served as the "Retreat Captain," overseeing the year's religious rally. These spiritual commanders included men such as: Special Agent W. A. Branigan, a specialist in Russian intelligence and counterintelligence; Special Agent Peter J. Wacks, an administrative assistant to J. Edgar Hoover and a supervisor of espionage cases; and Special Agent Carmine Bellino, an administrative assistant to Hoover, who Robert F. Kennedy dubbed "the best investigator in the country." These chosen men anointed "section captains" from each FBI division at headquarters. Special agents in the Identification, Training and Inspection, Administrative, Records, Investigating and Accounting, Domestic Intelligence, and the Technical Lab Divisions all had a section captain responsible for steering their respective colleagues to attend. These section captains included men like Special Agent Robert E. Lee. The Irish Catholic from Chicago was a trained accountant, educated at DePaul University. His priest considered him to be "honest and upright, and of exemplary character." The principled SA served as chief FBI clerk and administrative assistant to Hoover, maintaining a paper trail to document attendance (see figure 4).[21]

In this paramilitary structure, all of Hoover's white male special agents were "encouraged" to attend the retreats to seek God's will for their life and career. The male agents who embraced this religious vision

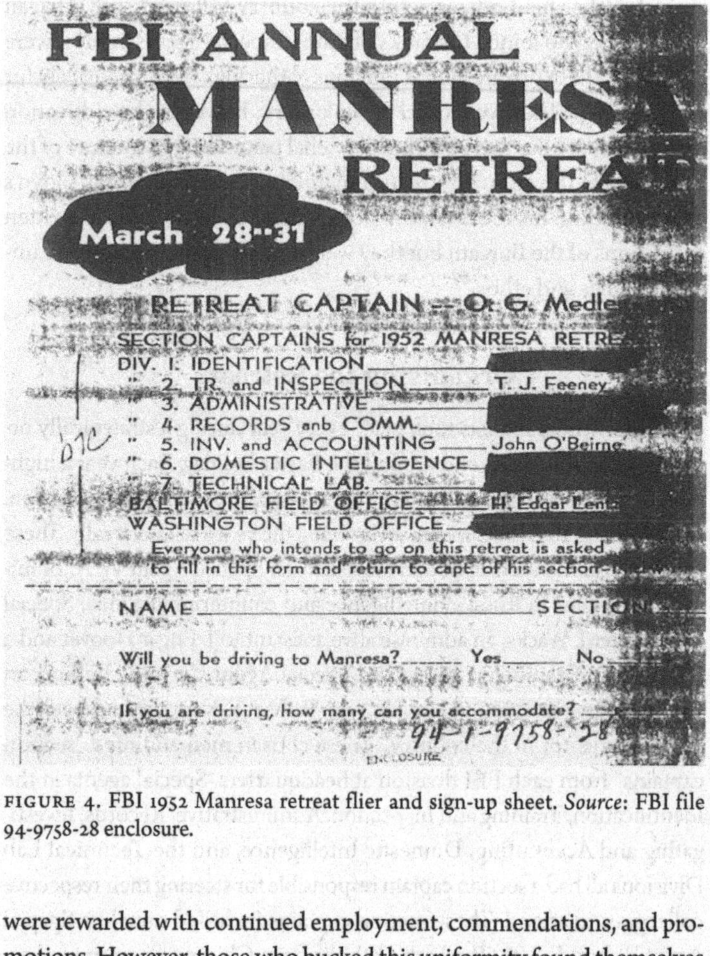

FIGURE 4. FBI 1952 Manresa retreat flier and sign-up sheet. *Source*: FBI file 94-9758-28 enclosure.

were rewarded with continued employment, commendations, and promotions. However, those who bucked this uniformity found themselves on the fast track to a stifled career or termination. In Hoover's regimented FBI, the best way to stand out was to fall in line.

The women of the Bureau had no need to sign up. The exclusively white female administrative staff were excluded. Women of the Bureau were not to be heard, save the sound of their typewriters. When they were seen, they were expected to be performing domestic and clerical labor and to be respectably adorned. The monthly FBI employee magazine,

The Investigator, made sure of it. The magazine, founded in 1932 for the purpose of enhancing "the mission of the FBI and to boost morale by showing cohesiveness of employees working as a team," featured a section dedicated to women. "The Feminine Slant" portrayed women fulfilling their part of the Bureau's mission: acts of faith, child rearing, party planning, and cooking. *The Investigator*'s "Miss Print of the Month," the Bureau's chaste version of a centerfold, featured "cheerful and charming" women of the FBI performing their clerical duties. The FBI viewed itself as the protector of women, shielding naturally pious women from the grime of war.[22]

Warfare was for men. After signing up for the retreat with the respective section captain, special agents were assigned transportation. Some G-men carpooled, while most boarded the Bureau's appointed buses. The Greyhound Bus Company provided "special buses" at a discounted rate to transport agents from FBI headquarters to their spiritual retreat. The buses, commandeered using taxpayer dollars, also made stops at the Washington, DC, and Baltimore field offices to pick up the faithful. Once the buses were full of federal spiritual seekers, the caravan made the approximate one-hour drive to Father Lloyd's retreat house for, as it was called at FBI headquarters, the annual "FBI Manresa Retreat."[23]

Manresa

Father Lloyd pitched his Manresa retreat house as a place of spiritual pilgrimage, where white men of all faiths could experience "the central touch of the soul with God." He assured visitors it was "not a retreat in the sense of a church retreat," nor a "Mission" seeking to win converts to Catholicism. In fact, he encouraged men "to remain true to your God and your church regardless of what church it may be and regardless of its religious denomination." At his retreat house, any man could retire from the world and in hallowed silence hear and speak to their God, and be "filled with strength and consolation for the battle of life."[24] Manresa was a place of spiritual refashioning for all of Hoover's men, a place to refurbish their spiritual armor; but there was no mistaking that the spiritual renewal was directed by a Jesuit priest who led men in the way of the soldier-saint.

The house was dedicated to St. Ignatius. It was named for Manresa, Spain, the location of the modest cave where the soldier dedicated his life and sword to Christ. In the cave, he began to formalize his spirituality in *The Spiritual Exercises*, the seminal text for spiritual formation for the Society of Jesus. It serves as the guidebook or manual for spiritual seekers to undergo a directed spiritual experience according to the ways of Ignatius. The soldier explained that the term "spiritual exercises" was purposeful. "For just as taking a walk, traveling on foot, and running are physical exercises, so is the name of spiritual exercises." They are a series of deliberate and structured religious practices of "examination of conscience, meditation, contemplation, vocal or mental prayer and other spiritual activities" to turn one away from sin and toward salvation and the discernment of God's will.[25] Manresa was the place where the soldier wrestled with God and emerged as God's soldier. Hoover made the analogy clear to his men: FBI special agents went to their Manresa to partake in the spiritual exercises to heal from the wounds of the battle afoot, seek divine guidance, and emerge as soldiers for God.

The retreat house, like Ignatius's cave at Manresa, was sequestered. It was built in 1926 in Annapolis, Maryland, on a triangular piece of land with a perpendicular drop down to the Severn River. Father Eugene McDonnell, SJ, acting on the behalf of the archdiocese, purchased the land from the Washington, Baltimore, and Annapolis Electric Railway for roughly $13,000 (a contemporary equivalent of $1 million). The property was covered with trees and brush with no road access. It was an ideal place for a Jesuit retreat house. St. Ignatius stipulated that his spiritual exercises should be conducted while in seclusion, preferably on a retreat away from one's natural surroundings, in order to attune the senses to God. Father McDonnell could not have chosen better. The twelve-acre plot, one observer noted, looked like "a jungle" where no human foot had trod. The priest had more than 150 trees cut down and removed to construct a road and a clearing in the wilderness to make way for a house of God.[26] The FBI convoys made their way from their FBI offices to Manresa via the plain, rough road hewn out of the wilderness.[27] The narrow path was the perfect metaphor for the convoys of G-men: the way of the soldier-saint is straight and narrow.

FIGURE 5. Manresa on Severn, view of buildings from river edge. *Source*: Maryland Province Archives Addenda Box 13, Folder: Buildings/Grounds, Georgetown University Special Collections.

The Manresa retreat house arose at the end of the narrow path; a holy shrine on the banks of the Severn River. The white pillared house was perched on a hill, seventy-one feet above the river. The house was like a spiritual beachhead, overlooking the US Naval Academy just one mile away. There Manresa stood—in the shadow and within earshot of one of the nation's most storied military academies. It was a perfect place for a house dedicated to the patron saint of all soldiers. Members of the US Navy performed military exercises on the lake-like portion of the Severn to train for battle, while special agents of the FBI went to the Severn to engage in their own exercises in preparation for the battle to come (see figure 5).[28]

Yet, the retreat house did not look like a training ground for war. It boasted welcoming accommodations. FBI agents ascended the holy hill like spiritual pilgrims, walking through the tiered manicured lawns dotted with white marble statues of Mary, St. Joseph, St. Patrick, St. Anthony of Padua, the Stations of the Cross, and the Grotto of Manresa.[29] White pillars greeted them at the entrance of the house, giving way to a lounging veranda over 1,100 feet long, the favorite resting place of the retreat house pet, a tan and white collie affectionately named "Lassie." The linoleum corridors and stairs led to sixty private rooms, each with hot and cold water. Brother Laurence Hobbs, SJ, and Ruby, one of two "colored girl[s]," labored in the "lightsome" dining room to cater to the physical nourishment of the spiritual seekers. The taste of savory chicken, sirloin, and ham regularly garnered standing ovations from the G-men. Little wonder a journalist described Manresa as having the aura of a summer resort hotel.[30]

However, the house was littered with relics to remind the government men it was not a vacation villa, but a house of prayer. The word "Manresa" loomed large over the weather-stripped front door. In each of the "simply furnished sleeping rooms" there was a crucifix, an icon, and a prie-dieu for prayer and meditation. Statues of St. Ignatius flanked the halls, leading to a small private chapel. The main chapel, however, was the crown jewel of the house. "Our Lady's Chapel" was constructed in the midst of the Great Depression in 1930–1931 for the substantial sum of $10,000 (a contemporary economic cost of approximately $2.2 million). The "small gem of architecture" had a seating capacity of approximately one hundred people. The quaint sanctuary was colored by six stained glass windows depicting the five Sorrowful Mysteries of Christ: Christ in agony in the Garden of Gethsemane, the whipping of Christ, the crowning of thorns, Christ carrying the cross, and the crucifixion and death. The final window portrayed the Resurrection. The altar was adorned with statues of the Holy Family: Mary, Joseph, and the infant Jesus[31] (see figure 6). The house was also outfitted with remembrances of Hoover. His autographed books were featured in the library. Father Lloyd prominently featured two awards Hoover gave him for his service to the FBI: the "FBI's Distinguished Service Cross," and a "beautiful plaque, setting forth the seal and the motto of the Bureau." And for worship, Hoover gave the priest an engraved "sterling silver, gold-plated" chalice and paten. FBI special agents, "non-Catholic as well as Catholic," donated money to purchase the gift known as "The Chalice of Salvation"

FIGURE 6. Manresa on Severn, interior of new chapel. *Source*: John Brosnan, SJ. Photographic Collection, Woodstock Theological College Archives, Digital and Special Collections, Georgetown University.

(see figure 7). It was engraved with the Bureau's seal. Father Lloyd graciously accepted the chalice, consecrated it, and pledged that it would "be lifted . . . daily at the altar, for Director Hoover and all the wonderful men and women of the FBI." "The FBI," he continued, "will be blessed daily in heaven and on earth. That is a true spiritual fact."[32] J. Edgar Hoover may not have been physically present at the annual retreats, but he was seemingly omnipresent. The house had the accommodations of a comfortable hotel, but FBI men could scarcely escape the sacred purpose of their visit. Everywhere they looked, it appeared that the eyes of the Lord (and their boss) were upon them.

Hoover trusted God to keep watch over his men, but he also verified. He left nothing to chance. Retreat captains organized every aspect of the annual federal ritual. They approved which topics were to be discussed and which priests would minister to their men. G-men were not

FIGURE 7. J. Edgar Hoover presents Father Lloyd with the FBI Chalice, Mr. Hoover's Office, FBIHQ, June 28, 1950. Standing left to right: Inspector John J. McGuire (despite his obvious height he was warned he was underweight); SA H. Edgar Lentz of the Baltimore field office; FBI Associate Director Clyde Tolson; Father Lloyd; Mr. Hoover; SA O. George Medler, Retreat Captain 1951; SA William C. Ryan of the Washington, DC, field office; SA James J. Bresnahan, Retreat Captain 1950. *Source*: Unprocessed collection, Father Stephen F. McNamee, SJ papers, Georgetown University Special Collections.

even permitted to select their room, or their roommate. Retreat captains assembled "a large detailed diagram of the house," indicating where every G-man was to lay his head, eat, and worship.[33] The Bureau's hierarchy also surveilled the retreating men. Special Agent Edward Tamm, the Bureau's third in charge from 1941 to 1948, made occasional trips to Manresa—not to worship with his men, but to check on them. The Georgetown law school alum was serious about his faith. His law school landlord described him as an "ardent Church member." As the Bureau's number three man, he was responsible for the Bureau's three investigative divisions: Domestic Intelligence, Investigative Division, and the Technical Laboratory. Special Agent Tamm added inspecting the

FIGURE 8. FBI Manresa group, March 13, 1955. *Source*: Photograph by W. Green, Maryland Province Archive Addenda Box 8, No Folder, Georgetown University Special Collections.

spirituality of the men in his division to his investigative duties. Special Agent Gerald J. Engert, the head of the Fingerprint Section of the Identification Division, did likewise. The impromptu visits by FBI supervisors not only surveilled the men, it also impressed upon them the importance of the yearly ritual.[34]

As a result, Manresa was bursting at the seams with FBI men. One special agent reported to his superior, "A few weeks ago when the first call was made for those wishing to attend, 145 men answered and it was then necessary to decline all subsequent requests. Consequently, many more were disappointed." Some of these men, he assured his boss, "will attend later on in the year with their parish or other spiritual groups." Eventually, the Bureau offered two retreat sessions—one in the spring and one in the summer, usually around the July 4 holiday weekend—to accommodate the demand (see figure 8).[35]

The Spiritual Exercises

During the retreats, Father Lloyd and a Bureau approved Jesuit priest led the ecumenical battalion through *The Spiritual Exercises of Saint Ignatius*. Hoover charged them with fashioning the G-men into soldier-saints. Retreat masters at Manresa did not offer direct advice. Rather, they followed the counsel of Ignatius to be "like the pointer of a scale in equilibrium, to allow the Creator to deal immediately with the creature and the creature with its Creator the Lord."[36] Father Lloyd took this charge seriously. He described his role as the spiritual director as simply "pointing the way through meditation to personal perfection and union of the soul with God. In fact," he continued, "Our Lord does most of the work Himself and the men just cooperate."[37] Father Lloyd and his priests likened the experience of the retreat to the transfiguration of Christ. The gospel story notes that Jesus and his disciples prayed on a hill, resulting in Christ being transformed, radiating like the sun. His disciples witnessed it and were changed forever. Special agents would also pray on the holy hill, see Christ anew, and, as one Manresan priest proclaimed, be "transfigured." This transformation, special agents were reminded, was "a grace from God," but it required their individual co-operation and effort. "You will be the one transfiguring yourself," they were told. This mission of guided self-transformation was framed in a maxim. G-men went to Manresa to receive the "guidance of the man who was reborn in a cave," that is St. Ignatius, so "they may be changed by the Man who was born in the cave at Bethlehem": Jesus Christ.[38]

Father Lloyd guided the G-men along this path. In the morning, special agents of the FBI attended Mass and received Holy Communion from the FBI's Chalice of Salvation. A priest led worship, but G-men served as acolytes, participated in every aspect of the service. Special agents looked after the vestments in the sacristy. Other agents infused the air of the chapel with incense by swinging the censer, while retreat captains led the gathering of soldier-saints in the rosary and the Litany of the Sacred Heart and the Litany of St. Joseph. Highly regarded special agents were torchbearers for the stations of the Cross, while the most respected special agents and captains literally carried the cross.[39]

Special agents were fully committed during Mass, as if their souls and jobs depended on it. Father James A. Martin, SJ, a storied basketball coach and athletic director at Georgetown University and St. Joseph's University, led the G-men in several retreats. He told Hoover that the FBI men always "give themselves one hundred percent to the purpose of the retreat." While most men struggled to "follow the regulations and the discipline entailed in going through a Retreat," the G-men went "through every part of the services as if it were in a manner born to this life."[40] FBI special agents, it seemed, were destined and perfectly fashioned for the ways of the soldier-saint.

Following the orderly worship, FBI special agents were individually assigned a time to take refuge in the chapel for private prayer. The chapel was hallowed ground, illuminated by the refracted light of the six stained glass windows and filled with statues of the saints and the real presence of Christ in the FBI Chalice. FBI men prayed at an altar that was devoted to the cause of "righteous" battle. The sacred space was dedicated to St. Francis Xavier. He was a companion of St. Ignatius and co-founder of the Jesuits. Xavier infamously proposed the Goa Inquisition, a violent militaristic and judicial campaign of the Portuguese colonial government in present-day India against non-believers. Men, women, and children were jailed, fined, and executed for their "unbelief." Accordingly, the crusading altar was adorned with red, white, and blue boxes containing the names of some two thousand Manresa men, living and deceased, who had enlisted in the armed forces to make the world safe for Christianity and democracy. The militaristic altar made it clear: the G-men were part of a long line of "righteous" crusading soldiers.[41]

Bureau soldiers were taught to take prayer seriously. It was not only central to the exercises, it was also key in the life of a G-man. Hoover attested, "Through the many years of sometimes overwhelming burdens I have become more and more a firm believer that prayer to Almighty God does result in sustenance to carry on in the proper performance of our duties from day to day." At Manresa, FBI agents were instructed to begin their supplication with the prayer, "You are alone in this chapel, yet not alone, for Christ upon the altar is here with you." Father Lloyd and the other priests at Manresa proudly watched "the G-men at prayer . . . hour by hour," as special agents communed with God, alone, like Ignatius at his Manresa, hoping to emerge anew.[42]

Following their prayer at the altar of St. Francis Xavier, kneeling agents were instructed to begin the "four weeks" of *The Spiritual Exercises*. These "weeks," Ignatius advised, were stages as opposed to an actual seven-day framework. Time was not the guiding principle; rather, bearing the fruit or grace that corresponds with each stage is what matters. The "weeks" can be lengthened or shortened according to the needs, temperament, age, and education of the retreatants. Ignatius believed in this flexibility, in part, because he trusted that God engaged individuals on a path that is befitting each individual.[43] Hoover embraced *The Spiritual Exercises*, especially at Manresa, because it was routinized spiritual labor for white men, just like his FBI.[44]

Special agents of the FBI focused on overcoming the self for the first "week." The men were encouraged to make decisions in accordance with the glory of God and not the "disordered affections" of sin. The corresponding spiritual exercises focused on the "consideration and contemplation of sins." Agents considered their individual sins as well as their participation in humanity's collective rebellion against God. This reflection was followed with the contemplation of the need for repentance and the joy that comes from forgiveness and the freedom to pursue God. The aspiration was to bring the special agent's desires and actions in line with the transcendent end of humanity: the glory of God and the salvation of the soul. As one Manresa priest summed it up, men should train themselves "to want what God wants and not to want what God doesn't want." Men should literally "beg Christ for intense hatred of sin."[45]

At FBI retreats, the sins of communism and materialism were often pinpointed as the sins that so easily led souls astray. Retreat masters often drew on their particular expertise to drive the point home. Father Dennis J. Comey, SJ, director of the St. Joseph's College Institute of Industrial Relations in Philadelphia, lectured at one retreat. He was "nationally known for his activities in settling labor disputes . . . which benefit both labor and management." He was no stranger to the Bureau, cooperating with the Philadelphia FBI field office on a number of labor disputes and investigations. At Manresa, he implemented his work with the labor movement and "rather detailed knowledge of the activities of communists" to instruct the G-men on the sin of communism and its role in producing disordered affections. The priest encouraged the men to put away worldly things in favor of pursuing righteousness, namely praise and reverence for God and service.[46] Legendary cross-country and track and field coach Reverend Francis J. Diamond, SJ, shared a similar perspective. He told Hoover's men about the dire need to train one's self to exercise "traditional spiritual and moral values to combat the materialistic influences of today."[47] Hoover praised Father Lloyd for overseeing this emphasis. "At a time when false ideologies and materialistic viewpoints are clouding the minds of many men," Hoover penned, "there is an increasing need for spiritual growth. All of us at the FBI are grateful that you so kindly afford this opportunity to our co-workers."[48]

Members of the faculty from Georgetown University, the nation's oldest Catholic and Jesuit institution of higher education, gladly preached to the G-men. Georgetown held Hoover and his FBI in high esteem. In 1939, the university presented him with an honorary law degree during an auspicious convocation celebrating the 150th anniversary of the school's founding.[49] The admiration was mutual. FBI men loved the male faculty of Georgetown. One Bureau retreatant reported to the Bureau's head of Domestic Intelligence, Special Agent William C. Sullivan, that the sermons and meditations of the school's theology department were always so "timely."[50] Special Agent W. A. Branigan was overjoyed by the visit of Georgetown ethics professor Father Stephen McNamee, SJ. SA Branigan was a counterintelligence specialist, instrumental in the infamous investigation that led to the Julius and Ethel Rosenberg espionage convictions and executions. The decorated sleuth found the meditations and sermons of the ethicist very "pertinent" to the moral problems of the day.[51] Another special agent praised Father Samuel R. Pitts, SJ, for utilizing "his background as Professor of Scripture at Georgetown University" to make his sermons and meditations "truly inspirational" for the personal and professional soul-saving work of the G-men. His effective presentations of biblical scholarship "contributed greatly to the success of the retreat."[52]

FBI men were encouraged to make a sincere confession of sin so they could recognize God's dominion and order. God was in charge, and his divine authority was expressed in American law, a societal arrangement the FBI was charged with keeping and enforcing. Father M. V. Jarreau, SJ, drilled this into the FBI men. One agent told Assistant Director in Charge of the Investigative Division SA Alex Rosen (1940–1972) that the white southern priest was a "dynamic" speaker. Jarreau, the first chaplain of the National Football League's New Orleans Saints, was a staunch believer in top-down authority, preaching, "God has complete and absolute dominion," and "All authority comes from God." Therefore, he told the men "reverence and respect for God includes respect for all legitimate authority." Breaking the law, whether it was a simple local ordinance or a federal infraction, was tantamount to sinning against God. The captain of the FBI retreat praised Jarreau for his words and for the way he "guided and directed the men through periods of meditation."[53]

FBI men were encouraged to believe that in their efforts to execute the law, they were working with and for God. In Ignatian thought, all labor is sacred. One should seek the glory of God in everything that one does. Hoover's rearing in the Protestant Reformed tradition shared this orientation. All vocations, not just ordained ministry, were callings; every vocation was a divine errand. One should always work as if working for the Lord. The work of an FBI special agent then was spiritual labor for the Kingdom of God. Being an FBI special agent was not just a job; it was, as Hoover noted in his law enforcement pledge, "a high calling."[54]

The "high calling" required agents to confess their sins, so they could be freed to be co-laborers with God. In the way of Ignatius, God is the creator of the world and the author of the created order. The world, and all that is within it, form the venue in which humankind cooperates with God in God's work to turn sinners back to God.[55] Hoover deployed the Manresa retreats to cultivate this sensibility within His Bureau. Special agents were soldiers and ministers working with God in and through the mundane to bring America back to God.[56] As one Jesuit priest assured Hoover, the retreats helped the G-men "reassess their sense of values so that they can fulfill their obligations to God, their country, and their own personal duties more fully."[57]

Being a special agent of the FBI, however, did not replace the love of God. The overall aim of the spiritual exercises, as Ignatius noted, is the "greater glory of God." True spiritual flourishing requires one to be free from "disordered affection or attachment," that is, trivial matters that compete with one's love of God, or worse, take the place of God. One's life and priorities should always be ordered toward the salvation of one's own soul and to glorify God. The primary aim in life, as the first soldier-saint put it, is "to keep as my objective the end for which I am created, to praise God our Lord and save my soul." Ignatius preached that "Divine vocation is always pure and clear, without any admixture of the carnal or of any disordered attachment."[58]

Manresa priests were sure to let the Bureau know that no one, not even priests, was above God's law and order. If a priest was out of line, the FBI had a God-given duty to restrain him. Reverend Neil J. Gargan, SJ, who served as president of Gonzaga College High School, the oldest boys' high school in the nation's capital, offered meditations and talks to FBI agents in which "he stressed the need for loyalty, adherence to order, and fidelity to responsibility to counteract the tendency so prevalent today to skirt responsibility and resist authority." The Jesuit priest reasserted his stance when members of the order, especially Father Daniel Berrigan, engaged in anti-war protests. He told the FBI he was embarrassed by the utter disregard for law and order and the "erratic behavior of the small segment of fellow clergymen which has brought shame and disgrace" to the Jesuits. He reassured the Bureau that he and the overwhelming majority of his colleagues were "wholeheartedly with the Bureau." The priest sermonized on the divine nature of authority and societal order to the very men who were pursuing his "erratic" Jesuit colleagues. Not surprisingly, the FBI agent reporting on the retreat noted that Father Gargan's sermons and meditations were "most inspiring and particularly applicable to our lives both private and professional."[59]

Celebrity Catholic televangelist Bishop Fulton Sheen declared a similar message to the G-men. The two-time Emmy Award–winning religious broadcaster and *New York Times* best-selling author was a close acquaintance and ardent admirer of J. Edgar Hoover. "You," he told Hoover, "have built up a tradition toward Divine Justice in this country which has been incomparable in the life of free peoples."[60] He told the Boss's men at Manresa that the "contemporary problems of our society such as the decline of morality, the lack of discipline generally, and protest for the sake of protest" were caused by "the general breakdown of society" caused by Christians who had neglected "the basic teachings of Christ." If America was to be fixed, Christians had to confess their sins and return to God's law and order. They had to recommit themselves to the very foundations upon which American society rested: the teachings of Christ. Special Agent Churchill F. Downing praised the retreat for emphasizing the role Christians should play in returning society back to God.[61]

Bishop Sheen helped SA Downing be self-assured of his role in this crusade. As chief of the Cryptanalysis-Translation Section in the Laboratory Division, he was in charge of translating and transcribing data obtained from one of the Bureau's covert surveillance operations. Codenamed "June Mail," the program obtained information through "sources illegal in nature" such as break-ins and mail intercepts. Such intel was sent to FBI headquarters under the marker "June Mail." It was routed away from the Bureau's central record system, placed in a "confidential file" in the Bureau's Special File Room, where it was maintained "under lock and key" for authorized personnel only—for men like Special Agent Downing. Downing, who was involved in countless June Mail operations including the bugging of the home of Nation of Islam leader Elijah Muhammad found Bishop Sheen's diagnosis of society empowering. He considered Bishop Sheen's weekend of spiritual guidance unparalleled "in content and in presentation, and particularly meaningful." Sheen's homilies, he concluded, were "stimulating and will not be soon forgotten."[62]

The focus of the first week of the retreat—the recognition and confession of sin coupled with respect for God's authority—was always a source of encouragement for SA Downing and his colleagues. When FBI special agents illegally monitored First Amendment–protected speech or unlawfully harassed American citizens, they were assured they were working with and for God to save American society. They had divine sanction to enforce and defend existing societal arrangements—the racial, gendered, classed, and sexual status quo—in the name of Jesus.

During the second "week" of meditation, special agents focused on the moral framework of their crusade. The G-men were charged with focusing on the life of Jesus Christ and pondering God's kingdom, the incarnation, and the public work of Christ. The men were asked three questions: "What have I done for Christ, the King in the Past?" Next, "What am I doing for Him Now?" And finally, "What do I intend to do for Him in the Future?"[63] These questions were fitting for the self-styled crusading G-men. It provided a spiritual frame for their work. In the Society of Jesus, spirituality permeates the mundane. God can be found in every aspect of life. Church attendance, sacred texts, and prayer are only a portion of one's spiritual life. For the Jesuit, nothing is outside the purview of the spiritual life. God is in all things, manifested and encompassed in the material world. All facets of life are spiritual: sex, suffering, relationships, family, friends, and, of course, working for the FBI.[64]

At Manresa, special agents were given the road map to navigate this world of all-encompassing spirituality. Jesuits were called to work in "secular" society and institutions. In the midst of this secular vocation, they had to be, the Society preached, "contemplative in action." Ignatian spirituality is for men on the move, soldiers who understand that the world, not the monastery, is where the spiritual life is practiced and lived, sometimes with little to no time to spare. The way of Ignatius did not teach a prescriptive spirituality, but rather a "way of proceeding." Soldier-saints were to be prayerful and mindful of God's way in the midst of daily life. It is a "calling" not simply to be something; but rather a "call[ing] to *do* something." This is essential for one who leads an active life, on a mission far from the authority that sent them. This was often the life of the G-men. Special agents on assignment—a stakeout, a surveillance detail, or an investigative trail—had little to no time to attend worship, pray, or seek guidance from their superior.[65] They were "called to do something," and to be "contemplative in action."

This spiritual practice provided FBI special agents with a "way of proceeding" during split-second decisions and ethical dilemmas. Ignatius taught that doing the will of God is clear in some situations. However, in others, the evidence is presented, yet the divine will is not obvious. In these situations, *The Spiritual Exercises* instructed SAs to pursue the decision that availed itself as emanating "solely for the praise of God our Lord and the salvation of my soul." Special agents were also directed to consider the final judgment of their souls during tough decisions. Ignatius advised that Christian soldiers should imagine and consider how they will feel about their moral choice on judgment day.[66] When FBI men confronted values and rules that conflicted with their federal vocational duties and personal morality, they were instructed to consider the glory and order of God and the eternal fate of their souls.

This moral instruction derived from the Jesuit teaching of casuistry. Jesuits on a mission far from traditional authority needed a method to confront moral ambiguity. The Jesuit "way of proceeding" espoused a rejection of universally applicable ethical rules and principles. Instead, casuistry prioritized the employment of analogous cases of ethical dilemmas to arrive at moral decisions that are consistent with a broader worldview, that is the ultimate glory of God, even if it might clash with traditional law and authority.[67]

Hoover made sure his G-men and the nation understood this well. In his first televised sit-down interview, Hoover cited the Bible as the analogous case and justification for the use of surveillance tactics, including paid informants and wiretapping. In the 1956 broadcast, Congressmen Kenneth Keating (R-New York) asked the FBI Boss if he believed there was any legitimacy to criticisms lobbied at the FBI for such questionable maneuvers. "No, I most certainly do not," Hoover snapped back. "The use of informants has existed for years and years ... and you will find reference to it in the Bible, in the time of Moses."[68] The trained lawyer did not cite the US Constitution for his defense, instead, he grounded his case in a biblical analogy. Moses followed God's command to appoint spies to gather intel on the enemies who were occupying the promised land and preventing God's chosen people from inheriting their promise. Hoover viewed his FBI as performing the same service. Whether legal or illegal, the FBI had a moral imperative from God to gather intel on all enemies, foreign and domestic, that stood in the way of God's chosen nation.

Such reasoning undergirded all of the Bureau's actions. SA John P. Mohr, the Assistant Director in Charge of the Administrative Division, laughed when a young law school student inquired about the legality of the Bureau's labor. "You're still in law school—which means you're still an idealist," he told the neophyte. The Bureau's number four man was in charge of the budget and all personnel matters. The man with the power to hire and fire fully expected and instructed special agents to break the law. He told the future special agent to always remember: extralegal and illegal methods were completely appropriate, because "When it's for the right reasons, the end does justify the means." There was no ambiguity in Hoover's FBI, the message coming from the top was clear: faithful special agents knew the Bureau's righteous ends justified any and all means. These moral ends were determined by the Bureau's Christian nationalism, not the US Constitution. "And if the moral values ran into conflict with the legal principles," one special agent noted, "the legal principles had to give way."[69] Former FBI agent G. Gordon Liddy (the mastermind of the Watergate break-in), who was educated in Jesuit schools, noted that agents were trained to "appear" to go by the book, but to "do" whatever was needed to "win," regardless of "the facts and circumstances." The DOJ could declare a particular investigative method to be illegal. But if the case was analogous to a similar case in which the method was legal and brought about Hoover's moral ends, the FBI special agent could proceed with the illegal action. It might be illegal for an FBI agent to bear false witness under oath, but it could be ethical and moral if it served this greater purpose. What mattered most was that the desired result was commensurate with white Christian nationalism.

To prevent self-interest and bias, Manresa taught the G-men that during difficult "cases of conscience," their course of action should not emanate from "disordered" motives such as egocentric pleasures, yearnings for career advancement, or any form of bias. Rather, their actions should spring from a desire to serve and please God. The way of the soldier-saint was the sure way to eschew all self-interest, in favor of the broader moral framework of the glory of God, that is, Hoover's God.

This moral taxonomy helped Hoover's FBI frame its activities, no matter how unscrupulous, as labor for the glory of God. The Bureau was on the side of law and order, that is, God's side. Therefore, whatever the Bureau did, it did for God. When FBI special agents such as Churchill F. Downing were seeking direction for an investigation—whether obtaining unlawful data from June Mail or performing extralegal counterintelligence—*The Spiritual Exercises* helped them confirm that their chosen path was to help maintain God's way. Breaking the law was permissible, as long as it was for the greater glory of God and the salvation of souls.

Special agents focused on the life and passion of Christ during the third "week" of their Manresa retreat. The men were invited to interrogate their life choices in the light of Christ. The aim was to help G-men strengthen their resolve to lead a life that mirrored that of Christ, especially in suffering. Bureau men were asked to explore whether their decisions had led them to experience the passion of the Christ.[70] Special agents solidified this shared understanding of suffering by ritually "read[ing] THE PASSION from the Gospel aloud" to one another. Reciting the gospel account of Christ's misery cultivated a unified view of the soldier-saint: to be a G-man was to suffer for Christ.[71] Father Jarreau told retreatants, "As we see Him in His great pain and suffering—let us be mindful that here He shows us a little something of what our life will be in some way or another."[72]

FBI agents received blessed assurance at Manresa. They were not just working for a federal agency, they were suffering for the sake of righteousness, and in doing so they were brought closer to Christ. The Manresa priests assured the G-men that their engagement of the sinful world was divinely inspired and guided. And in this work, they were not alone. Throughout these trying times, one priest noted, the consolation Christ offers is "the knowledge that we [are] with Him." Participating in "sin,"

associating with "sinners," and suffering to gather intel or establish informants was to share in the life of Christ. Long hours, low pay, or public
criticism were among the costs of discipleship.[73] Director Hoover took
solace in this. "It is gratifying that our people, who are so impressed in
the crass materialism of crime and subversion in the course of their duties, participate in this annual expression of faith," he proclaimed. It
provided his worldly soldier-saints with the chance "to enhance their
spiritual strength" for the ongoing battle.[74]

—

Finally, the joy and victory of Christ's resurrection and ascension were
celebrated during the fourth "week." It was geared to help special agents
experience the triumphant nature of Christ in every aspect of their
being.[75] Special Agent John J. (J. J.) McGuire, a graduate of the College
of Holy Cross and Fordham Law School, attested to this. In a report to
FBI Associate Director Special Agent Clyde Tolson he testified, "The
Retreat was highly successful from the standpoint of spiritual revivifica-
tion, mental relaxation, and physical benefit." Likewise, the Boss told
Father Lloyd following one retreat, "The men had a grand time . . . the
Retreat has improved them spiritually, mentally, and physically."[76]

The male physique was the canvas that displayed this all-encompassing
spirituality. The power of the resurrection was manifested in Christ's
risen and glorious body. Thus, the G-man's body—the appearance of
health and fitness—was the indicator of his spiritual state, character, and
morality. At Manresa, the physical prowess of a man attested to the condition of his soul. A fit soul was manifested by a fit body. Father Lloyd
told the men of Manresa in no uncertain terms, "The body simply cannot
radiate good health and true happiness, if there is a mortally sinful soul
within." Of no surprise, the retreat priests readily assured Hoover and his
retreat captains that they were "impressed by the . . . physical caliber" of
the FBI retreatants.[77] This was music to Hoover's ears. Like the pastor
of his youth, Hoover believed in muscular Christianity, where faith and
physicality were inextricably linked. Only white men who exuded masculine norms could be true patriotic male Christians.

Desirable Weight Ranges for Males			
Height	Small Frame	Medium Frame	Large Frame
5' 4"	117 - 125	123 - 135	131 - 148
5' 5"	120 - 129	126 - 139	134 - 152
5' 6"	124 - 133	130 - 143	138 - 157
5' 7"	128 - 137	134 - 148	143 - 162
5' 8"	132 - 141	138 - 152	147 - 166
5' 9"	136 - 146	142 - 156	151 - 170
5' 10"	140 - 150	146 - 161	155 - 175
5' 11"	144 - 154	150 - 166	160 - 180
6'	148 - 158	154 - 171	164 - 185
6' 1"	152 - 163	158 - 176	169 - 190
6' 2"	156 - 167	163 - 181	174 - 195
6' 3"	160 - 171	168 - 186	178 - 200
6' 4"	169 - 180	178 - 196	188 - 210
6' 5"	174 - 185	182 - 202	192 - 216

FIGURE 9. FBI weight program guidelines, 1960. *Source*: FBI file 67-308185-184.

This belief permeated the Bureau, and Hoover was the masculine mold. Hoover's pastor, Reverend Elson, idolized Hoover as the physical epitome of a godly man. In his estimation, Hoover was a "robust, manly, attractive figure . . . always impeccably groomed," he penned for a national publication. "With massive head, penetrating eyes, rugged jowls resting upon broad shoulders which taper to a slender waist and hip line, with his feet firmly on the ground." He concluded, "Look at him standing there—every inch a man. And you have a feeling down deep inside you that he is God's man."[78]

The boss wanted FBI special agents to be molded accordingly. He instituted an FBI weight program to make it so (figure 9). The plan specified weight guidelines for each special agent according to his height, regardless of his fitness. As one special agent recalled, the strict program "caused real problems for big-boned husky ex-football players and others of this type." Using the Metropolitan Life Insurance standards of the day, a special agent of six feet four inches could weigh no more than approximately 210 pounds for his annual physical exam. Hoover, at five feet ten inches and roughly 200 pounds, was consistently 20–30 pounds overweight for a man his height. However, he exempted himself from stepping on the scale. Other agents were not so lucky. If a man "had not an ounce of fat and looked wonderful," SA Milton Jones complained, but exceeded the guidelines, he was ordered to lose weight. "I frequently would be a few pounds over as examination time neared," he confessed, so "a crash diet with reduced liquid intake was in order." If the sudden diet failed, some veteran special agents could depend on a sympathetic physician to overlook a few pounds, or even give an agent a magical growth spurt of "about one-half inch if that was what it took to comply with the rigid weight chart." It was the only way to circumvent the Boss. Direct challenges were not allowed. When one physical examiner warned Hoover of the possible dangers of one agent's ordered weight loss, the FBI director called for a second opinion and ordered his employees to never visit the physician again. All that mattered in Hoover's Bureau was that a special agent could respond affirmatively to "the standard question: Make the weight?"[79]

Special agents still had to remain vigilant after their examination. A few sections and divisions at headquarters were known to "have impromptu weigh-ins ... between physical examinations." Missing weight, like any other Bureau infraction or faux pas, resulted in the SA receiving "a confidential letter from the Director drawing his attention to this fact and warning him to be back in shape by the time the next physical is taken." Special agents called them "'fat man' warning letter[s]." Such reprimands came in the form of censures, probation, demotion, transfer, or termination. A censure notification, the mildest punishment, "outlined one's dereliction in a formal tone," alerting the agent that "additional misconduct or carelessness would not be tolerated, and that performance would be observed carefully in the future." The formal reprimand became a permanent part of the special agent's personnel file and was considered during evaluations. Probation, which included a letter of censure, barred the offending special agent from receiving raises, commendations, or monetary incentives until they were removed from probation, usually a three-month period, provided the agent's record was deemed satisfactory during the interim. Demotions were accompanied with a pay decrease, while transfers were sent to undesirable and remote offices. A journalist bore witness to this disciplinary regime while visiting FBIHQ (FBI headquarters): "the slightest sign of a paunch brings a curt warning to get more exercise—or else," he observed. The "or else" was harsh. One SA, a former football player, was transferred for being five pounds overweight. He protested with an official statement from his physician indicating his weight was medically proper. This was an affront to Hoover's judgment. The "over-weight" agent and his surplus five pounds were "put on the bicycle," Bureau-speak for a series of rapid transfers from one unfavorable post to another. The agent eventually resigned.[80] The Boss questioned medical opinions when it came to the physical health of his special agents, because he was firmly convinced that only lean bodies housed the abundant spirituality required for the job.

Yet, being underweight was no safe haven, either. Special Agent J. J. McGuire's annual examination concluded that he was "capable of performing strenuous exertion" and had "no physical defects that would interfere with participation in raids or other work." However, Hoover told the towering, lanky Catholic special agent he was found to be twelve pounds underweight (see figure 7). The Boss warned him, "With regard to your underweight condition, please be advised that the standards of the Bureau require that you increase your weight during the next six months' period." McGuire had six months to discipline his body in compliance with Bureau standards, or else.[81] In Hoover's FBI, the relationship between a healthy body and a pious soul was like one's belief in God: it was a narrow yet measurable and exact science.

Sexuality was treated similarly. Christian masculine men performed heterosexuality, no exceptions. Suspicions continue to abound concerning Hoover's sexuality. He never married and he never had children. He and SA Clyde Tolson were inseparable, riding to work as well as eating lunch and dinner together everyday and annually vacationing together. Hoover's secretary Helen Gandy swore SA Tolson "hate[d] all women," but stopped short of commenting on his sexuality. In the FBI, Hoover's relationship with SA Tolson, at best, was considered a reflection of the platonic relations within the special agent corps. At worst, it was ridiculed in hush tones. Some FBIHQ employees whispered that J. Edgar Hoover and Clyde Tolson were actually "J. Edna and Clyde." Nevertheless, expressing same-sex romantic desire was never tolerated. That was a cardinal sin of Christian masculinity in the Bureau, punishable by immediate excommunication—no questions asked. "Generally, the FBI was most successful in getting the highest type personnel," Baptist SA Milton Jones remarked about sexuality in the Bureau, "but occasionally a 'bad apple' would slip through." A special agent from his section "made improper advances" to a plainclothes police officer "at a notorious hangout for homosexuals." The offending special agent was brought to FBIHQ where he relinquished his FBI credentials and was promptly fired. "He knew and we knew he was through," SA Jones remembered. The Baptist layman called the ordeal his "most embarrassing FBI experience."[82]

Even proximity to homosexual desire was shunned. Washington field office SA John Richard Nichols found out the hard way. In 1966, the Bureau received a report that Nichols's son, famed gay rights activist John Richard Nichols Jr., was gay. The younger Nichols lived and worked in DC, and expressed his same-sex desires as a teenager. When the Bureau confronted SA Nichols about his adult gay son, he told his superior he did not think it was necessary to address the issue. He did not raise the young man. He divorced the younger Nichols's mother in 1946, and was remarried in 1948. He pleaded with his son to change his name so as to avoid embarrassing the family name or harming his father's career. Nobody would suspect that "Warren Adkins," the name his son used in public, was the offspring of a prominent G-man. Nevertheless, SA Nichols never gave up on converting his son. He saw his son occasionally, hoping to convert him to a "normal male." He swore to his supervisor that he had desperately tried to "lead his son into a Christian way." He agonized for his son's soul, seeking counsel and "advice from clergymen." It was all to no avail. He told his superiors in the Administrative Division "that he hopes that he might continue to occasionally contact his son but if the Bureau desires, he will stop seeing him." Yet in the FBI, his willingness to sacrifice his relationship with his son was not enough to cover his sins. "SA Nichols's failure to advise the Bureau of this problem is inexcusable," his supervisor screamed. "Although his son is using an alias . . . this situation could develop into a source of great embarrassment to the Bureau." SA Nichols was censured, put on probation, and transferred to an unspecified and unfavorable field office for his "flagrant" behavior.[83]

This appearance and performance of Christian masculinity assured that Hoover's soldiers were detached from any "disordered affections." They pledged to perform their duties, seeking not to glorify themselves or any "disordered attachment," but the sacred virtues revealed in the risen Christ. His G-men took an oath "to testify without bias" and to approach their job as "a sacred trust" and to always "bear true faith and allegiance."[84] They were to keep as their objective the end for which they were created and hired: to minister to the nation and to wage warfare against "sin" wherever it lurked.

The annual weekend of spiritual formation concluded with a blessing, the Benediction of the Blessed Sacrament and the recitation of prayers. As special agents exited the Chapel for the last time, decorative wallet-sized cards were distributed bearing the words of the "Alone with Christ" prayer they uttered at the martial altar.[85] G-men descending from the holy hill, boarded their chartered buses and car pools, and drove down the straight and narrow path. Equipped with the way of the soldier-saint, they departed their Manresa prepared to labor for and with God.

Retired Special Agent Alan Ouimet spoke for many when he recalled his first FBI Manresa retreat. "I walked out of the retreat house at sunset . . . it was almost like I was feeling the divine." The Bronx native recalled that the 1958 retreat ushered him into a "spiritual epiphany," an unsurpassed "feeling of divine inspiration." He departed Manresa feeling that he was "at one" with God, forever convinced of his Christian vocation, noting that America "could not build a Christian society, without a Christian police force."[86]

Father Lloyd and the Manresa spiritual retreats played a central role in facilitating such divine revelations. The ecumenical troops of special agents were "composed of many men of many nationalities and of many religious faiths," Reverend Lloyd told readers of his newsletter. Yet, these men, "Catholic, Protestant, and Jew . . . slept under one roof, supped together at table, relaxed on the porch," and worshipped in "the chapel with real fidelity and deep devotion." Despite the religious differences, Lloyd said in amazement, "the Bureau ha[d] moulded [sic] these men, as if by magic, into one man, into one family."[87]

It was not magic; it was Hoover baptizing the Bureau in his own image. This spiritual formation created a uniform white male soldier and a unified white family, one in faith: the religious culture of the FBI. Or, as Father Lloyd noted, men of the FBI were "the special fruits, not only of an excellent system of training, but especially of a personal leadership that has fashioned them for Country and God."[88]

The spirituality of St. Ignatius of Loyola, the soldier-saint, took root not just in the hearts of the G-men, but also in the organizational culture of the Bureau. From the FBI Chalice to the spiritual exercises, the yearly ritual helped to form special agents, entrenching the militaristic faith of St. Ignatius in their lives and in the very DNA of the FBI. When duty called, Jesuit spirituality provided Hoover's men with a way to proceed. It helped special agents cast judgments about who was godly and who was subversive. It provided a moral framework for legal and illegal maneuvers, and solidified an image of Christian masculinity. It prompted special agents to see themselves as soldiers of God's nation. In the end, it sacralized the Bureau's politics of white male supremacy and Christian nationalism, all in the name of God and national security.[89]

Hoover was forever thankful to Father Lloyd and his retreats for shepherding his agents along this path. He told the priest, "Your words bring joy, consolation, and encouragement to all of us who are engaged in the struggle against the forces of Godlessness which seek to destroy our American democracy." He confessed that the retreats had consistently afforded his G-men "an opportunity to obtain in quiet retreat the divine inspiration" that was required for their jobs. Manresa gave his white male troops "the spiritual energy and zeal for principles of righteousness." For Hoover, the Jesuit retreat was part of the Bureau's arsenal in "the unending warfare against the menace of ungodliness." Without Father Lloyd and Manresa, Hoover concluded, the FBI would not have been able to "successfully carr[y] out [its] responsibilities in connection with the internal security of the nation." Hoover was confident that his men departed Manresa with a blessed assurance: the battle for the soul and security of the nation was "a fight which we cannot lose, since God is on our side."[90]

Father Lloyd died in 1960, but the FBI retreats soldiered on, outlasting both Father Lloyd and Hoover. Hoover's successor, Clarence Kelley, bore witness to the enduring centrality of the retreats in the Bureau. Shortly after assuming the mantle of FBI director in 1973, Director Kelley announced, "The effects of these spiritual exercises . . . not only enrich the lives of the men who attend the Retreat but also permeate and enhance the very fabric of the FBI itself."[91] The retreats ensured that Hoover's FBI produced soldier-saints of Christian America.

And before Hoover was done with them, they would also be lay ministers of Christian America.

CHAPTER 3

Ministers

Mr. Hoover has always sought high minded, clean-cut . . . [men] who will approach the business of law enforcement with the spirit of sacrificial consecration befitting a missionary or minister. . . . The FBI wants only people of high moral standards and religious devotion.

—HOOVER'S PASTOR, REVEREND ELSON, 1950[1]

"It is gratifying to me personally," J. Edgar Hoover told the first annual FBI Mass and Communion Breakfast, "that large numbers of my associates in the FBI have joined together in a special way, on this Sunday morning, to worship Almighty God." He assured the gathering of FBI employees, family, and friends, "It is this inextinguishable belief in and reliance upon our Creator which will enable all of us to carry out our responsibilities in a true Christian fashion." He closed his greeting with a conspicuous suggestion. "I hope that the purposeful spirit which has prompted this gathering of FBI employees will be kept alive in the future." FBI employees received Hoover's invocation with a round of applause, followed by decades of strict obedience.[2]

Beginning in 1950, the FBI began hosting "The Annual FBI Employees' Mass and Communion Breakfast" for FBI headquarters and the surrounding field offices. Field offices across the country followed suit.[3] While the Bureau's Manresa retreats were exclusively for special agents, the FBI Mass and Communion Breakfast was "for all employees of the FBI." That is, all white employees, including male special agents, the white female clerical staff, as well as their respective families and friends. They gathered annually for Mass to express their reliance on God and to affirm the divine sanctioning of their labor. They did so in an auspicious place: the Cathedral of St. Matthew the Apostle, the "Mother Church" of the Archdiocese of Washington, DC, and the seat of the Archbishop of Washington, DC.

This yearly FBI revival took on a Protestant form as well. The Bureau hosted an annual Protestant Vesper Service strictly for white Bureau employees and their families and friends. The service was held at various white Protestant congregations every year. The FBI deliberately avoided white fundamentalists, counting them as "sincere," but marginal "crackpots."[4] Instead, the Bureau focused on "respectable" white conservative Protestant congregations, restricting their worship services to the seven mainline Protestant denominations. Alternating the service between the nation's white mainline denominations was practical. The Bureau was, after all, comprised of white Protestants from across the denominational spectrum. But it was also savvy, displaying the Bureau's network of support among conservative white Protestants.

In all, the FBI Mass and Communion Breakfasts and the FBI Vesper Services, served as rituals of affirmation. Hoover's Christian nationalism cared little about denominational differences and theological debates. He viewed the worship services as the "traditional manifestation[s] of faith on the part of the men and women of the FBI, their families, and friends." In reality, the FBI worship services were a collection of federally approved and financed revivals that were scripted according to Hoover's two central ideals for his FBI and the country. First, the services reaffirmed the Bureau's Christian fidelity and purpose. As Hoover told his employees, the Bureau should take pride in "fulfilling [their] responsibilities to defend and perpetuate the dignity of the Nation's Christian endowment."[5] When Bureau men and women took part in the FBI worship services, they reasserted their roles as crusaders, religious actors in the ideological drama that was the Cold War.[6] Second and closely related, the annual revivals announced the priesthood of the G-men. Prominent white Catholic and Protestant clergy bestowed the blessings of God and the Church upon the work of the FBI. They authenticated the G-men as ministers, moral custodians anointed to help the nation maintain its Christian underpinnings against all enemies, foreign and domestic.

Special Agent J. J. McGuire "sparked" the FBI Mass and Communion Breakfast. The perpetually underweight Manresa man pushed for the service, and he easily gained a critical mass of followers.[7] A committee was formed to implement the sacred affair, comprised of members from every division at FBI headquarters and one representative from the Washington, DC field office. It was overseen by a chairman, a position that rotated through all the Bureau's divisions (see figure 10). The group typically met in December and January to plan every single aspect of the annual spring event. The worship service was held during one of the holiest times in Christian practice: Lent, the forty weekdays preceding Easter. The Bureau family typically worshipped on Palm Sunday, commemorating Christ's triumphant entry into Jerusalem, the seat of civil and religious authority. Once all the details were settled, each committee member was responsible for proselytizing employees in their division, compelling and organizing attendance.[8]

The Records and Communication Division drafted a "floater," a flier that was posted and distributed throughout the Bureau to spread the word of the FBI revival. The handbill listed the details of the event, as well as the names and office numbers of every committee member (see figure 11). The evangelistic efforts worked. The worship services were "heavily attended," with upward of a thousand special agents attending with their families, friends, and relatives.[9]

Black employees were not among them. The FBI had "an unwritten policy" against hiring Black special agents. For years, the FBI paraded five Black employees as special agents, even arranging a special issue of

TWENTY-FOURTH ANNUAL FBI MASS
AND COMMUNION BREAKFAST COMMITTEE

CHAIRMAN - Joseph W. Montefiore

DIVISION

Executive Offices	Nancy A. Mooney
Identification	Susan Kopacko
Administrative	SA John P. Dunphy
Files & Communications	Susan Rusnak
Domestic Intelligence	SA Robert A. Bermingham
General Investigative	SA Joseph G. Kelly
Laboratory	Eleanor Jackson
Special Investigative	SA Loy A. Wagoner
	SA John P. Kenney
Legal Counsel	Marguerite Devine
Computer Systems	Nelson Switzer
Office of Planning and Evaluation	SA William Y. Doran
WFO	SA Patrick O'Donnell

FIGURE 10. FBI Mass and Communion Breakfast Committee list. *Source*: FBI file 94-462870-123 enclosure.

Ebony magazine in 1947, extolling "Negro FBI Agents in Action." In reality, the men were exclusively "chauffeurs" and valets, deputized not to fight crime, but to serve as avatars of Hoover's supposed commitment to racial equality. This included James Crawford, Hoover's chauffeur and personal valet. After serving Hoover for nearly decade, Crawford was abruptly made a special agent. "It was in 1943," he remembered, "it was during the time when the NAACP was pressuring the Bureau because they didn't have any Negro agents." When Crawford went to training at Quantico, he was the only Black man, and he was forbidden from rooming with the other white agents. After completing his special agent training, he returned to work as Hoover's driver and gardener.[10]

Eighteenth Annual

FBI Mass and
Communion Breakfast

FBI Employees, Their Relatives and Friends

Sunday April 9, 1967

at St. John's College
2607 Military Road, N.W.

Military Mass at 10:00 A.M.
Breakfast at 11:00 A.M.

Speaker

HONORABLE JOHN W. MC CORMACK

The Speaker of the House of Representatives

Tickets ... $2.50   For those under 21 years ... $1.50

FOR TICKETS CONTACT THE FOLLOWING:

EXECUTIVE OFFICES			
DIVISION 1	HELEN MARTIS, Ext. 555	DIVISION 6	JOSEPH G. KELLY, Ext. 387
DIVISION 2	FRANCES C. LOMEDICO, Ext. 362	DIVISION 7	ERNEST J. LANDREVILLE, Ext. 726
DIVISION 3	WILLIAM M. MOONEY, Ext. 2511	DIVISION 8	DONALD G. HANNING, Ext. 653
DIVISION 3	JOHN P. DUNPHY, Ext. 2007	DIVISION 9	JOHN E. KELLY, Ext. 527
DIVISION 4	LAWRENCE W. BRADY, Ext. 562	DIVISION 10	O. JANNETTE SLUSHER, Ext. 2401
DIVISION 5	ALBERT B. KNICKREHM, Ext. 2181	WFO	LAWRENCE S. MOHR, Ext. 391

For needing transportation from downtown to St. John's, contact any Division Representative set forth above.

FOIA # 50210 (URTS 16233) Docld: 70104460 Page 133
ENCLOSURE 94-46287-96

FIGURE 11. FBI Mass and Communion Breakfast flier. Occasionally, the event was held outside of St. Matthew's to accommodate differences in the schedules of the Bureau and the parish. *Source:* 94-462870-96 enclosure.

This provided cover for the Bureau for decades. Even President Truman's Executive Order 9980 did not penetrate the Bureau's racial segregation. The 1948 directive mandated federal hiring practices to abandon racial discrimination and adopt hiring "based solely on merit and fitness." Hoover systemically turned down Black special agent applicants, claiming they lacked the requisite qualifications. We "hire Negroes on the basis of merit," SA Cartha "Deke" DeLoach assured President Eisenhower's Presidential Committee on Government Employment Policy (the precursor to the modern US Equal Employment Opportunity Commission). The FBI changed its tune when confronted by the threat of a fair employment investigation by the Kennedy administration. Hoover claimed colorblindness when Attorney General Bobby Kennedy demanded to know how many Black FBI special agents were employed. The FBI could not answer the question, Hoover maintained, because the Bureau did not keep employment records "according to race, creed, or color." Yet, in 1962, Hoover begrudgingly hired his first crop of trained African American special agents: James W. Barrow, a graduate of Brooklyn College of Law; and Aubrey C. Lewis, a Notre Dame University football and track star. The Bureau slowly added to their numbers. By 1965, thirty of the Bureau's more than six thousand special agents were Black. These Black SAs were tracked, given sequential employee ID numbers beginning with "9," while all white special agents were given numbers that began with "1," alerting all Bureau offices of the racial identity of a special agent without saying a word. Such covert practices aided the Bureau's efforts to exclude Black men from their worship services. Black SAs were neither invited nor encouraged to worship alongside their FBI "family." In fact, they were deliberately ignored for decades, ensuring the Bureau's religious culture was an all-white affair.[11]

One Black Catholic special agent was not deterred. Special Agent Allen Jordan joined the Bureau in 1968. SA Jordan was reared in the Catholic Church, but he found the FBI made him even more devout in the faith; not because of the FBI's religious culture, but in spite of it. Enduring the daily discrimination in the Bureau, he noted, "made you real spiritual, sometimes all you can do is pray." The FBI provided him with plenty of opportunities to pray. Despite being a Catholic SA, he was never invited to the worship services. The advertising "floaters" were floated past him without his knowledge. He quickly learned that his colleagues believed "they didn't make Catholics in two colors, just like they didn't make FBI agents in two colors." Nevertheless, he recalled, "I went to some of the Catholic friends and family worship services . . . I would go to the worship service sometimes, to be honest, just to piss them off," he admitted. "They didn't want me there, but I didn't care . . . they didn't confront me. There's a special place in fucking hell for anybody who would try to stop someone from going into the house of God! But they didn't try to stop me, it was easier for them to just avoid me."[12] White special agents took the easy way out. When it came to the binding ritual of worship, the FBI was sure to place Blackness outside its divine sanction and mission. Blackness was, at best, a gadfly; and the worshipping sleuths did everything in their power to overlook Black employees.

In addition to monitoring who came to worship, the Bureau took stock of where to worship. The Cathedral of St. Matthew the Apostle was nationally famous, a place where religion and politics were common bedfellows.[13] St. Matthew was "the patron saint of civil servants and all who serve government in some capacity." In the Gospel story, Matthew was a government worker who Jesus called into service. The civil servant did not just decide to follow Jesus, he was chosen to be a member of Christ's inner circle of twelve disciples, anointed as a representative of Christ. He was charged with spreading the "good news" of Christ to "make disciples of all nations."[14] Given its significance, several US presidents made it a point to worship in the hallowed church while in office: Cleveland, McKinley, Taft, Teddy Roosevelt, Wilson, Harding, Hoover, Eisenhower, and Kennedy all kneeled before the altar.[15] It was the church where the nation's political elite bent the knee to show American Catholics their civil service was an outgrowth of their faith. The FBI joined them. It was the perfect canvas for the federal agency dedicated to justice to illustrate its own brand of religious fidelity and service. When FBI employees and their families and friends went to the Cathedral of St. Matthew, it was for one primary purpose: the employees of the FBI were civil servants, called by Christ to do the work of God.

From the moment the Bureau faithful walked into the 1,000-seat sanctuary, they were surrounded by exquisite reminders of their calling and duty as civil servants. The doors and columns of the entryway featured an impressive red mosaic of St. Matthew the Apostle hoisting his written Gospel. He resembled a special agent taking note of all who crossed the threshold.[16] The sanctuary flickered with mosaics and murals completed by renowned artist Edwin H. Blashfield, known for his work on the dome of the Library of Congress. Murals of St. Matthew glistened with colorful marbles from around the globe. A royal purple mosaic of Matthew reigned down from the dome; a mural depicting his calling to follow Christ covered the west transept, while his martyrdom adorned the east.[17] The Cathedral was perfectly suited for the civil servant ministers of Hoover's FBI. Like Matthew, they would follow Christ, even unto death.

The Bureau's top brass surveilled attendance. Assistant Director in Charge of Training and Inspection Special Agent Quinn Tamm, Assistant Director in Charge of the Identification Division and the FBI Laboratory Special Agent Stanley Tracy, and Assistant Director in Charge of the Domestic Intelligence Division Special Agent Alan H. Belmont—a member of the Episcopal Church—faithfully attended the worship service.[18] Perhaps the most conspicuous and powerful worshipper was Special Agent John P. Mohr. To say he had tremendous power in the Bureau was an understatement. He oversaw all personnel matters—including hiring, promotions, and evaluations—and expected special agents to resort to extralegal and illegal means when necessary to accomplish their work. The stocky former college football star was "gruff" and possessed a legendary "quick temper." His law school classmates found him smart, but conceited, while Bureau executives found him "self-confident," intelligent, and handsome. SA Mohr's self-assessment was as gruff as the man: "I'm a hardheaded Dutchman," he boasted, "and nobody pushes me around." He parlayed it all into a successful career in the Bureau. He made friends and allies through the regular poker parties he hosted. By 1959, he played his hand into Hoover's inner circle, rising to Assistant to the Director overseeing all of the Bureau's administration and budget, having the power to make or break a G-man's career. He was known in the Bureau as an "inveterate gossip," a database of Bureau tales, rumors, and narratives that he selectively dispensed and planted to serve his own purposes. No special agent wanted to trip SA Mohr's short fuse or be the subject of one of his tales. Being present and seen at worship was one way to remain in Mohr's good graces. For safe measure, Methodist layman Special Agent Louis B. Nichols, the head of the Crime Records Division, kept the tally, compiling careful notes on attendance, the sermon, and the flow of the worship service. Worship was assessed like a headlining criminal investigation: Nothing went unnoticed. And it was all reported back to Hoover.[19]

Collectively, Special Agents Tamm, Tracy, Belmont, Mohr, and Nichols represented almost every division of the Bureau. Their presence incentivized the attendance and pious performance of their white workforce as well as their family and friends. To be seen at the FBI worship service went a long way in shaping an employee's image. Worship had the power to aid a special agent's placement, evaluation, commendation, compensation, and promotion in heaven and on earth.

The priest of St. Matthew's was cut from the same cloth as the FBI top brass. Monsignor John Keating Cartwright was an ardent anti-communist crusader, and an outspoken critic of "sham liberalism." Ordained in 1916, the Rome-educated priest led St. Matthew's from 1948 to 1968, rising to the prominent position of Protonotary Apostolic, the highest-ranking position in the archdiocese after the archbishop. From his perch, the wavy white-haired priest took aim at labor unions, clergy, politicians, and prominent citizens such as Eleanor Roosevelt for their lack of patriotic faith and their attempts to "eliminate social prejudice by federal bayonets," instead of the gospel.[20] Conversely, Cartwright offered praised for men like Senator Joseph R. McCarthy, eulogizing the eponym of McCarthyism as a "hero" whom history would honor with "enduring fame."[21] Clearly, he was the ideal priest for the FBI.

If his Gospel of Christian nationalism and personal salvation was not enough to secure his place in the Bureau's religious culture, the word of his brother did. The priest's younger sibling, Special Agent Robert F. Cartwright, assured Hoover, "if his brother handled the service he would preach on the general subject of propagation of American ideas." Hoover responded with one word: "Excellent." Monsignor Cartwright coordinated with the Bureau and assured headquarters the 9am Mass would be geared toward the men and women of the FBI, capped by his personal delivery of "a special sermon for the occasion."[22]

The Monsignor did not disappoint. The service was perfectly scripted to honor God and the FBI as God's ministers on earth. The priest walked down the center aisle toward the white marble altar. The all-white employees of the Bureau, seated in the "FBI" reserved center section of the Cathedral, stood to honor the priest who honored them. When Monsignor Cartwright reached the altar, the women and men of the Bureau kneeled, while the priest beseeched God's blessing for the service. Next, Cartwright departed from the norm and permitted the FBI to minister in song. A group of Bureau employees known as the FBI Choir offered musical selections, with Special Agent John W. O'Beirne serving as the featured soloist. As a firearms instructor and later a member of the office inspection staff, he was known by virtually every agent as a sharpshooter with guns and a straight shooter when it came to Bureau protocol. His "rich, full, baritone voice" annually blessed the service with deep "renditions [that] were most effective." Following the Bureau's music ministry, Cartwright celebrated the Mass and then celebrated the Bureau. His homily consisted of his standard sermonic fare, mixed with the sacralization of the FBI. The priest, who believed "there is nothing in the world more dangerous than a sense of vocation without belief in God," championed the FBI for its crusade against the ungodly and disloyal. The nation, he bemoaned, was full of citizens who had gained "PhDs in disloyalty," neglecting their civic and religious duty to Christ. The FBI and the Church were teammates in the war against disloyalty, and there was nothing more godly than waging battle against ungodly forces. "It is never given to the church on earth to be anything but militant . . . the glory of the Church is that of steadfast warfare . . . our struggle is against flesh and blood," he preached. Faced with such a spiritual and carnal battle, the FBI was the nation's only hope.[23]

After Cartwright's moral address, the FBI family recited the Nicene Creed: the statement of belief professing faith in God the Father, in God the Son, the Word made flesh, in God the Holy Spirit, and in the Holy Church. Cartwright then prayed for the FBI, both living and dead. As a sign of conformity, the G-family made the sign of the Cross with Cartwright whenever he made it upon his person. The Bureau men and women then bowed on the kneeling rails of the pews, as the preacher raised the "chalice of salvation" to consecrate the bread and wine as the body and blood of Christ. He prayed that the FBI men and women who received the body and blood of Christ "may be filled with every grace and heavenly blessing." Cartwright closed the service by offering a blessing to the genuflecting FBI faithful. "The Lord be with you . . . Go, the Mass is ended. May almighty God bless you, the Father, and the Son, and the Holy Spirit." The civil servants who had committed themselves to be co-workers with God responded, "Amen."[24]

The service was a success. Hoover loved how Father Cartwright preached to his employees. "The references you made to the FBI in your sermon were indeed magnificent and I am deeply appreciative for the encouragement you have given to all of us in our daily work," he told the Monsignor. "As you pointed out so succinctly, ours is a task of individual responsibility to our God and to our country, to live and do justly accordingly to the teachings of the Master."[25] Bureau executives praised Father Cartwright for the way his sermon "handled the tremendous responsibilities . . . [that] have been placed upon the Bureau in connection with our national security and protection of our American way of life."[26] Even Methodist layman Special Agent Nichols called the Catholic's preaching "splendid" and "inspirational." He proclaimed the worship service was "enthusiastically received and was considered a memorable highlight" for the Bureau. "There is no question that the event . . . was one of the outstanding events participated in by Bureau employees during the year," he noted. "A great number of employees urged their respective supervisors to make the event an annual occasion."[27]

The sacred template was set. The FBI Mass became a yearly ritual. Attendance swelled as employees, their families, and friends drove, walked, and boarded chartered buses to worship at St. Matthew's. As one special agent noted, the annual event was "one of the highlights of Bureau activity for the religious welfare of our employees."[28]

The Mass was so popular that some employees believed the annual service was held too infrequently. FBI headquarters employees started a "First Friday Group." "I thought you would like to know," Episcopal Special Agent Alan Belmont told Hoover, that a group of headquarters employees "attended 7:30am Mass and received Communion as a group at Saint Patrick's." The Protestant explained to Hoover that attending Mass and receiving Communion on the first Friday of the month "is a special devotion suggested by the Roman Catholic Church." As the Assistant Director in Charge of the Domestic Intelligence Division from 1950 to 1961, he proudly let the Boss know the role his division played in forming the FBI's First Friday Group. "The formation of the group, as well as the arrangements . . . were instituted by SA Joseph G. Deegan of the Espionage Section, Domestic Intelligence Division." The master sleuth informed the Boss that he had spied similar First Friday groups starting in several major FBI field offices including New York, Detroit, and Los Angeles. The Episcopalian reckoned, "I believe this endeavor is most noteworthy." He closed his government letterhead memorandum with a prediction that was, in reality, more like a directive. "It is expected that the number of employees participating in the First Friday Group . . . will increase in the future." Hoover exclaimed, "An excellent idea."[29] Whether it was held monthly or yearly, the FBI Mass was a hit with the Bureau's white employees, ritualizing their labor as civic ministers of Christian America.

Breakfast

After the annual Mass, the Bureau held a Communion breakfast. The spiritual nourishment of the Mass—the body and blood of Christ— was free; the physical nourishment at the Communion breakfast was not. Rank-and-file members complained that the cost of the Communion breakfast prohibited their attendance.[30] The Bureau decided to subsidize the meal, charging a maximum of $2.75 per ticket, regardless of the cost and quality of the food. Nevertheless, several of the lower salaried employees—clerks, receptionists, and administrative aides—found the subsidized meal still too costly for a family affair. The Bureau responded with another subsidy. Using a surplus in funds maintained at the Department of Justice Credit Union, tickets were priced at $1.50 for each qualifying employee. The socialized plan, the FBI justified, would "make it possible for many lesser salaried employees to attend."[31] The FBI was determined to eliminate any and all excuses and hurdles that hindered employees from following the religious spur, to the point of incurring a financial deficit. It was considered money well spent because the Mass and Communion Breakfast provided the lower paid employees "motivation in their daily tasks of assisting Mr. Hoover and the Special Agents of the Bureau in keeping this Nation secure."[32] What peer pressure from the Bureau's organizational culture could not accomplish, the Bureau's socialized subvention did.

Government subsidy in hand, the FBI faithful took the three-minute stroll down Connecticut Avenue from St. Matthew's to the historic Mayflower Hotel for their Communion breakfast. Built in 1925, the storied guesthouse hosted several government dinners, leading President Harry Truman to tag it "Washington's Second-Best Address." FBI Director J. Edgar Hoover and Associate Director Clyde Tolson agreed: for more than twenty years the two had lunch at the Mayflower virtually every weekday. The Mass and Communion Breakfast Committee decided to do likewise. G-families and friends dined in the stately 700-person capacity main ballroom at more than a 50 percent discount per person. But it was not a cheap affair. The hotel spared no expense, serving the FBI just as it did the global political elite. Corneal Mack, the Vice President and Managing Director of The Mayflower Hotel and later Vice President of the Hotel Corporation of America, took care of all the arrangements. He was on the Bureau's special correspondents list for good reason. He made sure the ballroom was adorned with stately decorations, provided "gratis" by the Mayflower, all arranged around a banquet table and dais with name placards according to the Bureau's exact specifications. The tables were graced with the hotel's "superior food and service," complete with white-gloved wait staff and the elite catered breakfast menu of assorted juices, coffee, eggs, bacon, fruit, and toast. The R. J. Reynolds Tobacco Company, one of the nation's largest tobacco companies, known for its iconic Camel cigarettes, joined in. Constance Criss Howe, the company's local representative, supervised the placement of "individual sample packets of cigarettes at each place setting." Everything was set—from deeply discounted gourmet food to free cigarettes—nothing was too good for the Bureau's sacred affair.[33]

Nothing, except Hoover's physical presence. The Boss authorized the entire extravaganza, but did not attend. The worship committee continually invited Hoover to the event, happy to have Hoover simply "stop in." Bureau executives bolstered the invitations, telling the director his attendance "would, of course, be a very great honor," and "give a tremendous lift" to the rank and file and their families. He repeatedly declined, electing to spend his Sundays with Special Agent Tolson or in his garden with his African American driver, James Crawford. Hoover never attended the mass; but like a special emissary of Christ, he sent his word.[34]

The director "gave" the invocation at every breakfast. These supplications were actually written by Southern Baptist layman SA Milton Jones, the chief of the Crime Research Section from 1944 to 1973. SA Jones's section was, as he put it, "an adjunct of Mr. Hoover's office." He was responsible for making policy recommendations for FBI operations as well as FBI publications. He authored book reviews for the Bureau's library and issued the FBI employee magazine *The Investigator* as well as the industry-leading *FBI Law Enforcement Bulletin*. He served as a consultant to authors who wrote books about the FBI and was responsible for all outgoing public correspondence under Hoover's signature, including the Bureau's press releases, radio scripts, as well as the director's articles and speeches. He was the perfect ghostwriter for Hoover's religious addresses. SA Jones was a man of the church, preparing and delivering Bible lessons and homilies his entire life. Like Hoover, he taught the "Intermediate Boys Sunday School" class at his church and served as "junior deacon" during high school. As a student at Western Kentucky State Teachers College (now Western Kentucky University), he voluntarily attended chapel every day and was president of the Baptist Young People's Union. His college pastor described him as "moral ... studious," and "above all else ... genteel." He kept the faith while matriculating at Harvard Law School, attending chapel and joining the Baptist student association. The pious Jones, who admittedly lacked "the native ability" of his Harvard classmates, counted his graduation from law school nothing short of a miracle. He prayerfully passed the state bar exam, landing near perfect scores in evidence and criminal law.

Ironically, and perhaps tellingly, the Baptist lawyer's lowest score was in Ethics. When the Baptist Sunday school teacher became a Special Agent at FBIHQ, he joined First Baptist Church of Washington, DC, the congregation of President Harry Truman and later President Jimmy Carter. SA Jones enjoyed several prominent roles at the church. He was elected to several terms as a Church Deacon, eventually becoming Church Moderator, "the highest church office aside from the paid ministerial staff." The church recognized SA Jones's lifelong service with the President Harry Truman Award for Christian Service. When SA Jones was asked to put pen to pad to ghostwrite Hoover's religious addresses, he was able to effortlessly and skillfully proclaim the gospel in Hoover's name.[35]

After SA Jones completed Hoover's homily, he submitted it to his supervisor, Methodist layman SA L. B. Nichols, the head of the Crime Records Division (1941–1957). As head of the Bureau's public relations arm, SA Nichols reviewed the draft, signed off, and submitted it to Hoover for his approval. The Baptist ghostwriter and his Methodist supervisor did their best to channel Hoover's faith: an ecumenical grievance over the loss of Christian America and the sacralization of the Bureau as the nation's only hope. Hoover expected to have the draft of his invocation as soon as possible, reprimanding the Southern Baptist for submitted it three days before the FBI Mass. "Hereafter, I must be furnished such drafts sooner," he scolded Jones. After Hoover's cosmetic edits and his defining signature, the statements were deemed blessed, printed, and placed inside the front cover of the event programs and distributed at the annual event.[36]

The director's formulaic invocations and homilies were too important to be brushed aside as words on a printed page; they had to be read out loud. A designated Bureau executive, usually the toastmaster of the breakfast, heralded Hoover's words like sacred text. The carefully crafted ecumenical supplications repeatedly mentioned "our Savior," assuring everyone that Protestants and Catholics worshipped the same God.[37] Hoover also continually reminded the Bureau faithful that they were members of an organization that was heaven sent, a family of men and women who were partners with God. The name of the organization said it all. He acknowledged "FBI" had an honorable triple entendre. Known as the Federal Bureau of Investigation since 1935, FBI also served as an abbreviation for the agency's motto: Fidelity, Bravery, and Integrity. The FBI Mass and Communion Breakfasts, the director announced, made it clear that the letters also stood for "Faith, Blessings, and Inspiration." He explained, "By your attendance this morning, you are exhibiting a strong *Faith*, His *Blessings* will follow, and it is certainly *inspiring* to have so many pay tribute to our Savior."[38] Hoover's invocation also assured the men and women they would be successful at whatever he ordered them to do because they were on God's side. "The fact that you have joined together to honor our Lord on this occasion is convincing proof that his teachings remain uppermost in your mind as you carry out your daily duties. With faith such as this, we cannot fail to succeed in the performance of our duties."[39]

The duty was to protect the soul of the nation. Hoover always identified the Bureau and the unwavering faith of the G-family as the only things preventing the nation from losing its soul and being swallowed up by its physical and metaphysical foes. At the 1964 breakfast, he told the Bureau family:

> Belief in God and His teachings is vital in the fight we daily wage against the insidious forces seeking to engulf us. Without this belief, crime would soon be rampant. Without it, communistic atheism would rob us of our spiritual existence. Let us model our lives in His image and likeness and strive to uphold the Christian ideals upon which this great Nation was founded.[40]

In God's name, the Bureau protected democracy, but it did not operate like one. Hoover had to approve every breakfast speaker. Following his rousing invocation, the toastmaster introduced Hoover's anointed. The honoree was always someone who had endured a deep investigative dive into their private life, techniques usually reserved for criminal suspects, real or imagined.[41] All speakers were nominated by the worship committee. After three speakers made it past the nomination stage, the committee chair performed a thorough check of Bureau files and indices. The background check went beyond assuring that the Bureau held "no derogatory" information on the individual that would embarrass the Bureau. Worship chairs had to ensure the nominees passed the Bureau's piety test and enjoyed a "cordial" relationship with the FBI. Three candidates in rank order were then forwarded to the director's office for approval. Hoover had sole veto privileges. There was no override provision.[42]

Hoover's iron fist was present from the beginning of the annual event. One of the earliest top choices of the worship committee was five-time Academy Award–nominee Irene Dunne. The recommendation was daring. Hoover's commitment to complete male authority, especially in matters of religion and politics, was known throughout the Bureau. Yet the committee presented the Boss with Dunne's name. Her resumé was impeccable, particularly when it came to her Catholic commitments. "The first lady of the Talkies" was the epitome of anticommunism. In 1949, the University of Notre Dame awarded her the Laetare Medal, "the most prestigious award given to American Catholics." The annual honor crowned an American "whose genius has ennobled the arts and sciences, illustrated the ideals of the Church and enriched the heritage of humanity." President Eisenhower even appointed the pious star as an alternate delegate to the United Nations. She was good enough to be honored by the American Catholic Church and even to represent the nation on the global stage, but not good enough for the FBI. Hoover vetoed her nomination, the first and last female candidate to be nominated. Women needed the guidance and direction of men, not the other way around. The Boss did not bother providing the worship committee with an explanation. He did not have to; the committee knew why.[43]

Hoover's veto authority ensured the Gospel his employees witnessed, mirrored him. The roster of breakfast speakers was a cast of white Catholic men who parroted and authenticated Hoover's every word and action. They praised him and his Bureau, consecrating the Bureau's labor as Gospel business. They were congressmen, federal civil servants, prominent clergy, religion professors, Hollywood elites, celebrities, captains of industry, authors, and professional athletes.

The speaker invitations were delivered with the direct simplicity and authority of a federal summons: "Dear Sir, During the spring of each year . . . our personnel at headquarters have held an Annual FBI Mass and Communion Breakfast in Washington D.C. We would be highly honored if you could see your way clear of your many pressing personal and official commitments to address our group on this occasion." For a more personal touch, the Bureau also made in-person invitations, with one or two special agents presenting the invitation in person. Speakers were offered an honorarium or "cuff links and a tie tack," eerily bearing the speaker's fingerprint impressions.[44] Few declined when the FBI summoned.

Senator John A. Danaher, whose son was a special agent, was the first breakfast speaker in 1950. The Connecticut senator praised the FBI and gloated about his long-standing connection with the Bureau, citing his "intimate knowledge of [the Bureau's] operations." After praising Hoover as the consummate leader, he "gave an intensely interesting talk on Communism and Catholic action," Agent Louis B. Nichols relayed to the director's office. The senator "completely won over at the outset the entire audience by his style and his most sincere references to the Bureau."[45]

Catholic clergy followed suit. Archbishop of Washington, DC, Patrick O'Boyle told the 1954 gathering, "a strong faith in God and country is a necessity" for FBI employees. Bureau men and women needed "a real, lively faith that vitalizes every action of your waking hours." The FBI had succeeded in forming such an ethos as a "moral entity," because Hoover directed the Bureau's "disciplines and destinies." Like Hoover's law enforcement pledge, he told the gathering it was faith in God that enabled them to understand their "calling as an indispensable cooperator" with God. It was faith, he continued, that "enable[s] you to see God in every action that you perform while in the pursuance of your duty whether it be the fascinating apprehension of a notorious criminal before the flashing bulbs of newspaper photographers . . . or in the silent drudgery of the laboratory or office."[46] No matter what labor the Bureau carried out, it was working with and for God.

The Most Reverend John J. Wright, Bishop of Pittsburgh, went further, likening the FBI to the Church. In his 1960 address, he named the Bureau and the Church as "the two most disciplined organizations in the world." He further noted that the men and women of the FBI comprised a much needed spiritual and intellectual aristocracy. "It's no sin," he preached, to recognize the necessity of such an elite force. It was the spiritual and intellectual aristocrats "who will use their greater intelligence and greater integrity to save the inept, underprivileged and incompetent from themselves."[47] The spiritual elite of the FBI and the Church were the saving force of America.

Celebrity was a very present force at the breakfast. NFL Hall of Fame coach Vince Lombardi "enjoyed excellent relations" with the Milwaukee FBI field office during his victorious time as head coach of the Green Bay Packers. Lombardi, whose long list of superlatives included "Mr. Professional Football," was "known to greatly admire the Director and the Bureau." It was quickly confirmed, "No derogatory information was located in Bureau files concerning Lombardi." When Milwaukee special agents approached him in Green Bay "concerning his availability as the Communion Breakfast speaker, Lombardi stated he 'would be glad to do it for the FBI people.'" The guru of professional football happily addressed the G-family in 1969, echoing Hoover's stump speech. Before more than 700 of the Bureau faithful, plus their loved ones, he "decried the violent anarchism and lawlessness" in society, and hailed the FBI as a godsend.[48]

Efrem Zimbalist Jr. ratcheted up the celebrity factor, as the 1970 speaker. He was the star of the hit ABC Sunday evening television series *The FBI*. Hoover handpicked him for the TV role, unashamedly crowning Zimbalist Hollywood's "most brilliant star." Hoover based his opinion on more than just the actor's gift for drama, but also his piety. Hoover demanded "that actors cast in the role of FBI Agents must look the part" and the show be "inclined toward Puritanism." Zimbalist was perfect. During the show's run from 1965 to 1974, Zimbalist embodied Hoover's FBI: white, male, religious, and clean shaven. The actor played the role of, as Hoover put it, a Puritan "in an increasingly permissive world." The chosen actor and breakfast speaker addressed more than 750 FBI employees, plus their friends and families. They listened intently as the man who played Special Agent Lewis Erskine peppered his homily with quotes from Thomas Jefferson and J. Edgar Hoover, decrying "the wave of permissiveness" sweeping the country. The TV G-man expressed his "awe and admiration" for the actual G-men and their dedication to "country, humanity, and God." Only intermittent applause from the faithful interrupted the momentum of his lay sermon. The actor who played a G-man on television received an extended standing ovation from the real G-men and their families. When the acclaim subsided, reporters remarked, the handsome Hollywood actor "was besieged by young women FBI employees and employees' daughters, and signed autographs for more than forty minutes."[49]

The stars of televangelism made an even bigger splash with the Bureau. Father James Keller was a favorite at the Bureau. In 1945 he founded The Christophers or Christ-bearers, a movement rooted in the Roman Catholic tradition, but ecumenical in scope. The organization aimed to stimulate at least one million "men and women of all creeds" to assume "personal responsibility for restoring to the market place the spiritual truths upon which the nation is founded and without which it cannot survive." In 1952, Keller brought The Christophers's crusade to the airwaves, broadcasting a popular weekly half-hour religious eponymous television show on ABC. The show also enjoyed free airtime on more than 350 stations across the country, coupled with 980 radio stations. The Maryknoll priest reached the entire nation with his message of personal responsibility to God and country. In his written work, he called the Bureau the model of a God-fearing government agency. His 1953 book, *All God's Children*, was not only approved by the Archbishop of New York, but was also heartily endorsed by Hoover. At the author's request, Hoover consecrated the book with an inscription: "The recognition of the reality of God and His inexorable moral law is basic in a free, democratic society . . . This book is at once thought provoking and challenging to those who are concerned about the religious instruction of tomorrow's citizens." Following the book's publication, Father Keller's presence was requested at FBIHQ. "While in conversation on other matters" with the FBI's Crime Records Division, his appearance as the principal breakfast speaker was confirmed for Palm Sunday in 1955. The televangelist's "inspiring talk" in which he proclaimed the FBI was an example of "integrity" and "devotion" was "well received" by the Bureau faithful. Hoover told the leading religious broadcaster, "From the remarks I have heard concerning your talk, I am certain that you gained . . . disciples for the Christopher movement."[50]

Keller was not the only televangelist to have disciples in the FBI. Bishop Sheen was the speaker in 1956. He was the Communion breakfast speaker for the Bureau's New York City field office in 1947, calling it "the finest looking group that he had ever spoken to." When the committee nominated the religious broadcaster for the more august FBIHQ Communion breakfast, Hoover quickly approved, invoking his favor upon the committee. "I should like to see this event made a real success. It is so worthwhile."[51] The popular televangelist drew the largest crowd, with more than 1,250 FBI employees plus "a small gathering of employees' families and friends." It was a real family affair, with the ten-year-old daughter of an FBI worship committee member dressed in an angel costume assisting the Bishop.[52] With the FBI's angel by his side, Bishop Sheen told the Bureau that the Eucharist allows Christians "to possess Christ in the inside," and empowers them to be ambassadors for Christ. It was the Bureau's emphasis on worship and communion that made the FBI the "noblest and greatest of all" departments in the federal government. The Bureau, he reminded them, worked with and for God, "for there is nothing in the service of God more important than the preservation of justice."[53] The *Washington Post* took note of the affair, providing the headline "FBI Work Is Praised by Sheen." America's leading Catholic televangelist let the world know he was in lockstep with the Bureau. Hoover gleefully told his executives, "This was excellently handled."[54]

Inviting Protestant clergy to speak, however, was not so easily handled, a detail that Assistant Director in Charge of Domestic Intelligence SA William C. Sullivan learned the hard way. When the Irish Catholic was elected Chairman of the Mass and Communion Breakfast Committee, he bucked tradition and nominated a Protestant clergyman to give the breakfast address. In a lengthy US government letterhead memorandum, the head of the Bureau's spying, counterintelligence, and surveillance operations levied his Protestant supervisor SA Belmont, "In view of the ecumenical movement going on—which is the most significant step of the century in the field of religion—it was voted unanimously to extend an invitation to an outstanding Protestant theologian or leader." Sullivan argued that the theological differences between Catholics and Protestants paled in comparison to the potential influence an ecumenical FBI event would have upon Christianity specifically, and society more broadly. "The impact of Christianity throughout the world in resolving social problems which communists exploit has not been as effective as it could be for lack of agreement even on fundamentals in the social order," he explained. In light of the modern changes coming out of the Second Vatican Council, Sullivan believed inviting a Protestant clergyman to speak at the 1965 FBI Mass and Communion Breakfast would "indicate that the Bureau employees have manifested sufficient interest in the ecumenical movement and the necessary broadmindedness and vision to take steps to support the dialogue now going on between Protestants and Catholics." He continued, "Certainly it will show that Bureau employees are not living in the sixteenth Century but rather [the] twentieth and are progressive and interested in current issues of their time; they are abreast of efforts being made to resolve issues." The move, he argued, was the much needed "constructive step" for the Bureau to take, helping right all the wrongs between Catholics and Protestants.[55]

"The overwhelming majority" of the worship committee, he continued, "voted to invite Baptist Reverend Dr. R. H. Edwin Espy, General Secretary of the National Council of Churches (NCC), the largest ecumenical body in the United States." Sullivan testified to Reverend Espy's appropriateness. "I know this man personally and vouch for him as a gentleman of loyalty, integrity, and good will toward the FBI." Indeed, Reverend Espy had been extremely friendly and cooperative with the FBI, in hopes of establishing a reciprocal relationship with the Bureau. He provided the Bureau with intel on all the NCC's social gospel activities, especially its involvement with the Civil Rights Movement, in exchange for the Bureau's public stamp of approval. The general secretary believed the FBI's Cold War endorsement would help the NCC weather attacks from the right charging that the NCC's moderate and reform-minded social stances were evidence of communist infiltration. However, Espy always ended up empty handed, giving the FBI far more than he received. Sullivan counted on that. He held out the Bureau's approval like a carrot on a stick, always just out of Espy's reach. The spy chief boasted about it to his superiors, assuring them "Dr. Espy has been extremely helpful in the past . . . and I can count on him to continue to do so."[56]

Sullivan also reminded his bosses, "A review of Bufiles [Bureau files] failed to show any derogatory information concerning Dr. Espy." Agent Sullivan knew these Bufiles well. At Hoover's request, the Domestic Intelligence Division had recently concluded an intensive investigation of the NCC. Completed in the spring of 1960, the investigation was compiled in a three-volume manual entitled "Communism and Religion." Domestic Intelligence concluded the Communist Party USA (CPUSA) had been "able to influence the thinking of ministers with respect to the communist propaganda involved in the petitions they signed." The majority of this small group of "Comsymp," or communist sympathizers, had been "duped" into affiliating with communist front organizations, lending their names to causes sponsored by the CPUSA or objectives in which the CPUSA had interests. However, Sullivan and his colleagues in Domestic Intelligence concluded, "There is no indication the CPUSA is dictating the national policy of the NCC today." In a lecture tour of American congregations spanning the early part of the 1960s, Sullivan repeatedly professed, "It can be stated factually, and without equivocation that any allegation is false which holds that there has been and is, on a national scale, any substantial Communist infiltration of the American clergy . . . The truth is that the Communist party has not achieved any substantial success in exerting domination, control or influence over America's clergymen or religious institutions on a national scale."[57]

Therefore, SA Sullivan concluded his plea for Reverend Espy by comparing the NCC to the FBI. "The NCC, like the FBI, occasionally has been involved in controversy," he wrote. "Like the FBI, it has its supporters and its detractors." However, the record was clear: just like the FBI, the NCC had "taken a strong stand against communism, and there is ample documentation to show that in the way of statements and publications issued." Self-assured, he closed with a torrent of pejoratives. "This is no time in history for any of us to be petty, narrow, intolerant, timid, fearful, self-protective, and visionless." His colleagues called him

"Crazy Billy" for a reason. "Unless advised to the contrary, an invitation will be extended to Dr. Espy."[58]

He was quickly advised otherwise. His superiors were not convinced. Any threat, no matter how small, of communist infiltration in the NCC or the presence of fellow travelers in the ecumenical organization was a bridge too far. What did light have in common with darkness? Reverend Espy's organization was not possessed by the CPUSA, but the whole posture of FBI domestic intelligence, especially under the leadership of Special Agent Sullivan, presupposed suspicion and a subplot mentally. Anyone, especially clergy, was prone to communist capture or deception. The demons that SA Sullivan helped to create haunted his ecumenical dreams.[59] SA Tolson, the Bureau's number two man, would hear nothing of SA Sullivan's dreams. He dismissed the proposal as yet another one of Crazy Billy's wild ideas. SA DeLoach agreed. As head of the Crime Records Division (1959–1965), DeLoach was responsible for the Bureau's public image. He saw nothing good in SA Sullivan's proposal. He did not trust some of the members of the NCC and he feared that hosting one of their leaders "could needlessly cause embarrassment." He continued, "While Mr. Sullivan's desire to promote the Ecumenical spirit is admirable, I do feel that we should invite someone other than an official of the NCC."[60]

Hoover followed SA DeLoach's advice. The Bureau would invite a Protestant clergyman, but only one Hoover knew and trusted. The lot fell to Reverend Joseph R. Sizoo. He was the former pastor of New York Avenue Presbyterian Church in Washington, DC. Hoover was familiar with the congregation known as the "church of the Presidents." He attended the church during his youth. In addition, and perhaps more important, Reverend Sizoo was the father of FBI Special Agent and Methodist layman Joseph M. Sizoo, an Agent Supervisor in the Domestic Intelligence Division. Reverend Sizoo was also the uncle of Special Agent Joseph A. Sizoo, an inspector in the Domestic Intelligence Division, an elder in the Presbyterian Church, and delegate to the general assembly of the Presbyterian Church. Reverend Sizoo was theologically, professionally, and personally the ideal Bureau choice. In his address, the father and uncle of Bureau spies praised the Bureau and his progeny for their faith and dedication, calling them the torchbearers of "Freedom's Holy Light." In addition to Sizoo, Methodist layman Dr. Raymond W. Miller was also invited. The Harvard Business School professor offered the closing prayer.[61] In the end, Crazy Billy's contentiousness got him an ecumenical service that blessed the FBI, just not the one he wanted.

Catholic Whispers and Protestant Vespers

Reverend Sizoo was not the only Protestant clergyman to lead the G-men in worship. In the Spring of 1954, the FBI launched an annual interdenominational "FBI Vesper Service." Outwardly, the service helped to dismiss rumors that the American Catholic Church had taken over the FBI. By 1948, one popular Catholic publication noted that Hoover was so beloved and known by Catholic America, he might as well be a "Catholic priest or bishop." Famed author and journalist John Gunther was convinced Hoover was Catholic. "I presume you are a Roman Catholic," he asked Hoover during a 1950 interview. Gunther was part of a trend; as a 1952 issue of *Our Catholic Messenger* pointed out, most Americans believed Hoover was a Catholic.[62]

Some of the leading conservative white Protestants were among them. In March 1954, Reverend Donald Grey Barnhouse began spreading the word of a "Catholic conspiracy" in the FBI. The white evangelical radio preacher, pastor of Philadelphia's Tenth Presbyterian Church, and founder and president of the Evangelical Foundation, was emboldened by purported secret intelligence "from a highly placed person in the Department of Justice." Reverend Barnhouse announced in his *Eternity* magazine that the informant told him "77 percent of all agents of the FBI are now Roman Catholic," while the "secretaries and clerks were entirely Roman Catholic, without one exception." This was an alarming development, the radio evangelist presaged, because Catholicism was a greater threat to the nation than communism and "atheistic absolutism." And he placed all the blame on Hoover's beloved Jesuits. Jesuits were "behind the scenes," building a coalition to take over America and the FBI was ground zero.[63]

Hoover was livid. "Quite frankly," he confessed to his pastor Reverend Edward Lee Roy Elson, "I am ashamed of the fact that members of my denomination can be so bigoted and false in their presentation, particularly when a minister of my own faith is involved." The FBI released a statement declaring the Bureau did not possess an official tally of the religious affiliation of FBI agents. The only thing that mattered was the Bureau's Americanness, a loaded and all-encompassing concept for Hoover. "The personnel of the FBI represents a good-cross section of the best of American manhood and womanhood," the Bureau Boss announced. *The Pentecostal Evangel*, the official weekly magazine of the Assemblies of God, quickly came to the director's defense. "A survey of the top ten officials of the FBI disclosed that eight are Protestant, one is Roman Catholic, and one is Jewish," the Pentecostal organ noted.[64] Hoover's denomination also came to Hoover's rescue. "May I express my personal regret that one of our Presbyterian ministers, in good standing, would embarrass you and the Department [of Justice] by repeated misstatements of fact," Reverend Eugene Carson Blake, the Stated Clerk of the Presbyterian Church in the USA, confessed to Hoover. The chief executive of the denomination's governing body assured Hoover "through the years your fellow Presbyterians have been very proud of the quality of the administration of the Federal Bureau under your leadership." He reminded Hoover that *Eternity* was "a private publication and has nothing to do with any official Presbyterian organization." The chief executive told Hoover that the Presbytery "would be more than willing to take this whole matter up with Dr. Barnhouse with a view to possible discipline, if you feel that it should be done."[65] When it came to choosing between Hoover and one of its ordained clergy, the denomination made its loyalties clear.

However, Reverend Barnhouse had fellow travelers along this conspiracy road. The National Association of Evangelicals (NAE) was among them. The NAE was founded in 1943 in opposition to the Federal Council of Churches, later the NCC. NAE accused the NCC of harboring "anti-Christian" theological stances, attacking capitalism, and working toward "the creation of a new social order." The NAE positioned itself as the "united voice" of "over ten million Bible-believing

Christians."[66] In 1956, Reverend Clyde Taylor, the longtime Secretary for Public Affairs for the NAE (1944–1963) and founding member of the National Religious Broadcasters, reportedly told the third Annual Banquet of Christ Mission in New York City, "Catholics [are] close to controlling the government" with "key positions . . . in the Federal Bureau of Investigation." Reverend John E. Kelly of the National Catholic Welfare Conference played the role of spy, bringing the remarks to Hoover's attention. "I know that you have more than once disposed of such false charges," the priest told the FBI director. "I thought that you might like to know that a supposedly responsible chairman continues to repeat the accusations."[67]

Hoover thanked the Catholic priest for the spiritual information and promptly wrote Reverend Taylor a personal letter. It was the first interaction between the two men, and it was not pleasant. Following the tactics he used against Reverend Barnhouse, Hoover attempted to shame the white evangelical preacher. "Your statement pertaining to the FBI is certainly a source of disappointment coming from a man in your position, as it has no foundation in fact," Hoover lectured. The FBI Boss reminded him it was the "official policy of the United States Government" to "keep no record of the religious affiliations of our employees." However, an emboldened Hoover reasoned, "even if you were correct, if a man is otherwise competent, the way he worships is not the test of his ability to serve." All that mattered is that the man worshipped the God of American nationalism. The Boss concluded his rebuke with a strong ecumenical claim, "It seems to me that if all Christians would devote more of their energies to furthering the Kingdom of God instead of bickering among denominations, we would come closer to making the Kingdom of God a reality."[68]

Reverend Taylor was deeply alarmed. Unlike Reverend Barnhouse, he wanted to settle the matter privately. He called the Bureau, explaining he was the victim of a misunderstanding. He desperately sought an audience with Hoover. From his NAE office in DC, he promised he could be at Hoover's office "within 3 minutes." The two men could then sit down and hash it out. The Boss was not moved by the preacher's pleas. He was convinced Reverend Taylor's remarks were based "on the authority" of

Reverend Barnhouse. The men were one in the same in Hoover's mind.
The Boss refused to see or even talk to the white evangelical leader, telling
his executives, "He will have to see someone else. I have no time for such
bigots." SA Robert E. Wick of Crime Records lent a sympathetic ear to
Reverend Taylor. Wick was an Episcopalian who, according to his supervisor, took "church work very seriously." He was eventually elected to
the Board of Vestrymen of St. Andrew's Episcopal Church in Arlington,
Virginia. The religious appointment involved managing the temporal affairs of the church, a perfect position for a man who performed the same
duties for the FBI. The concerned Anglican relayed to Hoover that Reverend Taylor was only requesting four or five minutes to "get this thing
straightened out." After several weeks, Hoover attempted to show himself
as a benevolent dictator, telling his executives, "I [will] only deal with such
a rat in writing and he certainly can put in writing anything he has to say
to me." Reverend Taylor's comments about the government were forget-
table, but his remarks about the FBI were not. "I don't care what he says
about the IRS and Int. Rev.," the Boss harangued, "but when he imputes
a conspiracy whether Catholic or Protestant within the Bureau, he is beyond the pale with me." After several failed attempts to visit the FBI Boss,
Reverend Taylor finally gave up. All he wanted, he told Hoover's executives, was for the Boss to know "that he knows personally all key officials
in the FBI are Protestant, not Catholic."[69] Hoover would hear none of it.

The FBI Boss continued to hear whispers, and they grew louder and
more colorful. Later that year, a writer, Avro Manhattan, offered commentary proclaiming the FBI was "blackened with the thickest layers of
Catholic termites," compromising the structure and integrity of the Bureau from the inside out. The Catholic Church, the critic later reasoned,
was "an invisible secret agent at the F.B.I."[70]

Hoover attempted to squelch the rumors. In 1954, he swore to readers
of Reverend Barnhouse's *Eternity* magazine that the FBI "did not know
and has absolutely no desire to know the religious affiliations of our
employees."[71] He pledged the Bureau's commitments to fairness, "Since
I became Director of the FBI in May 1924, it has been my strict policy
to judge a man solely upon his ability, his qualifications, and his character." The director conveniently failed to mention whiteness as an

exclusive hiring criterion. He attempted to publicly shame and discredit any preacher challenging his Americanness. "To inquire into [a G-man's] religion," Hoover continued, "would be personally abhorrent," and inconsistent with government policy.[72]

It was not a secret. Hoover's conspicuous praise of the Catholic Church and the extensive deployment of Catholic practices in his Bureau were fertile ground for the seeds of such nativist "Catholic" rumors. After all, Hoover crowned a Jesuit priest the FBI Chaplain, and oversaw his men attending annual Catholic retreats, Mass, and Communion breakfasts. However, as a Christian nationalist, Hoover was not concerned with denominational affiliations, only the depth of one's commitment to white Christian America. Hoover's commitment was unquestionable. But for many white Protestants, it was not sufficiently Protestant. Something had to be done.

The Bureau initiated and heralded the FBI Protestant Vesper Service in 1954, in part, to quiet such noise. An FBI Protestant Vesper committee was formed to plan the worship services and even distribute press releases to "friendly newspaper sources . . . [and] contacts for the purpose of gaining some publicity for this significant undertaking by FBI employees" (see figure 12). The establishment of the Vesper Service calmed the conscience of many concerned Protestants. As Hoover's pastor, Reverend Elson, noted in his diary, the FBI Vesper Service "was a good answer to the charge the FBI is R[oman] C[atholic]."[73]

The annual Protestant revival empowered FBI special agents to display how they were ministers, not just according to the Protestant notion of the priesthood of all believers, but ministers and custodians of Christian America. In the process, the ritual further cultivated an ethos of a unified federal family that ministered to the nation. One white special agent explained, "The primary purpose of these services is to reach the greatest number of our employees possible in order that we can meet together as a family in Christian worship."[74] Hoover referred to the service as the Bureau's "annual service of Christian fellowship" that "represented a quality of deep spiritual unity within our organization."[75] Hoover considered church attendance a very important public ritual for Christians. It constituted a public pledge. "Through his presence,

May 17, 1967

FBI VESPER SERVICE

The fourteenth annual interdenominational FBI
Vesper Service will be held at 3 p.m. Sunday, May 21st, in the
Capitol Hill Methodist Church, Fifth and Pennsylvania Avenue, S. E.,
at Seward Square, Washington, D. C.

The Reverend Edward Bradley Lewis, Minister of
this Methodist Church, will deliver the sermon "Values that Last."
Assisting in the worship service will be United States Senate Chaplain
Dr. Frederick Brown Harris, FBI Assistant to the Director John P.
Mohr, and FBI Special Agent Steve Sziarto.

The church's Sanctuary Choir will sing under the
direction of Professor Paul Hill. A reception will follow the service.

This vesper service for FBI employees, relatives
and friends has added significance in this year's setting. Located on
the birth and boyhood homesite of FBI Director J. Edgar Hoover, the
newly constructed Capitol Hill Methodist Church last June dedicated
in his honor its sanctuary window. The window and its theme, conceived
by the Reverend Mr. Lewis, symbolically depict in stained glass art,
"Statesmanship through the Christian Virtues."

FIGURE 12. FBI Protestant Vesper Service press release, 1967. *Source*: 94-46705-49
enclosure.

whether it be in the humblest chapel or the loftiest cathedral," Hoover
lectured, "man registers his acceptance of the duties and obligations
which Christianity imposes." Church was not the place for unbelievers.
Only the redeemed of the Lord needed to make their way to the house
of God.[76] This, of course, included Hoover's men.

The FBI Vesper Service was established as an evening ritual, organized in a similar fashion to its Catholic counterpart. Representatives from every Bureau division served on the worship committee. They were charged with determining the date, location, preacher, food, and publicity, all of which was subject to the director's approval. Once Hoover signed off, committee members then drafted a mark-up for the flier and submitted it for approval. Bureau protocols stipulated "that no poster or flier shall be printed or distributed" without obtaining permission from Hoover or SA Tolson. Once permission was granted, the worship committee printed and circulated at least 1,000 handbills to share the good news with their white colleagues (see figure 13). The few African American special agents were completely ignored. They were never invited, evangelized, or encouraged to attend. In fact, the existence of the service was actively hidden from them. Retired SA Wayne Davis, one of the Bureau's "first fully qualified school trained" Black special agents, recalled that during his time in Washington, 1967–1979, he was never invited to worship or even witnessed a handbill heralding the annual revival. "I have no recollection of it," he noted. However, white Bureau employees as well as their families, friends, and relatives filled the worship service. It was seemingly required. The retired Black agent noted, "At least among the Administrative Division employees—the FBI's most powerful division (personnel matters, promotions, etc.)—attendance was pretty much mandatory."[77] What was good for the influential Administrative Division was good for all, that is, all white special agents.

Hoover arranged for the first service to be held on May 23, 1954 at his home church, the National Presbyterian Church. The National Presbyterian Church was "the representative Church of the Presbyterian Church in the United States of America." The church, Hoover's shepherd proclaimed, was "a focal point dramatizing the influence of the Presbyterian Church in national life." It "symbolize[d] the inseparable relationship between true religion and noble patriotism." The principal congregation was just a short three-minute march from where the FBI held their annual Mass at the Cathedral of St. Matthew the Apostle and less than a five-minute drive from the White House.[78]

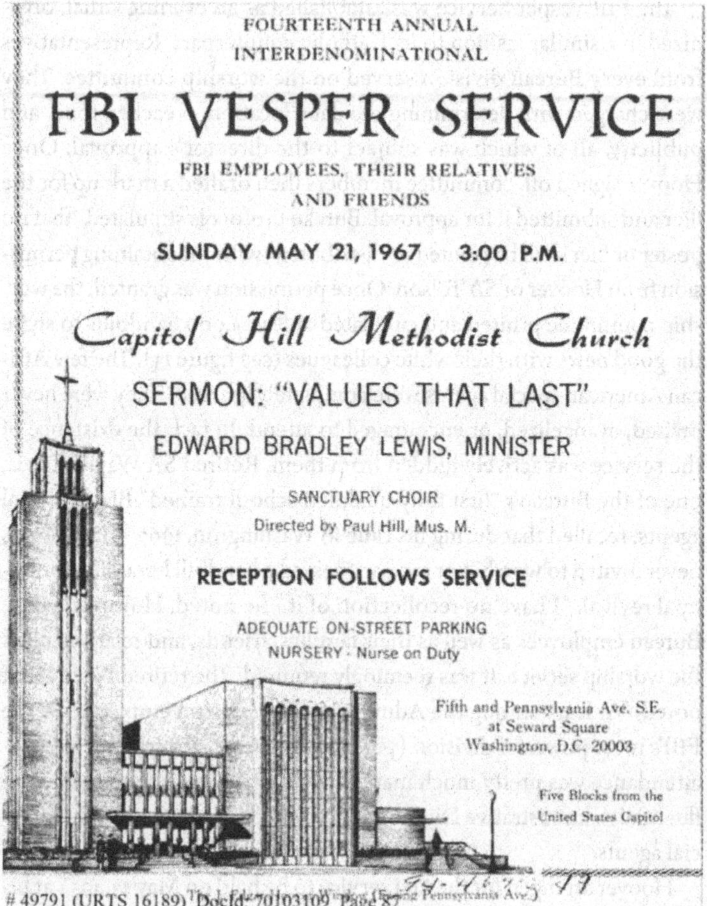

FIGURE 13. FBI Vesper Service flier. The flier also advertised the J. Edgar Hoover Window. *Source*: FBI file 94-46705-49 enclosure.

The physical location of the church was not the only reason Hoover chose the National Presybterian Church. The Boss was thoroughly involved in the life of the congregation. The self-described "Presbyterian layman" taught adult Sunday school at the church and served as a trustee where he was elected, time and again, by his church peers to serve, beating several other candidates on the ballot. The position of trustee was a sacred office in the Presbyterian church. Alongside elder or deacon, a trustee was called by God to utilize their gifts in the service of the local congregation. Hoover joined the small group of white Presbyterian men, including the first director of the CIA, Rear Admiral Sidney William Souers, who met periodically to make decisions concerning the church's business affairs. He served on numerous church committees, including the National Church Affairs Committee, Policy and Planning Committee, the Advisory Committee, Legal Committee, the Housing Committee, and the Acquisitions and Operations Committee. In addition to offering his talents, Hoover was a generous contributor to the church. He faithfully paid his pew rent, gave to the annual fund, and even supported "special projects," including the erection of a new National Presbyterian Church complex. J. Edgar Hoover was a man of the church.[79]

More than one thousand members of the Bureau family showed up to worship at the church Hoover helped to build and run. Known as the "Hagia Sophia of Washington" by architectural historians, the church featured "a massive vaulted interior," similar to the famed Byzantine cathedral in Constantinople. Bureau men and women entered a sanctuary with sweeping vaulted arches and ceilings, stained glass windows made by Tiffany, a pulpit sculpted out of wood from the Holy Land, and a grand, 15-foot wide, gas-powered Byzantine-style brass chandelier shining down from the center of the sanctuary.[80]

The grandest feature of all: the worship bulletin that was distributed to every worshipper. The FBI Seal was affixed on the front of the worship bulletin, replacing the customary seal of the Presbyterian Church. Beneath the seal, Hoover's words, not those of Christ or Holy Scripture, were printed: "What we need most in this country," the Boss declared, "are the things unseen—spiritual development, moral power and character" (figure 14). Sacred marching orders in hand, worshippers

The
National Presbyterian
Church

Connecticut Avenue, at N Street
Washington

"What we need most in this country are the things unseen—spiritual development, moral power and character.

"The answer to Communism lies in the love of God. This Nation was founded on the simple—upheld by every generation of Americans—that man shall be free to worship as he chose. We must unite today—one and all—to hold aloft the torch of religious liberty. It is the hope of America, the hope of oppressed millions behind the Iron Curtain, the hope of the entire world."

J. EDGAR HOOVER
Before the Military Chaplains Association
of the United States, May 5, 1954

Federal Bureau of Investigation

Vesper Service

May 23, 1954

FIGURE 14. FBI Vesper Service worship bulletin at The National Presbyterian Church, Washington, DC. *Source*: The Ervin N. Chapman Memorial Archives, The William Smith Culbertson Memorial Library, The National Presbyterian Church, Washington, DC.

scurried to sit in the named pews of Presidents Jackson, Polk, Pierce, Buchanan, Cleveland, Harrison, Grant, and the newly anointed pew of President and Mrs. Eisenhower. Especially motivated or perhaps fortunate G-men and women sat in the prized rented pew of their boss, J. Edgar Hoover.[81]

The Bureau faithful filled the ornate 950-seat sanctuary, while latecomers were sent to the overflow space in the Sunday school room. The service began with a processional and coronating hymn "All Hail the Power of Jesus' Name." Next, a Bureau executive ministered to the faithful. It became standard operating procedure for Hoover or "one of the Assistant Directors of the FBI" to lead the responsive reading, prayer, and scriptural lesson at every Vesper service.[82] In Hoover's absence, Assistant to the Director Special Agent Louis B. Nichols was the first to receive the honor. The Methodist layman walked to the front of the Presbyterian church and led the G-family in the scripture lesson. FBI men and women responded to the holy recitation by singing "Glory Be." Next, in unison, the FBI petitioned God, "Grant unto us with Thy gifts a heart to love Thee; And enable us to show our thankfulness for all Thy benefits; By giving ourselves to Thy service; And delighting in all things to do Thy blessed will; Through Jesus Christ our Lord. Amen."[83]

After the FBI pledged themselves to God's service, "the handsome" Reverend Elson ascended the cedar, oak, and olive wood pulpit, ready for the task at hand. He was perfectly suited for the task. The former military chaplain conducted his ministerial duties with military precision, causing his Catholic friends to jokingly accuse him of being an undercover Jesuit priest, as "only a Jesuit could run his religious office with such discipline and thoroughness."[84] Reverend Elson's relationship with Hoover also made him the ideal Bureau clergyman. The pastoral relationship between the two men grew more intimate as FBI Chaplain Reverend Lloyd, SJ, ailed from his stroke. The preacher followed a routine during the week of sitting in the respective pew of each famous parishioner to pray for them. "Sitting in the pews of my own parishioners," Reverend Elson reflected, "and praying for them as individuals gives me a sense of reality and communication when, on Sundays, I stand before them in the pulpit as God's spokesman." Reverend Elson sat in the rented pew of powerful men such as President Eisenhower, who joined the church in 1953—making Reverend Elson the first minister to baptize a sitting president—and members of Congress and three justices of the Supreme Court. Yet he shared publicly that he made a special effort to pray in the rented pew of J. Edgar Hoover. He vouched that Hoover's faith was "the reflection of his whole philosophy of life," and "in accord with the rest of his life." The pastor continued, saying of Hoover, "When he speaks of personal morality, of the religious life, or of God it is with a depth of feeling that comes from the center of a man whose entire being is focused upon the God he loves and serves." This heartfelt dedication led Reverend Elson to crown Hoover "a model of manhood."[85] The Presbyterian made it an annual ritual to make "pastoral visits" to Hoover on Hoover's birthday. Elson recorded these meetings in his personal diary, recounting Hoover's casual uniform of "tieless sports shirt and slacks," and his "bounding" energy. Elson always greeted Hoover with birthday gifts: books, devotionals, and even recordings of Christian music. During these sojourns, the two men sat and engaged in "sustained heart to heart" conversations about personal life, religion, and politics. "I pledge to you my steadfast pastoral care and my warmest affection," Reverend Elson promised Hoover. "Please call upon me . . . and command me for any service I may render."[86]

The feeling was mutual. Hoover was close with his shepherd. He confessed to his pastor that he was "deeply privileged to be a member of your congregation," and he was not afraid to show it. The FBI Boss annually sent his pastor meaningful Christmas gifts pertaining to faith and politics: new editions of the Bible, the Gospels "in exquisite limited edition," and rare copies of national documents including the Constitution. For his pastor's birthday, Hoover annually sent birthday cards and notes accompanied by an assortment of "usable accoutrements for travel." He also sent his pastor autographed self-portraits. He invited Reverend Elson over to his house for "all male" suppers and evening gatherings. Theirs was a close relationship. It was more than shepherd and sheep. Hoover called it a "valued friendship."[87] If anybody could impart J. Edgar Hoover's spiritual intimacies into the FBI, it was Reverend Elson.

Hoover's pastor and friend ascended the pulpit with the spiritual heart of the FBI. He was a Christian nationalist. "Our origin, our instruments of government, and our institutions," he was known to repeat, "are dependent upon faith." After the FBI choir sang "Faith of Our Fathers," an ode to the faith of past patriarchs as the ideal faith, Reverend Elson preached his sermon. It was a fitting sermonic hymn for Elson's address, entitled "The Ramparts We Watched." The sermon, previously championed as the October Sermon of the Month in a local ministerial magazine, was one of Hoover's favorites.[88] The decorated FBI preacher, who was often criticized as "a 'baptizer' of national policy," set his sights on Christian nationalism, taking aim at the decline of America's "democratic Christian society." The master pulpiteer delivered the sermon in his famous controlled "staccato tempo," issuing sacred marching orders like "Napoleon giving an order of the day," with a style that was "a well-thought out campaign, from premise to triumphant finality." The church, he sermonized, was the "undergirding organism" of American democracy. Only men "produced by the Christian Gospel" could be "trusted with their own destinies." He surmised, "Unless we re-establish life on a spiritual foundation, our future generations are doomed." Throughout the sermon he periodically ad-libbed "commendatory references to the Bureau" and to his beloved parishioner and friend J. Edgar Hoover. The sermon made it clear: Hoover and his men were the ministers who would ensure the nation's ramparts remained intact.[89]

At the conclusion of the FBI-themed sermon, Hoover's shepherd descended from the pulpit and recessed from the sanctuary as the faithful sang, "Stand Up, Stand Up for Jesus." "Ye soldiers of the cross," they sang in unison, "lift high his royal banner, It must not suffer loss. From victory unto victory, His army He shall lead, till every foe is vanquished, and Christ is Lord indeed." The apropos pledge was affirmed with a collective "Amen." The faithful then followed Hoover's pastor to a reception in the "Church Hall."[90]

The service was universally praised. SA Louis B. Nichols, with no shame, praised his own involvement, telling Special Agent Tolson, "I thought it was excellent." Reverend Elson gushed in his personal diary, "F.B.I. Vesper Service packed the Church. . . . Choir was superb. Big reception in Church." *Religion News Service* authenticated the Bureau's genuine Protestant character. The all-American federal outfit, the news agency reported, "jammed the church and overflowed into the Sunday School." The success of the event ensured the FBI Vesper Service would be an annual event.[91]

Hoover's pastor continually offered his church for the revival. The FBI worship service had capped off a wonderful year for the preacher. The Religious Heritage of America awarded him the "Clergy Churchmen of the Year" for 1954. The religious spotlight seemed to follow Reverend Elson, and he basked in it. The FBI director, however, reminded his shepherd on more than one occasion that the Bureau instituted a "policy . . . of rotating the services among the various denominations in th[e] area." He promised his pastor, "You may be sure, we will keep your invitation in mind."[92] As Hoover's home church, the National Presbyterian Church did host the Bureau for worship three more times during Hoover's reign. However, the Bureau had virtually every white Protestant congregation in the DC metro area bidding for the privilege of hosting and worshipping with the FBI, for the opportunity to crown the Bureau as divine ministers and agents of faith and patriotism. However, only churches the Bureau deemed appropriately Christian were granted the privilege.

The National City Christian Church was the second congregation to receive the FBI's blessing, hosting the 1955 revival. The neoclassical church with a monumental façade was the national church of the Christian Church, Disciples of Christ (DOC), and the foremost DOC church in the Washington, DC metro area. The DOC churches in the local area were racially segregated. The FBI took note, however, that despite opposition, the local DOC churches had recently agreed on a tepid resolution to "take definite steps toward eliminating segregation" in their respective Sunday schools. The National City Christian Church preached a lukewarm commitment to racial integration, but its support for the FBI was white-hot.[93]

Reverend Dr. J. Warren Hastings, the pastor of the representative church, anointed the FBI as America's salvific force. His sermon, "Fire in My Bones," was based on Jeremiah 20:9: "His word was in my heart like a burning fire shut up in my bones; I was weary of holding it back, and I could not." Like Jeremiah, Reverend Hastings could not contain his burning desire to speak the word of the Lord and praise the FBI. In a "very stirring" preaching style befitting the title and text, he proclaimed "the FBI ha[s] saved the country." At the reception, he told Special Agent Nichols, his only regret was that he was unable to spend the entire worship service glorifying the FBI for "saving the country."[94]

The church was chosen again several years later, featuring a new and more effusive pastor. Reverend Dr. George Davis opened his sermon by confessing the "great deal of pride" he felt in leading the Bureau in worship. Reverend Davis, known nationwide as the Washington, DC, minister of President Lyndon Johnson, laid all his cards on the table. In his 1968 sermon, he told the Bureau that not even the attendance of President Johnson outranked seeing the FBI at his altar. "I know of nothing," he confessed during the FBI Vesper, "I have looked forward to with greater interest during the seven years of my ministry than this service."[95] His sermon, "Religion and Law, the Universal Twins," confirmed both his admiration of the Bureau and the sacredness of the FBI. "I believe you are in a sacred profession," he told the G-men. "Indeed, you dare never look upon it as being secular. You dare never look upon it as being just a job paid for by the United States government—you dare never look upon it as just another occupation to which you go each day—you look upon it as sacred commitment under God." Hoover could not have said it better.[96]

He blessed the Bureau's lawlessness in its efforts to maintain "law and order" under God. The nation was full of "an element of criminality that [is] so dangerous in our time that it is unsafe to walk the streets—unsafe to even think about walking," he declared. The Bureau should not be handcuffed by the law. The FBI had to fight fire with fire. People of genuine faith understood and endorsed this. "My friends I must say to you bluntly . . . with all the force I have," he strained, "I'll choose . . . some men in the law enforcement agencies violating laws to uphold the law . . . over against criminal brutality running rampant across the nation." All of the FBI's lawlessness was blessed under God.[97] Reverend Davis then called all FBI employees to the altar to receive a special anointing. He gave them a charge to keep: "Not to a job—not to a secular profession—but to a sacred commitment under God." His call for the sacred men and women of the FBI to break the law for the love of God was lauded by Hoover. "Your sermon," the FBI Boss told Reverend Davis, "was an excellent portrayal of the dual roles played by religion and law in maintaining a stable society."[98]

The Episcopal Church followed suit, hosting the FBI at the Washington National Cathedral, the American Cathedral of the Episcopal Church, in 1959. The striking neo-Gothic edifice, the second-largest church building in the nation, is the seat of the Presiding Bishop of the Episcopal Church and the Bishop of the Diocese of Washington, DC. Reverend Francis B. Sayre, the Dean of the Cathedral, "was enthusiastic" about hosting the Bureau. However, the excitement was not reciprocated. Bureau files had written him off as "somewhat a liberal." The chief resident cleric of the Cathedral gave a commencement address in 1952 in which he "commented unfavorably" about loyalty investigations in Hollywood. To make matters worse, he made the comments at George Washington University, Hoover's alma mater. Reverend Sayre's participation in the 1957 Prayer Pilgrimage was the final nail in his proverbial liberal coffin. The pilgrimage was sponsored by the NAACP, the Brotherhood of Sleeping Car Porters, and Martin Luther King Jr.'s Dexter Avenue Baptist Church, with the aim of commemorating "the third anniversary of the ruling of the United States Supreme Court against racially segregated public-school systems" and to call all believers to assemble at the Lincoln Memorial to "give thanks for the progress to date, and pray for the wiping out of the evils that still beset our nation." However, Hoover, with virtually no evidence, was convinced that "communists" were going "to practically take over" the solemn assembly. He financed informants from across the country to surveil the prayer meeting. Infiltrators with covert names such as "the cat from Detroit" were given cash advances and gas money to travel to Washington, DC, to spy on the Prayer Pilgrimage and Reverend Sayre. Yet, the Bureau's worship committee persisted with their proposal. "Despite the connection of Sayre with the Cathedral," they proposed, "we should explore the possibility of holding Vesper Services at the Cathedral because of its national prominence."[99]

The Bureau did indeed secure the Cathedral and its national prominence, yet they managed to remain insulated from the "somewhat liberal" Sayre. The Bureau sent two special agents to the Cathedral, where they were greeted by Reverend Luther Miller, the Canon of the Cathedral. The former Chief of Chaplains of the US Army was "extremely cooperative and enthusiastic" about the FBI Vesper. He told the special agents he was "a great admirer of the Director and the FBI. He "conferred at length" with the FBI envoy, promising the Bureau that if they brought their annual religious affair to the Cathedral "the entire service could be arranged as [the FBI] saw fit." He suggested the FBI even invite their own preferred preacher. Reverend Dr. Norman Vincent Peale was the first suggestion. He was known at HQ as "an excellent friend of the Bureau." He had already conducted Vesper services for the FBI field office in New York, making him a safe and ideal choice.[100]

Hoover overruled it. "I think it is somewhat of an imposition to ask Dr. Peale," he told the committee. The committee came back with another name: Lutheran clergyman Dr. Franklin Clark Fry. Reverend Fry was the ecumenical man of the century. He was the president of the United Lutheran Church in America, "the largest and most theologically relaxed group in U.S. Lutheranism" during its time. The man with "a mind like an I.B.M. machine" also presided over the constituting convention of the National Council of Churches, became chairman of the World Council of Churches, and "the first American ever elected president of the 50-million-member Lutheran World Federation." Despite his global and ecumenical commitments and association with the NCC, the committee assured Bureau superiors, "We have a brief reference to him in Bureau files, nothing unfavorable." The Bureau found his politics to be pleasant, but the man was not. Similar to Hoover, he was "impersonal," yet respected for his "efficiency," "zest for combat," and the power he wielded. His colleagues reckoned him as "not exactly a warmhearted shepherd." Rather, the hefty six-foot-one preacher employed his "brisk impatience" and "tendency to kick the rumps of the sheep, rather than lead them" to get things done. He was never in danger of being "voted the best-loved churchman of the year," but he was known as "Mr. Protestant" for his tireless ecumenical work. It vaulted him to the cover of *Time* magazine in 1958, and to Hoover's approved preacher for the FBI worship service in 1959.[101]

The service was held on May 10, 1959, to commemorate the thirty-fifth anniversary of the appointment of J. Edgar Hoover as director of the FBI. The service, just like Hoover's FBI, was scripted. Everybody had assignments. The Lutheran clergyman arrived at the National Cathedral of the Episcopal Church and played the part that had been prepared for him. The presence of the man *Time* magazine dubbed "the most influential leader of world Protestantism" signaled the Bureau's status as a key force of ecumenicalism, an agency all Protestants and Catholics could collectively champion. Special agents from the Washington field office handled the nursery, ushers, and the flowers, while FBI Assistant Director C. Lester Trotter, the head of the Identification Division, read scripture. The Bureau muzzled the "liberal" Reverend Sayre. He could not be left to his own devices. Instead, the Dean of the Cathedral was regulated to chanting the scripted prayers of the service, while the entire service boldly praised the FBI for its gospel labors and thanked God for Hoover's thirty-five years of leadership.[102]

Similarly, the United Church of Christ (UCC) bent over backward to display its allegiance to Hoover and his leadership of the FBI. The congregational UCC did not have a national representative congregation. However, the Westmoreland Congregational Church was close enough. The congregation gained prominence within the denomination and the nation as "the church attended by the Vice President of the United States, Richard Nixon." The Bureau approached the church to host the 1960 worship service. In addition to political clout, the congregation was a short drive from FBIHQ, had a sizeable sanctuary, and the pastor, Reverend Thomas Chalmers Dick, "was very enthusiastic" to host the FBI. It was seemingly a perfect fit. There was just one problem: a perusal of Bureau files and a thorough background check revealed that Reverend Dick had previously served as president of a branch of the American Civil Liberties Union (ACLU). He resigned from the position, not for ideological reasons, but because he was simply "too busy with other duties." This was cause for concern.[103]

However, Special Agent Stephen Sziarto, the chairman of the worship committee, calmed all fears. Sziarto was a graduate of Lancaster Theological Seminary and a former ordained pastor in the Hungarian Reformed Church. He knew theology and he knew how to talk to ministers. The clergyman turned G-man interviewed Reverend Dick. Reverend Dick pledged that his ACLU branch had not been involved in any un-American activities, nor was it a subversive front organization. "To show his full cooperation," the worship committee reported, Reverend Dick "offered to furnish a membership list of the American Civil Liberties Union." With that offer of intelligence, Hoover approved the pastor with a terse, "Ok."[104]

The worship service, however, was more than okay. It was, by all Bureau accounts, exceptional. Having put Reverend Dick securely in the Bureau's hip pocket, the pastor of the UCC church led the FBI family in a "most inspiring service." His "challenging sermon was entitled 'We Too, May Be Forefathers,'" a call to be progenitors of a renewed commitment to God and country. Assistant to the director, Special Agent Mohr was tasked with reading the scripture. The notoriously boastful Bureau executive was on his best behavior administering the "word of God." One special agent reported, Special Agent Mohr's "pulpit demeanor . . . left nothing to be desired. All of us who attended were in unanimous agreement." There was evidence to support their assessment. Mr. William J. Hudgins, the Bureau's photographer, took photos, alongside "a cameraman of the *National Geographic Magazine*."[105] SA Mohr's preacherly manner and the chorus of holy affirmations of his Bureau colleagues were all caught on camera, making it possible for all to behold the priesthood of the FBI.

The Bureau turned to the Methodists during the high holy days of the Civil Rights Movement to affirm the sacredness of racial segregation.

The FBI was not interested in enforcing the 1954 *Brown vs. Board* Supreme Court decision overruling the doctrine of Separate but Equal. It was the prerogative of Hoover's FBI to aggressively pursue and investigate even the slightest hint of a federal violation; however, when it came to civil rights cases, Hoover deferred to the DOJ, awaiting direction. The Bureau's indifference to the *Brown* decision was not hidden. In 1955, Thurgood Marshall, executive director of the NAACP Legal Defense and Educational Fund, informed the Bureau that SA Marvin A. Reynolds of Little Rock, Arkansas, had publicly expressed his disdain for the *Brown* decision and voiced fervent support for racial segregation. Marshall's complaint was corroborated by a Little Rock school official. SA Reynolds was not fired for expressing his failed allegiance to federal law. Instead, the Bureau instructed all personnel to not express their views on the law, in stark contrast to every other federal statute.[106] Bureau personnel may have been silenced on the *Brown* decision, but their commitment to segregation was anything but muzzled. The FBI viewed segregation as part of God's law and order, and they solicited the Methodists to help them sacralize this view. The Methodists obliged, hosting the Bureau at several segregated congregations as well as their national representative churches.

The Foundry Methodist Church was a favorite of the Bureau, hosting the FBI faithful twice. The church was established in 1814 by wealthy Methodist layman Henry Foxall "as a thank-offering to God because his Georgetown iron foundry was saved from destruction by the British in the War of 1812." God, Foxall said, provided his business with "the protection of divine providence," so he returned the favor by building Foundry Church. Beginning in 1924, the church was led by Reverend Frederick Brown Harris. The segregationist pastor and longest serving Senate chaplain (1942–1947, 1949–1969) was a very well-known minister, and one of Hoover's personal favorites. President Truman dismissed the Senate chaplain as a "headline hunter and showman." However, Hoover loved the headlines and embraced the show, placing Reverend Harris on the FBI's special correspondents list. FBI files labeled him "a very good friend of the Bureau." Reverend Harris returned the favor, reckoning Hoover and his FBI a parachurch organization, calling the

FBI director "a great citizen and public servant . . . [and] the partner of every preacher of justice and righteousness." He told Hoover, "Against the forces of darkness, you, a truly great American, are as terrible as an army with banners. . . . It is a deep satisfaction to march by your side in the great battle that is raging." As a member of Hoover's army of the Lord, Reverend Harris railed against communism and "liberal churches," meaning those he deemed insufficiently anti-communist. The FBI director made a habit of saving the Senate chaplain's national syndicated sermons and editorials. The sermons often praised the FBI and its director as the arbiter of true Christian faith and allegiance. Reverend Brown noted in one published homily that Hoover and his FBI were the most "effective antidote to the tragically mistaken attitude of some church leaders." His published addresses also advocated for individual moral reform, while warning of the communist conspiracy that lurked behind every social protest. He was especially suspicious of Black civil rights protests, calling African Americans the decedents of "savage tribes of Africa" and the reality of racial inequality a "lie." American democracy might have some "growing pains," but it was better than the "malignant foe" of communism, he argued. Some African Americans might struggle to obtain voting rights, the moral locus of the US Senate reasoned, but if communism had its way, everyone would be denied "the sacred right of the vote." Hoover routinely distributed the homilies to his executives. He called one of Reverend Brown's moralizing homilies "a great sermon," telling his soldiers the sermon was "as applicable . . . to the FBI as it is to an individual."[107]

The ministry of the racial segregated congregation was so applicable, "about 1,000" FBI worshippers marched into the Foundry Church sanctuary for the 1956 FBI Vesper Service. The Bureau worshipped at Foundry for a second and final time in 1964. The next year, the church's new pastor, Reverend Edward W. Bauman, began the process of welcoming Black worshipers and unleashed a number of "liberal" reforms at the church. Once Black worshippers showed up, the Bureau left, never to worship at the Foundry Methodist Church again.[108]

The Mount Vernon Place Methodist Church gladly stepped in, hosting the Bureau in 1965. The stately church was constructed in 1917 as the national representative church of the Methodist Episcopal Church, South. The denomination was founded in 1844, splintering from the "Northern" Methodist in support of owning enslaved Africans and the institution of slavery. The northern and southern factions united in 1939, under the condition the newly unified denomination would maintain racially segregated jurisdictions. Despite the merger, Mount Vernon Place proudly laid claim to its legacy in name and practice. Church stationery, worship bulletins, and promotional materials still declared the congregation "The South's Representative Church." Church bulletins declared "We welcome all visitors," but in reality, the congregation policed its racial composition, deliberately remaining an exclusively white church.[109]

The Bureau embraced the church, describing it as a "pro-Bureau" congregation. The worship service was a success. Pastor Albert P. Shirkey expressed "his pleasure" at having the Bureau's head of Domestic Intelligence SA William Sullivan, a Catholic, read the scripture lesson. The Bureau's white Catholic G-man was welcomed at the church, while Black Protestants were not. The FBI and Mount Vernon Place saw their reflection in one another. Like the FBI, Mount Vernon did not welcome African Americans, but flung its doors wide open to white men and women, Protestant and Catholic alike. The Bureau continually sent speakers to the church, especially G-men who had been raised in the church or attended the congregation, men such as SA Leonard Walters and SA Forrest Burgess. The church had an open-door policy toward the FBI, and a closed-door policy toward African Americans.[110]

However, the FBI had little need for the Southern Methodist congregation once the shrine to Hoover was constructed at Capitol Hill Methodist Church in 1966. The church built on the birth site of J. Edgar Hoover hosted the 1967 FBI revival. The worship committee put all the Bureau heads on notice, "The annual Vesper Service has been a meaningful occasion for the FBI employees and their families since 1954, but is uniquely significant this year since it is to be held in the new church which stands on the site of the Director's birthplace and has the large and beautiful J. Edgar Hoover Window, dedicated in his honor." Hoover announced his plan to attend; it was the only Protestant Vesper he joined. The committee chairman advised the Bureau division heads of Hoover's attendance. It was the first detail that went out to the Bureau. "Additional details and posters for bulletin boards will be forthcoming," the worship chair noted, "but the Vesper Committee wanted you to have this information immediately in order that employees under your supervision . . . might reserve the date and make their plans accordingly." The Boss went to worship at the church with the stained glass window in his name, and the FBI, as well as Bureau family and friends, fell in line, filling the church to capacity. Basking in the light of his own Christ-like image, Hoover called the service a "significant worship experience."[111]

It would take an FBI agent turned clergyman to convince the Bureau to worship at the seemingly more progressive national representative church of the former Methodist Episcopal Church, North. Reverend Merrill W. Drennan became pastor of Metropolitan Memorial Methodist Church, "the National Church of Methodism," following a six-year career as an FBI special agent. During his time in the Bureau, Drennan divided his time between investigating financial crimes and serving as a Methodist Sunday school teacher, superintendent, and later lay leader. He heard "the call" to ordained ministry while he was still an FBI special agent, "partially as the result of an appeal Dr. [Reverend Joseph R.] Sizoo had made in a sermon." Drennan recalled that Sizoo, a favorite Bureau minister, compelled people to move beyond volunteer church work. The G-man recalled, "From my active work as a layman and realization that the church needed help at this point, I decided to try." Drennan told Hoover he heard the call of the Lord to "turn from the FBI to the ministry to apprehend persons seeking spiritual security." Hoover was understanding. He gave Drennan his blessing, "remembering how he almost entered the ministry himself." After attending Westminster Theological Seminary (now Wesley Theological Seminary) and serving smaller churches, the former agent was catapulted up the church appointment ladder. In 1967, against the congregation's wishes and votes, the Bishop appointed SA Drennan to Metropolitan Memorial Methodist Church, the district's wealthiest Methodist congregation and the second largest. It was an all-white church, and unapologetically so. In 1965, the church prevented fellow Methodist Dorothy Horton, a decorated Black soprano, from singing during worship. Reverend Drennan opened the doors of the racially segregated church to his white FBI colleagues in 1970, and put on quite a show. One called the untitled sermonic ode to Hoover and the Bureau "inspirational," another scribbled to the Boss, "Drennan makes an outstanding impression."[112]

The Baptists had no such luck with Hoover's FBI. The G-men only visited one Baptist Church during Hoover's reign. Calvary Baptist, "the stately red-brick church" on Eighth and H streets, Northwest in Washington, DC, received the honor in 1957. It was the founding congregation of the Northern Baptist Convention (now American Baptist Churches, USA). Yet, the pioneering congregation also had an affiliation with the Southern Baptist Convention, the denomination founded in 1845 based on its pro-slavery stance and opposition to the equality of African Americans. Calvary Baptist claimed it was the first white congregation in the nation's capital to admit an African American member in 1955. However, US Representative Lawrence Brooks Hays, a staunch Southern Baptist and segregationist, found the political stances of the congregation welcoming, even joining the church. The Arkansas congressman was among eighty-two Southern Representatives and nineteen Southern Senators to sign the 1956 "Southern Manifesto." The declaration pledged to exert "all lawful means" to fight and reverse the Supreme Court's desegregation decision, appealing to Southerners to do likewise. His anti-integration posture helped to catapult him to the presidency of the Southern Baptist Convention (1957–1958). Whether or not African Americans were actually members of the church is questionable. But Hays, the segregationist and outspoken president of the Southern Baptist, certainly felt very comfortable joining and worshipping at Calvary.[113] And so did the FBI.

Calvary's pastor, Dr. Clarence W. Cranford, "delivered a stirring message entitled 'The American Dream,'" a FBI special agent reported. "Throughout this message and during the remaining portions of the service, Dr. Cranford was highly complimentary of the Director and of the work being done by the FBI and its employees." Despite the homiletic skill of "the preacher with the eloquence of sincerity," the highlight of the service "from the Bureau employee's standpoint . . . was the reading of the scripture, which was performed by Assistant Director Parsons," the man who oversaw the Domestic Intelligence Division as well as the Investigative and Laboratory Divisions. Nothing was more important than the glorification of the Bureau, its labor, and the priesthood of its white men. The subsequent relationship with Calvary was telling. As the church's pastor became more involved in civil rights activism, Congressman Hays left Congress as well as the congregation, and Hoover's FBI followed suit, never worshipping at Calvary again.[114]

—

A few months before J. Edgar Hoover died, the Billy Graham Evangelistic Association asked him about the religious nature of the FBI. "Mr. Hoover," the standard-bearer of mainstream white evangelicalism asked, "What are the Christian qualities you seek to inculcate in the young agents whom you train, and how do you go about it?"[115] The answer was simple: J. Edgar Hoover exclusively hired white male special agents and took them to church to worship according to the dictates of white Christian nationalism, cultivating the men of the FBI into the soldiers and ministers of Christian America.

Hoover credited the worship services with providing "a quality of spiritual unity within our organization of which I am most proud."[116] No matter Catholic or Protestant, nor the congregation or denomination, the Bureau kept their revival not only spiritually unified, but also uniform. The worship services were always led by white male clergymen, and restricted to white employees. The segregated Bureau packed every church. The Bureau's white male leaders sang, ministered the word, led the responsive readings and prayers as well as the scriptural lessons. The chosen white preacher offered unequivocal praise of the FBI as the nation's ministering army and ultimate bulwark against godlessness, communism, crime, and immorality. With sermon and lecture titles such as "Spiritual Security," preachers and speakers alike made sure they praised the Bureau as the moral custodians of the nation's Christian soul.[117] Despite their many theological differences, every church, whether Catholic or Protestant, agreed on one thing: the FBI was the vanguard of one nation under God. In the process, Hoover established conservative Christianity as the bedrock of the FBI and American national security. As a result, he became a leading spokesman of conservative white Christianity, a brand of faith that would become known simply as modern evangelicalism.

Promoting Faith: The FBI and White Evangelicals

PART 2

Promoting Faith:
The FBI and
White
Evangelicals

Religious stimulation, prayer, and adherence to the commandments of God are to me the outstanding "musts" of the postwar era.

—FBI DIRECTOR J. EDGAR HOOVER, *THE PENTECOSTAL EVANGEL*, MARCH 16, 1946

In 1942, J. Edgar Hoover offered the nation his diagnosis and solution to all that ailed the nation. "The present situation," he told a nationwide NBC radio audience, "is similar in many respects to those dark days in the early thirties when crime ran rampant and threatened to corrupt the very blood stream of the decency of America." Similar to the crime wave, the present crisis of communism and fascism, he noted, was nothing more than a manifestation of "the forces of the Anti-Christ." Therefore, the plan of attack against the Anti-Christ was the same as it had always been: religious revival. Hoover's promotion of Christian nationalism reformed the FBI, and it could do the same for the nation. "We should resurrect the plain strong ideas of our God, our home, and our country," he told radio listeners. He closed his homily by quoting Psalm 121, telling the NBC audience, "I will lift up mine eyes unto the hills from whence cometh my help. My help cometh from the Lord."[1] As Hoover looked to God, the fledgling movement of modern evangelicalism looked to Hoover.

J. Edgar Hoover emerged as a leading religious figure during the Cold War. His enduring tenure, coupled with the authority and visibility of his office, anointed him the American face of anti-communism. He was a perennial federal crusader for revival since his early days as head of the Bureau. He had been a steadfast voice, calling for a religious rededication for decades. When crime was the national scourge, Hoover was the hero. It would be no different with communism. He called for revival then, and he would do it again. The Cold War was a particular battle, but not a new war. Communism was an old foe, "the Anti-Christ," dressed in new clothes.

On its face, the Cold War was a clash of economic systems and a geopolitical contest between America and Russia. However, Hoover saw such notions as subplots to a bigger existential war. He saw the Cold War primarily as a religious struggle, a cosmic war that pitted Judeo-Christian civilization against the "religion" of atheistic communism. "Communism is more than an economic, political, social, or philosophical doctrine," Hoover declared. "It is a way of life; a false, materialistic religion" that sought to rob the American citizen of "his belief in God, [and] his heritage of freedom." It was faith versus faith. Hoover was not alone in his spiritual assessment. Government agencies, elected officials including President Eisenhower, captains of industry, and Hollywood elites were also Cold War spiritual warriors. They comprised a "spiritual industrial complex," deliberately utilizing public and private resources to promote a religious revival during World War II and its immediate aftermath.[2]

But they were new converts to the cause. Presidents came and went; civil servants departed government, celebrities and evangelists rose and fell in popularity, but Hoover remained. He utilized his public and political limelight as FBI director to call for revival for nearly half a century. His FBI was also the most visible federal agency, embedded into the public and private lives of American citizens, complete with radio and TV shows, and consumer swag. The religious culture of the Bureau fashioned its members into soldiers and ministers of Christian America, preparing them to fight for the soul of the nation. As the nation's top cops and domestic security force, Hoover's Bureau was America's expert and front guard against communism and all things Anti-Christ. The Bureau held unprecedented power and near omniscience. Highly classified intelligence allowed them to see, hear, and know information the American public could not and would not ever know. As the nation scrambled to establish an intelligence superstructure in its war against godless communism, Hoover's FBI became the seemingly all-knowing, all-seeing eye against any signs of godlessness. The Bureau's spiritual discipline, combined with its specialized knowledge and omnipresence, convinced the public that the FBI was the good physician of the body politic, detecting the malady and prescribing the cure. Hoover was the nation's spiritual general in the Cold War.

He utilized the traditional jeremiad to pronounce his marching orders. Named after the lamentations of the biblical prophet Jeremiah, this rhetorical form declares there is a moral decline from an imagined pious past, highlights a cause of the decline, and then identifies a social ill as divine punishment. Political and moral reform, namely replicating patterns of the past, is presented as the cure. American preachers and politicians, from Increase Mather of the seventeenth century to today, have utilized this form of religious and political speech. However, Hoover remains the nation's most voluminous and prominent, yet forgotten Jeremiah. He continually lamented the present, recalled the past as the ideal society, and called for a return to past social practices as the only way to avoid certain destruction.[3]

Hoover's jeremiads were light on prophecy and historical accuracy, but heavy on political punditry. The powerful symbolism of decline and return allowed Hoover to cloak everything he did, legal or not, as a means to maintain the godly nation and bring American back to God. Political concerns deserving robust democratic debate—gender equality, voting, sexuality, segregation, racism, capital punishment, surveillance, labor—were reduced to conservative Christian morality plays with cosmic consequences. He argued that the nation had divine origins and there were dire consequences if the nation turned to the right or the left. "This nation was born out of faith in God," he repeated, "it can continue to exist in freedom only as that faith remains forthright and strong."[4]

Hoover never stated exactly when America was an undefiled Christian nation; it was a time that resisted precise periodization. The structural arrangements of that greatness, however, were very well defined: a time when white Christian men governed the nation according to conservative white Protestant norms. Therefore, Hoover recognized the advancements of modern society—technology, secularism, increasing rights for African Americans and women, and shifting sexual mores—as the culprits that chipped away at America's Christian democracy, producing a national decline. He pitched rising crime and subversion as the natural consequences of the nation's departure from its godly origins and practices. He refused to accept sociological explanations for crime or protests. Rather, Hoover offered a theological explanation: all moral failings were the result of individual and societal abandonment of spiritual moorings. As he plainly put it in 1948, "The criminal is the product of spiritual starvation. Someone failed miserably to bring him to know God, love Him, and serve Him." Hoover continually lamented that Americans had relinquished "The Faith of the Fathers." Whether it was crime or communism, protests or progress, the answer was always the same: rededication to God. No matter what ailed America, revival was always the answer. Going back was always the only way forward.[5] He would focus on shaping public opinion, always ready to launch a holy crusade against social problems, presenting himself and his men as the respectable, divinely sanctioned antidote.[6]

Hoover's image and homilies were ubiquitous in postwar America, saturating the burgeoning market of white evangelical print and broadcast media. His squadron of efficient Protestant and Catholic ghostwriters in the Crime Records Division, which included men such as SA G. Gordon Liddy, pumped out material at an astonishing rate, exceeding that of the most popular white evangelists, and all paid for by taxpayers. He was featured in *Our Sunday Visitor*, the nation's most widely circulated Catholic weekly, as well as the popular *Sunday School Times*. Nothing, however, surpassed the influence and prominence of Hoover's presence in *Christianity Today*. The upstart outlet was the brain trust and organizing platform of modern white evangelicalism. The magazine connected disparate white evangelicals, forging a shared identity, and a unified political battle cry that would transform religion and politics in the United States.[7] Hoover's invited contributions to the leading literary voice of modern white evangelicalism established him as a bona fide ally and accomplice of white evangelicals, even as his presence authenticated the upstart group of conservative white Protestants. Hoover, his FBI, and white evangelicals were woven together into a united front. They partnered to promote the faith of white Christian nationalism to win the battle for the soul of the nation.

CHAPTER 4

Christianity Today

On December 18, 1962, Reverend Carl F. H. Henry, the editor of *Christianity Today*, wrote to FBI Director J. Edgar Hoover, "We honor you for your dedication in your strategic post of national service." The overseer of the literary voice of mainstream white evangelicalism thanked Hoover for his latest essay prescribing white evangelical conservatism as the remedy to all that ailed the nation. "It is always a privilege and pleasure to carry your essays in *Christianity Today*," the architect of modern white evangelicalism told Hoover. Reverend Henry hoped Hoover's article would be "widely quoted" in the press, as well as from the pulpit to the pew. The managing editor spoke for many white evangelicals when he closed the thank you letter, "You" he told the FBI Boss, "have a part not only in the message of *Christianity Today* but in its mission, and we appreciate this greatly."[1]

Beginning in the 1950s, J. Edgar Hoover, the FBI, and the newly formed Protestant community known as white evangelicals became close collaborators. They saw themselves as allies in the battle for the soul of the nation. The collaboration began with *Christianity Today*, the intellectual mainframe of white evangelicalism. The FBI director used his office to aid the fledgling flagship evangelical magazine. He abetted the message and the mission of white evangelical conservatism. His partnership with *Christianity Today* helped to bolster the magazine's sales and prominence. In the process, Hoover authenticated white evangelicalism as the rightful religious and political heir and custodian of postwar America.

The partnership between Hoover, his FBI, and white evangelicals was timely. The US government was in the midst of establishing a "spiritual industrial complex," promoting, managing, and financing "religion-in-general," a generic faith to promote national revival for the purposes of Cold War survival.[2] However, the FBI believed the majority of America's clergy were asleep at the wheel, unable to properly steer the nation's soul.

The Bureau had concluded the National Council of Churches (NCC) was a trojan horse. The white mainline Protestant organization was "either knowingly or unknowingly" supporting communist front groups, "Communist propaganda," and "Communist causes," such as labor reform, pacifism, or the Black freedom struggle. The FBI director was, his pastor rightly surmised, "a little impatient with clergymen who appear better versed in Marxism than Biblical religion and whose public utterances are made in the context of a secular socialism rather than revealed religion." Hoover, he continued, "is so much a part of the Christian church that he finds it difficult to have confidence in the judgement of churchmen in ecclesiastical matters if they have had the poor judgement to be associated with Communist front organizations."[3] Hoover and his FBI almost single-handedly shaped and decided what constituted a communist front organization, giving the Bureau the power to determine who was a member of the true Christian church and who was not. The NCC and its social gospel were labeled out of bounds.

White fundamentalists also failed to measure up. The Bureau had long dubbed leading white fundamentalist ministers such as Carl McIntire and his fundamentalist American Council of Christian Churches, and Billy James Hargis and Christian Crusade, as "crackpots" and "hillbilly" evangelists. They dismissed this growing network of virulent anti-communist conservative white Protestants as extremists on the right. The Bureau even released public statements on the matter announcing "the far right [is] every bit as subversive to the United States as the far left."[4]

The FBI needed a trusted network of Protestant partners. With the NCC "communist front" on one end of the Protestant spectrum, and religious "McCarthyism" on the other, the choice for a new religious syndicate became clear. The FBI saw *Christianity Today*, and the "respectable" Protestant evangelicalism it represented, as the sensible, patriotic, and preferred Protestant collaborator. *Christianity Today* spoke for white Protestant conservatives who styled themselves as every bit as anti-communist as white fundamentalists, but adorned with the respectability of white mainline Protestants. The magazine gave Hoover a direct line to this emerging community of white religious conservatives. He used the pages to express his long-standing commitments to anti-communism, revival, and Christian nationalism, finding a multitude of fellow travelers and supporters along the way.

The partnership was also a boon to *Christianity Today* (CT). The magazine was founded in 1956, with a sacred charge to keep: to be the intellectual mainframe and standard-bearer of white evangelicalism. The founders of *Christianity Today* aimed to use the pages of the magazine to engage the burgeoning conservative intellectual print culture of the era in order to gain mainstream respectability for the movement and ultimately establish white evangelical conservatism as the nation's moral and political custodian.[5] J. Edgar Hoover was just the man for the job. He was the ideal modern white evangelical leader: a white Presbyterian male who was every bit as anti-communist as he was respectable. The FBI director occupied a seat of religious and moral authority, one that he used to prescribe an old remedy to new problems: the revival of the faith of old.

The FBI Boss provided the magazine with a steady flow of his Christian commentary. From 1958 to 1960, Hoover contributed five articles to *Christianity Today*. Each essay was immensely popular. His tried and true epistles did not present a new message, but that was their strength. Hoover's stature brought new life to an old jeremiad, producing three phenomena. First, the FBI director authenticated the gospel of white evangelical conservatism with the authority of the US Department of Justice (DOJ), the expertise of the FBI, and the subsidy of the US

UNITED STATES DEPARTMENT OF JUSTICE
FEDERAL BUREAU OF INVESTIGATION
WASHINGTON 25, D. C.

COMMUNISM:

The Bitter Enemy of Religion

J. EDGAR HOOVER

Not long ago I read a Communist magazine. There was an article on a famous Bulgarian monastery. It told of the shrine's historic beauty, gorgeous mountain setting and significance in the nation's history.

Then the author, with bitter atheistic scorn, commented about the "new trends and tides" in Bulgarian life. The monastery, he happily proclaimed, "once a center of religious activity," was now "mainly a haunt of artists and art lovers." He added: ". . . it will no doubt attract fewer and fewer devotees. For our young men today have set out to build heaven on earth, and they would rather go in for engineering, medicine and aviation than for theology."

This article is typical of Communist propaganda against religion. The "new trends and tides" refer to communism, of course. Spiritual edifices such as monasteries and churches are mere antiques of history! Theology is the babbling idiocy of diseased minds! The job of building "heaven on earth" means the establishment of communism throughout the world.

Communism is a bitter enemy of religion. Karl Marx was an atheist. He violently attacked religion as an opiate. To him, God was only a figment of the imagination, invented by the "exploiting classes" to drug men's minds. Lenin was also an atheist, as is Khrushchev. For this reason the Communists attack Western morality and seek to substitute a code of values destructive of the Judaic-Christian way of life.

J. Edgar Hoover has been Director of the Federal Bureau of Investigation since 1924. He holds the LL.B. and LL.M. degrees from George Washington University, and seventeen honorary degrees from colleges and universities across the land. He first entered the Department of Justice in 1917.

The Communists would like to extirpate religion. However, even behind the Iron Curtain, they have found this most difficult. Hence, they attempt, wherever possible, to deride, scorn, and ridicule religion as an old wives' tale or superstition which is contrary to the "modern" mind. "We Communists," they say, "have outgrown the religious stage of history. Man no longer needs God." "Bright young men find religion pure foolishness." Religion is equated with ignorance; atheism with intelligence.

This bitter Communist campaign against religion is world-wide, extending also throughout our nation. The Communist Party, USA—though not as openly vocal as Iron Curtain Communists—is a believer in atheism. It works to weaken the tenets of religion. Every possible device—propaganda, front organizations, literature —is used to attack the believers of God.

THE FATE OF CHRISTIAN VALUES

What does the acceptance of atheistic communism mean in terms of the individual? What happens to the concept of man when Marxism-Leninism gains control? What is the fate of Christian values?

The answer: the individual is not a creature of God, loved and cherished, but a blotch of skin and bones to be trained, manipulated, and exploited for reasons of state. Love, mercy, and justice become meaningless symbols, mocked as "bourgeois weaknesses." The state becomes supreme and man exists to serve a supreme master whose every whim is final and irrevocable. Man becomes a tool without personality or individuality. In other words, our Judaic-Christian history is completely reversed.

94-51060-32

(Reprinted from "Christianity Today," June 22, 1959)
ENCLOSURE

FIGURE 15. J. Edgar Hoover, *Communism: The Bitter Enemy of Religion* (Washington, DC: US Government Printing Office, 1959), reprinted from *Christianity Today*, June 22, 1959. *Source*: FBI File 94-51060-32 enclosure.

government. After his essays were published in *Christianity Today*, the Bureau reprinted them on DOJ letterhead, with the FBI emblem and "reprinted from *Christianity Today*" affixed on every copy. They were distributed throughout the country to preachers, evangelists, laity, and white evangelical publishers alike, free of charge, courtesy of US taxpayers (see figure 15). His essays, stamped with the US Department of Justice insignia, amounted to one of the best endorsements for which white evangelicals could have hoped. *CT* quickly became the voice of respectable white Christian conservatism, speaking to and for a broad public. The magazine even boasted a higher circulation than *National Review*, the periodical that claimed to be "the Bible of the conservative movement." *National Review* was founded just one year prior to *Christianity Today*, yet by 1964, the print circulation of *CT* was more than double that of *National Review*.[6] The *National Review* may have been the Bible of the movement, but it was *Christianity Today* that held the bullhorn for the national revival of white religious and political conservativism. The magazine of white evangelical conservatism rose to such prominence, in part, on the pen of J. Edgar Hoover.

Second, and closely related, Hoover's epistles corroborated the political claims of white evangelical conservatism, aiding and abetting the notion that white evangelical racial, theological, and moral ideals should sit at the center of national life. White evangelical conservatism, they preached, was the only way to achieve salvation, liberty, and justice for all. Finally, as a result, Hoover became more than just another contributor for the white evangelical magazine; he quickly emerged as a welcomed national spokesman for white evangelical conservatism.

Masters of Deceit

Special Agent Fern Stukenbroeker, PhD, was key to building the Bureau's relationship with *Christianity Today*.[7] The Missouri Methodist arrived at the Bureau in 1942. The balding white man stood only five feet six inches, and weighed a shaky 140 pounds, looking more bookish than strapping G-man, and he had the background to prove it. He had extensive journalistic and research experience. He entered Washington University in St. Louis (WUSTL) at the age of fifteen, graduating with a BS in Journalism, while serving as the managing editor of the WUSTL News Bureau. The precocious writer matriculated through WUSTL, completing an MA in History with a thesis on "The Attitude of Great Britain Towards Turkey, 1908–1914." He continued his studies at WUSTL, earning a PhD in Modern European History in 1942. His dissertation was entitled "British Public Opinion Upon Austria Hungry, 1900–1914."[8] SA Stukenbroeker's studies equipped him with a profound understanding of the importance of public opinion and war. He was the perfect employee for the FBI—a federal agency that utilized its own propaganda machine for its war against sin and evil.

In 1948, the bookish special agent was appointed to the Bureau's PR engine, the Crime Records Division at FBIHQ. SA Stukenbroeker's kind nature and expansive professional skills made up for his short stature in an agency that was obsessed with Christian masculine appearance. His section chief and close friend, Baptist SA Jones, remembered, "Though somewhat short, he presented an excellent physical appearance, he had an outstanding personality, and got along exceedingly well with others." Methodist SA Louis B. Nichols, the director of the entire division, was equally disappointed in the special agent's appearance, but remained impressed with his skills. "His physical appearance was average," the Methodist noted, but SA Stukenbroeker was "a research man who had a very distinct flair for original writing."[9] During his thirty-two-year career, SA Stukenbroeker's work was "used by FBI officials in policy statements and widely disseminated as of [sic] great practical value in preserving and furthering public welfare against crime and subversion." SA Stukenbroeker was dubbed "the most outstanding Special Agent from the standpoint of original composition."[10] He was the Bureau's resident scholar.

SA Stukenbroeker was also a popular Methodist lay preacher and Sunday school teacher. After arriving at FBIHQ, he immediately joined Trinity United Methodist Church in nearby Alexandria, Virginia, where he was named Chairman of the Official Board, elected to the Board of Trustees, and appointed the congregation's historian. When he delivered a lay sermon at both Sunday morning services on October 20, 1957, SA Jones reported that SA Stukenbroeker's sermon, "'My Father's Business' . . . was an inspiring message which reflected great credit both upon himself personally and the FBI as well." Several other sources reported that "SA Stukenbroeker exhibited a scholarly knowledge of his topic which was most effectively presented to the congregation." SA Stukenbroeker approached Sunday school in the same fashion. He was named Superintendent of the Church School, where he taught more than one thousand lessons for the church's adult Sunday school class. The religious academic G-man even turned his colleagues into disciples. SA Gordon A. Nease, the head of Crime Records from 1957 to 1959, occasionally attended Sunday school classes at Trinity Methodist. "Frankly," he told Associate Director SA Tolson, SA Stukenbroeker's preaching and teaching "was far superior to that of anyone I had heard before [at the church], including the Minister." He added, "he not only knew his subject but did a masterful job in putting it over to the class." Even SA Stukenbroeker's pastor agreed, at least with the latter point. SA Stukenbroeker, he noted, had "the unique ability to enable a class to accompany him in reliving Biblical experiences."[11] Stukenbroeker's professional research skills combined with his religious vocation made him an excellent FBI ghostwriter for all things faith and politics. He employed his gifts to transport readers to Hoover's vision of and for America. It was entitled *Masters of Deceit*.

SA Stukenbroeker inherited the manuscript from Catholic SA Sullivan of the FBI Domestic Intelligence Division and an eight-person research team. The team, SA Sullivan later complained, worked on the project "during the day at the taxpayers' expense" for several years, producing a draft of 815 pages. SA Stukenbroeker took the tome, cut it down, and made it attractive for a general audience.[12] In a historical tour de force, the Methodist lay preacher presented communism as a growing false religion, complete with its own moral standards and godless "theology" of atheism. Drawing on biblical imagery, he portrayed communism as the serpent in the Garden of Eden. It enticed racial minorities and clergy with false promises of knowledge, freedom, and social "progress." Communism slithered its way into reform organizations, infiltrating civil liberty groups, pacifist organizations, as well as churches, schools, colleges, and labor organizations. Institutions that advocated for social change—especially those comprised of African Americans, Jews, and women—could not be trusted. They were likely infested with communists at worst, or were actually a "communist front" at best.[13]

The only way to inoculate the nation against this plague was through Christian nationalism, a faith predicated upon Americanism and individual biblical devotion. "All we need is faith," were the words SA Stukenbroeker put in Hoover's mouth. "Suppose every American spent a little time each day . . . studying the Bible and the basic documents of American history, government, and culture?" Hoover asked. "The result would be a new America, vigilant, strong, but ever humble in the service of God."[14]

Like a long-winded sermon, the more than 300-page treatise concluded with an altar call. "I have tried to make the tactics of the Communist Party as clear as possible," Hoover surmised. To "stay free," Americans had to have a collective "reawakening." "The call of the future," he concluded, "must be a rekindled American faith." If readers missed the message on how to best fight communism, the photo on the original back cover of the book made it clear. It featured a pensive J. Edgar Hoover in the posture of prayer—hands clasped, kneeling, and looking up.[15] SA Stukenbroeker, the scholar-agent, took Hoover's religious worldview and gave it the respectability and modern rigor of a professionally trained historian, all without sacrificing traditional fervor. He was Hoover's religious messenger.

The message was well received. Hoover's ghostwritten handbook on communism and Christian nationalism was published on March 10, 1958, as *Masters of Deceit: The Story of Communism in America and How to Fight It.* The book was required reading for new agent training at the FBI Academy in Quantico, Virginia, and quickly reached a similar place among white evangelicals. The FBI playbook topped 250,000 sales in hard cover, holding the number one spot on the *New York Times* Best Seller List for nearly ten weeks, staying on the list for another twenty weeks.[16] The book went on to sell two million copies in paperback, going through twenty-nine printings in twelve years. The high school textbook version, *A Study in Communism*, became required reading in high schools across the country.[17]

The book's mainstream popularity cemented Hoover as America's undisputed spiritual Cold War champion. Hoover had previously flooded smaller Protestant and Catholic publications with similar jeremiads and religious screeds against communism. Yet, *Masters of Deceit* vaulted Hoover's musings on communism and religion to a broader and more cosmopolitan audience. He joined publisher Henry Holt and Company's stable of respected and lucrative authors including Robert Frost and Walter Lord, making Hoover, the author, a household name.[18] The Chaplain of the US Senate, Reverend Frederick Brown Harris, summarized the book's popularity among conservative white Protestants. The Methodist clergyman pronounced from his lofty perch, "I would that every church, as its bounden [sic] duty, would have its entire membership familiar with every chapter of J. Edgar Hoover's *Masters of Deceit*."[19] Book sales indicated that millions of churchgoers did just that.

Christianity Today

Reverend Dr. Carl F. H. Henry was one of those readers. The Professor of Theology and Christian Philosophy, and Dean at Fuller Theological Seminary, called *Masters of Deceit* "a timely and very worthwhile book for every citizen of the U.S. to read and study."[20] "The message was so important," the Baptist minister told Hoover's aides, he "wanted to do more than a review . . . he wanted to devote the first portion of his magazine—4 or 5 pages" to Hoover's gospel of Christian nationalism.[21] His magazine was *Christianity Today* (CT).

Christianity Today was birthed from the dream of famed evangelist Billy Graham. He envisioned a periodical that would serve as a "flagship" magazine of mainstream evangelicalism, and as a means to institutionalize his ministry. Some ministers erected churches, schools, or universities to establish their legacies. Graham chose *Christianity Today*. It would be an enduring, respectable gospel labor and, like his ministry, it would bring America back to God, "one soul at a time." Graham was the founder and the acknowledged head of *Christianity Today* for fifty years. *Christianity Today* was the name of the periodical, but there was no doubt that it was Graham's journal, or as one board member affectionately dubbed it, "Billy's magazine."[22] The comment was not in jest. Graham personally chose the founding editors with whom to lock arms: Fuller professor Reverend Carl F. H. Henry, Graham's father-in-law and avid pro-segregationist and white supremacist Dr. L. Nelson Bell, and Presbyterian Pastor J. Marcellus Kik made up the team.[23]

The white male founders made themselves the brain trust of evangelical theology. They outlined the faith as belief in "the Bible as the authoritative Word of God and the norm of judgement in faith and practice" and they gave primacy to saving individual souls.[24] The contributing editors would not just define "biblical" Christianity, they would stoke its revival. The magazine pledged to train an interdenominational vanguard of ministers in evangelical faith and practice. "There are many ministers who have been trained in liberal theological seminaries who want to believe biblical Christianity but cannot because they lack theological education which supports the position," the magazine argued. "To reach these ministers with the rationale of biblical Christianity is the objective of *Christianity Today*." What the *Christian Century*—the most popular religious publication of the time—was for liberal and mainline Protestants, *Christianity Today* would be for evangelical Christians.[25]

CT also had a political agenda. The magazine endeavored to be a "symbol of the place of the evangelical witness in the life of the republic," preaching that the answers to modern social and political problems were only "found in Christ and the Scriptures." Protestant Fundamentalism had failed to address modern spiritual problems because it was stuck in a defensive posture of anti-intellectualism and separatism. Protestant liberalism, Nelson Bell argued, was equally flawed because it preached "social reform rather than soul redemption," exulting "the autonomy of the human mind" over the Bible. Evangelical Christianity had to be at the center of the nation and its governance at home and abroad, or the nation and the global order would crumble. Reverend Harold J. Ockenga, PhD, founder and first president of the National

Association of Evangelicals (NAE), put it this way: "What the Communist party is in the vanguard of the world revolution, the evangelical movement must be in the world revival."[26]

Yet, the task to save the soul of the nation went beyond theological particulars and biblical fidelity. Rather, the evangelical army also operated under the broader cultural norm of whiteness. The designers of mainstream evangelical conservatism did not include Christians of color as they crafted and molded their new movement. Many Black, Latinx, and Asian American Christian faith communities fit the magazine's stated evangelical mold, yet they were not included in the "new evangelicalism." The self-appointed spokesmen, leaders, and definers of so-called historical biblical Christianity were deliberately and exclusively white. Whiteness was the norm in their midst. It was an unmarked category that functioned as the organizing principle for the magazine and the movement it represented. Whiteness was never questioned, named, or even debated during the formation of the magazine. It just, simply, was.[27]

Maleness was the same. As the magazine pulled together its contributing editors and broader network, Nelson Bell reminded everyone, "We must examine each *man* in the light of the effect his name will have." Maleness was assumed, never questioned. Women were outright disqualified, as were members of the charismatic and Holiness movements, placing white Pentecostals such as Oral Roberts and Kathryn Kuhlman on the outside. Pentecostals and Holiness folk shared the evangelical theological stance, but many also embraced female leadership, as well as divine healing and speaking in tongues. These practices were seen as lacking respectability. They were viewed as uneducated, backward, and lower class; anything but respectable. "If we do not eliminate these men," Bell noted of Pentecostals and Holiness folk, "we are not going to have the stature we must have." Graham agreed with his father-in-law, noting that the magazine must "restore intellectual respectability . . . to evangelical Christianity."[28] The contributing editors of CT were the watchmen on the wall. They not only defined the faith, they also decided who was in and who was out.

J. Edgar Hoover was in. He did not fit their theological profile. He did not believe in being born again, but he met the more weighty requirements. He was white and male, performing militant patriarchal authority. His law degree and position within the federal government conferred the intellectual credentialing and respectability the magazine and movement so desperately craved, and he believed in white Christian nationalism. He hearkened back to the fundamentalism of the old Christian right: belief in the Bible, conversion as the answer to all social ills, and America as God's chosen nation. Yet, he baptized these commitments in whiteness, civility, respectability, and political power. He was everything neo-evangelicals needed to gain traction in America's religious landscape, and gain admission into the technocratic halls of power.[29]

Armed with a white Christian nationalist vision, CT set up corporate offices in the nation's capital near the main political thoroughfare, ready to bring the nation back to God. A proud Reverend Henry boasted from the magazine's editorial perch at the 1014 Washington Building, Washington, DC, "the editors daily look down Pennsylvania Avenue," and lay eyes on all the "strategic centers of national life." The White House and FBIHQ were among them. The magazine's white Christian nationalist stance, along with its strategic physical location in the nation's capital, put J. Edgar Hoover and his FBI in the figurative and literal vision of Christianity Today.[30]

Christianity Today and Hoover

Christianity Today planned to publish as many of J. Edgar Hoover's words as possible. Reverend Henry wanted to reprint the majority of the chapter "Communism: A False Religion," from Masters of Deceit. SA Tolson quickly doused that flickering idea. "Dr. Reverend Henry should be told that Mr. Hoover appreciates his interests very much but that since the book is going to be syndicated the publisher would not be willing to have an entire chapter reprinted at this time."[31] Reverend Henry and the Bureau compromised on a book review. There was just one last hitch: Reverend Henry, true to white evangelical anti-Catholic sentiment of the day, was concerned about Hoover's perceived fondness for white Catholics. The troubled editor read a *Religion News Service* report relaying that Hoover gave an inscribed copy of the book to Archbishop Richard Cushing of Boston, telling the Archbishop that he was "the inspiration" for the book. Reverend Henry called the Bureau, stressing that he had "no personal feelings one way or another," he simply wanted to know if the news story was true. Yet, his persistence betrayed him. He asked "if there have been other similar inscriptions to religious leaders of other faiths." Hoover was irate, barking to his staff, "It's none of his business!" With SA Jones serving as translator, he politely informed Reverend Henry that such inscriptions were "personal matters," and no further comment would be given. Undeterred, *CT* published a summary of the director's book as the lead article in the news section of the March 17, 1958, issue.[32]

But the upstart magazine wanted more. Reverend Henry wanted the FBI director to write directly to his white evangelical audience, to join the brain trust. A book review was one thing, but an article for evangelicals was another. Hoover's authoritative voice would help to fortify the walls governing who was an evangelical and who was not. "I'm wondering," Reverend Henry wrote to Hoover, "whether a piece from your pen, perhaps on the theme 'If I were a Clergyman,' would serve the purpose even better." The FBI Boss could simply repeat *Masters of Deceit*, but "in a fresh way." Reverend Henry did not care. "The important thing," the editor noted, "is to get this material—under your influential signature—before the Protestant ministers of America and Britain." Hoover's pen held the power and respectability to endorse *CT* and authenticate the white evangelical religion and politics it sought to build.[33]

Hoover agreed. Re-presenting the material from his book for an evangelical audience would be easy. SA Fern Stukenbroeker handled it. The Methodist layman elected not to use Reverend Henry's suggested title. "If I Were a Clergyman" was too limiting. Instead, he drafted marching orders for America's clergy, entitled "The Challenge of the Future."

Hoover's first article for the evangelical flagship magazine announced that youth crime and communism threatened the soul of the nation.

From the seat of government, he diagnosed the solution. "America stands in great need of spiritual guidance." Ignoring the sociological diagnoses of the day, Hoover laid blame on a lack of faith. "These youngsters need religious training. They need to know the teachings of the Bible . . . The alternative is an ever-increasing crime rate." Likewise, communism could only be defeated by religious revival. Clergy had to be the leaders and shock troops in the battle against crime and communism. "The clergymen of America have a vital role in meeting this challenge of the future," Hoover announced. "The Church is the heartbeat of America. By urging men and women to rededicate their lives to God, clergymen are striking against these evil enemies." He closed his traditional jeremiad with a call to return. "The teachings of religion have guided us in years past, they must continue to be our guide in the future. An America faithful to God will be an America free and strong."[34]

The epistle was edited by the Crime Records Division and then sent on to Luther Huston at the US Department of Justice (DOJ) for formal approval. Lu, as he was affectionately called, was the DOJ Director of Public Information, responsible for the department's public facing materials and overall public image. He took the post in December 1957 following a storied career as the New York Times's Washington, DC, bureau chief and principal legal correspondent. The FBI cheered his appointment, perceiving him as a favorable reporter, as "one of the few decent persons at The New York Times office." Lu did not disappoint. He gave Hoover's essay the literal DOJ stamp of approval. Presbyterian SA Jack Keith then hand delivered the official DOJ treatise to Reverend Carl Henry.[35]

The article was featured as the lead essay in the May 26, 1958, issue of CT, adjacent to a storied address from conservative Presbyterian stalwart and Princeton Theological Seminary professor Reverend Dr. Charles Hodge. Historic figures aside, Hoover was the man of the hour, and his essay was the main attraction. Reverend Henry even added an editorial note at the conclusion of Hoover's essay, extolling his faithful service and ability "to arouse the citizenry" to save the nation.[36]

The essay was a hit from the halls of power to the grassroots. Congressman Glenard P. Lipscomb, representative of California's 24th District, inserted the article into the *Congressional Record*, telling his elected colleagues, "I commend this timely article to the attention of all Members of Congress."[37] The general public also took notice. Reverend Henry told Hoover, "We had a good flurry of correspondence on the piece and I am sure that it commended the moral vision of the FBI in a constructive way."[38] This was not news to Hoover. Americans across the country also wrote to Hoover, requesting copies of the essay. The FBI chief wrote Reverend Henry requesting permission to reprint the article, because the essay addressed "subjects about which we frequently receive requests for information." Executive Editor L. Nelson Bell gladly responded. "My dear Mr. Hoover . . . we will be delighted to have you make reprints of your challenging article . . . and to have you make any use of same you feel wise." The pro-segregationist closed with a personal note of admiration, "May I extend to you a personal word of appreciation of that which you are doing and also of your willingness to share your views with our readers."[39]

The FBI was pleased with the outcome. They trusted Reverend Henry as a dependable representative of the "very conservative and respectable sector of the religious publication field." They crowned him "a valuable contact," placing him on the coveted "special correspondents list," noting that he had "been very cooperative with the Bureau." The FBI embraced Reverend Henry as a trusted, like-minded soul. SA Jones surmised, "it is believed that he will do complete justice to the Director and the FBI in any editorial he may write."[40]

The FBI was right. Reverend Henry told the Bureau he came to the nation's capital with the intent to stay with the magazine "for only about a year until it was established and then return to Fuller Theological Seminary." However, he noted, "the magazine ha[s] been successful above and beyond [my] most optimistic expectations," so much so, "Dr.[*sic*] Billy Graham and other Protestant leaders . . . prevailed upon [me] to continue as editor." No longer interim editor, he alerted the Bureau he was "not content to be an interested observer but would like to assist the Bureau if possible."[41]

He was a man of his word. "Perhaps the time has come for another bold article," he wrote to Hoover in February 1959. It was indeed a crucial time. The Bureau was reeling from what it called "the Smear Campaign against the FBI." Investigative journalist Fred J. Cook was the chairman of this so-called campaign. Cook investigated the investigators in a widely circulated ten-part exposé published in *The Nation* in October 1958. The Bureau, he argued, was an institution "which Americans should try to understand before they worship [it]." Cook concluded that the FBI was more myth than hero. The Bureau had modernized crime fighting with scientific advancements, but, he argued, it also claimed undue credit for crime solving. The Bureau had bumbled major cases, allowed organized crime and racial violence to flourish. Moreover, the FBI used forged statistics to dramatize the threat of crime and communist subversion, placing itself at the center of a developing American police state. Yet, Hoover and his FBI had managed to be inoculated from federal scrutiny and public accountability. The mythos and "worship" of the FBI, Cook concluded, was not patriotic but had actually muzzled democratic practices and perpetuated a pervasive culture of fear and suspicion.[42]

Hoover saw red. He ordered the Crime Records Division to deconstruct and refute every claim within the sixty-page "communist" feature. In less than two months, Crime Records, led by Baptist SA Jones, produced an astounding 443-page manuscript "to expose Cook as a prevaricating character assassin and virtual intellectual prostitute." However, the director and SA Clyde Tolson were inconsolable, calling the tome "inept." The Boss wanted a report that could be used "before a Congressional Comm[ittee]." Instead, he found the lengthy memorandum "valueless," surmising, "It is a sad commentary on our staff." Hoover turned to Catholic SA Sullivan to "bring order out of chaos," a harmony that was not completed until April 1959. In the meantime, the Bureau turned to CT. An embarrassed Crime Records Division suggested the Bureau approach CT because, SA Jones posited, the "publication would be an excellent source for a short article regarding the current smear campaign against the Bureau, and SA Keith believes that Dr. Reverend Henry would be amenable to a suggestion that his magazine set forth the facts of the attack against the FBI." Presbyterian SA Keith, armed with reprints of Cook's exposé, was dispatched to "personally contact" his "personal friend," Reverend Carl Henry, to discuss the matter.[43]

Reverend Henry was under no pretense concerning the FBI visit, he was ready to join the fray and provide cover for the FBI. "We are troubled," Reverend Henry attested, "over the widening criticism of . . . the FBI as a Federal investigative agency, on the part of those who would dissolve or discredit the independent fact-finding agencies that have done so much to hinder the penetration of Communism in our land." Reverend Henry suggested Hoover "write an editorial" in *CT* addressing the evil campaign. Reverend Henry reminded the FBI Boss, "No other journal has the access to the Protestant ministry that *Christianity Today* does, and it would please us immensely to carry a forceful essay from your pen at this strategic time." The magazine editor suggested Hoover's editorial "be addressed to the theme of 'The Communist Use of a Religious Front.'"[44]

The two men came to an agreement. Hoover agreed to write the article, telling Reverend Henry, "It is indeed encouraging to all of us in the FBI to know that you were alert to the attacks against us." He continued, "I am pleased to advise that I will be glad to write an article along the lines you suggested."[45] The letter prompted Reverend Henry to issue an abundance of flattery for the FBI director. "The sparks from your anvil always seem to glow at white heat, and we are glad to waft them across the land where they will get the attention of those who so often grow starry-eyed in the presence of some of the alien ideologies that crowd our horizon today."[46]

Both men understood the benefit of the other. *Christianity Today* provided Hoover an evangelical endorsement and access to an eager audience of evangelical clergy and laity during his time of need. Criticism of the Bureau, Hoover argued, was not healthy democratic scrutiny, it was an assault of the shared conservative religious worldview of the Bureau and white evangelicals. Publishing in *Christianity Today* would drive the point home. On the other hand, Hoover's commentary gave *CT* and, by extension, the developing network of white evangelicalism the respectable legitimation the founders so deliberately sought and the federal promotion they so desperately desired.

Crime Records, led by Methodist SA Stukenbroeker and Baptist SA Jones, drafted the essay "Communism: The Bitter Enemy of Religion." It was approved by the DOJ office of public information and hand delivered to Reverend Henry by SA Keith on April 29, 1959. The magazine had an editorial policy of avoiding personal attacks, therefore the essay indirectly responded to Cook and the "smear campaign." Hoover argued that communism was godless. Its hallmark was attacking "Western morality" in order to "substitute a code of values which will destroy the Judaic-Christian way of life." Communist onslaughts came by way of "every possible device—propaganda, front organizations, literature." The devices were varied but united in their attack on "the believers of God." Advocates of this false religion "appeal to a better world, to a heaven on earth, to elimination [sic] of racial, economic, and political injustices." Liberal Protestants and other advocates of structural reform comprised the indicted group. Indeed, he argued, "The minds of thousands of men and women, including many in our own country, have succumbed and are today furnishing world communism the incentive, intelligence, and dynamic power to make it a master of millions of human souls." Americans, he ordered, "must be willing to devote the same amount of time and devotion to our beliefs, to reading the Bible, to working for Christian values, as the communists do for their institutions." The Protestant ministry was key in his expert diagnosis. "You as ministers stand on the front line in our battle of survival . . . No group in our population can do more to defeat communist man than the clergymen of America." The foremost expert on communism instructed ministers to stand up, gird their loins, and prepare for battle. America's fate was in the hands of white evangelical ministers. Their marching orders were simple: preach freedom under God. "Sermons represent one of the most potent forces for good in the Nation today," he told white evangelical ministers. Any kind of preaching would not do. Their sermons had to be traditional jeremiads. "You must urge a rededication to Christian beliefs," Hoover told them. "By faith in God this Nation was created. By faith in God this nation shall endure, strong and free. By faith in God communism can be overcome."[47]

Hoover's logic was simple. No matter what the critics said about the Bureau, the communist threat in America was real. Only communists, or fellow travelers on the road to perdition, would say otherwise. These lost souls were bent on destroying America and the Judeo-Christian way of life. The FBI, along with ministers loyal to the FBI's version of America, were the only entities standing between a godly nation of freedom and a godless wasteland of communist-controlled souls.

Christianity Today was thrilled. The article was published in the June 22, 1959, issue, once again, in the lead position. Hoover's essay echoed and authenticated the stance of the evangelical flagship. Reverend Henry told Hoover the article was "virile," helping thousands of Protestant ministers and laymen "to reinforce their sense of conviction on the side of high and holy things." *CT* issued a press release, heralding their partnership with the FBI: "FBI Director J. Edgar Hoover says that clergymen can do more to defeat Communist man than any group in our population." Newspapers, including the *Washington Post*, picked up the press release, announcing Hoover's religious prognosis and cure for all to grasp.[48]

The publicity was effective. SA Jones reported that Hoover received "numerous" letters praising the article, "many from members of the clergy." The Baptist special agent confirmed the same phenomenon was occurring at the office of *Christianity Today*. He reasoned, "this would be an appropriate article to distribute to citizens who write us requesting information regarding communism." Reverend Henry happily relented. Hoover's epistle to white evangelical ministers was printed on official government printing office paper featuring the Bureau's emblem and official header: "UNITED STATES DEPARTMENT OF JUSTICE FEDERAL BUREAU OF INVESTIGATION, WASHINGTON D.C." The small print at the bottom of the official government document gave praise where praise was due: "Reprinted from *Christianity Today*, June 11, 1959."[49] The Bureau's official reprint and distribution of Hoover's essay gave his religious marching orders to the Protestant clergy of the country the imprimatur and authority of the federal government, while the inclusion of *Christianity Today* on the government-issued document as the source lent the magazine specifically, and evangelicalism more broadly, a very conspicuous federal endorsement.

The fruits of their labor increased. The Freedoms Foundation awarded Hoover the George Washington Honor Medal for his article.

Founded by advertising executive Don Belding, the foundation aimed to recognize citizens who promoted "the American Way of Life." The foundation honored Hoover with its principal award because his essay increased "the understanding" of the "American Way of Life," and reflected "the best of the American spirit of volunteerism by offering constructive solutions to contemporary problems." Reverend Henry called the FBI and requested that a photograph for *CT* be taken at once. He made the short trip over to FBIHQ and was welcomed with open arms. The two men were photographed in Hoover's office as the spectacled editor presented Hoover with a replica medal. It was a moment Reverend Henry cherished. "Thank you," he told Hoover, "for the treasured photographs, one of which will be mounted for our offices here at *Christianity Today*." The other photo, Reverend Henry promised, will be "of course in our February 29, [1960] issue." The issue proudly announced Hoover's award, alongside awards given to two Presbyterian ministers, but only Hoover's picture was featured. The photograph of the leading religious editorialist and Reverend Henry was published in the news section of the magazine, nestled next to an advertisement for "Scripturally Sound Sunday School Papers." It was a fitting placement for the former Sunday school teacher.[50] The picture was worth a thousand words: The Bureau, *Christianity Today*, and the white religious conservatives the magazine represented were all in lockstep.

Hoover's Evangelical Magnum Opus

Reverend Henry told Hoover his contributions had "struck the deep note of Judeo-Christian heritage and its significance for an enduring civilization." *CT* and its expanding readership wanted more. "I hope," Reverend Henry tendered, "we shall be able to carry something from your pen—addressed to the 160,000 Protestant ministers and lay leaders of America—in 1960 also." Indeed, by 1960, the magazine had a circulation almost five times that of the conservative political periodical *National Review*. Hoover's pen, by way of leading Methodist layman SA Stukenbroeker, was helping to shape white evangelical conservatism. It was a task Hoover relished. "It has been a pleasure for me to prepare articles for your publication," the FBI Boss relayed to Reverend Henry, "and I am looking forward to the opportunity of writing another one next year."[51]

Hoover went above and beyond. In 1960, he pledged to write a series of three articles for *CT*. They turned out to be his evangelical magnum opus. The articles were the product of a microcosm of the new white evangelicalism: Presbyterian SA Jack Keith, Methodist lay preacher SA Stukenbroeker, and Baptist Reverend Henry gathered for a small "personal conference" on July 25, 1960. The magazine editor continued to push for the FBI director to take on the role of a religious authority and give white evangelical ministers and laymen their battle plan. Reverend Henry firmly believed Hoover's "long experience in fighting communism could certainly be put to excellent advantage in informing the clergymen of America just how to combat this menace." He pledged "to run an introductory editor's statement" that pointed readers to Hoover's *New York Times* best-seller and remind them "that Mr. Hoover's lifetime of experience in fighting communism has uniquely enabled him to give advice and share his convictions with the readers of *Christianity Today*." Reverend Henry and his readers were well aware that Hoover's words were more than mere advice and convictions. America's top cop had the power and authority to investigate, surveil, arrest, and charge any American for anything resembling a federal violation or disloyalty. When it came to the nation's top threat, Hoover's words were gospel, and Reverend Henry counted on it. He wanted Hoover to instruct clergy on their religious duties and police the boundaries of the proper morals and manners of the laity. He laid out these goals in a series of three propositions. First, he told SA Stukenbroeker and SA Keith that he wanted Hoover's essay to "draw the battle lines between the Judaic-Christian heritage and the communist way of life." Any person who was a communist or shared the slightest affinity for so-called communist ideals could not possibly be a Christian. Second, Hoover's epistles should "set forth communist efforts to hoodwink and deceive the clergy and emphasize just what the churches can do to remain alert toward communist propaganda." Finally, "emphasize primarily the need for Americans in all walks of life to rededicate themselves to our Judaic-Christian

heritage . . . point out the responsibility of every clergyman and layman
to do his share in fighting communism."[52] Hoover was not ordained, nor
was he trained in theology. Yet, Reverend Henry beseeched Hoover to
take his rightful position as America's Christian bishop, overseeing the
response of the Protestant ministry to the global crisis of communism.

J. Howard Pew pressed further. Four days after the Bureau's confab
with *Christianity Today*, Pew sent word to Hoover, giving the FBI director a charge to keep. The oil giant and trustee of the General Assembly
of the Presbyterian Church, and financier of the new white evangelicalism did not believe that Protestant ministers were actually communists.
But he was convinced the liberal theological positions of some mainline
Protestant ministers ran parallel to those of the Communist Party, jeop-
ardizing the ability of Protestant churches to lead the charge against
communism. Liberal stances had to be exposed for the evil that they
were, and then corrected. He saw the pages of *Christianity Today* as the
perfect venue for this rebuke and correction. "J. Howard Pew advised
me," the Special Agent in Charge (SAC) of the Cincinnati, Ohio, field
office wrote, "that he feels that it would be tremendously important for
Director Hoover to point out in his articles the utter brutality of the
Communists." Pew's perspective was that "the American people are too
lethargic, too docile, too willing to tolerate and not understand Communism." Pew's solution: the politics of fear. Hoover's essay, the wealthy
oilman pressed, should "put fear into our people and thus cause them
to understand the enemy." The SAC agreed with the self-interested ty-
coon. "If the Director can see his way clear to get such a message in
brutally frank terms in to his proposed articles, it will make a great hit
with Pew," he wrote. "In my humble opinion, I think this is precisely
what the American people need."[53]

SA Stukenbroeker went to work supplying this need and more.[54] He
began by drafting Reverend Henry's introductory editorial statement.
The words the Bureau put in the preacher's mouth read, in part, "At the
invitation of *Christianity Today*, the distinguished director of the FBI,
J. Edgar Hoover speaks his mind on the Communist threat to the Christian heritage. Based on his long experience in dealing with subversive
forces, Mr. Hoover here relates for *Christianity Today*'s wide readership

how the Communist Party operates against the American religious heritage. He expresses some firm convictions on how churchmen and churchgoers may effectively confront the Red Menace in prayer, thought, and action." To further bolster Hoover's authority, the spiritual preface closed with a reference to Hoover's book. "Readers of Mr. Hoover's best-selling book *Masters of Deceit* have found it to be a definitive analysis of the Communist menace facing the world today." Reverend Henry embraced the Bureau's ghostwritten statement, making only a few cosmetic changes. His preface ensured white evangelical readers understood: J. Edgar Hoover was America's General in the global war against communism.[55]

With Hoover's Christian and political authority established, Stukenbroeker went on to define communist goals and true Christian behavior. The first essay, "Communist Goals and Christian Ideals," told readers, "In the final analysis, the communist world view must be met and defeated by the Christian world view." Clergy, he wrote, quoting Matthew 6:33, "truly" had one responsibility: "to urge that 'seek ye first the kingdom of God and his righteousness'" was the heart of their ministries. Social protest and change were not in the wheelhouse of faithful clergy. Such things were, in fact, the goals of communists. He closed the essay explaining, "Strong, responsible, and faithful Christians, wearing the full armor of God are the best weapons of attack against communism and the other problems of our day."[56] Revival was the answer for everything.

In the second essay, "Communist Propaganda and the Christian Pulpit," the Methodist lay preacher made Hoover the arbiter of faithful preachers, pastoral leadership, and sermon topics. "Have you, as a minister, preached any sermons describing the frightful challenge which communism poses for the spiritual heritage of America?" He continued, "Have you urged the formation of discussion groups to acquaint men and women with this challenge." The "anti-communism serum" he noted, was "the strength of our Judaic-Christian Tradition, the power of the Holy Spirit working in men . . . *the tremendous power of God* to turn men toward good." The Christian church possessed "The spiritual firepower . . . to destroy all the Soviet man-made missiles and rockets and extirpate this twentieth century aberration." However, ministers and churches also had to beware. Their spiritual munitions also made them the bullseye, ground zero for all communist attacks. "The communists realize that unless the Christian pulpit—that mighty fortress of God—is liquidated, pitilessly, and mercilessly, the very existence of communism itself stands in jeopardy." Americans had to guard and protect their churches and their pulpits, and be vigilant for those who claimed to come in the name of the Lord. To this end, Hoover closed by outlining the proper mission, duty, and job description of a faithful minister. "The job of you, as clergymen, is to help channel this divine power into the hearts, minds, and souls of men . . . *That should be your mission*" (emphasis in original).[57] Any minister who claimed to do more or less than this should be viewed with great suspicion.

The final essay put the crisis in stark existential terms: "Communist Domination or Christian Rededication." Americans had two choices: the immorality of the "faith of communism" or the revival of traditional Christian faith and mores. "The future, to a large extent, will be determined by what we, as Christians, have to say and do," Hoover told readers. "You, as ministers of the gospel, can help determine this fateful decision: shall it be a world of communist domination or Christian rededication? Shall it be the cold world of communist inhumanity, sterility, and conformity, where the bodies, minds and souls of men become as stone, lifeless in the darkness of atheistic perversity, or Christian regeneration, where the power of the Holy Spirit floods with joy, love, and harmony." It was death or life; there was nothing in between. "A God-centered nation," the Bureau instructed white evangelicals, "can keep alive freedom, justice and mercy. This is the heritage of America."[58]

The series of jeremiads was edited by Southern Baptist SA Jones and Catholic SA Sullivan. It was then approved by Hoover, and then the DOJ. Finally, the essays were hand delivered to Reverend Henry's office on September 8, 1960. The magazine made slight editorial changes, publishing the first article as "Red [instead of "Communist"] Goals and Christian Ideals." "Red Goals" was a more capacious and apt description than the narrow "Communist Goals." Fellow travelers may not be communist per se, but their ideas and aims were, nonetheless, just as red.

The second essay was published without a name change. However, the magazine failed to mention Hoover's book. Reverend Henry was reprimanded for his sin. "I . . . chided Dr. Reverend Henry for making no mention of *Masters of Deceit* in the second article," Presbyterian SA Jack Keith reported, "and told him this was not living up to our agreement when he had requested the articles." Reverend Henry was reportedly "very apologetic," but refused to take all the blame, "stating that he had been in Europe when the second article was issued and his instructions simply had not been carried out. He promised to remedy this situation in the third and final article in the series." Reverend Henry did indeed correct the error of his way, sending Hoover proofs of the essay with a note attached. "You will note on page 2 we again included a boost from *Masters of Deceit*." The final essay was printed as "Soviet Rule or Christian Renewal" (instead of "Communist Domination or Christian Rededication"). The three essays were published in three successive issues, hitting newsstands, churches, public libraries, schools, seminaries, and mailboxes across the country on October 10, October 24, and November 7, 1960.[59] Reverend Henry viewed the opportunity to publish the series as nothing short of "a privilege," calling the essays "among the finest we have carried." They "dealt forcefully, intelligently and accurately with the communist challenge toward the Christian Church." In doing so, the director, he surmised, "had rendered a public service."[60]

Hoover's essays did indeed perform a service for white evangelicalism. His epistles were placed squarely in the middle of all that was the new white evangelicalism. His homilies were pitched alongside ads for the in-color full-length features of Billy Graham Evangelistic Films, announcements for Billy Graham's urban revivals, and updates on white evangelical organizations such as World Vision and the National Association of Evangelicals. The magazine that branded itself "Protestantism's fortnightly magazine of evangelical conviction" was the place where Americans learned the gospel of J. Edgar Hoover, America's high priest of Justice. In the process, *Christianity Today* and its white evangelical network received yet another indication that their gospel was indeed the true and original nature of America, God's chosen nation.[61]

White Evangelicals and Hoover's
Evangelical Magnum Opus

Hoover was well pleased with the project. "Dear Mr. Stukenbroeker," he wrote in a letter of commendation, "I am writing to thank you for the excellent research you conducted in connection with a series of articles on communism which has appeared in *Christianity Today*. You did a splendid job in handling this matter and your service reflected a high degree of intelligence and skill."[62] Compared to Hoover's reprimands for the slightest grammatical errors, a short letter of praise from the Boss was nothing short of effusive.

Hoover had reason to praise Stukenbroeker. His partnership with *Christianity Today* received unprecedented coverage—and in the process gave Hoover and *Christianity Today* free advertising. Louis Cassels, a senior editor and religion columnist for United Press International (UPI) and Episcopal layman, covered Hoover's words for the international news service. The Hearst Headline Service, a news feature agency of the Hearst newspaper empire, went further, announcing the series and even carrying portions of the essays. Newspapers such as the *New York Journal American*, the *Dallas Morning News*, and the *Milwaukee Sentinel* featured the series.[63]

Readers who did not have a paid subscription to *Christianity Today*, but subscribed wholeheartedly to white evangelicalism, pleasantly encountered the series in the press. Reverend V. C. Frank of the Sherman Park Evangelical Church in Milwaukee read the series in one of the "Hearst papers," and considered it "a well-done series." He was "pleasantly surprised by the reaction of local readers." Citizens "clipped" Hoover's words from the newspapers and brought them before the preacher "with much satisfaction." He assured Hoover some of the "thought and material" would be used at the church "in a variety of ways."[64]

Politicians followed suit. Reverend Frank's US Senator, Alexander Wiley, read Hoover's series in the Milwaukee newspaper and moved to have the series printed in the *Congressional Record*. "Over the years," the long-serving Republican announced to his colleagues on Monday

January 9, 1961, "J. Edgar Hoover, Director of the Federal Bureau of Investigation has carved a unique role in our history as a guardian of our internal security." In light of Hoover's status as a moral custodian, he told his fellow senators to take heed of Hoover's sermons on communism. "All of us," he pronounced, "need to be more thoroughly oriented on the techniques and practices of this atheistic ideology." He requested unanimous consent for Hoover's first CT article to be printed in the Appendix of the *Congressional Record*. There was no objection. Emboldened, the veteran senator completed the job the next day. "The Nation, I believe, can be particularly gratified that the Director of the FBI, charged with investigation of violations of Federal law, possesses such a deep concern for development of the spiritual aspects of our way of life. At this time, I ask unanimous consent to have printed in the Appendix of the *Congressional Record*, the second and third articles." His wish was granted.[65]

The following month US Republican Senator Styles Bridges of New Hampshire did the same. The four-term senator told his colleagues that Hoover was "a tower of moral strength." He added, "I know of no person with greater knowledge as to the inherent dangers represented by that false and godless philosophy [of communism]." "There is not," the Joseph McCarthy supporter continued, "one more competent to alert the American public in meeting its challenge." The articles, he argued, "forcibly" lay out "the spiritual basis for the structure we know as democracy." "Mr. Hoover," he continued, "makes it abundantly clear that Christianity is one of the great forces at our command, with which to meet the greatest menace of our times. I commend these articles to the attention of all Americans." He requested unanimous consent to have the series printed in the *Congressional Record* at the conclusion of his soliloquy. As the highest-ranking Republican in the Senate, no one dared challenge the redundant gesture. Hoover's essays were, once again, printed into the *Congressional Record*.[66] Three months later, Republican Congressman Don L. Short of North Dakota requested 400 copies of the director's series. The congressman planned to give them to "a small group of private citizens who desire to combat the fight against communism." The copies were sent to his office immediately.[67]

In February 1961, the national praise reached its zenith when the series was awarded a George Washington Honor Medal, a second for the duo of Hoover and *Christianity Today*, this time receiving the award alongside states-rights advocate Senator Barry Goldwater. J. Howard Pew congratulated Hoover, while managing to pat himself on the back. "I am proud of the small part which I played," he noted, "although it was only that of helping to inspire you to write the articles."[68] Pew may have provided the inspiration, but SA Stukenbroeker actually wrote the words, while Hoover became the object of white evangelical affection, admiration, and authentication.

White evangelicals across the nation registered their excitement with *Christianity Today*. Reverend Henry noted that the series "received a highly enthusiastic reception." He told the Bureau, "We are constantly receiving requests for additional copies." Indeed, Curtis H. Willey from Terre Haute, Indiana, demanded *Christianity Today* "mail reprints . . . to every preacher in the United States." Reverend Henry was quick to respond, telling SA Keith, "The series has been so popular and influential" that *CT* "deemed it necessary to have the series reprinted for distribution purposes." In fact, the magazine had "prepared more copies of the reprint . . . than any other reprint in the history" of *CT*. They created an "extremely attractive brochure" of Hoover's epistle, priced at ten cents. Those looking for larger quantities of the coveted gospel tract received the discounted price of twenty-five copies for $2.00; fifty copies for $2.50; and one hundred copies for $4.00. Crime Records Division proudly informed Hoover that the three articles brought in a whirlwind of "very favorable publicity and comment from the clerical field."[69]

The major white evangelical publishers also sought a piece of the pie. The storied Gospel Light Publications firm received Hoover's blessings to reprint. Henrietta C. Mears (1890–1963), one of the founders of the National Association of Evangelicals's National Sunday School Association, founded the publishing house of "Christ-Centered Bible Materials" in 1933. As the director of Christian Education at First Presbyterian Church of Hollywood, California, she established the company and ministry to print and distribute her self-authored Sunday school graded curriculum, materials, and teacher training aids. White evangelical purity was her brand. The company's insignia was the firm's name enclosed in a pyramid, instructing seekers, "Look for this emblem—it signifies quality." Both her publishing firm and summer Bible conferences at her Forest Home Christian Conference Center were interdenominational. By 1960, her organization forged and served an evangelical network of more than 20,000 churches in approximately sixty denominations. Her ministry had one simple mission: "Equipping the church with Christ-centered resources for making and teaching disciples who obediently transform today's generations." That transformation did not involve transcending America's racist norms. Her publications and ministry readily featured the word "nigger," racist jokes, exaggerated physical features of African Americans, and blackface entertainment. Gendered norms fared similarly. Mears refused to call herself or any other woman a preacher. Preaching, she believed, was exclusively for men. She was, by her own estimation, only a teacher; but she was one of the most important teachers in modern white evangelicalism. A young Billy Graham attended and preached at her summer Bible conference center. He later confessed that Mears was one of the most important female influences upon his life and ministry. "I doubt if any other woman outside of my wife and mother has had such a marked influence," he confessed. Bill Bright, the founder of Campus Crusade for Christ—the largest modern white evangelical campus ministry—was converted under her watch. He ran his rags to riches evangelical "student Christian movement" out of her home for more than a decade. "Apart from my mother," Bright declared, "no one has influenced my life for Christ so profoundly as has Dr. Henrietta C. Mears." Harold J. Ockenga credited her teachings as being formative in his ministry. Mears was, as *Christianity Today* put it, the "Grandmother" of modern white evangelicalism.[70]

The Grandmother counted Hoover as a prominent member of the white evangelical family. Two weeks after the *CT* series was published, a managing editor wrote to the FBI Boss. "We have been greatly impressed by your excellent series of articles on Communism that appeared in the October 10, October 24, and November 7 issues of *Christianity Today*," Fritz Ridenour wrote. "We are hoping that it might be possible to arrange for reprint privileges." The team at Gospel Light Publications chose *Teach*, the firm's quarterly "Sunday school idea magazine" started in 1959, as the right place for Hoover's essays. The goal of the magazine, Ridenour explained, was "to provide practical, down-to-earth training and inspiration for Sunday school teachers, superintendents and other workers." In just over a year the magazine accomplished its mission, quickly building a circulation of 30,000. In 1960, the Evangelical Press Association recognized *Teach* with the "Periodical of the Year Award." Reprinting Hoover's series, the editor continued, "will do the most good—in the hearts and minds of those who are directly cooperating and working with pastors in the teaching of God's word and Christian principles." In addition to Hoover's words, the managing editor also requested permission to use Hoover's photo on the cover of the award-winning "evangelical Sunday school" magazine. Hoover consented, supplying them with his preferred photo. Hoover's glossy face, stamped with the Gospel Light Publications marker signifying evangelical quality, took up the entire cover of the Summer 1961 issue. In the lead essay of the evangelical Sunday school magazine, the editors touted Hoover as the "internationally respected Director of the FBI." Portions of Hoover's important statements, similar to the words of Jesus in the King James Bible, were set apart and printed in red. Not even the words of the founder, Henrietta Mears, received such attention. The FBI Boss was presented as the ultimate teacher, instructing and affirming white evangelical Sunday school students, teachers, superintendents, and everyday parishioners in the evangelical Gospel way.[71]

Bill Bright and his Campus Crusade for Christ International (CCC) followed the Grandmother's lead. Bright, a former confectionary business man, found the white evangelical Christ in 1947. He established Campus Crusade for Christ in 1951 on the campus of UCLA while he was a student at nearby Fuller Theological Seminary. Approximately 250 students "committed their lives to Christ" during the first school year. The powerful officers and advisory board, which included Henrietta Mears, Harold J. Ockenga, and Billy Graham, helped fan the flames to other campuses across the country. By the mid-1960s, the organization had a paid staff of more than 300 and had established its international headquarters on an 1,800-acre estate in San Bernardino, California. The facilities included a six-story luxury hotel, ten bungalows, two dormitories, four professional tennis courts, and two swimming pools, all to train young adults in evangelism. "The college campus," Bright told Hoover, "is one of the most important and strategic mission fields in the world, and represents the greatest source of manpower of our time for fulfilling the Great Commission." Bright desperately desired to draft Hoover into his crusade. "Your name," he told the FBI director, "is a symbol of integrity, honor, and patriotism to millions of loyal Americans."[72]

He asked Hoover if he could reprint portions of the *Christianity Today* series for *The Collegiate Challenge*, the official magazine of CCC. The monthly was designed specifically to "appeal to the non-Christian student and professor on the secular campus." Hoover agreed to the article request, but only after he investigated Bright, CCC, and the magazine. Unbeknownst to the preacher, the Los Angeles and Minneapolis FBI field offices each performed "a discrete background check on Dr. Bright, his organization, and publication." Hoover ordered the surveillance "be limited to contacts with appropriate police and credit agencies, as well as established contacts and a search of office indices. Under no circumstances," Hoover decreed, "should Dr. Bright become aware of your interest in him or his organization and publication." Bright passed the Bureau's white glove inspection with flying colors. Hoover published "Freedom Begins with Christ," for the May–June 1962 issue of *The Collegiate Challenge*. The epistle was a compilation of quotes from the *Christianity Today* articles combined with a Hoover homily for college students. Bright called the article "vital" and made it the cover story of the issue. It was released to the magazine's audience of approximately 38,000 university presidents and professors on more than a thousand campuses, and an additional 75,000 copies were "mailed to almost all of the fraternities, sororities, and dormitories in the United States and Canada."[73]

Next, the William B. Eerdmans Publishing Company came knocking. William B. Eerdmans founded the eponymous evangelical stalwart publishing firm in 1911 in Grand Rapids, Michigan, after dropping out of nearby Calvin Theological Seminary. Labeling itself as "The Reformed

Press," Eerdmans focused largely on literature published in his native Dutch language, on Reformed Protestant texts in particular. In a savvy business decision, the publisher expanded his business market share to native English speakers in an effort to spread what he called his "book ministry" to a broader audience. In addition to treatises on reformed theology and biblical studies, Eerdmans curated and published non-fiction and fiction works from authors outside of the Dutch reformed network, especially conservative Presbyterians. He published and blessed these complementary views in hopes of immersing and educating readers on proper Christian living. Readers were taught how to be true Christians and navigate their lives and faith in the midst of a permissive theological liberalism on the one hand and an unbending fundamentalism on the other. The expansion of his religious and commercial market share made his brand synonymous with what he called, "good, wholesome, character-building, Christian books." With a stall of Presbyterian and reformed authors and distinctive branding, he was able to weave together a common community of white conservative Christians. By the 1940s, the company was established as a significant organ of the interdenominational network of the "new" white evangelicalism, declaring itself "a leader among evangelical publishers." Not only did Eerdmans oversee a cash-prize competition for the "Evangelical Book Award," they published landmark books by white male evangelical luminaries such as Reverend Carl Henry's *The Uneasy Conscience of Modern Fundamentalism* in 1947. Eerdmans was a seat of respectable white evangelicalism.[74]

Hoover would aid Eerdmans's evangelical authority and market share, and the chief editor, Calvin Bulthuis, knew it. The personable and unassuming Calvin College alum joined the publisher in 1957. With his English degree, Bulthuis brought a renewed literary professionalism to the publisher. He knew the faith, he knew the evangelical publishing market, and he had the founder's trust. He went to FBIHQ less than a month after Hoover's last essay struck evangelical hearts and minds. He had a proposition for the FBI chief: let Eerdmans publish his *Christianity Today* series in book form. The offer was tempting. Americans trusted the Eerdmans brand for "good, wholesome" white evangelical literature, putting Hoover in the position to receive sizeable royalties. Nevertheless, he turned down the leading evangelical publisher. "While I deeply appreciate your suggestion," Hoover told Bulthuis, "I do not feel that it would be appropriate at this time since the original articles are of such recent date. I hope you will understand my position in this regard."[75]

Legality aside, Hoover relished his position of evangelical authority and adoration. He did not need Eerdmans's money or blessing. He was raking in royalties from *Masters of Deceit*, while his *Christianity Today* essays were enjoying unprecedented praise and circulation within white evangelical networks. The Bureau began receiving a flood of reprint requests from white religious conservatives. Allowing free reprints would spread Hoover's gospel farther and wider than any publishing deal. Hoover wanted his gospel to be free and accessible, to give his religious musings the broadest reach possible.

—

By 1965, Hoover had become so identified with *Christianity Today* and white evangelicalism, Reverend Henry asked Hoover to take part in one of *Christianity Today*'s half-hour televised panel discussions. The filmed series was produced for public service television stations across the country and for nonprofit use by churches, college students, and home discussion groups. Reverend Henry wanted Hoover to participate in a panel on Christianity and national issues. The editor explained he would serve as moderator. Reverend Henry desperately desired to appear on TV alongside the FBI director because Hoover ranked as someone who had "the most to give on these themes." He pleaded with Hoover to stand in his rightful "role of Christian influence in our national life" and join luminaries of the white neo-evangelical movement in the televangelist endeavor. The plan was to pair Hoover with Samuel Richey Kamm, an NAE leader and Wheaton professor of political theory and constitutional history, and Reverend Harold J. Ockenga, founder and first president of the NAE and chairman of the board of *Christianity*

Today. "We have an opportunity," Reverend Henry told Hoover, "to help set a national mood and individual response on the ultimate issues of modern life."[76]

Hoover declined; he was too busy for another public appearance, and he granted television interviews sparingly. But Hoover did not need to appear on Christian TV. His *Christianity Today* articles had already set the "national mood" and influenced the "individual response" of countless white evangelicals on the "ultimate issues of modern life." *CT* made sure that Hoover's homilies were carefully and deliberately placed in *CT*, positioning Hoover as one of the most trusted and vetted theologians, Bible expositors, and evangelical witnesses of "international reputation." He had nothing to prove. Seemingly overnight, *CT* had made the FBI director a standing figurehead of "Protestantism's fortnightly magazine of evangelical conviction."[77] He was an evangelical spokesman and a member of the white evangelical brain trust. It was a phenomenon that made white evangelicals—from the pulpit to the pew—rejoice.

CHAPTER 5

Message to the Grassroots

"My Dear Christian Executive," Reverend Clinton F. Criswell, LLB, wrote to J. Edgar Hoover, "I have just read your article in the current issue of *Christianity Today*. . . . Your pen is indeed mightier than a Thompson submachine gun!" The Wisconsin preacher loved all the articles Hoover wrote for the evangelical flagship magazine, but he saw something special in Hoover's September 11, 1964, jeremiad, "The Faith of Our Fathers." Reverend Criswell predicted that Hoover's call for a national return to the faith of old would be "widely quoted and under God . . . greatly blessed." The preacher had only one suggestion for the "Christian Executive" of the FBI: "Contribute more oftener [*sic*]." He closed the fan mail with a blessing for Hoover, "May God continue to keep you close to His heart."[1]

Reverend Criswell may have been a prophet, or perhaps he was just observant. Either way, he was right. Mainstream white evangelicals were convinced that Hoover was close to God's heart. From 1960 until his death in 1972, all of Hoover's *Christianity Today* essays were "widely quoted" and distributed in white evangelical crusades, pulpits, institutions, publications, newsletters, and home study groups. Hoover's essays helped to stitch together the religious and political vision of an otherwise disparate community of evangelicals. He helped them become a united political front. For the white men and women of the growing religious network, Hoover's essays did indeed have the impact of a "Thompson submachine gun." And the foot soldiers in the white evangelical army of the Lord found ammunition, cover, and a unifying battle cry in each and every word.

Beginning in 1960, Hoover became a regular contributor to the evangelical flagship magazine. The popularity of his 1960 three-part series sealed the deal. He wrote at least one annual essay for the magazine until his death. The process was routinized, becoming as predictable as Hoover's faith. Methodist SA Stukenbroeker or Presbyterian SA Keith would periodically visit Reverend Carl Henry, and "plant" article ideas with him. Reverend Henry would then "request" the article from Hoover. The FBI director would piously refuse the magazine's $100 honorarium, in exchange for the Bureau's right to republish the articles, careful to credit *Christianity Today*. Methodist SA Stukenbroeker would then get to work, drafting the homily. It would be relayed to the desk of Baptist SA Jones for editorial gloss, and on to Hoover for approval. Once the religious missive was authorized, it was submitted to the US DOJ Director of Public Information for the final rubber stamp of approval. The respective essays were then hand delivered to Reverend Henry on official US DOJ letterhead to be published in *Christianity Today*. The process became a ritual, one that enabled J. Edger Hoover to reach countless white evangelicals.[2]

Once published, the Bureau's propaganda machine went to work, reprinting the essays and answering the mass of "inquiries from the public." The Bureau distributed the essays to each FBI field office. Hoover's essays were like epistles, and his Special Agents in Charge (SACs) carried and spread his words to the public. SACs were told the essays were perfectly suited for dissemination to "educational institutions and religious groups and organizations" and other important contacts. When SACs needed more reprints, they made their requests known to FBIHQ.[3] Soon the bureau's federal printing office could not keep up with the demand. The growing network of white evangelicals rushed at the chance to preach, distribute, and study Hoover's words in the name of Jesus. He became a central preacher to the white evangelical grassroots.

The FBI and Grassroots White Evangelicalism

As word of Hoover's essays spread throughout white evangelical networks, the faithful from across the country bombarded CT with requests for "free" copies of Hoover's epistles. The cost-conscious magazine directed all such requests to the FBI.[4] It saved Christianity Today money and served as free advertising and legitimation of the magazine as an essential partner in statecraft and national security. The glory would go to CT, but the bill would be paid by taxpayers.

The FBI seized the opportunity to evangelize the nation with its massive government printing capacity. On November 18, 1960, less than two weeks after the three-part series appeared in print, the Bureau received permission from Christianity Today to reprint the essays. The Bureau's Mechanical Section got busy making copies. They started in-house. On December 7, the Bureau sent out copies of Hoover's federally sponsored epistles to each FBI field office across the country, every Legal Attache office (legats) around the globe, and to every person on the special correspondents list. Hoover's homilies were also sent to graduates of the FBI National Academy. Hoover wanted his entire army to know his gospel, especially local law men. In addition to their signed Pledge for Law Enforcement Officers, graduates also had Hoover's gospel in their arsenal. This was especially helpful for graduates who became icons of the religious anti-civil rights crusade. Men such as Albany, Georgia, Police Chief Laurie Pritchett (who kept a framed picture of himself arresting Martin Luther King Jr. next to his FBI Academy graduation certificate), credited with successfully quelling King's 1961 crusade in the city; Birmingham, Alabama, Police Chief Jaime Moore; and the city's mayor Arthur Hanes (who was a former FBI special agent and the son of a Methodist minister), opposed King's 1963 efforts to desegregate the city's public accommodations. All three men were shaped and empowered, in part, by Hoover's gospel of white nationalism, delivered to their doorstep courtesy of the US DOJ.[5]

With the DOJ stamp of approval, Hoover's essays were the official religious and political positions of the US Department of Justice. White Christians wrote their FBI requesting multiple copies of Hoover's articles. The FBI educated them accordingly, supplying every need, sending copies of Hoover's religious essays, free of charge. In less than six months, the Bureau distributed thousands of copies of Hoover's jeremiads, complete with the seal of the FBI and DOJ. SA Jones calculated in March 1961, just four months after the publication of the series, that "Reprints have been distributed by the tens of thousands and many requests are still being received." Indeed, within a year, the Bureau's circulation of Hoover's *Christianity Today* essays surpassed the general circulation of *Christianity Today*.[6]

The Bureau became a significant outlet and dispenser of certified white evangelical literature of the highest order and thus a central and unifying institution for evangelical faith, connecting evangelicals from across the nation. And the evangelizing crusade was all underwritten and subsidized by American taxpayers.

The requests for copies of Hoover's essays came from thousands of white male ministers and white male and female laity alike. Some crusading white evangelicals were not satisfied with simply reading Hoover's words. They wanted to preach them. The transdenominational network embraced Hoover, preaching his words as gospel truth. It began with Reverend Billy Graham. The leading evangelist took to quoting Hoover in his sermons. Ever the humble Southern "plain folk" preacher, Graham was careful not to explicitly cite the *CT* essays. However, he deliberately cited J. Edgar Hoover by name during major urban crusades in cities such as Chicago, Minneapolis, Pittsburgh, and Los Angeles. He also cited Hoover during addresses before state legislatures and the Presidential Prayer breakfasts. In his often-repeated crusade sermon, "The Lost Frontier," Graham used Hoover's jeremiad to authenticate his own revival sermons. In another often-repeated address, entitled "Siren Songs," the evangelist cited Hoover's reflections on the atheistic and revolutionary "New Left," the subject of Hoover's 1967 contribution to *Christianity Today*. The address was marked in Graham's notebook as a sermon "to carry at all times."[7]

"At all times" included Graham's broadcast ministry as well. During one broadcast of the international radio show, *Hour of Decision*, Graham explained to his audience of twenty million listeners, "Most of us would agree with J. Edgar Hoover." The ABC, NBC, and Mutual radio sermon, "Rioting or Righteousness," paraphrased Hoover's *CT essay* "The Faith of Our Fathers." Graham preached, "'Let the hoodlum, the demagogue, and the exponent of anarchy know that the great, quiet power of this nation lies in her law-abiding citizens, and they will stomach no more. The choice is ours. The time is now.'"[8] Graham's consistent references and deference to Hoover sent a signal to readers of *Christianity Today* and the broader network of white evangelicals: Hoover was one of their own, on their side, leading the fight for the soul of America.

Naturally, other white evangelical preachers followed Graham's lead. The Pittsburgh SAC reported that Dr. J. Davis Illingworth of Vance Memorial Presbyterian Church in Wheeling, Virginia, peppered his pre-Thanksgiving Sunday sermon with quotes from Hoover's essay, just a few weeks after it was published. "Make Your Blessings Count" was broadcast over local radio on November 25, 1960. "Dr. Illingworth is a prominent minister in the United Presbyterian Church," the vigilant SAC reported, "and has been a leader in the community." The prominent minister gave Hoover's words ministerial approval, while the radio provided an even broader audience. The FBI director, never one to miss a compliment, made sure to thank the preacher. "I have learned of the honor you paid me on November 20 in quoting from my recent article in *Christianity Today* and want you to know of my personal appreciation for calling my remarks to the attention of your congregation." Hoover continued, "Certainly, it is vital in our struggle for survival that Americans turn to the teachings of Christ for moral strength and guidance." Enclosed in Hoover's note of thanks were four of his essays that addressed communism and religion. The Presbyterian minister was left assured of two things: he had plenty of material from which to preach, and the FBI would surely be watching and listening.[9]

Some white ministers from the Sunbelt went even further, preaching Hoover's essays from the pulpit, word for word. These parsons were leading flocks of transplanted white Southern folk who fled the South but took their brand of Christian conservative politics with them, transforming the region into a sprouting stronghold of modern white evangelical conservativism.[10] The clergy and their sheep received the FBI's gospel with open hearts and open ears, heeding Hoover's words as marching orders to take America back for God.

Baptist Pastor A. Barnum Hawkes of suburban Atlanta proudly wrote to the FBI about his Sunday sermon. "Yesterday morning, I preached on 'Guidelines for a Civilization in Peril,'" which was Hoover's lead essay from the June 22, 1962, issue of *Christianity Today*. On June 28, 1962, the pastor of the "white flight" suburban congregation mounted the pulpit, armed with the issue of *Christianity Today*. Following the church hymns, "Guide me, O Thou Great Jehovah" and "Jesus, my Lord," the preacher commenced his eponymous sermon, which, he admitted, consisted of simply reading Hoover's article. The preacher parroted Hoover's words, "We need to make sure that guidelines which served us so well in creating sturdy, self-respecting, self-reliant and God-fearing citizens in the past are not discarded." The copied jeremiad was broadcast over local radio in Waycross, Georgia, as Hawkes's original sermon. In reality, he had simply lifted and laundered Hoover's words as the word of God. During the course of the sermon, Pastor Hawkes was sure to express his gratitude to the FBI and to Hoover for his "excellent leadership . . . as a Christian Statesman."[11]

Robert S. Neuenschwander, MD, a churchgoer from the southern California city of Covina, loved hearing Hoover's words as Sunday gospel. The physician was exemplary of modern evangelicalism. He was a formally educated white transplant to the Sunbelt, living near Orange County, California, a "prototype" milieu of the emerging white evangelical conservatism, the soil that eventually proved so fertile for the political rise of Ronald Reagan.[12] From Dr. Neuenschwander's perspective, Hoover's essays spoke the "plain-folk" Gospel truth. He told *Christianity Today*, "Our minister . . . always uses a scriptural text," but on the most recent Sunday, the pastor "used [Mr. Hoover's] article instead." Hoover's epistle, he enthusiastically reported, was "an excellent sermon." Speaking for his minister and fellow parishioners, he thanked God for Hoover's inspirational Christian witness. "America should be

deeply grateful," he declared, "for a man with such insight and high
Christian ideals."[13]

Other pastors requested Hoover's gospel to educate themselves and
their congregations. Reverend W. M. Dennison of the First Christian
Church of New Port Richey, Florida, beckoned the Bureau for copies.
He wrote to Hoover in late November 1960. The letterhead of the Sun-
belt church proclaimed, "Where the Bible speaks, we speak; where the
Bible is silent, we are silent." The Bible was silent on communism, but
Reverend Dennison still wanted to hear what Hoover had to say. "I am
writing to request your three articles on [sic] *Christianity Today*," the
Florida pastor told Hoover. The Bureau happily sent him three copies
of each essay and six other essays on communism and religion for good
measure.[14] Likewise, Reverend Al Casebeer, pastor of First Christian
Church in Anaheim, California, requested 525 copies of Hoover's 1967
CT essay, "The New Left: A Gospel of Nihilism." The preacher called it
"one of the most important presentations of recent years." He sent one
copy to every family in the church.[15]

White evangelicals seeking to convert their pastors from Protestant
liberalism received an especially gracious response from the FBI. They
set out to use the authority of the FBI to police and rein in the religious
practices and theologies of their ministers and point them toward the
white evangelical cause. They saw themselves as righteous religious reformers. Creola L. Paradise of Sioux City, Iowa, requested permission
to reprint the essay to disseminate to all local clergy. Many of the clergy
had lost their way, and their membership in the ACLU was proof.[16]

Mrs. Wallace K. Dyer wrote to the FBI, identifying herself first as a
member of the First Presbyterian Church of Evansville, Indiana, and
second as an evangelist of Hoover's words. "They are so succinct," the
retired public welfare social worker told Hoover, "to the point and perfectly phrased to get the message across to church groups." Mrs. Dyer
was a member of the church's Social Action committee, the Christian
Life Commission, and the local Women's Association. Mrs. Dyer took
each of her roles to heart, but she was particularly committed to her
self-appointed role as an evangelist for Hoover's words. She relayed
Hoover's message to unwilling ears, and passed around her sole copy

of Hoover's essays to any interested soul. One earnest reader did not want to part ways with the dog-eared copy. Mrs. Dyer had to retrieve her sole cherished copy from her friend Ed Marshall, who was "a wonderful little man" who had "almost memorized the first 2 articles." But willing listeners like Mr. Marshall were not Mrs. Dyer's prime audience. Her pastor was the target. "Our minister," she confessed to Hoover, "thinks our church could co-exist with communism; that communism would be a 'gentle' share. The wealth type thing if it were to triumph here etc. etc." Nevertheless, she persisted. "We haven't given up on trying to keep him [sic] see the light! How can people be so naïve." She saw it as her mission to help her pastor "see that Communism, should it triumph in this country, would not be peaceful, share the wealth type of government." She wanted more copies of Hoover's essays to pass along to her pastor to help him "see the light." Moreover, she planned to distribute them to local church groups, her fellow parishioners, and to members of the anti-communists and states rights study group she hosted at her house. Mrs. Dyer was the kind of Christian Hoover believed every citizen should be, while her pastor was the kind of duped minister Hoover believed was plentiful in the Protestant mainline. Seven days later, the FBI sent her one hundred pamphlets as well as three other essays on religion and communism.[17]

Mrs. David W. Smith was similarly rewarded the following week. The suburban Columbus, Ohio, mother of three was concerned that "many ministers . . . heed the word of the *Christian Century*." The magazine, she confessed, "frightens me as it is considered the voice of all Protestant churches." This was especially true of her own pastor, a fact that placed the minister in her sights as the "first target" of her local anti-communist crusade. The unnamed parson, she admitted, was "most excellent in the pulpit," his sermons made "a great impact" on her and her family. The community agreed, and the church grew numerically and financially. Yet, his good works and influence made him all the more dangerous. He possessed tremendous influence, but did not measure up to the anti-communist plumb line. He was a "firm believer" in the *Christian Century* and Dr. Martin Marty, noted church historian and associate editor of the Protestant mainline journal. Despite Mrs. Smith's pleading, the pastor refused to preach on communism, admitting that he was "afraid" of getting caught up in the controversy. "This is very hard for me to understand in a minister in the church of God," she scrawled. She blamed the *Christian Century* for his lack of will and ability to understand the stakes. *Christianity Today*, the magazine that billed itself as the evangelical answer and corrective to the liberal *Christian Century*, was the answer. She asked Hoover for copies of his *Christianity Today* essays and the magazine's address, so she could subscribe to the magazine and get the "help" she believed her minister and faith community desperately needed. The Bureau was slightly troubled that it did not have a record of Mrs. Smith or her pastor, with no quick remedy in sight. However, the Bureau did have a record on the *Christian Century*, and that was all it needed. The magazine, the FBI internally noted, "has approved of the position taken by pacifists and has condemned the treatment of Negroes." It was a prototypical "communist front organization." The Bureau quickly responded to Mrs. Smith, thanking her for her concern and interests, calling it "reassuring." They directed her to buy *Masters of Deceit*, sent her two copies of Hoover's series—one for her and one for her pastor—and a few of Hoover's other essays addressing the crisis.[18]

Likewise, Mrs. D. A. Kemp, a church secretary in Baton Rouge, Louisiana, requested copies for her minister and the churches in her community because she was convinced communism was attempting to "infiltrate our churches." African Americans were the biggest threat of all. She wrote to Hoover in 1960, during nonviolent sit-ins by Black college students seeking to desegregate the city's downtown stores. She was sure the students were communists. Her feelings, not facts, constituted her only evidence. And as far as she was concerned, that was sufficient. "I feel that the NAACP and all of the race disturbances are Communist inspired." In her opinion, America treated its darker citizens just fine. African Americans were simply ungrateful and lazy. "The negro has been given better treatment, more money, and better schools in the South than they have had anywhere," she surmised. "They do not assume any responsibility for helping themselves or improving the morals of their race." Hoover felt the same. In response, the FBI did not inform her that protesting racial discrimination was constitutionally protected speech, or a patriotic act in line with the nation's highest ideals. Rather, the FBI simply thanked her for "the benefit" of her observations, and assured her they were "indeed appreciated." The FBI sent her the *Christianity Today* essays, as well as six additional Hoover homilies.[19]

The requests of evangelical "kitchen table activists" in the Midwest and Sunbelt were also zealously fulfilled. Local kitchen clubs, reading groups, and study collectives of white evangelicals looked to *Christianity Today* for their religious and political education. These groups were particularly important to suburban white women, offering opportunities for leadership and avenues of political and religious activism outside of the parameters of male-led institutions such as churches, church-affiliated schools, corporations, and machine politics. *Christianity Today* schooled evangelical white women and supplied them with "expert" talking points with which to proselytize their respective communities. This shared stock of literature and intellectual touchpoints weaved local groups of "suburban warriors" into a national movement.[20] And J. Edgar Hoover was one of their favorites.

Regina Olbertz of Milford, Iowa, belonged to a small group of women studying the "Facts of Communism." The group had "very limited" financial resources. She requested free copies from Hoover during the spring of 1961 to serve as training curriculum for her battalion. Hoover sent the free copies and a host of his other writings so Mrs. Olbertz and her friends could "help combat communism."[21] Mrs. Kyle McDaniel requested copies, as her First Baptist Church of Maryville, Tennessee, was forming an anti-communist reading group.[22] Fran A. Smith, Education Chairperson of the Baton Rouge Laymen Association, requested 500 copies for a "planned study program."[23] After hearing about the series at a local study group in the spring of 1962, Mrs. E. R. Katzorke of the southern California city of Torrance requested a copy of the pamphlet from the FBI. She was so impressed, she passed it along to her pastor. The cleric was so moved, he directed Mrs. Katzorke to write back to the FBI to procure "a large quantity" for the church and broader community. "May God Bless you," she wrote to Hoover. "We remember you in our prayers daily." Hoover remembered her and ordered copies of the pamphlet sent to her church along with four of his other publications.[24]

Male activists also reached out to the FBI to sustain their souls. Floyd F. Suder, Jr. of Bellaire, Texas, requested sixty copies to distribute to his study group of white conservative activists and neighborhood evangelists during the Christmas holiday season. "It will be our purpose to get them into the hands of the clergy," he professed. The Bureau sent copies, with a note attached. "If we can be of further service, please do not hesitate to contact us."[25] Hoover also went above and beyond for Dr. Robert Null. The Garden Grove, California, physician requested an astounding one thousand copies for his community. The Bureau did not hesitate, sending the free copies with pleasure. "There is no charge for material which this Bureau is privileged to send to the public," the FBI assured him, "and if you have a need for additional copies of these articles or other materials, please do not hesitate to let us know."[26]

The requests continued to pour in from all over the Midwest and Sunbelt. Clarence Brueggeman, a member of the conservative Lutheran Church, Missouri Synod in Saint Louis, requested "a stack of free copies for distribution." The Bureau sent him twenty-five copies of the series and fifty copies of Hoover's other epistles.[27] Likewise, the president of the First Methodist Church Men's Club in Yuma, Arizona, requested one hundred copies to distribute to the men of the church and the local Kiwanis club. If Hoover would send the articles, the police sergeant promised, "the men in these two organizations will enjoy the article and also help to fight the Communist Menace." His need was met.[28] Police Captain W. G. Cook of Ford City, Pennsylvania, requested 1,000 copies to "distribute them all over the entire county."[29] Gene Darnall, a land surveyor in Columbus, Indiana, asked Hoover if he could have copies of the "sermon to the Christian ministers of our country" to send to every minister in his community.[30]

The number of distributed copies to local white evangelical activists would have been even greater had the Bureau not been so judicious. The Bureau did not permit every willing activist to go forth in Hoover's name. Only those the Bureau deemed respectable and possessing an identifiable conservative religious witness were given Bureau approved copies. The ever-vigilant Hoover instituted a policy: "The Bureau desires to know the identity and reputation of those persons to whom we furnish material on the subject of communism in volume." Special agents at FBIHQ and field offices investigated questionable religious seekers using "brief, discreet inquiries," making sure the subject did "not become aware of the Bureau's interests."[31] The Bureau wanted to protect its witnesses and do its part to police those who belonged in the white evangelical community.

The Bureau found Mrs. Nicholas D. Davis, a Sunday school teacher in Jackson, Mississippi, acceptable only after some deliberation. She received Hoover's series in pamphlet form from the FBI field office in New Orleans. The pamphlet was the discipleship she was desperately seeking, answering all "the questions" she had about religion and communism. She asked Hoover for five hundred copies of the pamphlet to distribute to the local Women's Society of Christian Service. "I am not interested in joining the John Birchers in labeling those who disagree with me as Communists," she noted. "But I would like to know as much as I can about what communism is and what I can do constructively to strengthen the cause of freedom." The mention of the John Birch Society (JBS) raised suspicion at the Bureau. Founded in 1958 by Robert Welch, the national mass-membership organization aimed to educate citizens against communism—which for Welch was any form of federal regulation or activism with which he disagreed, making the organization a wellspring of unproven conspiracy theories. The Bureau labeled JBS an extremist organization. Hoover proudly noted that he had "no respect" for Welch's politics. However, Mrs. Davis's status as a Sunday school teacher secured her respect at the Bureau. "It appears she is a Sunday school teacher," SA Donald C. Morrell told his supervisor, "and is active in church affairs." He concluded, "It appears that Mrs. Davis is a sincere individual . . . She also appears to be conservative in her approach to combatting communism." Her request was granted.[32]

Mr. and Mrs. William T. Wood did not provide much background in their request, only that she and her husband were "comparatively new citizens" who wanted to use Hoover's series for the church study group they started in the southern California city of Torrance. Whether immigrants or simply transplants, Hoover did not trust their "new" status. He directed the Los Angeles (LA) field office to investigate the couple. The LA office investigated their employment, credit history, and even performed a background check with the local police. "No derogatory information was developed." The Bureau happily sent along the requested twenty-five copies for the Woods's study group.[33]

The FBI outright rejected the request of James F. Davis Jr. He requested free copies of the series for the Anti-Communism Association of Harrison County, Texas. *Christianity Today* said yes, and directed him to the FBI. The Bureau was more cautious. They had no record on Davis. Hoover directed the FBI field office in Dallas "to designate an Agent to conduct a discreet inquiry regarding the general reputation of Davis and his Anti-Communism Association. Under no circumstances," Hoover ordered, "should David become aware of the Bureau's interest." The Boss gave them five days to complete the mission—it only took four. The Dallas SAC reported Davis was an unemployed engineer with extremely poor credit, with "quite a number of past due and delinquent accounts." He was penniless and reportedly lived off the money he received from his married daughter. His organization was equally hampered and paltry in the Bureau's estimation. The anti-communism group "was ultra conservative," advocating the impeachment of the entire US Supreme Court. While it was led by the county judge, "no really responsible citizens" were members, only those of the "defunct White Citizens Council." The group was anti-communist but lacked respectability and was associated with a violent racist group. It was settled: FBIHQ marked his request for copies "killed." The rejection letter was sent by Hoover's secretary Helen W. Gandy, "so that Davis [would] not have the opportunity to utilize a letter from the Director to the embarrassment of the Bureau." The shrewd Gandy informed Davis they did not have any copies of the essays and any reprint request would have to come directly from the requesting publication.[34]

Dr. Leslie K. Campbell received the same treatment. In a handwritten note, the registered Arcadia, California, republican asked *Christianity Today* for permission to quote Hoover at length in a book he was publishing. He was, he told the magazine, "in the final stages of a manuscript ... a serious critical analysis of our society which has led us to our present-day apostasy, immorality, dishonesty, etc." He wanted permission to reprint Hoover's work "as much as would seem feasible." The magazine passed the request to Hoover. Hoover answered by having the LA field office "conduct a discreet inquiry" on the retired dentist. Dr. Campbell had a clean background, good credit, and was known to be of "excellent character and reputation." However, the Bureau investigation found the republican was "very to ultra conservative in political beliefs." The Los Angeles field office advised FBIHQ against giving Dr. Campbell anything. The Bureau informed CT of their denial via telephone to prevent the magazine from "making a copy of a written communication from the Director available to Campbell, which might prove to be embarrassing to the Bureau."[35]

The FBI loved disseminating Hoover's gospel ways, but it drew a line. The Bureau decided who was sufficiently pious and conservative. Those who lacked respectability or overtly endorsed white supremacy were rebuked. The Bureau had an image to protect and a white Christian nationalist movement to police. As far as the Bureau was concerned, men like Davis and Campbell could continue to spout their racist and anti-communist views, just as long as they did not seem to have the official endorsement of the FBI. "Never embarrass the Bureau" was more than a saying, it was the eleventh commandment.

A Small Remnant

There was a small remnant of white evangelicals who felt they were suffering the most embarrassment. They were disgusted by the movement's embrace and hero worship of J. Edgar Hoover. Irvin Andres of Goshen College told Hoover he had been "enjoying" the articles by the FBI Boss. "However," the Mennonite sarcastically confessed, "this morning they have begun to give me a headache."[36] The headaches were caused by a scandalized evangelical mind. Hoover was outside the evangelical theological camp, yet the magazine and the broader movement embraced him. How could a movement purportedly founded on theological specificity give up its theological integrity in exchange for political access, authentication, and power?

From 1960 to 1972, a small but fierce storm of theological criticisms rained down on the magazine. Leo L. Riddle of Spruce Pines, North

Carolina, called Hoover's theology "Holey." He admired Hoover's commitments to "patriotism, morality, law and order," but he was dumbfounded as to "how an 'evangelical' magazine could give such prominent billing" to Hoover's "unevangelical" theology. "I am only a layman," he confessed, but he could still "see the many perforations in Mr. Hoover's theology." Hoover was not born again, and thus failed to acknowledge that salvation through faith in Jesus Christ was the only way to fix America.[37]

A weary writer from suburban Chicago chastised the magazine for being so "eager to accept moral, religious, and philosophical judgements from respected, famous, government officials." The anonymous writer believed Hoover was "a sincere Presbyterian Christian," but the magazine's dependence on Hoover to validate white evangelicalism was the same mistake the church made "in Constantine's day."[38]

A believer from Newark, Delaware, also berated the magazine for its embrace of Hoover. The six-year subscriber found Hoover's place in the movement "shocking!" The confused Lutheran sternly wrote, "I know that some of Mr. Hoover's theological concepts must be repugnant to you!" Were Hoover and his anti-communism and power so dear, the evangelical asked, "that you should be compelled to print such a theological disaster?" Hoover's "political religiosity," he continued, confused "political necessities with deeper theological realities." No matter how patriotic one's soul may be, the writer concluded, "even the brave and the free need Jesus Christ."[39]

The shared commitment to whiteness also came under fire. Vernon Geurkink of the Madison Square Christian Reformed Church of Grand Rapids, Michigan, called on all "reflective evangelical Christians" to see the error of Hoover's ways as it related to religion, race, and citizenship. Hoover demanded that "we must be loyal to America because it is Christian, not because we are Christians." Geurkink asked how Hoover specifically and evangelicals more broadly "overlook the racial discrimination that perpetuates the mental, societal, political, and economic enslavement of almost an entire race of people." Hoover's "blind patriotism" and "uncritical devotion to the American dream" allowed the FBI director to "praise a romanticized past that never existed," enabling him to "ignore the shooting of black militants to protect white supremacy while the Mafia runs wild."[40]

A soul from Oakland, California, offered the harshest criticism of the white Christian nationalism preached by white evangelicalism and the FBI. The indignant reader called Hoover's writings pure "absurdity," a continual "diatribe" riddled with "fatuous" beliefs. Hoover's epistles amounted to "hatchet job[s]" that were "inaccurate, biased, selective, and viciously distortive." They were made worse by the magazine's editorial commendation and refusal to rebut anything Hoover wrote. How could one who was not properly Christian adequately "define the mission of the church?" It was the height of "hypocrisy." Hoover's prominent presence in the magazine, the Oakland native argued, was proof that white evangelicalism was nothing but a "masquerade [for] . . . conservative political philosophy under the cleaner banner of Christianity."[41]

These detractors bore the minority report. They were too credulous. They actually believed white evangelicalism and its institutions were exclusively founded upon theological particulars. The reality could not have been further from the truth. Whiteness and nationalism were the foundations from which modern white evangelicalism sprang.

The majority of white evangelicals were like Mark F. Bartling and Duane H. Anderson. Bartling, a candidate for ordained pastoral ministry at Redeemer Lutheran Church in Philadelphia, assured Hoover in 1962, "While I know that there are men, even in the church, which are attacking [you] . . . I want you to know that there are some who support and are praying for you. May the Lord continue to give you the courage to carry on your witness."[42] Anderson, a principal of the Seventh-Day Adventist's Portland Union Academy, went further. In 1970, he pronounced a white Christian nationalist blessing on Hoover. "May God bless you in your continuing vigilance as you, with your dedicated force, guide and preserve the real values of this country which are based upon Biblical values of God's creation."[43] The two men symbolize the majority of evangelical opinion. Hoover was praised by most, critiqued by very few, but nevertheless, heralded as the movement's political champion.

SA Jones foresaw how the Bureau's relationship with *Christianity Today* would play out. On February 14, 1958, the Southern Baptist told Hoover that *CT* possessed an outstanding yet untapped opportunity to proliferate the Bureau's religious and political views. *Christianity Today*, he advised his boss, reached "an important segment of church leaders and molders of public opinion." When the magazine approached Hoover to be a regular contributor, SA Jones proffered, "I think we could safely assume that literally hundreds of sermons pointing out the dangers of this false religion [of communism] would result and that real benefit would accrue."[44] And it was so.

J. Edgar Hoover's essays became gospel in white evangelical pulpits, congregations, crusades, publications, newsletters, institutions, and study groups. J. Edgar Hoover—and by extension his FBI—became a widely accepted and central figure in the construction of modern white evangelicalism. Hoover, as founding editor Reverend Carl Henry noted, was an important part of the message and mission of modern white evangelicalism. Hoover became a spokesman of white evangelical conviction and identity.[45] Every time the Bureau distributed Hoover's essays, it did so on DOJ letterhead featuring the FBI emblem and the name of *Christianity Today*. Readers were assured, not only of the magazine's patriotism and the central role white evangelical faith should play in the fate of the nation-state, but also of the importance of the FBI's place in evangelical faith and politics.

Policing Faith: Hoover, the Author and Adjudicator of White Evangelicalism

PART 3

Plotting Faith:
Hoover, the
Author
and Adjudicator
of White
Evangelicalism

Mrs. Joyce Carter of Augusta, Georgia, was spiritually lost, so she reached out to J. Edgar Hoover. The Independent Missionary Baptist Church member desperately desired to live a wholesome evangelical Christian life, but she did not know where to turn or what religious authority to trust. She was a bewildered sheep, feeling herself going astray. She needed a good shepherd, so she turned to J. Edgar Hoover. Joyce poured out her heart to the FBI director in a four-page handwritten letter on August 10, 1962. "When I was really and truly saved (accepted Christ as my personal Savior)," she confessed, "I pulled out of the Southern Baptist Convention of which I'd been a member about 15 years . . . [I] Just couldn't go along with atheists teaching in their schools." She wanted someone to adjudicate true evangelical faith and allegiance. However, there was just too much theological and political chatter on the religious and political right. Everybody had something to say about which Bible to read, the threat of communism, and the path to the way, the truth, and the light. "Goldwater, Billy Graham, and everybody or group that wishes to, runs a daily column in newspapers nowadays," she complained. "Christians are getting to the point where they fight among themselves so much, it's sometime difficult to know who to believe." She looked to Hoover to author the last and final word on her faith and politics. "There just isn't anyone all different church groups would believe, as well as Republicans or Democrats, except the F.B.I." Only Hoover and his shock troops knew the truth and possessed the religious authority to set the record straight on all things pertaining to life and godliness. She begged Hoover to speak out more, to shut down all the false prophets, and send her the truth. She promised she would herald his words and make certain "everyone" in her church community was enlightened. She concluded her plea by reminding the FBI Boss that Christians were ready to fight, they just needed his leadership. "P.S.," she wrote, "People wouldn't mind fighting this thing and many are anxious to, but its [*sic*] like 'beating the air.'" The only way forward, she told Hoover, was through his leadership and through his FBI. "I don't believe some folks will believe anything," she told him, "unless its from the F.B.I."[1]

Mrs. Joyce Carter was right. White evangelicals and their institutions were ready to fight for the soul of the nation, but they did not know how best to wage the war, and they did not know who to trust as their spiritual general. Many white evangelicals looked past local clergy, evangelists, and religious professionals. They could not be trusted to answer such queries, because they were vulnerable to being duped by communism, or led astray by every wind of doctrine.

Instead, white evangelicals turned to Hoover and his FBI to police their faith. Hoover's outspoken faith as well as his print ministry in *Christianity Today* solidified his place as an icon of white evangelical faith. A broad constituency of white conservative Protestants and institutions recognized Hoover as the nation's leading evangelical statesman. He was not born again, seminary trained, or ordained; but his commitment to white Christian nationalism and political power made him perfectly suited for the position. His education and mainline background bequeathed respectability, while his knowledge of the Bible rivaled any fundamentalist barnstormer. As FBI director, he had the expertise and confidential knowledge of white Christian America's existential threat: subversion. All of this positioned him in the seat of white evangelical power and authority.[2] The white faithful turned to him for gospel advice and spiritual guidance, believing he possessed the wisdom and power to police the faith that would lead the faithful and the nation back to God.

The Bureau was deluged with such requests. The number of existing letters in Bureau files, let alone those that were destroyed, is immeasurable. However, the tone of the thousands that remain is very discernable. The faithful wrote him, seeking his guidance, approval, and favor in matters of faith and politics. Their questions largely avoided the topic of conversion as well as personal moral dilemmas and failings. They turned to Hoover for the weightier matters of religion and politics. The faithful sought his godly approval of which version of the Bible they should use, which evangelist was capable of guiding their souls home, and even the religious and patriotic legitimacy of the Civil Rights Movement. They sought his guidance and spiritual counsel for all things pertaining to life and godliness. They expected Hoover to act as a righteous judge and political champion.

Hoover gladly accepted the position. Like a Bishop, he assumed jurisdiction over the purity of evangelical faith, adjudicating its godly standards. Hoover responded to the faithful, sending his word, namely in the form of his own published religious writings. Similar to popular white evangelists like Billy Graham or Oral Roberts, Hoover also had a team that fielded white evangelical concerns, offering efficient responses. The ecumenical Crime Records Division, with Hoover's approval, offered routine yet relevant answers to the countless sacred queries that poured in to FBIHQ. Each of these epistles concluded with the authoritative and heartfelt sign-off, "Sincerely Yours, J. Edgar Hoover." The letters enabled Hoover and his FBI to know the heart of white evangelical America, while the Bureau's responses helped them to control the pulse.[3]

CHAPTER 6

Bishop

In late 1951, Hoover attempted to use his knowledge of the Bible to comfort President Truman. Both men agreed Protestants should embrace Catholics for the sake of Cold War unity, but their theological and biblical agreement went no further. After the president confessed that he felt betrayed by some of the very men he had appointed, Hoover consoled the Baptist president, reminding him that even Jesus was double-crossed by a disciple. The biblically astute Commander-in-Chief quickly corrected the Sunday school teacher: not one, but three disciples betrayed Jesus—Judas deceived Christ, Thomas doubted him, and Peter denied him.[1]

Hoover left the Oval Office incensed. Unknown to the president, the seemingly casual exchange on the Bible was not so casual to Hoover. The FBI Boss was zealous for scripture. Since his youth, Hoover prided himself on rote memorization of the sacred text. Scripture was, after all, the foundation of the nation's laws. Hoover approached all mentions and discussions of the Bible with the passion of a crusader, stopping at nothing to battle and prove his superiority of biblical knowledge and interpretation. His zeal often imprisoned him in wars of his own creation, but he refused to suffer alone. Hoover perceived President Truman's correction as both an attack on the Bible and on his knowledge of the same. He immediately directed Crime Records to launch an FBI investigation on the betrayal of Christ. The directive spread throughout headquarters like a mighty rushing wind: "The Boss wants us to investigate Jesus Christ?" The answer was a resounding yes. Hoover was so perturbed, he told his pastor about the matter. "Holy wrath" and "righteous indignation," he told Reverend Elson, were required to defend biblical truths. The FBI investigation was completed by an ecumenical team of Methodists, Baptists, and Catholics. They sided with the president. Arriving at a conclusion was the easy part, informing the FBI director of the error of his ways—about the Bible, no less—was the hard part. The Boss waited anxiously to know the results. After days of intentional delay, Crime Records delivered the results of their investigation on Jesus Christ to their sanctimonious Boss. The lot fell to Catholic SA William Sullivan, aka Crazy Billy. Hoover, surprisingly, took his defeat in stride. But he never forgot. At home, he displayed photographs of every president under which he served, except for President Truman.[2]

Hoover's battle with Truman was not the last time the FBI director sought to ensure his righteous judgment of all things pertaining to God, the Bible, and Christian America. As he did unto President Truman, he would do unto the nation. Beginning in 1953 with the publication of a new version of the Bible until his death, white evangelicals sought Hoover's judgment and guidance on all things religion and politics. In response, Hoover gladly dispensed his gospel of white Christian nationalism, and white evangelicals joyfully received it.

In January 1953, the FBI launched a Domestic Intelligence investigation of the Revised Standard Version of the Bible (RSV). The translation and publication of the "new Bible" was completed by a select group from the Division of Christian Education of the National Council of Churches (NCC) on September 30, 1952. The Bible committee was exclusively comprised of white men hailing from elite eastern and midwestern universities and seminaries, hailing from ten Protestant denominations, and one Reform Jew. The first copy of the new Bible was presented to President Truman in the White House, followed by celebratory worship services and ceremonies across the country in more than 3,000 communities. The affair signaled that the ecumenical team of liberal churchmen were the respectable and commendable representatives of white Protestantism, and their Bible was the "new authorized version" of sacred text for white Protestantism.[3]

However, for the FBI and conservative white Protestants it was no time for celebration. The composition of the team and its entrée into the Oval Office was cause for cosmic concern. The anxiety centered on the "liberal" translation of what conservative Protestants believed was a Messianic prophecy in Isaiah 7:14. The King James Version renders the text, "Therefore the Lord himself shall give you a sign; Behold, a virgin shall conceive, and bear a son, and shall call his name Immanuel." However, the NCC's council of Hebrew scholars relegated "virgin" to the footnotes, opting for the more accurate interpretation of "young woman." Conservative Protestants read the NCC's attempt at scholarly precision as just another sinister communist plot to deny the pure and divine nature of Christ's birth, crushing the faith that undergirded the nation.[4]

Conservative Protestants were fired up. Reverend Carl McIntire provided the intellectual accelerant. The president of the fundamentalist American Council of Christian Churches published a small, twenty-three-page pamphlet outlining the biblical sins of the NCC. At ten cents a copy, *The New Bible: Why Christians Should Not Accept It* was extremely popular across the country. It listed the names of the translators, warning that many had ties to communist front organizations. The removal of "virgin" from Isaiah was all the proof real Christians needed. True Christians, he declared, could not accept the RSV. Those that embraced the Bible were members of another religion, an un-American faith. "The people and the church that feed upon this new Bible will be a different people and a different church," the pamphlet proclaimed. Reverend McIntire listed twenty-nine denominations that belonged to the NCC "which authorized the printing and copyrighting of the Revised Standard Version of the Bible," and then issued an alert. "*If you are a member of one of these churches, you are in the National Council (NCC) and the new Bible was presented in your name.*"[5]

Pastors across the nation were not pleased. They cited Reverend McIntire's leaflet as the grounds of their righteous indignation. To the alarm of local fire chiefs everywhere, some ministers hosted public burnings of the RSV Bible. An assortment of ignitions were used; blow torches, matches, and bonfires, anything to burn away the chaff. Reverend Martin Luther Hux, a Missionary Baptist pastor in North Carolina, made his disdain a public spectacle, announcing the deed would take place on November 30, 1952. On the day of judgment, the former Southeastern Baptist Theological Seminary (Wake Forest, North Carolina) student delivered a two-hour sermon with the straightforward title, "The National Council Bible, the Master Stroke of Satan—One of the Devil's Greatest Hoaxes." After the hellfire sermon, the congregation and the gathered press were led outside and given American flags as Reverend Hux set the blaze. He was careful not to burn the entire Bible, which would have been as sacrilegious as the NCC offense. Rather, he only burned the "fraud" pages of Isaiah 7:14. "This," he screamed from the bed of a pickup truck, "has been the dream of modernists for centuries, to make Jesus Christ the son of a bad woman." Two months later, Reverend Bill Denton from Akron, Ohio, went further. The radio preacher and pastor of the Furnace Street Mission took the name of his church literally, and incinerated the entire Bible. He collected the ashes and sent them to Luther Weigle, former Dean of Yale Divinity School and chairman of the translation committee. The registered mail was accompanied by a note, "Dear Sir: You will find enclosed the ashes of a book which was once called the Revised Standard Version of the Holy Bible."[6]

An FBI Domestic Intelligence investigation rose from the ashes. The FBI agreed with McIntire—the RSV was red. The Bureau was, however, "most circumspect" about its relationship with McIntire. The FBI abhorred his "very controversial reputation and statements," especially his tendency to take "issue with other religious leaders in a rather blatant manner not generally considered to be in good taste," and his "rather vitriolic" publications. They dismissed him as a member of the "extreme right-wing element in the country." The Bureau even stopped responding to McIntire's letters and requests.[7] Nevertheless, the FBI agreed with McIntire's assessment, and the chorus of conservative Protestants that joined in, including Hoover's beloved *Sunday School Times*. The FBI labeled the new Bible a product of communists and communist-affiliated clergy. All of the men were subject to an investigation by the FBI.[8]

Matters grew worse in 1960 when the RSV communist conspiracy appeared in a US Air Force Reserve Training Manual. The military countersubversion handbook instructed reservists to be on alert for the red Bible. It was to be avoided at all costs. Homer H. Hyde, an eighteen-year veteran of the air force's educational unit and member of Grace Baptist Church in San Antonio, Texas, was responsible. The air force educator accepted "intelligence" from M. G. Lowman—a Methodist layman and executive secretary of the Circuit Riders, an anti-communist organization that prided itself on collecting intelligence on socialists and communists—laundered it and inserted it into the Air Force Reserve Training Manual, not as one man's opinion, but as verified gospel truth. "From a variety of authoritative sources," Hyde inscribed in the manual, "there appears to be overwhelming evidence of communist antireligious activity in the United States through infiltration of fellow travelers into churches and educational institutions." The NCC's affiliation with the new bible was identified as the source of the contagion."[9]

All hell broke loose. The NCC dispatched a letter to Thomas Gates Jr., secretary of the Department of Defense, on February 11, 1960, demanding the manual be retracted. The air force withdrew the manual on the same day. Mr. Gates as well as Dudley Sharp, the secretary of the air force, and officials at the Pentagon issued public apologies to the NCC, expressing regret that the manual ever saw the light of day. Connecticut Republican Senator Prescott Bush, the father of President George H. W. Bush, excoriated the manual. The Episcopalian labeled the accusations "unjustified and outrageous," articulately calling its publication "inexcusably stupid." Pennsylvania's Democratic Congressman Francis E. Walter, the chairman of the House Committee on Un-American Activities, naturally disagreed. He criticized the air force, the Department of Defense, and the Pentagon for apologizing and retracting the manual without investigating the claims. It showed great weakness and dereliction of duties. Besides, Congressman Walter confidently smirked, the translators did have ties to communism.[10]

All along, conservative white Protestants looked to the FBI for evidence to corroborate their suspicions that the new Bible was a subplot to a bigger domestic intelligence emergency. From 1953 to 1970, pastors and churchgoers alike wrote to J. Edgar Hoover seeking the light. Their respective denominational authorities could not be trusted, they were complicit at best, while many elected officials belonged to churches of the NCC. Only J. Edgar Hoover possessed the power, knowledge, and truth to set them on the right biblical path. The envelopes filled with the desperate hopes for cosmic guidance did not even bear an address, they were simply directed to "Mr. J. Edgar Hoover, Washington D.C."[11]

Requests from ministers like Reverend Shelburn A. Trent of Erwin, Tennessee, were typical. The minister attempted to speak for all Americans in his handwritten letter of January 20, 1953. "I am but a country minister," he humbly announced, "but I represent the sentiment of millions of real American citizens who see a great danger before us but find that unless we find help from a higher source we shall not be able to combat the forces of Communism." He encouraged Hoover to read McIntire's enclosed diatribe—marked "pass this around to your friends and family to read also." Reverend Trent then unleashed his own tirade. "Our country stands today and has been blessed of God on the grounds of our Faith in God and in His Son Jesus Christ. If the Communist or modernists can succeed in undermining the faith of the American people they will have won the greatest battle of the Ages. To send out a new Bible and have it preached that Jesus Christ was only a man and not a Savior is their first attempt to destroy us without Guns." He requested that Hoover investigate the matter, immediately. He closed with a strong suggestion. "The National Council of Churches . . . to my mind is un-American, subversive and headed by these men associated with Communists, [they] should be declared subversive by our Government, outlawed and charges brought against these men for attempting to destroy the American way of life." Reverend Harold Pierce, a pastor overseeing several churches in West Virginia, embodied the more reserved pastors. He requested "some information in regards to the Revised Version of the Bible." The local newspaper noted the communist allegations, but he wanted to know the truth, and he knew J. Edgar Hoover possessed it. His petition concluded, "I want to lead my churches in the correct way if this be true [I] would appreciate [illegible] much something explaining there [sic] background."[12]

Reverend Allen Newman, pastor of Ocean Beach Baptist Church, told the FBI director the controversy was "disturbing the spiritual harmony of my church and many other churches in the San Diego area." He flat out asked America's top cop to adjudicate the gospel truth, pleading "What is the truth in this matter?"[13] Reverend Carl Yoder felt the same way. The Church of the Brethren pastor in West Virginia reached out to Hoover for help. "I am preaching to Mountain People," he told the FBI, "they believe the Revised Standard Version of the Bible is written by Communist and fellow travellers [sic]." He asked Hoover to settle the religious debate. "I sincerely would appreciate plenty of help along this line."[14] Reverend Billy Doyle Gaither of Wesley Chapel Methodist Church in Mobile, Alabama, was deathly concerned as a member of the indicted group. "I think it is only fair to tell you that I feel that these accusations are irresponsible," he proffered, "but I would like to get any information that you are at liberty to give."[15]

Laypeople did the same, looking to Hoover as the adjudicator of their faith. The faithful continually bypassed their pastors. The clergy, trained or untrained, could not be trusted to know the way. Instead, they turned to J. Edgar Hoover and his FBI. Mrs. Ralph M. Ryckman of Pennsylvania wrote to protect her church from liberalism and rescue her denomination from atheistic communism. "Since the issuance of the revised version of the Bible and its acceptance by the Methodist Church," the Bible Study leader wrote, "I have learned to my dismay that leaders of the Federal or National Council of Churches and officials in our own denomination as well as the translators of this godless book are members of Communist organizations." She continued, "Some of the members of a study class on missions which I teach are taking the word of such men that there is no difference made in the Bible." She asked Hoover for help, she wanted to prove to her class that the translators of the RSV "have no love of God in their hearts." "I am so desirous of this information," she pleaded, "that I may prove definitely to my class that this thing which they have been asked to accept is written by men with the purpose of destroying their faith. . . . I shall anxiously await your answer."[16] While Ted Miller from Findlay, Ohio, simply asked, "Could you give me any more data, to help me in my trials to keep the St James version [sic] in our church."[17]

Harold Owings of Springfield, Ohio, wrote to Hoover. Harold addressed Hoover as "friend in Christ." He desperately sought salvation amidst the cosmic crisis. "I respect your understanding of both the essence and authority of God," he wrote, " [I] simply want help in a decision which, I feel, will have drastic results." He outlined his shifting perspective on the RSV, from embracing it "as absolute scripture" to "disregarding it as Scripture" and throwing it "in the trash can with the Russian flag." He highlighted his grievances in a typed three-page single-spaced letter. He concluded the acceptance of the RSV would erase the "Truth an inch or a degree at a time," resulting in a "common peace . . . between Christianity and Communism." Yet, he still wanted Hoover's opinion on which was the righteous path: acceptance or rejection of the RSV. He distressingly implored Hoover, "Please help me . . . to know what stand to take . . . Just simply say that you feel that I can accept it and teach it. Or that I must, as a free American citizen, reject it because of possible dangerous effects on the public."[18] All Hoover had to do was send his word to Harold Owings and it would be so.

Frances K. Ludwick seemed to believe Hoover was endowed with religious omniscience. She was, admittedly, "a very religious person" with "deep convictions about God and the Bible." She proudly devoted her time to "working for the salvation of souls." However, the RSV controversy had shrouded the truth. Some of the members of her Brethren Church were using the RSV, while others refused to attend worship and Sunday school if the RSV was used. She asked ministers of several denominations, but she was still lost. She turned to Hoover, the all-wise one, to settle the matter. "I have endeavored to find out the truths of these things," she confessed to Hoover, "but never got a definite answer so that is the reason I'm coming to you for I know that you are very truthful and will give me an honest answer and of course you above all people know the answers to all questions." Therefore, she asked, "I'd appreciate you telling me . . . if the Revised Version of the Bible was partly written by Communist people."[19]

George Hieb granted J. Edgar Hoover the power to determine Holy writ in his house. He and his family were "Protestants" in Vallejo, California, who "read the King James Version of the Bible." He wondered if there was "any truth" to the controversy surrounding the RSV. If the rumors were true, he pledged, "we would not be interested in reading it or have such a Bible in our house."[20]

Others wrote to Hoover as a means to convert their pastors and keep the parsons on the straight and narrow path. Mrs. Ellen Forson of New Jersey reached out to Hoover after she read Reverend Carl McIntire's pamphlet. "I took it to my Pastor," she complained, "and he called it rubbish and threw it on his desk." She asked Hoover to respond and clear up the matter. Whatever Hoover wrote, she promised, "I intend to show it to the pastor of my church who refuses to believe such a thing. I will also make good use of it among the members of my church."[21]

Mrs. Merrill K. Abernathy in Mississippi chastised her husband for bringing the RSV into the house. The fact that the Bible was a gift from his Sunday school class was irrelevant. The RSV was contraband in the Abernathy house. Mr. Abernathy asked his wife for proof of the communist conspiracy, so his wife turned to Hoover. "The history of the United States will record that J. Edgar Hoover was one of her truly great men," she flattered. "Our country has been stronger and more secure against its enemies because of your many years of service." She asked the great man for proof, and copies to boot, to send to her wayward pastor, Sunday school head, and the newspapers in Jackson, Mississippi.[22]

Hoover routinely offered a savvy yet regimented response to these pleas of piety and salvation. He tiptoed on what amounted to a high-wire act of religion and politics. The Bureau was convinced the NCC was a communist front. Its RSV Bible was a tainted project attempting to dethrone the Bible as the word of God and foundation of the nation. Yet, Hoover refrained from directly informing the faithful. Publicly branding the Protestant Establishment a communist front organization was political suicide for Hoover. The FBI needed mainline Protestants who were elected officials, like Prescott Bush and others, to approve the Bureau's ballooning appropriations requests. Instead, he offered a subtle response to the controversy surrounding the RSV. He continued to maintain, "The FBI is strictly an investigative agency." He apologized to believers: "I regret that I am unable to help you and hope that you will not infer in this connection either that we do or do not have data in our

files relating to your inquiry." However, true to form, he dropped a political morsel, leading to the desired political destination. He responded
to concerned Protestants from his portfolio of religious reflections.
They included a healthy portion of his *Christianity Today* essays. The
essays were taken from the pages of the leading white evangelical magazine which staked its identity, in part, on two crucial fronts: belief in the
"Bible as the authoritative Word of God" and opposition to the NCC.
Christianity Today even claimed the RSV Old Testament possessed
"serious defect[s]," including poor translations of the Messianic proph-
ecies, concluding, "We believe it to be imperative that conservative scholars prepare a revision." When Hoover sent concerned conservative
Protestants his essays from *Christianity Today*, his seemingly neutral
position on the matter became clearly partisan: Hoover sided against
the RSV and its authors. He routinely wrote with each response, "Enclosed is some material which I trust will be of interest to you." The literature was certainly of interest to inquiring Protestants. The faithful
accepted Hoover's responses and heralded them throughout their
churches and communities. Hoover's simple, routine gesture enabled
him to say a great deal about the issue, without saying a direct word.[23]
It became abundantly clear which Bible patrotic white evangelicals
should read.

Shepherding Pastors

Galvanized by the RSV controversy, pastors from across the country
sought Hoover's approval and guidance on a host of issues. They fashioned
Hoover a pastor to pastors. Clergy wrote for guidance pertaining to the
purity of their ministries and denominations, and the propriety of their
personal piety. They looked to Hoover to police and purify the faith.

First and foremost among clergy seeking Hoover's guidance was
Hoover's pastor. Reverend Elson admitted "on numerous occasions"
that he went to Hoover "for counsel." He made a habit of requesting
Hoover's clearance on books and religious material for the church. He
asked if Hoover would investigate certain books and authors and report
back to him "whether or not any of the books or authors are on the

subversive list, or are in any way implicated in subversive activities."[24] The pastor did not trust his own judgment as much as he trusted Hoover's adjudication of theological purity.

Reverend Elson even looked to Hoover, like a Bishop, to police church membership. Reverend Elson described the most "ticklish" occasion, involving Larry Motherwell, a young ordained elder in the congregation. The pastor's suspicions were awakened when Motherwell, the leader of the Sunday Evening Club, began collecting money from the club's twenty- to thirty-five-year-old parishioners for a trip abroad. The pastor asked Hoover for help. "For months," the pastor proudly recalled, "FBI agents attended church dinners and services, sitting near Motherwell, without anyone in the church knowing what was going on." When the taxpayer-funded investigation concluded, a disappointed Hoover stopped by the church office, a folder full of investigative memos in tow, and baldly asked his pastor, "How did this bird get into our church, let alone get elected an elder?" Motherwell's real name was John Cavender, a carpenter who had served time in prison for impersonating a naval officer. Reverend Elson rendered the man's ordination null and void and dismissed him from the church for impersonating a committed Christian.[25] Hoover was well pleased.

Pastors across the country did likewise. They wrote Hoover for religious guidance, hoping he would help keep them and their flocks and denominations on the straight and narrow. Reverend Jospeh E. Humerickhouse, pastor of First Baptist Church, Fowler, Colorado, got straight to the point in his March 24, 1960, letter. He asked the FBI Boss to answer one simple but profound question: "Is the American Baptist Convention . . . in any way officially connected with the Communist Party . . . An official statement from you will be greatly appreciated."[26]

Others asked about specific theological and ecclesiological issues. Reverend Karl E. Blake, pastor of Redeemer Evangelical Lutheran Church in Lebanon, Connecticut, requested Hoover's theological position on church raffles. "As a Christian pastor for 40 years I am opposed to all forms of gambling including raffles, because the word of God states: 'Thou shalt not steal,'" he told Hoover. He asked the FBI director for his position, "pro or con or both on raffles."[27] No issue was too small.

Pastor Tyler Terry of the Evangelical Free Church of Oroville, California, wrote the director in 1968 seeking validation on the religious claims of Reverend David Noebel's *Rhythm, Riots and Revolution: An Analysis of the Communist Use of Music, the Communist Master Music Plan.* It did not matter that Noebel was the pastor of the Fundamental Bible Church in Madison, Wisconsin, as well as the executive assistant and heir apparent to the famed anti-communist crusader Reverend Billy James Hargis. Reverend Terry wanted approval from a higher power. He asked Hoover if the claims in the book were true: have the Communists "set up Record Companies which are geared to making records which will break down the minds of our children? As a pastor," he continued, "and as a parent I am very much concerned." Pastor Terry asked Hoover if he possessed any "proof" that authenticated such claims. "In these days of real crisis," the pastor confessed, Hoover's trustworthiness and expertise were a godsend.[28]

Some ministers just wanted encouragement from Hoover. This was especially true for pastors who found themselves in the crosshairs of Carl McIntire and the host of extreme right-wing anti-communist ministers. The beleaguered pastors just wanted reassurance that their ministries were in fact acceptable in Hoover's sight. "My church members," one Methodist minister wrote, "are deeply upset by his [McIntire] attacks on the Methodist Church and its leaders." The pastor then poured out his heart to the FBI Boss, revealing the state of many ministers. "I am sick at heart over what is happening among our churches these days. Some of my fellow ministers are afraid to say anything about social questions, and some few are resigning their pulpits and their ministry." The young minister understood their plight, confessing, "I know that temptation myself. Why should I stay with it, when I am still young enough to get out and earn a living where my services will be appreciated and much more generously rewarded? And yet, here on the second day of Holy Week, 1962, I cannot avoid the challenge of my Lord and Savior, Jesus Christ, who took the worst possible thing the world could do to him and turned it into the best possible thing that could happen to the world. We need any encouragement you can give us."[29]

Similarly, in 1966, Reverend John C. Calhoun, named after the pro-slavery senator from South Carolina, beseeched Hoover for guidance.

The pastor of First Methodist Church of Albertville, Alabama, wrote, "I have often desired to prevail upon your time . . . How can I as a Methodist minister, who greatly appreciates the Constitution and sees a grave danger in Communism, civil disobedience, and its attendant disorders, most effectively serve as a citizen?"[30] In dark times, when evangelical pastors did not know which way to go, they turned to J. Edgar Hoover and his FBI to shepherd their souls.

Pastoring the Faithful

The faithful also wrote to Hoover seeking guidance and approval. New Christians inquired about righteous living, while others wrote with questions concerning the Christian patriotism of white radio evangelists, pastors, evangelical parachurch groups, and everyday gospel labors. "I am a new Christian," one restless soul wrote to Hoover on March 7, 1961. After hearing and reading "The Communists are getting in our churches, colleges and schools," he was lost. "I don't know what to think," he confessed. "It's enough to scare you to death." The seeker implored the FBI director for religious guidance, hoping Hoover would put his religious doubts to rest. He was in desperate need of pastoral care and assurance that the pillars of Christian America—churches and schools—would survive. The new believer pleaded with Hoover. "I know you are a very bussy [sic] man Mr. Hoover but if you will only take 5 minutes to answer my letter. I must know one way or another. so [sic] I can sleep at night . . . Than [sic] you so much. I will be waiting for your answer. God be with you."[31]

One letter dated October 10, 1962, was more specific, requesting Hoover's judgment on two of the most famous evangelists in the land. "Dear Mr. Hoover," a young Georgia man wrote, "I would like any information on the two religious or Evangelistic associations. One is the Billy Graham Evangelistic Association and the other is Oral Roberts Crusades." He admitted, "I have heard thing [sic] about both groups." Yet, the spiritual seeker turned to Hoover to adjudicate whether the men preached a gospel of pure patriotism. "Mr. Hoover you are a very religious man . . . your opinion of them would be appreciated. . . . Yours in Christ."[32]

Around the same time, Paul O. Hamer, a resident of cosmopolitan Arlington, Virginia, wrote Hoover after receiving an unsolicited religious publication. "*The Christian Beacon* has been coming to my house for several months, although I have not subscribed to it," Mr. Hamer noted of Reverend Carl McIntire's magazine. He validated his concern with his Christian testimony. "I have been a Christian during my life time infact [*sic*] I was brought up in the Presbyterian Church in a small town in Pennsylvania." After grounding his faith, he asked Hoover, "What is this Beacon—a real religious paper or just a tendency to confuse and divide our religious thinking?"[33]

"I have read articles you have written," one evangelical wrote on March 19, 1963, "and you are often quoted by the *Sunday School Times* of which I am a suscriber [*sic*], so you were the only one I could think of to write to concerning the conflict I have been going through." The conflict sat at the intersection of religion and politics. The writer's pastor asked each and every church member to sign a petition to have the US State Department investigated for allowing "Russian churchmen" to visit the country. "My problem is this, I am a born again Christian and I want to be loyal to this country and to Christ. . . . I would very much like to hear from you as to your opinion as to whether Christians should sign such a petition."[34]

Hoover handled all these letters the same way: he sent them his *Christianity Today* epistles, pastoring them with his own words.

Hoover adjudicated the godliness of evangelical institutions as well. Campus Crusade for Christ (CCC) received a great deal of attention. Students from universities across the country wrote Hoover asking for guidance about Bill Bright's organization. "I would like to inquire about an organization known as Campus Crusade," wrote Miss Martha Wald of Boston University in 1966. "They say they are a Christian movement," she told Hoover, but she also heard otherwise. She did not trust her own opinion or that of supposed experts in the field. "I have spoken to my religion professor," she confessed, "[he] believes they are Fundamentalists." Nevertheless, she knew she could count on Hoover for proper religious guidance. She enclosed CCC materials for Hoover's inspection. "Could you please send me any information on them," she closed her plea, "since, if they are a subversive group, I would like to know before I become too involved."[35]

J. Robert Ashton trusted his instincts on CCC, but his fellow churchgoers did not. The president of a small college-age study group at Richardson Park United Methodist Church in Wilmington, Delaware, wrote the FBI in 1971 to obtain information on the CCC. Many in his small group wanted to donate to CCC at the University of Delaware, but there was division within the ranks. Methodists at Southern Methodist University notified Ashton's small group that CCC was barred from their Methodist campus. The group was deemed "dangerous." Ashton's confidence in CCC as a worthy investment was not swayed. He was the president of an insurance underwriting corporation, he weighed financial risk for a living. However, his co-religionists were not convinced. Therefore, he reached out to Hoover to settle the matter once and for all. "It is my understanding that Billy Graham has endorsed this organization. If this is correct, this would be sufficient to satisfy me," he noted. Yet, for some in the group, Billy Graham's evangelical approval paled in comparison to Hoover's word. Ashton confessed, "However, this is not enough to satisfy a couple of our class members . . . We would really appreciate you advising us concerning information, other than what you must keep confidential, of course, you might have concerning this organization."[36]

White parents were also terribly concerned about their college-age children joining Campus Crusade for Christ. "I would like to have you investigate the Campus Crusade on nearly all campuses as far as I know," wrote Mr. and Mrs. R. B. Paine of Junction City, Oregon, in 1962. Their daughter, a student at Oregon State, "was ok until the end of her Freshman year when some one [sic] persuaded she and others to attend Religious Meetings. Since then it has gone on and on until she and other girls have become more or less fanatical on God etc." The campus crusader went from majoring in home economics to working a poorly paid job at a Christian radio station. Bill Bright's organization was to blame. "I feel some one is brainwashing these young girls' minds . . . These leaders go into the Dorms and Fraternities and work on the girls' minds. . . . They are told and trained to witness to people for Campus

Crusade." The Paines were convinced there was something wrong with the organization and they wanted Hoover's religious advice and federal insight. "I believe this should be investigated," the concerned parents told the director.[37]

Two families in Paris, Texas, approached their rector, Reverend James W. O'Connell, about their children who had joined CCC at the University of Texas, Austin in 1967. The rector of the Church of the Holy Cross knew exactly where to turn. "I wonder if you have any information on an organization calling itself Campus Crusade for Christ," he wrote the FBI. "I have no definite cause for suspicion . . . but I feel that if there is anything shady about this organization you will know it . . . At the same time, if it is fully respectable, that information will help us, too."[38]

The Bureau's regimented responses reminded the faithful the FBI was simply an investigative agency that did not comment on organizations or individuals. The company line was followed by some form of note, for example: "The Campus Crusade for Christ has not been investigated by this Bureau. This should not however be construed as clearance by the FBI." Yet, Hoover's 1962 essay "written especially for" CCC's *The Collegiate Challenge* magazine provided the faithful with all the clearance they needed.[39]

Mr. A. B. Cowen of Henderson, Nevada, was concerned about the liberal drift of the American Baptist Convention (ABC). The ABC was a member of the NCC. If the NCC was filled with communists, what, he wondered, did it mean for his faith and his local church? Beyond guilt by association, Mr. Cowen was concerned for the soul of his community and his "small Baptist church." He told Hoover on February 28, 1960, "The one thing we want to believe beyond all else is that we can depend upon our Church group to be sound and above any taint whatsoever." He asked Hoover to set his mind at ease. "Could there in fact be some Communists in the American Baptist Convention? If so, how are we to know . . . and what can good Church people do to stem this tide?"[40] Mrs. J. R. Whisman went further in 1964. The faithful member of First Baptist Church of Auburn, California, believed her church was

"100% sound and fundamental," but the future was bleak. First Baptist was in danger of being led astray by the ABC. "You are probably wondering why we stay in this church, but," she hedged, "we feel that splits in churches are a poor testimony to the unsaved—they don't understand and use it as an excuse." Her pastor was not as concerned about the unity of believers. In fact, she begrudgingly confessed, the parson had "washed his hands of the whole thing," yet had the audacity to appoint a pro-ABC committee to investigate the issue. She was not satisfied. She and her fellow avid anti-communists presented the committee with irrefutable evidence, including letters from other Baptist pastors who left the ABC. First Baptist was not moved; instead the church invited an ABC leader from Northern California to calm the troubled waters. "Naturally, he isn't going to admit [it] ... or he'd lose his job," she confidently predicted. "So you see," she told Hoover, "we need your help and soon." Only the righteous judgment of Hoover could solve the matter once and for all. "Please reply as soon as possible because we are most desirous of having all of the facts possible before our next meeting."[41]

By 1966, Ruth B. Tanner was alarmed by a new development at her Baptist church. The San Diego Baptist was concerned that her church was considering adopting the "The Cell Plan." Modeled, in part, after John Wesley's small class meetings, the cell plan is a form of church organization in which parishioners are divided into small groups, referred to as cell groups, for personal Bible study and discipleship. Ruth, a member of the local church board of Christian education, saw something else afoot. "To the best of my knowledge, the suggested structure of the church cell plan is the same as the Communist cell plan. I think that it is a lullaby for Communism to teach this to our church." Ruth told Hoover she was "considerably concerned" about the ordeal. She sent the church literature to Hoover for his righteous "appraisal." In addition to his opinion on the particular matter, she asked, "Are there any other authors in our denominational literature that we should beware of?"[42]

White evangelicals also sought Hoover's approval of their personal piety. Mrs. J. L. Barry, "a housewife of a Navy sailor and mother of two young children," in San Diego, California, wrote in 1959 for advice in holiness on behalf of herself and her close friend of the Episcopal Church. "Could you please give me correct information regarding communism in our churches," the Methodist wrote. Mrs. Barry and her friend had read a flurry of material on religion and communism, and even heard Reverend Carl McIntire on the radio. All of it left the two women confused. She confessed they did not trust their respective mainline denominations, so they asked Hoover. "How," she pleaded, "can I be an intelligent, well-informed person in regards to these matters?"[43]

One couple wrote in 1961, asking for Hoover's approval on their religious giving. "My wife and I are adult counselors for the senior high school youth in the Methodist Church of our town," one man explained. "The group will trick or treat for UNICEF . . . Would you consider it to be un-American to send money to UNICEF." He continued, "The same question is in order for . . . the Daughters of the American Revolution and for the American Council of Christian Churches." The couple requested Hoover's religious judgment, even as they were frustrated by the Bureau's religious hierarchy. "We called you [sic] agent in Oklahoma City, [redacted] regarding this problem. Apparently, his position did not permit him to comment. . . . It appears that an FBI agent should be authorized to give more aid on a problem of this nature than we received." Regardless, they added, "Your immediate help on the above questions will be appreciated."[44]

Letters from white evangelicals show that J. Edgar Hoover was seen as an authority on all things pertaining to godliness. Whether questioning which version of the Bible to read, or the righteousness of the ministry of Billy Graham or Oral Roberts, or asking questions concerning personal piety, or the godliness of white evangelical parachurch organizations, white evangelicals positioned Hoover's authority as superior to clergy and church officials. White evangelicals anointed him their Bishop. And Hoover functioned accordingly, dispensing his gospel guidance.

One woman wrote to Hoover and said it best. She praised evangelical preachers for "waging a magnificent battle" to save the church and the nation's soul. Yet, nobody compared to J. Edgar Hoover. "There are a lot of people (and I am one of them) who feel that . . . the only man we can trust in the nation is you," she wrote. The evangelical foot soldier closed her note with a stern warning, "Don't argue the point because you know that being a woman I'll get in the last word."[45]

For most white evangelicals, there was no argument to be had.

CHAPTER 7

Champion

On April 27, 1956, the Chicago Bible Society gathered to celebrate J. Edgar Hoover. The society was founded in 1840. The Chicago chapter, similar to its parent organization, the American Bible Society (ABS), aimed to promote "the study and understanding of the Bible" as "God's Word . . . the touchstone of assurance in a changing world." Their goal was to distribute Bibles across the country and globe to establish a "Christian civilization in the United States and, eventually, around the world." The Chicago Bible heralds established the Gutenberg Award to celebrate this mission. The award was "named in honor of Johann Gutenberg (1397–1468), the inventor of the printing press and publisher of the first printed Bible," to recognize an individual "whose life and work have contributed to the promotion and understanding of the Bible." On that spring day, the Windy City's chapter of the ABS awarded FBI Director J. Edgar Hoover its Gutenberg Award.[1]

The award citation announced that Hoover had "repeatedly lent his high office and great influence to an endorsement of causes associated with the Scriptures." He had proven to be a towering figure in promoting the Bible, God's Word, as the foundation of American citizenship and society. "J. Edgar Hoover," the gold-lettered scroll concluded, "has shown himself to be an example of true justice based on the full implications of the moral and ethical principles of THE HOLY BIBLE and has consistently proclaimed in life and word his unfaltering faith in the teaching of the Scriptures as a guide for the fullest Christian citizenship and happy community life."[2] The Chicago Bible Society passed over

Billy Graham for the award. Instead, they crowned J. Edgar Hoover the
leading man for God and country. And they were not alone.

———

The embrace Hoover received from grassroots white evangelicals was
matched by their parachurch organizations and denominations. The
FBI Boss received more awards and honors from this broad network
than any white clergyman, rivaling Billy Graham as one of the most
widely praised names in white evangelicalism during the 1950s and
1960s. During this time, Hoover's collection of awards and public
honors—which included major white evangelical groups such as the
Chicago Bible Society, National Religious Broadcasters, the Jesuits,
the Assemblies of God (the largest white Pentecostal denomination),
and the Billy Graham Evangelistic Association—confirmed his status
as the political champion of white evangelicalism.

National Religious Broadcasters

In 1962, the National Religious Broadcasters (NRB) honored J. Edgar
Hoover. The NRB was an affiliate organization of the National Association of Evangelicals (NAE). As the "official radio arm of the NAE,"
the NRB rented office space in the nation's capital by the mid-1950s. The
aim of the NRB was to shore up evangelical political influence and preserve their space on the national airwaves. Their annual convention was
held in Washington, DC, complete with a newly formed "Congressional
Breakfast," where convention delegates invited their respective congressional representatives and senators.[3]

Reverend Dr. Eugene R. Bertermann, head of the NRB from 1957 to
1975, led many of these efforts. He was a natural leader of the organization: white, male, heterosexual, and theologically and politically
aligned with white evangelicalism. In 1940, he was ordained in the Lutheran Church, Missouri Synod, a separate Lutheran denomination
founded in the nineteenth century, predicated upon what it saw as historic orthodox Christianity. The Lutheran minister also possessed a

respectable education, completing his MA and PhD from the Greek Department at Washington University in St. Louis (WUSTL). His 1940 dissertation was entitled, "The Theology of Euripides." The scholar of Greek drama had extensive experience in broadcasting trendy radio dramas. The bespectacled, chubby preacher was the brains behind one of the era's most popular religious radio shows: *The Lutheran Hour*. As director of radio for the Lutheran Church, Missouri Synod, he produced the chart-topping radio show from 1938 until 1959. The commercial religious broadcast was one of the most lucrative and wide-ranging radio shows in the country. By 1951, "the free-will offerings" of listeners annually supplied the $1.4 million broadcasting budget and then some. Pitched as "absolutely non-sectarian . . . a simple Gospel message dedicated to the moral and spiritual upbuilding of our world," it was heard in fifty-nine languages and more than 1,300 stations in the United States, Canada, and sixty-nine territories and foreign countries. The radio wunderkind even testified before Congress to advocate for increased radio time and access for white evangelicals. Reverend Dr. Bertermann brought his Midas touch to the NRB with a clear vision to create popular white evangelical broadcasting.[4]

Bertermann saw J. Edgar Hoover as part of that vision. He understood Hoover was key to respectable postwar religious broadcasting. The religious media guru believed that Hoover's work was "consecrated service."[5] When Reverend Bertermann became NRB president, he sought Hoover's blessings. On November 17, 1961, he began a campaign to recruit the FBI director. From his office in Saint Louis, he sent telegrams to FBIHQ and a personal summons of "somewhat greater length" to Hoover's home. He left no stone unturned. "I should like to invite you most earnestly and cordially to address the 19th annual convention of National Religious Broadcasters," the overture began. The 1962 convention was slated for Hoover's favorite lunch spot, the Mayflower Hotel. Reverend Bertermann explained that the NRB was "an organization of men active in the religious broadcasting field." Among its membership were the two most popular radio ministries in American history, *The Hour of Decision* with Dr. Billy Graham, and *The Old-Fashioned Revival Hour* with Dr. Charles E. Fuller. The organization of leading white evangelical preachers "earnestly" sought Hoover to preach at their annual meeting.[6]

There was more. The NRB also wanted to honor Hoover's Christian service. "At the same time the [NRB] organization should also like to have the honor of awarding a special citation to you," the NRB president declared. "Our men are keenly conscious of the far-reaching leadership you have given to the moral and spiritual upbuilding of the nation." Hoover, according to the NRB man, was accomplishing the exact mission as *The Lutheran Hour*. The director was a foundational force of "moral and spiritual upbuilding." The dates of the convention were set, but the NRB president stressed that the organization was "more than happy to re-arrange the schedule" according to Hoover's convenience, as his presence was paramount. "It would be a great honor for our organization to be able to present this citation to you in person," Reverend Bertermann noted.[7]

Hoover was not sold. Bertermann he knew, but the NRB was an unknown in Bureau files. As was customary, Hoover had his secretary Helen Gandy acknowledge the overture, promising an official response when Hoover returned to the city.[8] The stall tactic provided the Bureau time to conduct "discreet inquiries" into the NRB. Hoover gave the Saint Louis SAC six days to engage "established sources to determine [the] reputation" of the NRB. "Under no circumstances," he ordered, "should [the NRB] become aware of Bureau's interests."[9] The Bureau completed background checks and interviewed trusted ministers and attorneys. The Saint Louis office quieted Hoover's paranoia, assuring him the NRB had an "excellent reputation."[10] Hoover was satisfied.

The Boss accepted the invitation, in part. The convention was scheduled for Tuesday evening, January 23, 1962, through the afternoon of Thursday January 25, 1962. Hoover was scheduled to testify before the Congressional Appropriations Subcommittee on January 24. The NRB had to take a back seat. Hoover required time to prepare his justification for his ballooning budget and his pleas for more federal largesse. Hoover told the NRB he was "honored" but "prior commitments" precluded his presence. "However," he pivoted, "I would be pleased to designate an assistant to fulfill this engagement in the event this would meet with your approval."[11]

Reverend Dr. Bertermann and the NRB executive committee as well as the board of directors approved, but with a caveat. They agreed to receive SA DeLoach as Hoover's stand-in, but they insisted on honoring Hoover in the flesh. "Would you be willing, please, to receive a delegation of several officers of [NRB] . . . and permit us the privilege of presenting our citation to you," they pleaded. "We will be deeply grateful if you will grant us the privilege of awarding you the citation in person."[12] Hoover agreed.

It was all set: NRB top brass would tour FBIHQ and present the director with the white evangelical citation at 3pm on Tuesday, January 23, 1962. Dr. James D. Murch was tapped to trumpet the affair. The founder of the Evangelical Press Association was the former NRB front man and managing editor of *Christianity Today*. The savvy media man was charged with drafting press releases and drumming up publicity. NRB also requested a photographer be present "to take appropriate pictures" the NRB could deploy in both the mainstream and religious press. The celebration of Hoover's white evangelical bona fides warranted such press. The crowning of the FBI director would mark the beginning of the entire annual convention of leading white evangelical media men. Before the men would gather to ask God's blessing on the convention, they would first seek the blessing of J. Edgar Hoover.[13]

The squadron of white male evangelical clerics arrived at FBIHQ in dark suits and ties, resembling special agents reporting for duty. They were armed with adulation and a glistening plaque. The eight white men were the intellectual mainframe of popular white evangelical broadcasting: NRB President Reverend Bertermann; Walter Bennet, NRB executive committee member whose ad firm handled all the public relations for Billy Graham's radio and television programs; Reverend Theo Elsner, a nondenominational evangelical broadcaster and pastor who served as NRB chairman of public relations; Reverend T. W. Willingham, executive director of the Nazarene Radio League and NRB treasurer; Reverend Ralph Neighbour, a Baptist pastor and NRB first vice president; Reverend Charles Leaming, a Pentecostal minister and NRB executive committee member; Reverend D. V. Hurst, the Assemblies of God secretary of radio and member of the NRB board of directors; and Reverend Earl P. Paulk, state overseer for the Church of God, Cleveland, Tennessee, and NRB second vice president.[14] After their tour, they were escorted to Hoover's private office, where the admiring men presented Hoover with a citation:

> National Religious Broadcasters Presents this Special Citation to Dr. John Edgar Hoover Director of the Federal Bureau of Investigation in thankful recognition of the distinguished service he has rendered our nation in the execution in his important responsibilities; In Grateful appreciation for the courageous leadership in the battle against crime, corruption and vice; And in the fight for morality, decency, and virtue; And with the prayer that Almighty God May continue to grant him continued strength and benediction and many more years of leadership and service to our beloved country.[15]

Hoover thanked the gathering of NRB men for the honor. Then he returned the favor, telling the men they were "Without a doubt the most influential group in the battle against world atheism." His prepared remarks, drafted by Baptist SA Jones, went further, offering the group an unfettered endorsement. "I am, of course, aware of the splendid work being done by the National Religious Broadcasters. In this time of world crisis, a spiritual reawakening is absolutely necessary . . . The efforts of you and your associates are a most important influence in this regard, and it is my hope that you will enjoy every success in your endeavors." The NRB men departed Hoover's office en route to their convention, buoyed by the FBI's blessing upon their white evangelical mission.[16]

SA DeLoach kept their spirits high the following evening. The head of the FBI Crime Records Division aimed to preach to the preachers and the vast white evangelical audiences they represented. "I, of course, had in mind," he told his supervisor, "that some of the ministers present might possibly perhaps use these remarks later in their sermons and thereby attract public attention."[17] He was not shy about it; it was his desired outcome. The Bureau's gospel was standard fare in America's pulpits. He told the NRB convention, "I sincerely hope, in speaking to you tonight, that I speak, through you, to the American people." His evening keynote address was a textbook jeremiad, a form of preaching

his audience knew well, especially when it came time to interject a ritualized and heartfelt "amen." Crime, he declared, was increasing because
faith was decreasing. He rattled off crime statistics in rapid fire, painting
a bleak picture of carnage, with God's judgment awaiting sinners. Continuing his literal interpretation of the Bible, he told the preachers that
Christians should follow the "Divine example until the return of the
Christ." All others were lost forever. This was especially the case with
lawbreakers and parole. "When the Devil sneered 'I will not serve,' he
was cast into hell for eternity. To my knowledge, no one has as yet urged
that the Devil be paroled," he smirked. "For I am aware of the effect of
the fall of Adam and know full well that there shall always be among us
men who choose the path of evil." He told the National Religious Broadcasters their "inspired programming" was "proof" of God's work in the
world. "In your broadcasts, manliness and love replace manslaughter
and lust," helping to "immunize" society from the viral sins of immorality and communism. He closed his sermon with hope and a charge for
the evangelical broadcasters to keep. "These situations need not continue to exist. Your microphones can daily pierce the veil of apathy . . .
With the work of the National Religious Broadcasters to constantly
remind us that 'In God We Trust,' America can continue to walk in the
light of His countenance." SA DeLoach made it clear: the cosmic fate of
the nation depended on white evangelical broadcasters and their working relationship with the FBI. The ministers present were challenged to
tell their listeners the same.[18]

The NRB men returned home with their hearts aflame. Reverend
Bertermann praised Hoover as soon as he returned to Saint Louis. It
was the "first" thing he did. In a tone reminiscent of meeting a celebrity
or idol, he told the FBI Boss, "There was not a clergyman in the room
who had not quoted you scores of times in sermons and addresses. You
can well imagine what a tremendous thrill it was to have the privilege
of meeting you personally." Like a nervous fan, he told Hoover the men
were "honored" to have had "the privilege of shaking your hand and
meeting you personally." The once in a lifetime moment was captured
for the ages. The director graced all of the white evangelical media men
with an autographed copy of the group photo. Reverend Bertermann

received a special dispensation of grace: a signed "close-up." He told Hoover, "The picture occupies an honored place here in my office." The effusive NRB president closed his letter with a prayer. "We join in the prayer that our Heavenly Father may richly bless you and your associates in the magnificent work you are doing . . . With heartfelt personal greetings and a prayer for God's rich benediction."[19]

Reverend Dr. Earl P. Paulk, second vice president of the NRB, was not content to let the NRB president speak for him. The Tennessee state overseer of the Church of God, Cleveland, Tennessee, wrote to Hoover as soon as he got home. The autographed photo moved him. "I count this as one of my most precious possessions," he told Hoover. "My prayer is that God will continue to guide and protect you as He has in the past. I think you are one of the most outstanding citizens in this great nation." The Pentecostal overseer then pledged his allegiance, "If at any time I can be of any assistance to your department, do not hesitate to call on me."[20] Reverend Paulk stood ready to be an informant or a confidential source, whatever the FBI needed.

Reverend Paulk also dispatched a note to SA DeLoach praising the special agent's homily. "I really thought your address was the most outstanding of the entire convention," he told SA DeLoach. It was high praise coming from a preacher who had attended a gathering of leading preachers. "I trust that our Heavenly Father will protect and guide you in your work to protect our nation."[21] Missionary Bob Hammond of Pasadena, California, agreed. *The Voice of China and Asia* broadcaster told SA DeLoach his address on Hoover's behalf "was one of the high lights" of the NRB convention. He was so moved, he wanted to share his FBI joy on the air. He asked the Bureau for any information ministers could use for the broadcast. Hammond received several Bureau items, including one of Hoover's *Christianity Today* articles.[22] Likewise, NRB treasurer and Nazarene cleric Reverend T. W. Willingham wrote the FBI for materials to aid in a sermon series he was writing on the life of the biblical character of Lot and its relationship to humanity's modern entrapment to material things and spiritual neglect. He thanked Hoover for his "consistent stand" for "righteousness," adding, "May God give to you strength to carry on the good work." Hoover replied, "enclosed is some literature containing my views on this general topic." The enclosure consisted of several essays, including "The Role of the Sunday School."[23] The NRB laundered Hoover's religious views. They took his words and presented them not as the politicking of a government official, but as Gospel truth, securing Hoover's place as an anointed warrior of white evangelical broadcasting, defending Christian America.

Jesuits

American Jesuits also crowned Hoover their leading spiritual soldier. The FBI Boss was Protestant, but he checked all the right boxes: white, male, anti-communist, and a fervent believer in the cosmic struggle that engulfed humanity. And most important, he oversaw the nation's federal army of moral custodians, and made certain these men knew the way of St. Ignatius. He was the right man for the hour. Loyola University Chicago did the honors on November 24, 1964. The city's leading Jesuit university named the FBI director the first recipient of the Sword of Loyola Award (figure 16). The Jesuit university inaugurated the annual tribute as its highest non-academic honor. A copy of the sidearm of St. Ignatius of Loyola would be given to a person of national or international prominence who exhibits to a high degree the qualities of St. Ignatius of Loyola. The university selected Hoover as the inaugural honoree because the FBI Boss had acted with "authority and dispatch to effectively implement the goal of life," as defined in Micah 6:8, Hoover's favorite verse: "And what doth the Lord require of thee, but to do justly, and to love mercy and to walk humbly with thy God."[24]

The celebration of Hoover's humble walk with God was anything but humble. The black-tie celebration was held in the Grand Ballroom of the Conrad Hilton Hotel, just off Chicago's posh Magnificent Mile. The cavernous room, adorned with French crystal chandeliers, was used to host stylish dinners and receptions for celebrities, US presidents, and world leaders. It was now J. Edgar Hoover's turn. Wishful attendees had to consider the cost—and at $250 per plate (a relative value of approximately $2,500 today), it was no simple consideration. Yet, more than

FIGURE 16. "Hoover's Sword of Loyola, 1964." *Source*: Loyola University Chicago Digital Special Collections, http://www.lib.luc.edu/specialcollections/items /show/320.

one thousand guests paid the price to bear witness to J. Edgar Hoover's coronation as God's soldier-cop. The wealthy audience was entertained by Don McNeill, the host of the radio hall of fame variety show *The Breakfast Club*.[25] The famed radio man presented the tuxedoed Hoover the warring memento. He explained to the gathered elites that the sword was made in Toledo, Spain, just like the sword St. Ignatius carried into battle. Loyola dedicated himself "to the service of God," and offered his sword to God "as a symbol of becoming a spiritual soldier of Christ." The soldier and his sword, McNeill's booming voice declared, symbolize "the distinctive spiritual qualities associated with St. Ignatius of Loyola." The sword was laid before the FBI Boss to signify that he "personified" the life and characteristics of the soldier-saint.[26]

Hoover unsheathed his sword and unleashed a torrent of words. "To every man and every nation there comes a time when decisions must be made about grave problems," he announced to the packed ballroom. "That time has come for the United States." Hoover's jeremiad "Time for Decision" warned that if the nation did not come back to God, it would be destroyed by the virus of sin. He pleaded with the crowd, "I trust you will give consideration to my remarks and not dismiss them as typical of the traditional age-old lament." It was a customary lamentation, but Hoover's words were not in danger of being shelved. He was surrounded by an admiring army of white Christian folk.[27]

"We are courting disaster," he told the sea of bowties and ball gowns. The supposed increase in crime and lawlessness was proof that the nation and "the whole of creation" was ailing, separated from its "divine purpose." Public "indifference" was salt in the nation's wounds. "Today, patriotism seems to be out of style. Those who express their love of country are often looked upon as paranoiac patriots or rightwing extremists," Hoover complained. "This breakdown in our moral standards can only render us impotent as a people and as a Nation." America was on the verge of "destroy[ing] itself." He told the enthralled gathering, "We badly need a moral reawakening." Revival was the singular diagnosis for the nation's multiple infirmities. "We must," he preached, "return to the teachings of God if we are to cure this sickness."[28]

The Boss embraced the sword as confirmation of his holy orders as the director of the FBI and moral custodian of American faith and governance. "I sincerely hope the 'Sword of Loyola' will mark the beginning of a new and enlightened era in the United States," he said, enlisting himself in God's army. Finally, hoisting the blade like the battle-worn soldier-saint for which it was named, he announced the nation's path to victory in the cosmic battle. "America stands at the crossroads of destiny," he stated. "Man is blessed with the liberty to choose between opposing factors . . . between good and evil, between God and the Devil," he preached. "As Americans, we should learn to trust God, to know His teachings. And to live in His Ways. This is truly a time for decision."[29]

The homily was well received. Illinois Republican Congressman Harold R. Collier "heartily endorse[d]" the speech in Congress. "Mr. Hoover conveyed a message to which all should heed and practice," the former ad man lobbied. His colleagues agreed. The speech was entered into the *Congressional Record*.[30] Bill Bright, president of Campus Crusade for Christ International, also loved the speech. He sent a copy to each of his 300-person staff of workers, officers, and advisory board members—which included influential ministers like Reverend Billy Graham. He hoped his staff would "find it as interesting and informative as I have," telling Hoover, "I want you to know, again, of my admiration for your fine work with the F.B.I. and the Christian testimony which you have upheld."[31] Midcentury Catholics and white evangelicals did not trust one another. Theologically they disagreed about much. But they agreed about one thing: they could trust J. Edgar Hoover, the soldier-saint to lead the nation into the promised land.

Pentecostals

The Assemblies of God (AG) also lionized Hoover. In 1965, the largest white Pentecostal denomination on the planet announced, "John Edgar Hoover is not only a lawman but he is also a philosopher and a man of God." The AG crowned Hoover with the biblical title "man of God" because he embodied the revival faith and politics of white Christian America.[32] The white Pentecostal group was founded with a revival spirit in 1914, when a group of white Pentecostal ministers separated from the African American–led Pentecostal denomination, the Church of God in Christ. The white ministers severed ties with their Black spirit folk, sounding the death knell of interracial Pentecostalism, while ringing the alarm for Protestant revival under a new all-white banner: The Assemblies of God.[33]

The AG was a partner in white mainstream evangelicalism. The denomination did not possess the influence within the movement that white Baptists, Methodists, and Presbyterians enjoyed, but it was present from the beginning, joining the NAE in 1943.[34] Its emphasis on print culture aided its climb to respectability. *The Pentecostal Evangel*, the AG's first official weekly publication, was founded in 1913 (as *The Christian Evangel*). The founding charter maintained that the magazine be purposely "slanted mainly toward laymen rather than ministers of the gospel," in order to help knit disparate white Pentecostals into a tight network of white Pentecostal believers. The linkages steadily grew, as did readership. The postwar years saw significant growth. From 1940 to 1960, the circulation more than doubled, increasing from 70,000 to more than 170,000, making it the most widely circulated weekly Protestant magazine in the nation. In 1971, circulation topped 200,000. The revival paper was distributed to the highways and byways, churches, depots, jails, prisons, public libraries, and other public spaces considered devoid of the word of the Lord. The wide readership was treated to missionary updates, Pentecostal Sunday school curricula, testimonies, sermons, profiles in faith, and of course news and signs of revival. True to its name, *The Pentecostal Evangel* was integral to spreading the Gospel. "The Assemblies of God," one AG pastor noted, "was born in revival, and it is sustained by revival. Hence, whatever contributes toward keeping the fires of evangelism burning among us is of vital importance to us all." *The Pentecostal Evangel* did just that. It rekindled "flagging revival fires" by fueling, fanning, and reporting where the fire could, would, and should spread. All reports of revival fire were printed under the words of Zechariah 4:6, "Not by might nor by power but by My Spirit says the Lord."[35]

The AG saw the spirit of the Lord resting on J. Edgar Hoover and the flickering of revival fire in every word he uttered. The journal began quoting and highlighting his speeches in the 1940s. In 1965, the magazine published a feature on Hoover, entitled "He Trusts in the Lord." *The Pentecostal Evangel* hailed the FBI director as a man who trumpeted personal faith since his "youth." J. Edgar Hoover experienced opposition, the sanctified puff piece promised, but through it all, the man of God remained faithful and dependent "on the Almighty." The Pentecostal weekly asked him, "What makes a man strong?" Hoover, ever the Sunday school teacher, quoted Proverbs 3:5: "Trust in the Lord with all thine heart, and lean not unto thine own understanding." Hoover relayed his faith to the Pentecostals, with no regard to the theological differences. He prayed, he read his Bible, and he attended church. "I have a pew at the National Presbyterian Church and attend service whenever possible," he noted.[36] Rented pews were anathema to Pentecostals, but that did not matter. The AG overlooked the theological differences, just like the broader white evangelical movement. There is no room for internal bickering when one's army is under siege. What mattered most was that Hoover believed America was a white Christian nation, and he fought to keep it that way.

The interview lobbed softball "questions concerning crime and subversion," allowing Hoover to belt out his matter-of-fact solutions—cure-alls that made the AG say "amen." A disaster was nigh, Hoover told the magazine. America was "conceived under God," but "crime and godless communism [were] striv[ing] to rob our nation of its cherished beliefs." He continued, "It has become quite sophisticated in certain circles to ignore the teachings of Christ and treat the Ten Commandments lightly." Moreover, "the aspirations of Negroes for equality," he warned the white Pentecostal denomination, were prone to communist exploitation. As if hoping to be misquoted, Hoover pivoted. Such hopes were not necessarily "communist inspired," he interjected. However, "America's 20 million Negroes and all others in this struggle are major targets for communist propaganda and subversion." This armada of "alien forces" were "seek[ing] to undermine our freedom and Christianity," he cried. The nation, especially parents, needed to "revive . . . spiritual standards." The road map was clear. "Adhere to the Bible," and "take time from material pursuits to find Christ in the home, at church," and "teach Christianity to children." The Boss had spoken. The feature closed praising Hoover's faithfulness. "Regardless of how tough the going," the AG editorialized, "Hoover cleaves to his Faith."[37]

The AG continued to cleave to Hoover even unto death. The denomination's radio ministry, *Revivaltime*, presented Hoover as a leading witness for Christ. The denomination launched the weekly thirty-minute broadcast into the ether in 1950, seeing radio as God's providential tool to spread revival around the globe. Early measures suggested it was so. After just three months on the air, the National Religious Broadcasters (NRB) named the program one of its top three nationwide radio programs. Three years later, the highly touted media ministry became the first commercial religious program on ABC. For approximately $10,000 a week, the program was heard on more than three hundred stations in the United States and more than a dozen abroad, garnering an estimated

audience of three to four million listeners every week. The success made
the ministry's tagline fitting: "*Revivaltime* on the air coast to coast and
around the world . . . Let it be *Revivaltime* everywhere."[38]

Reverend C. M. Ward, a pastor from Bakersfield, California, was chosen as the man for the task. He was anointed the AG "National Radio
Evangelist" in 1953. He took the name of the program to heart. Every Sunday at 10:30pm, just as the ABC late evening news signed off, Ward signed
on, turning the studio into an old-time revival pulpit.[39] The program received 12,000 to 15,000 testimonials, letters, and prayer cards each month.
Even President Lyndon B. Johnson wrote to the broadcast. The NRB
recognized Reverend Ward's ministry of the air with the NRB Award of
Merit in 1964. He was later inducted him into the NRB "Hall of Fame,"
the "NRB's most prestigious award." Joining hall of famers Charles Fuller,
Billy Graham, and Eugene Bertermann, Ward was cited for his "invaluable
contribution to the field of Christian communication, exhibition of the
highest standards, and evidence of faithfulness in Christ." The NRB
placed Reverend C. M. Ward in its "showcase of warriors for Christ," for
"blazing trails and leaving paths for succeeding generations to follow."[40]

One enduring trail he blazed was a Gospel tract ministry based on
the testimony of J. Edgar Hoover. Beginning in 1965, Reverend Ward
drafted a series of three-cent booklets titled *Revivaltime Miniatures*. The
2 1/2-inch by 3 1/2-inch testimonial booklets focused on the personal
faith of "great Americans." The Pentecostals identified J. Edgar Hoover
as fitting the mold. The tiny revival booklets were a big hit. By 1969, the
AG National Radio Department claimed three million total orders.
The miniatures "seem to be just what concerned Christians want to use
in reaching unsaved friends," Reverend Ward boasted. "Scores of letters
from Christians tell how readily the unsaved accept these colorful little
books. Many who write say that they did not realize how easy witnessing could be until they started carrying a few 'miniatures' in [their]
pocket or purse."[41] White evangelicals could easily take Hoover's gospel
witness with them, wherever they went.

The national organ of the AG advertised *J. Edgar Hoover Testifies* as a
privilege, presenting him as a chief fanner of the flame of revival (figure 17). Hoover "allow[ed] *Revivaltime* to feature his personal Christian

REVIVALTIME'S
NEW
"MINIATURE"--

J. Edgar Hoover, director of the FBI, in an exclusive interview evaluates the attacks which seek at this hour to destroy faith.

In response to some pointed questions about violence, revolutionaries, subversion, the Bible, and personal faith, he penned his carefully written answers in this new miniature.

USE THIS COUPON TO OBTAIN YOUR COPY
- -
Please send me a copy of *Revivaltime's* new miniature witnessing booklet about FBI Director J. Edgar Hoover, called **J. EDGAR HOOVER TESTIFIES.**
I want to help *Revivaltime* take the gospel by radio into places that otherwise might not be reached. Enclosed is my offering.

FBI-A   Amount Enclosed $ _____

Name _____

Address _____

City _____

State _____ Zip _____

REVIVALTIME
P. O. Box 70, Springfield, Mo. 6580

FIGURE 17. Advertisement for *Revivaltime* miniature witnessing booklet, *J. Edgar Hoover Testifies*. Source: *The Pentecostal Evangel*, August 23, 1970. Courtesy of the Flower Pentecostal Heritage Center, Springfield, MO.

testimony in booklet form." It was pitched as fuel to set any unredeemed heart ablaze for Christ. J. Edgar Hoover was positioned as the ultimate evangelistic tool. "Those whom Christians encounter while witnessing are sure to know the name J. Edgar Hoover and will be receptive to learning more about this great American dedicated to his country. His name is certain to draw interest, and the strong, convicting testimony is sure to be instrumental in winning souls." Another ad posited, "Perhaps the copy you share with a neighbor boy might contribute toward his becoming a Christian leader, inspired by the fact that the FBI chief's testimony proves that a Christian can be a real *he man*." The accompanying order form compelled the faithful, "Don't miss this ideal opportunity to do something for the Lord and for our sin-sick country."[42]

Hoover represented the remedy. Reverend Ward praised the FBI director as an ambassador of "an old-fashioned faith." Hoover's miniature bore witness to the importance of the Bible as the "vital guidepost" of his life, his rearing in the faith, and his childhood pastor, Reverend Donald MacLeod; but he never strayed far from the jeremiad that was the basis of his faith. "I believe we need a renewed adherence to the historic values which have sustained this nation," he warned. "If we stray from these precepts, we invite disaster both for our present and future generations."[43]

Reverend Ward closed the palm-sized revival pamphlet with his own commentary. "This is strong, convicting testimony," he exclaimed. He compared J. Edgar Hoover to the biblical prophet Samuel, "one of the greatest advocates and law enforcers of all time." The radio preacher concluded by quoting the biblical prophecy that accompanied the prophet's birth, 1 Samuel 2:9, "He will guard the feet of his faithful servants, but the wicked will be silenced in the place of darkness. It is not by strength that one prevails." Samuel was anointed by the spirit of God to challenge Israel to remain true to the laws of God. He guided the faithful and silenced the faithless. The faithful believed in Hoover and the power of his witness. *Revivaltime* boasted selling 250,000 copies of Hoover's gospel tract in its first year.[44] The Pentecostals wanted the world to know: as God led Israel through Samuel, so God was leading America through the godly law man, J. Edgar Hoover.[45]

Billy Graham Evangelistic Association

Hoover's status as a champion of white evangelicalism was epitomized by his appearance in Billy Graham's devotional magazine, *Decision*, in 1971. The magazine's moniker reflected Graham's belief that religious conversion was a decision. Following Jesus was a willful act, a cognizant ritual. Hoover agreed. The FBI director was also very familiar with the magazine format. In the hopes of creating a more accessible version of *Christianity Today*, Graham founded the magazine in 1960 and modeled the monthly after *Our Sunday Visitor*, a magazine that was strewn with Hoover's words. Lead editor Sherwood Wirt made Graham's vision a reality. Wirt, who held a PhD in theology from the University of Edinburgh, guided the glossy, tabloid-sized monthly to a broad circulation, reaching a zenith of six million, publishing in six languages and braille. Outside of the publications of the Jehovah's Witnesses, *Decision* was the most widely circulated religious periodical in the English-speaking world. For roughly $2, seekers could obtain a year-long subscription to the self-professed monthly "Magazine of Evangelism, Inspiration, [and] Bible Study."[46]

The layout was simple, but effective. Every issue featured the text of a recent Billy Graham sermon. The devotional rendering was accompanied by inspirational stories, outsized photographs, and news and current events from a white evangelical perspective. Highlights of Billy Graham's crusades were also listed, alongside news and advertisements for his upcoming revivals. *Decision* was rounded out by listing several testimonials from the faithful. They bore witness to how Graham's ministry specifically, or the decision to follow Christ more broadly, had brought about a dramatic transformation, enabling souls to overcome personal challenges.[47] The sacred statements also highlighted how life in Christ empowered the faithful to accomplish great feats and reach holy heights, just like the FBI director had done in his life.

As *Decision* embarked on its second decade and a circulation of almost five million, they published an interview with Hoover.[48] The interview likely grew out of an undisclosed meeting Billy Graham had with him at FBIHQ on May 1, 1969. FBI files documenting the meeting have been hidden or destroyed. The topic of the meeting remains a mystery, but the mood does not. A photograph of the cordial meeting between the two white evangelical giants reveals them smiling and locking hands. Hoover sent Graham a copy of the snapshot with his autograph: "To Dr. Billy Graham with affectionate regards, J. Edgar Hoover." Both men kept their respective copies as a keepsake.[49]

Graham had peppered his sermons with quotes from the FBI director, but his magazine's interview with J. Edgar Hoover gave followers the chance to read about the man's personal faith. Graham's magazine lauded Hoover as the epitome of Christian integrity. The interview highlighted Hoover's Lutheran and Presbyterian upbringing and his personal "commitment to Christ" as the ground of his valor. Hoover's faith was the source of his public respect, while his leadership of the FBI was the fruit of his faithful spirit. *Decision* entitled the interview, "The Structure of Integrity."[50]

The interview provided space for the FBI Boss to flex his authoritative white Christian worldview. Always aiming for the devotional benefit of its readership, Billy Graham's magazine asked Hoover, "How can churches help re-instill character and morality in people today?" Hoover responded with his textbook jeremiad. Crime was up, because decisions to follow Jesus were down. "In my career as Director of the FBI," Hoover announced, "I have seen too frequently what happens when young people forget God, scorn the teachings of Jesus and mock the moral laws. Crime today is ruining the lives of thousands of young people . . . they lack a personal faith." This moral decline, he reminded his anti-communist spiritual comrades, was an issue of national security. Like Judas, those who had not made a decision to follow Christ would betray the Christ-loving nation "for a few pieces of silver." This was a recipe for Soviet invasion at best, a catastrophe at worst. "A nation which has lost its reliance on moral values is a nation doomed to extinction," he promised. The evangelism of faith communities was the only hope. "Church men and women should speak out forthrightly for what is right, good, and noble," he charged the white evangelical troops. "The voice of the church is a powerful and meaningful voice and it should ring forth loudly and clearly."[51]

The interview closed with Graham's magazine prodding the FBI director to give young adults explicit religious instruction. The magazine asked, "What would you say to a young person today who is considering the claims of Christ upon his life?" Hoover didn't hold back. "I would tell him to accept Christ fully and joyously and to do everything humanly possible to follow his principles. This is a lifelong commitment."[52] During Hoover's lifetime, white evangelicalism remained loyal and committed to him as their champion.

—

From the Chicago Bible Society to the Billy Graham Evangelistic Association, there was no question: Hoover was the leading white evangelical statesman from the 1950s until his death. He did not profess evangelical theology. He did not even believe in being born again. But he embraced and embodied everything that really mattered to white evangelicalism: white Christian nationalism. His status and all-encompassing worldview made him the unequivocal standard-bearer of white evangelicalism. He was their revivalist in chief, prodding the nation toward the spiritual awakening it needed for survival, while dispensing punditry like an evangelical sage. He was hailed as their anointed leader in the cosmic struggle against the enemy within. He was their hero and partner in the halls of power, fighting for the America in which white evangelicals believed. He was their soldier-saint, leading the nation into righteousness. His stature was particularly evident during the national crusade that became known as the modern Civil Rights Movement.

CHAPTER 8

Crusader

On Thursday, April 15, 1965, J. Edgar Hoover offered his sincere assessment of the Civil Rights Movement. In extensive "off-the-record" remarks to a gaggle of newsmen, the FBI director confessed that recent civil rights legislation—the 1964 Civil Rights Bill and the Voting Rights Bill under consideration in the US Senate—was the result of a coalition of "bleeding heart" judges and politicians who failed to understand the heart of the nation's racial predicament. Judges and politicians had succumbed to two groups of extremists. "The thing which has irritated me more than anything else," Hoover summarily barked, "has been the unreasonable demands of the extremists of the right and left—the Klan on the right, and Martin Luther King on the left." Hoover described the former as repugnant, "a group of sadistic, vicious white trash . . . You can almost smell them . . . in the areas where they live." They "must be weeded out," he snarled. He felt similarly about King and civil rights crusaders. He believed their religious demands were nothing short of "anarchy." King's nonviolent activism was, in actuality, Hoover noted, a "disservice to his own race and our country."[1]

Hoover believed the solution to America's racial strife was between these extremes. Violence and protest were both unacceptable, while civil rights legislation was not effective. A more moderate and gradual approach was needed, one in which Black freedom dreams took a back seat to white grievances. "White citizens are primarily decent, but frightened for their lives," Hoover diagnosed. While "the colored people are quite ignorant, mostly uneducated, and I doubt they would seek an education if they had an opportunity. Many who have the right to register very seldom do." He concluded his racist assessment with the carrot of gradualism. If African Americans proved themselves worthy, they would "in due time" garner the "acceptance" of broader white society and then proceed to gain "rights equal to those of the white citizens in their community."[2]

Hoover's gospel focused on the individual soul. The best way to fix America's race problems was not violence, protest, or legislation. Rather, individual and group piety was the best way for Black Americans to earn white respect and the eventual prize of equality. Equal citizenship was not given to Black Americans at birth, they had to prove themselves worthy of God and country. He perceived all other strategies as a subversive threat, seeing a communist conspiracy behind every call to rearrange America's racial social structure. And nothing, not even the law, would stop Hoover from trying to eliminate such threats. Hoover believed he answered not to the US Constitution, but to a higher calling.

Hoover and the white evangelical brain trust at Christianity Today (CT) were on the same page concerning America's original sin. The leaders of white evangelicalism christened their shared position as the "evangelical moderate" stance. CT argued that advocates of integration and segregation were both extremists. Compulsory segregation and compulsory integration were both wrong. Ironically, the fortnightly journal sided with white supremacist fears of miscegenation to ground their so-called moderate perspective.[3] Supporters of racial intermarriage, CT told its readers in 1959, were the same as the White Citizens Council. The magazine editors argued, "The persistent integrationist question: 'After all, what's wrong with racial intermarriage?' perturbs the evangelical moderate as much as the provocative slogan on letterheads of the White Citizens Council: 'Let's keep white folks white.'" Therefore, true evangelicals would not seek "to exact support of integration from every evangelistic convert as a test of true repentance." Commitments to capitalism, patriarchy, heterosexual marriage, and marital fidelity were the tests of true Christian repentance. Racial equality was not. The white evangelical mainstream refused to "give advance approval to some undefined integration as a Christian ideal or objective." Like J. Edgar Hoover, the magazine professed to be against both ardent integrationists and segregationists, yet it reserved its most severe criticisms for those "radicals" who called for integration. The brazen religious advocates of racial equality failed to "acknowledge that integration may not always be in the best interest of both races, nor do they readily grant that segregation need not always imply disbelief in the dignity and equality of fellow men." Such "hasty" calls for integration, according to the editors at *CT*, often dripped with "semi-collectivistic overtones," that is, communist-inspired ideology.[4] *Christianity Today* was clear: one could simultaneously be a faithful white evangelical and a pro-segregationist, who was "perturbed" by interracial unions and calls to dismantle segregation.[5]

The editorial board embodied this truism. Graham's father-in-law L. Nelson Bell published several articles supporting "separate but equal," in the *Southern Presbyterian Journal*, a periodical he founded and ran. When the government struck down Jim Crow laws, he did not consider it a step toward legal equality, he called it a ludicrous, unnecessary, and unbiblical practice mandated by the government. Bell and the supporters of his Christian journal signed a formal statement vowing "voluntary segregation in churches, schools, and other social relations is for the highest interests of the races and is not unchristian." The pro-segregationist physician believed integration would encourage the dreaded sin of interracial romance, as well as an unavoidable and warranted violent white backlash. Even after Bell accepted his son-in-law's stepwise practice of hosting some integrated crusades, Bell still enjoyed entertaining his fellow founders with supposedly "humorous anecdotes" about the innate inferiority of African Americans. Bible-believing Christians, he argued, understood that African Americans were the descendants of Noah's son Ham. Inferiority and servitude was the divine destiny of Black Americans.[6] With Bell at the executive head and empowered by Graham's blessing, there was no question which direction the white evangelical flagship was headed when it came to the "racial situation."

Christianity Today and Hoover agreed: the problem of racism exclusively resided in individual hearts, particularly the backward, uneducated, and unredeemed hearts of African Americans. Racism was therefore best addressed one soul at a time, not through legislation. And during the hot days of the Civil Rights Movement, the FBI and white evangelicals were busy collaborating to defend their shared worldview. Beginning in 1964, the Bureau began partnering with the National Association of Evangelicals' (NAE) Office of Public Affairs (OPA) to employ white evangelicals into the FBI. The OPA established offices in Washington, DC, near the US Treasury Building and US Department of State, and unapologetically served as the political "watchman" for white Christian America. It viewed itself as keeping "a close watch on legislation and the enemies of the Gospel operating in government circles." More than bystanders, the OPA advocated and lobbied for like-minded appointees, candidates, and legislation. They believed that earthly governments were ordained by their God, and it was up to white evangelicals to hold the government accountable to their God's moral laws. Ultimately, the clearinghouse of white evangelical political engagement aimed to place white evangelicals in federal service to accomplish this goal.[7]

The 1964 Pastors and Laymen Federal Seminar marked the formal beginning of the NAE-FBI employment collaboration. Outside of NAE General Director Reverend Clyde Taylor (who accused the FBI of being overrun with Catholics in 1956), the Bureau recognized the NAE as "pro-Bureau" and was happy to educate white evangelical pastors and leading laymen. The NAE federal seminars were created to help white evangelical college students, graduates, and faculty prepare for federal employment. According to the NAE, the constituency was "brilliant mentally," but "devoid of conviction and inclined too far to the left." The federal seminars aimed to assist faithful white Christians who attended evangelical colleges and seminaries to begin careers in the FBI. The FBI's Protestant men came from elite mainline Protestant universities such as George Washington and Harvard. By the 1960s, the NAE viewed these schools as bastions of "relativistic" teaching, producing men who lacked "ethical absolutes." The seventy Christian colleges participating in the federal seminar were the exact opposite. They taught "a decidedly Christian philosophy of life and behavior." These graduates embraced ethical Christian "absolutes" and "true patriotism and an appreciation for their American heritage." It was Reverend Taylor's dream that evangelical students would emerge as shock troops, prepared to attack the federal government as a mission field "where they will have an opportunity to witness for Christ" and "offset the sinister forces working within our government as well as the pagans coming in [to the government] from our great universities and colleges." Wheaton professor Earle Cairns offered a more vivid description. The Seminar on Federal Service, he noted, was similar to the nineteenth-century anti-slavery political campaigns waged by religious folk to rid the country of its original sin. Likewise, the NAE program was part of the white evangelical "strategy of infiltration of well-trained, devout Evangelicals into all branches of government."[8]

The NAE requested that the Bureau address "What the FBI looks for in personnel," with special attention to "Characteristics the FBI demands in its personnel," and "Characteristics which determine rapidity of promotion." The answers to these questions could be narrowed down to the maxim: be a white man that believed as Hoover believed.[9]

Methodist layman SA Dr. Fern Stukenbroeker led the seminars accordingly. The *New York Times* best-selling ghostwriter and noted lay preacher was a seasoned lecturer, traveling around the country to churches, high schools, colleges, and civic organizations giving seminars on "Subversion" and "Communism." Stukenbroeker's NAE seminars offered the white evangelical organization "scholarly" lectures and guidance, answering all questions pertaining to life, godliness, and employment with the FBI. The NAE thanked SA Dr. Stukenbroeker for addressing "the topics adequately and concisely." Reverend Taylor personally thanked Hoover for allowing the NAE to visit the Bureau and for their dividends. "From their evaluation sheets and our own experiences, the more personal contact that our church leaders have with the various agencies, the more directly involved they feel in the direction of our country's future. Thank you for your very significant part in this." The partnership was established as an annual affair. In another thank you note, he saluted the FBI as America's religious shock troops: "may God continue to effect righteousness through the work that you have established." As one NAE summary noted, "We trust that some of them [students] will make a real effort to get into the Department of Justice and possibly into the FBI."[10] Mission accomplished.

White evangelicals, slowly but surely, began to fill the ranks of the FBI. Meanwhile, the Bureau's cartel of white evangelical clerics such as Billy Graham and Dr. Bell continued to dole out a white Christian nationalist gospel that criticized the righteousness of the Civil Rights Movement and legislation. They denied their stance was steeped in racism. Rather, they argued their view was strictly theological, in line with America's Christian origins. What Hoover, the FBI, and evangelicals lacked was a Black evangelical clergyman to authenticate that their shared "evangelical moderate" stance against the Civil Rights Movement was not racist. It was purely Christian and American.

Hoover had just the man. His name was Elder Lightfoot Solomon Michaux, one of the most prominent and pioneering evangelical broadcasters in American history. He was the first clergyman, white or Black, to have his own television show. Like most African American evangelicals of his day (and ours), he was not invited into the inner sanctums of modern evangelicalism. He held evangelical political and theological convictions, yet his Blackness prevented him from being a member of the NRB, NAE, or the evangelical brain trust at CT. His belief that racism was solely a sin of the heart that could be overcome by Black piety actually sanctified and helped to preserve the dominant racial order. Whether willingly or unwillingly, his theological and political commitments aided and abetted the cause of white Christian nationalism. And Reverend Michaux made his stance known when he teamed up with the FBI to launch an evangelical anti–civil rights crusade against the Reverend Martin Luther King Jr.[11]

Elder Lightfoot Solomon Michaux was the ideal Bureau clergyman. Born in 1884 in Newport News, Virginia, Michaux preached that communism, not racism, was the nation's most dangerous moral foe. Communism would destroy America, he believed, unless the nation deployed all of its resources toward a spiritual awakening, one soul at a time. Individual conversion was also the key to ending racism. Similar to Reverend Bell, Michaux believed God ordained America's racial hierarchy. In one nationally broadcast sermon in 1958, he declared that people of African descent were born inferior, trailing the "intellectual culture of [their] White brother" by centuries. Slavery was God's way to save the souls of Africa's Black "heathens." American slavery and the subsequent introduction to Christianity enabled enslaved Africans to ascend to the "higher bracket" of civilization, a place white citizens seemingly occupied at birth. Eradicating anti-Black racism then required the individual salvation of Blacks, followed by the resulting social progress toward middle-class status and values. When whites recognized and approved the patriotic Christian progress of Black Americans, racial equality would be reached. African Americans progressed *because* of America's Christian democracy, not in spite of it.[12]

Michaux's gospel of soul salvation and attributing anti-Black racism to Black biological inferiority and sinfulness assured his place among the Bureau's anointed. Special agents warmly described him as a popular minister who was a "very vigorous exponent for race segregation. He believes everybody, White, Black, Yellow or Red has a definite place in life and *that each should keep their place.*" The special agent assured his superiors that Michaux was "handling the segregation problem."[13]

In addition to his congregation in the nation's capital, Michaux proclaimed his racialized Cold War jeremiad over his suite of media ministries. The converted businessman and minstrel show actor launched his *Radio Church of God* over CBS radio in 1932. The nationwide sustaining time (free airtime) program was broadcast over the network's national chain of fifty-eight stations. *The Radio Guide* called the preacher and his show "a marvel," concluding, "No feature on the air is talked about more." Similarly, *The Billboard* dubbed his radio ministry "one of the most novel programs on the air." For some, the minstrel performer offered more minstrelsy than gospel. In an open letter, George H. Mark, a prominent Baptist layman, told Michaux his radio sermons were akin to the "wise cracking and yelling" of *Amos 'n' Andy.* "I take the position that not only are you not advancing the cause of Christianity, but you are doing both the church and your racial group incalculable harm," he concluded.[14]

Whether Michaux was offering minstrelsy or gospel, television executives wanted it. Within months of launching commercial television in Washington, DC, on WTTG-TV on November 29, 1946, DuMont Laboratories offered Michaux free airtime. The fledgling network hoped the preacher's radio popularity would translate to television. He became the first minister (Black or white) to have his own weekly television show and the first African American to star in his own television series.[15] DuMont broadcasted the live thirty-minute Sunday evening show across its national network, while Washington's channel five aired the show locally at 6pm.[16] The Elder's television ministry was acclaimed. *The Billboard* noted that the television show "reproduces the practical down to earth religion for which he is famous." DuMont station engineer and general manager Les Arries Jr. recalled that Michaux "put on one heck of a show." More than four decades after the show ended, the industry insider maintained that the trailblazing television program "would survive, I think, even in today's times, because it wasn't just religion. It was really good entertainment."[17] Hoover agreed. He wrote to the televangelist in 1950, "Whenever I am home, I always endeavor to follow you on television . . . I think that you have been making a very fine contribution."[18]

Hoover also publicly proclaimed his appreciation for the preacher. On September 20, 1951, more than 20,000 gathered at Washington, DC's Griffith Stadium—the home of Major League Baseball's Washington Senators—to celebrate the Elder's more than twenty years of religious broadcasting. Michaux invited Hoover, but the Boss was unexpectedly called out of town. Nevertheless, Hoover made certain to dispatch agents to the event, and even sent Michaux a flattering Western Union telegram. "I wish to extend to you my heartiest congratulations," the $1.55 (approximately $15 today) direct telegram raved. "In the last twenty years . . . your dedication and devotion, as well as your timely messages, have been a real inspiration to countless thousands. Keep up the good work." Agents made certain the telegram, along with one from presidential hopeful General Dwight Eisenhower and US Attorney General J. Howard McGrath, was read aloud to the multitude of listeners on CBS radio and the admiring crowd gathered at the stadium affair.[19] It was no secret—the FBI and Michaux played for the same team. Michaux was a Bureau clergyman, a status that set him on a collision course with Martin Luther King Jr.

Michaux's partnership with the FBI was formalized on January 23, 1956. Assistant to the Director Louis B. Nichols set up a private meeting with the clergyman. The Bureau's head of crime records was accustomed to consulting with clergy at FBI headquarters. In addition to serving as the Bureau's liaison to Congress and chief public relations officer, Special Agent Nichols regularly enlisted prominent private citizens to aid the FBI. The tall burly man used his towering physique and "boisterous and outgoing personality" to build a network of cooperating private citizens. Clergy were particularly important partners for the Bureau during the Cold War, and Nichols was especially suited for the job. He was a committed Methodist who advocated for a "more militant and more effective" Methodist Church.[20] SA Nichols was also a strong believer in gradualism when it came to racism and segregation. "You cannot legislate against human nature and traditions, and customs cannot be changed overnight," the Methodist law man preached. He saw in Michaux a like-minded Black minister with tremendous public influence. He told Director Hoover, "The Elder has a very active mind. He effervesces with enthusiasm and it certainly can be said that he does have a most radiant personality." "I am convinced in my own mind." Special Agent Nichols gushed "that he [Michaux] has been a powerful influence for good."[21]

The admiration was mutual. Michaux believed the FBI director and his six thousand agents did God's work. They were his co-laborers in the Cold War battle for America's soul. He saw Hoover as "a minister of God" and the FBI as "second in importance only to the church." For Michaux, the FBI was a bulwark against crime and a powerful mobilizing force for America's only hope: religious revival.[22]

The top special agent and Black minister met on a wintry Monday to coordinate their responses to the Black civil rights crusade. Agent

Nichols told Michaux the FBI was "naturally busy" monitoring communist subversion within the movement. In the midst of the budding Montgomery Bus Boycott, the G-man admitted that the FBI was "fearful in view of all the emotion that is presently being generated." The movement was ripe for a takeover by atheistic communists. Therefore, with a sense of religious vocation, he told Michaux, "It might be necessary to call [you] into service." Agent Nichols assured the media preacher that serving the Bureau would help squelch the ungodly revolt and bring "some sanity back into being." The Elder did not need much convincing. Like the FBI, he believed that godless communists had a hand in all civil rights protests. He therefore departed Agent Nichols's office pledging his fidelity to the Bureau, noting that he would be "ready . . . at any time."[23]

Michaux's most prominent *service* to the FBI occurred during the Bureau's campaign to neutralize and publicly discredit Reverend Martin Luther King Jr. Following the momentous 1963 March on Washington for Jobs and Freedom (MOW), the FBI labeled King the nation's "most dangerous Negro" and immediately called Michaux into service. Michaux kept his promise: he was indeed ready. The Elder used his status and popular media ministry to illegally launder Bureau counterintelligence in order to publicly scandalize King's gospel labors for civil rights, while also defending the Christian virtues of the FBI.

King's Dream versus Michaux's Bible

The FBI's religious commitments influenced the decision to begin a direct investigation of Reverend Martin Luther King Jr. For years, J. Edgar Hoover was convinced that atheistic communism, not religious fervor, was fueling the fight for Black equality. "The Negro situation," he testified before Congress in 1958, is "being exploited fully and continuously by Communists on a national scale."[24] Hoover viewed this purported communist infiltration not simply as a political debate, but as an attack on America's Christian heritage. It was the duty of the FBI, he told his employees in 1961, to "reaffirm" the Bureau's "Christian purpose . . . to *defend* and *perpetuate* the dignity of the Nation's Christian endowment."[25] Christianity was the bedrock of the nation's heritage and the FBI was "the main line of resistance against all enemies of our heritage." Hoover insisted that the FBI soldier on, taking "strength in the Biblical quotation, 'If God be for us, who can be against us.'"[26] The FBI director saw his army, in part, as an agency of spiritual propagation and the nation's first line of defense against the "godless" forces of the Black freedom struggle. He expected ministers to join the FBI "on the front line . . . in the fight against communism" by helping to "preserve the dignity of man as the image of God and to mold the individual to be a worthy citizen in a democracy."[27] Black citizens were not sufficiently molded.

King certainly did not fit the mold. His religious calls for Black equality directed citizens to challenge, not preserve, the democratic status quo. Moreover, he kept two men in his inner circle—Stanley Levison and Jack O'Dell—who had murky ties to the Communist Party USA (CPUSA). The FBI began a formal investigation into Reverend King in 1962. The purpose was to determine if King was simply a misguided cleric who had fallen under the influence of godless communists, or if King was actually a committed communist in clerical disguise, bent on destroying the nation's Christian heritage. As one high-ranking Bureau agent later put it, "We wondered whether he [King] was, to use Lenin's phrase, 'a useful idiot' or someone acting on his own and deliberately attempting to foment riot and insurrection."[28] Regardless, Reverend King was clearly out of line. He was a threat to America's Christian foundation and it was the FBI's duty to protect the nation from him.

However, the FBI lacked corroborating evidence. On August 23, 1963, Assistant Director William Sullivan, the head of the Bureau's Division Five (Domestic Intelligence), drafted a comprehensive analysis on the "exploitation and influence by the Communist party on the American Negro population." After more than a year of investigation, the resulting sixty-seven-page brief entitled "Communist Party, USA—Negro Question" concluded that the Communist party had completely failed to influence the Black civil rights crusade. Agent Sullivan was in the best position to know. He had helped to significanatly weaken the party beginning in 1956 by spearheading a Counter-Intelligence Program

(COINTELPRO) against the CPUSA. The COINTELPRO was launched against the CPUSA when the DOJ deemed the Smith Act—a statute that essentially made it a crime to belong to the Communist Party—unenforceable. In 1957, the US Supreme Court ruled defendants could only be prosecuted for their actions, not their beliefs. Robbed of such prosecutions, the FBI launched a COINTELPRO against CPUSA members and those considered fellow travelers. "Crazy Billy" gained his nickname in part by helping to formalize COINTELPRO's covert, clandestine, extralegal, and illegal actions. No holds were barred. Top ranking SA Mohr told a special agent in training that COINTELPRO had one simple, distorted Christian principle: "Do unto others as they have done unto others." If the Bureau believed an organization or person was breaking the law—extorting, intimidating, or hurting the public—or simply had the potential to do so, then the FBI was divinely obliged to return the favor. Ideally, COINTELPRO did not wait for citizens to commit crimes. "You take direct actions against the enemy," SA Mohr noted. "You try to confuse him, disrupt his operations, sow dissension in his ranks, ruin his morale, steer him in the direction you want him to without him knowing that he's being manipulated. That's what COINTELPRO does." Through such direct tactics, the FBI learned that despite Levison's and O'Dell's suspicious connections to the CPUSA, the civil rights crusade King was leading was too religious for communist infiltration. King was neither a "useful idiot" nor a communist in clerical garb. The Boss, however, refused to believe the report. He chastised Division Five. King could not be a clergyman. Only atheistic communists desired to overthrow the nation's Christian status quo.[29]

The MOW occurred just five days later; it changed everything. Hoover was terrorized by the inability of Division Five to obtain direct evidence of communist influence in the Civil Rights Movement. It mattered little if Levison or O'Dell cut formal ties with the CPUSA. Not being a communist was insufficiently patriotic. One had to be anticommunist. Hoover was also disgusted by King's growing fame as the nation's moral and religious conscience. That was Hoover's throne. Following King's thunderous "I Have a Dream" speech, the nation's top cop admitted that he held King "in complete contempt." King was a religious fraud. The director's professed animus toward King took on biblical proportions. As one of Hoover's most trusted agents described, "Shortly after King's star ascended to these breathtaking heights, Hoover developed an intense animosity toward the civil rights leader, one that grew, like the biblical mustard seed from a small kernel into a huge living thing that cast an enormous shadow across the landscape."[30]

It was a long and persistent shadow indeed. Hoover's religious conviction that King was a communist enemy of the state completely shaded Division Five's verdict on the matter. After King articulated his dream, Hoover in turn dictated his own vision to Division Five. King was an atheistic revolutionary who needed to be destroyed. Despite lacking evidence, "Everybody in the Division," Agent Sullivan later testified, "went right along with Hoover's policy." After the MOW, a compliant Sullivan pivoted toward Hoover's view. Division Five had simply failed to "put the proper interpretation upon the facts which we gave to the Director." Facts are not meaningful by themselves, Sullivan noted. "They are somewhat like stones tossed in a heap as contrasted to the same stones put in the form of a sound edifice." Identifying King as public enemy number one became a cornerstone of national security. As Sullivan wrote to his direct superior two days after the MOW, "Personally, I believe in the light of King's powerful demagogic speech yesterday [sic] he stands head and shoulders over all other Negro leaders put together when it comes to influencing great masses of Negroes." The Bureau, he continued, should "mark" the preacher "as the most dangerous Negro of the future in this Nation from the standpoint of communism, the Negro, and national security." "The nation," Sullivan noted, "was involved in a form of racial revolution," and King was the leader. King was "a very real security problem to [the] country." Therefore, Sullivan concluded, it was "unrealistic" for the Bureau to "limit" their investigation of King to "legalistic proof or definitely conclusive evidence that would stand up in testimony in court or before Congressional Committees." The nation's top law enforcement agency devoted itself to stopping King by any means necessary, the law be damned.[31]

Hoover congratulated the repentant and "enlightened" Division Five. "I have struggled for months to get over the fact the Communists [are] taking over the racial movement but," Hoover complained, the Domestic Intelligence Division had simply refused to "see it." Nevertheless, the pleased director wrote, "I am glad . . . that 'light' has finally, though dismally delayed, come to the Domestic Int[elligence] Div."[32] Division Five had an awakening. It would follow Hoover's convictions, no turning back.

The Bureau shifted its investigation of King from focusing solely on his supposed communist ties to a crusade that would expose King as a "clerical fraud." The Bureau's blitzkrieg aimed to reveal that while King "purport[ed] to be a minister of the gospel," he was actually a "fraud, demagogue, and moral scoundrel" who was preaching a false gospel of American spiritual bankruptcy and racial inequality. The FBI commenced an onslaught on King, Agent Sullivan later testified, that resembled techniques they used against "Soviet Agents." The campaign had one guiding principle: "no holds were barred."[33]

Calling Michaux into service was one means the Bureau utilized. On September 25, Agent Sullivan returned from a leave to draft a memo indicating Division Five's next steps. The memo was "prepared not on official office memorandum but rather on plain bond" paper so the contents would not be included in the Bureau's "official record." Agent Sullivan's "plain bond" memo recommended that the G-men alert all FBI field offices, federal agencies, and prominent officials to the Bureau's renewed and intense focus on King and the Civil Rights Movement. He reiterated King's status as "the strongest of the Negro leaders" and "the most dangerous and effective Negro leader in the country." "We need to renew our efforts and keep the pressure on and leave no stone unturned," he noted. Hoover inscribed his infamous and authoritative "o.k." on the document.[34] On the same day, the G-men called Michaux into service.

Michaux immediately launched a coordinated public critique against King and the gospel the civil rights minister preached. On September 25, Michaux preached a radio sermon from the nation's capital on CBS Standard and FM radio affiliates criticizing the MOW and King's address. The homily opposed the march of "Saint Martin Luther King"—the name the Elder derisively gave King—and the historic "I Have a Dream" speech. The Elder took Luke 11:1-2 (commonly known as The Lord's Prayer) as his sermon text. Michaux preached that racial equality would only materialize when God's rule was established in the hearts of men. "Yes," the Elder quoted King, "righteousness will flow like a mighty stream." However, the Elder qualified, only "when the kingdoms of this world become the Kingdom of our Lord and Savior, Jesus Christ—but not until then according to God's Word." Advocating for legislative change was futile. Changing hearts was the only way to bring about racial equality. "God's will must be done on this earth before you are made equal," Michaux preached. "God spoke through His Prophet and told us," he reminded his audience, the day when "the sons of former slaves and the sons of former slave-owners will sit down together at the table of brotherhood . . . will come but not until His kingdom comes and His will is done on the earth as it is in Heaven." He closed the sermon, and seemingly settled racism in America, by telling his listeners to cease marching and simply "seek to do the will of God and be blessed. May God bless you. Amen."[35] King had a dream, but Michaux had the Bible.

Using radio to combat King's televised speech was cunning. Radio remained a key medium in American life, especially as a battleground for the nation's varying civil rights agendas. Radio persisted as the most effective medium for disseminating propaganda to the masses. Even King knew this. As late as 1967, King told dinner guests at the National Association of Television and Radio Announcers Convention that in his "years of struggle north and south," he came to learn that the masses, especially those who had been "denied and deprived educational and economic opportunity," were "almost totally dependent on radio as their means of relating to the society at large." He continued, "They do not read newspapers" and "television speaks not to their needs, but to upper middle class America." Michaux banked on it. The preferred narrative was clear: the best way to overcome racism was to live a holy life and pursue the conversion of individuals, not social revolution. It was one thing to hear this from white evangelists like Billy Graham, or even Hoover. It was a weightier matter to hear it from a pioneering Black cleric.[36]

In addition to the masses, the Elder and the Bureau also targeted the White House with the sermon. He transcribed the sermon and sent it to President Kennedy. "Inclosed [sic]," he wrote to JFK, "you will find a copy of the sermon I preached over the air concerning the March on Washington August 28, 1963. I felt that you would like to know the opinion more or less of those who reach the ears of the Public [sic] on such a vital subject." King's star was rising, but Michaux reminded President Kennedy that he was the preeminent Black cleric. "For thirty years I have been on the air on many of Columbia's Broadcasting Stations (CBS) and have also broadcasted over the major networks in this country and England." He closed with a gesture to distinguish himself from the godless and unpatriotic, signing the letter, "Respectfully yours in the service of God and country, Elder L. S. Michaux, Pastor." As the Kennedy White House moved closer to King, the Bureau and Michaux wanted the president to know that King's gospel was false and was not representative of the majority of the nation's Christians, especially Black Protestants. Michaux's sermon offered his gospel as the true religious and patriotic path to racial equality for one nation under God. King spoke for some, but not the patriotic children of God. King and the gospel of nonviolent direct action received a great deal of media attention because of the march. However, Michaux assured the White House that the gospel of revival and soul salvation held the hearts and minds of Christian America. The White House had a choice: side with either King's godless rabble-rousing or Michaux's Cold War revivalism.[37]

The White House took notice. Louis Martin, deputy chairman of the Democratic National Committee (1960–69) and political advisor to Presidents Kennedy and Johnson, advised the White House to respond to Michaux. Martin, whom the *Washington Post* crowned "the godfather of Black politics," coyly described his job as securing and preserving "the prestige and the stature of the President of the United States among the Blacks." He advised and guided the White House on several notable Black appointments, including the first Black Supreme Court Justice, the first African American to hold a White House cabinet position, and the first Black woman appointed to the US Commission on Civil Rights. Martin was, simply put, all things Black politics in the Kennedy and Johnson administrations. Aware of Michaux's prominence, he urged the White House to respond to the sermon.[38]

The White House never issued an official response to the Elder, but the Kennedy administration was far from idle. Within approximately two weeks of Michaux's sermon, on October 10, a concerned Attorney General Robert Kennedy finally relented and granted the FBI a long awaited gift: permission to conduct technical surveillance on King. The president's brother authorized the FBI to wiretap King's home "or at any future address to which he may move." The G-men interpreted Kennedy's approval broadly. In addition to King's home, the FBI also installed wiretaps and microphones wherever he went, including King's hotel rooms across the country and the home of friends with whom he occasionally resided. The Bureau also installed technical surveillance on the Atlanta offices of King's Southern Christian Leadership Conference (SCLC). The goal of the comprehensive coverage was to use King's political plans and private activities to prove that he was not a committed clergyman, but in league with godless communists.[39]

The Elder's sermon stirred a pot that was already boiling. He successfully utilized the nation's public bullhorn to provide air cover for the FBI. He discredited King's religious commitments and corroborated the intel the Bureau was supplying the Kennedy administration. King was an enemy of the Christian state, a godless subversive who warranted surveillance and containment. Michaux called both King's religious motivation and advocacy for racial equality into question. King's dream was not a biblical exposition or admonition for the nation to heed, but the naïve and perhaps sinister ruminations of a demagogue. The Kennedy administration heard the message loud and clear. The FBI was granted permission to use electronic surveillance to monitor King's every move and utterance. The Bureau's collusion with Michaux was a success.

Casting doubt upon King's religious authority became the cornerstone of the Bureau's campaign against him. Emboldened by their technological surveillance of King, Bureau executives from headquarters and the Atlanta field office met for a one-day conference at FBIHQ to coordinate their efforts against King. SA Sullivan led the nine-hour strategy session. The head of the Domestic Intelligence Division set the agenda: "The primary purpose of the conference [is] to explore how best to carry out our investigation to produce the desired results without embarrassment to the Bureau." Instead of investigating civil rights violations, the Bureau concentrated its efforts and resources on violating King's civil rights. The Irish Catholic and his squadron of special agents, which included Domestic Intelligence inspector and Presbyterian elder SA Joseph A. Sizoo, concluded the meeting with a clear objective. The Bureau should deploy a "discreet approach" to use counterintelligence measures to prove that King was "unfit to serve as a minister of the gospel." One avenue they pledged to pursue was the deployment of "ministers . . . who are in a position to be of assistance." The men departed the meeting in a self-congratulatory mood. SA Sullivan noted the men "were both enthusiastic about the case and stated the conference was of exceptional benefit to them and will be of assistance in setting the future course of the investigation." Elder Michaux matched their enthusiasm, willingly enlisting in the future course of the campaign. His opportunity came again when Hoover and King had a very public spat. Michaux quickly came to the Bureau's aid.[40]

"You Owe Mr. Hoover an Apology"

On November 18, 1962, King accused the Bureau of being a tool and protector of white supremacy. Following his sermon at New York City's Riverside Church, the guest preacher chatted with a *New York Times* reporter in the church's vestry. As he removed his vestments, he dressed-down the FBI, telling the journalist that the FBI was shrouded in white supremacy. "One of the great problems we face with the FBI in the South is that the agents are white southerners who have been influenced by the mores of the community," King noted. "If an FBI man agrees with segregation he can't honestly and objectively investigate." King believed the FBI could prosecute civil rights violations "if there was a determined effort," but the Bureau was plagued with the same racism it was charged with investigating. "You can't explain to a Negro," King commented later, "how it is that a plane can be bombed and its pieces scattered for miles and the crime can be solved, but they [the FBI] can't find out who bombed a church."[41]

Hoover was outraged. The Boss periodically refuted King's allegations, yet was careful not to mention King by name, telling anyone who would listen that such claims against the FBI were as "bigoted" as the KKK. Hoover knew attacking a private citizen, a famous minister at that, was risky. Instead, Hoover continued to tell the press and Congress that the Civil Rights Movement was under the influence of godless communists. It was a movement of subversion and destruction, simply un-American. King's criticism of the Bureau only exemplified the point. Real Americans were vigilant and faithful to God. Such personal piety was not only necessary for the survival of America's democracy; it was the very purpose of life. "The goal of life," he told the *New York Times* on September 23, 1964, was embodied in the Bible. Micah 6:8, his favorite verse: "'And what doth the Lord require of thee, but to do justly, and to love mercy, and to walk humbly with thy God?'"[42] The Civil Rights Movement may have been marching on, but according to Hoover, it was not walking with God.

Despite such veiled responses, the Boss still could not leave the issue alone. In Hoover's eyes, King had committed an unforgivable sin. "It is almost impossible to overestimate Mr. Hoover's sensitivity to criticism of himself or the FBI," former Attorney General Nicholas deB. Katzenbach testified before Congress. "It went far beyond the bounds of natural resentment to criticism . . . In a very real sense there was no greater crime in Mr. Hoover's eyes than public criticism of the Bureau and Dr. King's repeated criticisms made him a Bureau enemy." SA G. Gordon Liddy preferred to describe Hoover's penchant for revenge with the vivid maxim, "Nobody fucks with J. Edgar." Indeed, according to Hoover's closest aides, King's indictment of Hoover and his Bureau was seared in the Boss's mind. Baptist Special Agent M. A. Jones tactfully surmised the ordeal: Hoover felt wronged by King, and he left "no stone unturned in setting the record straight." The director found his opportunity on November 18, 1964, the anniversary of King's statement. The timing was apropos. As Hoover later admitted, President Johnson's presidential campaign had concluded, King had just been crowned the winner of the Nobel Peace Prize, and his book *Why We Can't Wait* had just hit stores. The Boss had had enough. His rage spilled over during a three-hour press conference with eighteen reporters from the Women's

National Press Club, headed by noted White House reporter Sarah McClendon. Admittedly, Hoover was "always . . . reluctant about holding press conferences." He did not trust the "jackals." In fact, he boasted, he had "only held one or two" while he was director. "However," he told SA Sullivan, he relented because the "women reporters [had] been most persistent to have a briefing on the work of the Bureau and there were a number of things that I wanted to also get off my chest at the sametime [sic]." Painting King as a false minister was foremost on Hoover's mind. King's "exposure," he later told Sullivan, was "long overdue." The director wasted little time before venting his pent-up righteous indignation. He began by offering what one agent in attendance described as the Boss's "standard lecture" of "canned data" delivered in a "staccato" style. Then suddenly, Hoover broke routine and began to address the FBI's civil rights record. The harangue announced that King not only had ties to godless communists, but that the civil rights leader had refused to meet with him, and even instructed Black Southerners not to cooperate with the FBI. King was no minister or righteous spokesman. He was, Hoover concluded, "the most notorious liar in the United States," and "one of the lowest characters in the country." One of Hoover's agents immediately passed him a note, pleading, "'Don't you want to say this off the record?'" Hoover promptly threw it in the trash.[43]

Hoover's accusations made front-page news. King responded in kind. In a telegram to Hoover (later made public), the civil rights minister maintained his criticisms of the FBI, noting that he was "appalled and surprised" by the director's statement "maligning" his "integrity." King's official public statement, however, was more biting. He dismissed Hoover's accusations as the ramblings of a paranoid old man who had "faltered under the awesome burden, complexities, and responsibilities of his office. Therefore," King concluded, "I cannot engage in a public debate with him. I have nothing but sympathy for this man who has served his country so well."[44]

The FBI possessed no such sympathy for King. The next day the Bureau sent him a threatening "anonymous" package, challenging his status as a minister. The bundle consisted of an edited audio recording and an ominous letter. The aural mix was prepared by FBI Laboratory audio tech John Matter. It contained several audio snippets of King's extra-marital sexual encounters and ribald comments the Bureau obtained through its hotel bugs. The written missive, drafted by SA Sullivan on un-watermarked paper, claimed to be from a fellow Black Christian who questioned King's Christianity. The letter volleyed, "I will not dignify your name with either a Mr. or a Reverend or a Dr. You are no clergy-man . . . you could not believe in God and act as you do." The note con-tinued, "The Church organizations that have been helping—Protestant, Catholic, Jews will know you for what you are—an evil abnormal beast." King and his associates were "pretend[ing] to be ministers of the Gos-pel." King's evil, the angry epistle concluded, was so severe, "Satan could do no more." The writer threatened to expose King if he did not commit suicide, refuse the Nobel Prize, or at least bow out of the Civil Rights Movement.[45] The Bureau used the pseudonymous mix and missive to attack King for what they perceived to be his lack of religious and cleri-cal commitments.

King, with no knowledge of the letter, lobbied leaders such as Doro-thy Height of the National Council of Negro Women, and the captains of the SCLC, the Congress of Racial Equality (CORE), the Urban League, and countless ministers to issue statements criticizing Hoover and the FBI's stance on civil rights. According to an FBI wiretap, King told one minister that Hoover should be "hit from all sides."[46]

The Bureau responded by coordinating with its own clergy to hit King from all sides. On the morning of Monday, November 23, 1964, two days after the Bureau sent King the notorious package, Michaux met with Director Hoover and Deputy Associate Director Cartha "Deke" DeLoach at FBIHQ.[47] "Deke" was the Bureau's third in charge and, like Agent Nichols before him, served as the liaison to the White House. He became a member of President Johnson's inner circle. The president even had a direct private phone line installed at Agent DeLoach's house, right next to the G-man's bed. One agent described him as Hoover's "protégé, almost a son" and "he, more than most, had Hoover's confi-dence." In addition to his dealings with the White House, he led the Bureau's Crime Records Division—the Bureau's public relations arm. He used his characteristic smoothness and sophistication to shape the

Bureau's image via FBI publications and courting public opinion leaders like Michaux.[48]

The Monday morning meeting was part of the Bureau's tenacious campaign to find journalistic and religious allies for their crusade against King. On the same day as the meeting with Michaux, Hoover sent presidential aide Bill Moyers two letters containing disparaging information on King's associates. The Bureau also attempted, but failed, to conscript journalists from the *LA Times*, *New York Times*, *Atlanta Constitution*, *Chicago Daily News*, and *Newsweek* to print transcriptions of FBI audio surveillance of King's private hotel room activity. Ben Bradlee, *Newsweek*'s Washington bureau chief, refused to even examine the transcript of the recordings, let alone accept it as a news source. According to Bureau files, Bradlee was outraged, stating that if the FBI carried out such acts against King, surely they would do the same to any other person for personal gain. Bradlee informed Attorney General Nicholas Katzenbach about the whole ordeal. The head of the justice department immediately flew to President Johnson's ranch to inform the president. LBJ, in turn, told the FBI that Bradlee could not be trusted. "I don't understand why we are unable to get the true facts before the public," Hoover incredulously wrote to his media man SA DeLoach. The Bureau went looking for other trusted outlets. They reached out to Edwin Espy, the General Secretary of the National Council of Churches. The Bureau "confidentially" informed him that King "left a great deal to be desired . . . from the standpoint of personal conduct." Reverend Espy did not air the Bureau's purported intelligence; however, according to Bureau files, he swore not to give King another cent. The same counterintelligence efforts were made with clergy from the Baptist World Alliance. While the journalists and ministers refused to publicly collaborate with the Bureau, Michaux was more amenable.[49]

Agent DeLoach described Michaux as having a record of being "quite cooperative and friendly over the years," and the Elder did not disappoint. During the morning meeting, Michaux assured Hoover and Agent DeLoach that he was "distressed to learn of Martin Luther King's false statements against the Director and . . . wanted to do something about the situation." The Elder vowed that he and his followers were strong supporters and believers in Hoover and the G-men. They were, he pledged, "Hooverites." They saw King, on the other hand, as "an insincere individual who was concerned only with self-aggrandizement," with a proven record of being "a liar," while Hoover was "one of the great leaders of our time." The Elder, at one point, desired to act as the "intermediary between the Director and Martin Luther King." However, he gave up on the idea. King was not trustworthy. The Elder explained, in opposition to King, "his theory of civil rights involves the ability of the Negro to qualify or deserve any newly won freedoms." He continued, "It is wrong for the Negroes of today to demand things they do not deserve." The Elder "deplored the activities of CORE in demonstrations, sit-downs, etc." Such activities, he claimed, did "the Negro no good." Marches and pressure groups could not bring about Black equality; only regeneration and the resulting self-improvement of Black Americans could earn that right.[50]

The day after Michaux's visit to headquarters, Hoover made similar comments during his acceptance of the first annual Sword of Loyola Award from Loyola University Chicago. In his first public address since eviscerating King as a "notorious liar," Hoover subliminally continued his onslaught.[51] His acceptance speech, "Time for Decision," noted that "pressure groups" were led by non-believers, "Communist and moral degenerates," who protested and boycotted under the guise of "liberty when they really mean license." There was little doubt to whom Hoover's jeremiad was referring. The balm the nation needed, Hoover sermonized, was not more collective action, but revival. "We must return to the teachings of God if we are to cure this sickness," he preached with the sacred sword by his side. This, he maintained, was faithful to "the American way." America had a decision to make: return to God or suffer the impending chaos. It was Hoover's way, that is, God's way, or follow King and the Civil Rights Movement down the path to destruction. The homily was well received. It was "heartily endorse[d]" in the US Congress and later entered into the *Congressional Record*.[52]

Seven days later, Bureau clergyman and pastor of Chicago's Quinn Chapel AME Reverend Archibald Carey Jr. brokered a meeting between King and Hoover (along with their respective aides) to help settle their public dispute. Carey, a minister on the Bureau's special correspondents list, set up the one and only meeting between King and Hoover for December 1, 1964, at 3:30pm. They met in Hoover's "lavish" FBIHQ office, a stately thirty-five-foot-long nest on the fifth floor of the DOJ building. The one-hour gathering was very cordial. A late arriving King was ushered past an exhibit of crime souvenirs—the weapons and paraphernalia of famous gangsters subdued by the G-men, even John Dillinger's death mask—a foreboding monument to FBI triumphs. Once seated, Reverend King explained that his criticisms of Hoover and the FBI were misquoted and misrepresented. He praised the Bureau's work in Mississippi and denied ever instructing "negroes" to not cooperate with the FBI. "My only complaint," King quickly hedged, "is the fact that I have seen FBI agents who have received civil rights complaints, consorting the next day with the local police officers who have been charged with brutalities." This reality, he added, made Black folk "sometimes on the verge of temporary despair." He continued in a conciliatory tone, pledging it was never his aim to launch a personal attack on the director. He simply tried to give voice to Black frustration. King then reassured the director that his strong Christian beliefs would never allow him to yield to the "crippling totalitarian disease" of communism.[53]

Hoover, however, would hear none of King's Christian testimony. The director abruptly interrupted the preacher's confession of faith, launching into a fifty-five-minute monologue from behind his elevated gleaming mahogany desk. Hoover was known to burst into such long soliloquies from behind his perch when he did not particularly trust an office visitor. The director became garrulous when King spoke of his faith. Hoover, similar to the pseudonymous letter the FBI sent King, refused to call King "Reverend." Hoover constantly gloated to the press, "I never addressed him as Reverend or Doctor." He reveled in the personal triumph even after King's death, telling anyone who would listen, "I never called him reverend." Instead, Hoover, with two American flags behind him and the large Bible that was known to occupy his desk during such visits, lectured "Mr. King" on the dangers of communism and the FBI's long history of civil rights work dating back to the 1920s, when the FBI "put the fear of God" into the KKK. Hoover dismissed the modern Klan as "white trash." He claimed his agents had "interviewed every Klan member in Mississippi and put them on notice that if trouble comes, the FBI plans to look into the Klan first." Hoover assured King, or perhaps threatened, that the FBI often knew of the Klan's plans in advance, leaving every Klansman to suspect that there was an FBI informant behind every white hood. He rejoiced at the infighting such suspicion had fostered.[54]

The Boss then assured King that the FBI supported the "sincere aspects of the Civil Rights Movement." The director confessed that he favored the desegregation of public accommodations and schools (it was, after all, the law of the land), but strongly opposed certain mechanisms to ensure the same, particularly school busing. Finally, Hoover offered King some advice: Black leaders should focus their efforts on Black voter registration and job training, not militancy and protest. Society and employers—especially the Bureau—could not lower their standards to accommodate African Americans. African Americans had to prove themselves worthy. It was only by "a complete change in community thinking," Hoover announced, that the race problem would be solved, "in due time." King despised Hoover's reference to a moderate gradualism. The preacher had constantly and publicly condemned the philosophy of white evangelical moderates, most famously in his 1963 *Letter from Birmingham Jail*. King criticized the perspective for being "more devoted to 'order' than to justice." White evangelical moderates like Hoover paternalistically believed they could "set the timetable for another man's freedom." Hoover was a high-ranking official at the US Department of Justice who was certainly concerned with order and believed he could indeed set the timetable for Black equality.[55] He was, after all, the decorated guardian of Christian America.

King departed the hour-long meeting and issued a prepared press statement from Hoover's reception room. Reverend King told the throng of waiting reporters—including James McCartney of the *Chicago Daily News*, who was offered FBI transcriptions of King's hotel surveillance while he waited for King's and Hoover's meeting to conclude—that the meeting was "very friendly, very amicable" and that the two sides had reached "new levels of understanding." King hoped the public would "forget the confusion of the past and get on with the job."[56] For the Bureau, King was the job. The FBI continued its attempts to prevent the publication of articles favorable to Dr. King, while it struggled to persuade "friendly" news sources to print unfavorable articles and public rebukes of King. The G-men found little success among journalists.[57]

The Elder, however, was once again happy to oblige. Michaux returned to headquarters on December 9, 1964 (eight days after King's meeting with Hoover), determined to lionize Hoover, help the Bureau, and publicly chastise King for bearing false witness. After meeting with the Boss and the Bureau's chief propaganda officer, SA DeLoach, it was decided that Michaux would "issue to the wire services a public letter which he would write to King . . . and state that the Director and the FBI have been extremely effective in the Civil Rights Movement. He will also call upon Reverend King to issue a public apology to the Director so that Negro people may realize who their friends are." Michaux believed the open letter was a must because King had "led many uneducated Negroes to believe that the FBI was not properly performing its responsibilities," namely, the defense and perpetuation of America's Christian heritage. Such falsehoods in the Black community, Michaux maintained, only hurt Black people because "a lack of cooperation . . . prevented the FBI from fully doing its job" on behalf of the nation's Black citizens. DeLoach concluded the memo noting, "I thanked the Elder for his interest concerning the Director and the FBI and told him that he, of course, could call upon us at any time for assistance."[58]

Michaux, with the dubious assistance of the FBI, composed a four-page open letter to King on December 22, a few days after King returned from receiving the Nobel Peace Prize in Norway. The release of the open letter was coordinated with the distribution of the Bureau's "strictly confidential" report on King's "immoral" personal conduct to a critical mass of politicos and government agencies, including the White House, Vice President-elect Hubert Humphrey, the secretaries of state and defense, the CIA, the US Information Agency, four military intelligence offices, and the National Science Foundation.[59] Michaux's dispatch served to buttress the Bureau's two-page report on King. It was one thing for the

Bureau to oppose King in the halls of power. It was even more conse-quential for the Bureau's concerns to be publicly corroborated by a Black celebrity minister.

The Elder's public missive rebuked King, while extolling Hoover's Christian witness. King may have won the coveted Nobel Peace Prize but Hoover, Michaux reminded King, was the inaugural recipient of the prestigious "Sword of Loyola." Hoover was not just the director of the FBI; he was also a faithful soldier in the army of the Lord.[60] The Elder lectured King on the proper relationship between the FBI and the Civil Rights Movement. He presented his findings as independently verified. "In my investigation, I found that the duty of maintaining law and order in the civil rights demonstrations . . . is the primary responsibility of local and state law enforcement agencies . . . the FBI is solely an inves-tigating agency as distinguished from a peace officer or police agency, and is without authority to maintain peace or provide protection." He then rattled off a complementary listing of FBI statistics and anecdotes concerning the number of civil rights cases the FBI had investigated in the pursuit of civil rights justice. He assured King, "In my investigation I included a visit to Mr. Hoover's office and had these above facts all confirmed." He failed to mention that such federal investigations rarely led to convictions. From 1960 until the time Michaux penned his open letter, the Bureau launched 11,328 civil rights investigations. They netted a paltry fourteen convictions.[61]

Michaux did not let facts get in the way. "Under these circumstances," he admonished King in the laundered letter, "you being the recipient of the famous Nobel Prize which brands you as the prince of Peacemakers among men of this day, portraying the image of Christ, I suggest that you apologize to Mr. Hoover for your suspicious remarks." It was King, Michaux argued, who instigated the whole affair. "Your statement based on suspicion only was a grave error on your part . . . And Mr. Hoover was provoked to call you a notorious liar." The Elder proposed that the answer to the dilemma was simple: "If you apologize to Mr. Hoover and the thirteen thousand FBI Agents if [sic] will be Mr. Hoover's duty to accept and to apologize to you." More than this, Michaux directed King to "cooperate with and aid the FBI." It was a Christian duty.[62]

The Elder concluded his public scolding by quoting Hoover's acceptance speech at the Sword of Loyola Award ceremony. Michaux had an advance copy of the evangelistic speech, compliments of the Bureau. "America stands at the crossroads of destiny in which we shall all finally stand or fall together," Michaux quoted. "Man is blessed with the liberty to choose between opposing factors . . . between God and the Devil . . . As Americans we should learn to trust God, to know His teachings and to live in His ways. This is truly a time for decision."[63]

In reality, Michaux did not investigate the FBI; he simply illegally laundered the Bureau's data. Following the Elder's November and December meetings with Hoover and Agent DeLoach, the Bureau illegally provided him with two documents meant for Bureau employees only: an internal monograph on civil rights and a flattering catalogue of FBI "accomplishments in the field of civil rights." In violation of federal law, the Elder simply copied the Bureau's confidential data, inserted it into his open letter, and sent the letter to King and the press, original spelling errors and all.[64]

Michaux's epistle was pure propaganda, not an olive branch. The Elder admitted as much to Agent DeLoach. When DeLoach showed Hoover a copy of the letter, he noted, "Attached is the letter issued by Elder Michaux in connection to the Martin Luther King matter. He gives us considerable credit concerning civil rights accomplishments but, as I mentioned on the phone, goes too far in his request that after King apologizes, he calls upon you also to apologize. The Elder has mentioned that he, of course, realizes that King will never apologize."[65] The vetted letter allowed the Bureau to leak information concerning its Christian commitments and civil rights work while receiving a Black clerical endorsement of the same. The Elder substantiated the Bureau's labor while authenticating his own status as the prophet of Black Protestantism. He presented the debate between Hoover and King as one of ultimate significance. Hoover was God's man and the FBI was an instrument of righteousness. King, on the other hand, was being used as a tool of the Devil and the godless, or worse, King was the embodiment of godless evil. The nation could not serve two masters. Americans could not support both their FBI and King's Civil Rights

Movement. It was either righteousness or godlessness. The fate of the nation depended on it.

Michaux and the Bureau were relentlessly committed to the cause. After the major papers did not print their open letter in its entirety, the Elder preached a sermon that echoed the same. News coverage was not lacking this time. On Sunday, January 3, 1965, the first Sunday of the New Year, Michaux explained to more than four hundred worshippers as well as journalists and thousands of radio listeners that the "breach" between Hoover and King was one that only King could repair. With a sardonic tinge, he explained it was King's responsibility because "King is the prince of peace-makers." The "feud," the Elder explained, was dire, one that "threatens America." King's recalcitrance opened "an avenue through which the Communists can infiltrate this country" and all Black citizens would be blamed as the "avenue" of communist infiltration and exploitation. Subsequently, Michaux reasoned, "This thing can cause the Negro in America to be put back 100 years." An apology from King, Michaux argued, "will not only lift him up, but will lift us up with him."[66] The Bureau and Michaux colluded to preach a sermon that made the issue plain: King was the avenue of godless communist infiltration. He had to repent and apologize; authentic Black Christianity, race progress, and, most important, national security depended on it.

The following day, January 4, Hoover thanked Michaux for the sermon. "I read the account of your sermon for January 3 as reported by the *Washington Post* and I want to take this opportunity to thank you for your support of my administration of the FBI. Your straightforward remarks concerning this Bureau's role in civil rights matters are a source of encouragement." Nothing was more encouraging than having the national press parrot the Bureau's own views under the guise of a minister. Hoover closed his thank you note, "You may be assured my associates join me in expressing appreciation."[67] The Boss was well pleased.

A "most friendly and cooperative" Michaux visited Agent DeLoach at FBI headquarters a few weeks after the January 3 sermon. The Bureau had just received fresh transcriptions from bugs in King's New York City hotel rooms. The Elder brought his own intelligence as well. He presented DeLoach with "numerous letters which [sic] he had received which expressed support for the Director and were against King." Michaux reportedly told Agent DeLoach the "numerous" letters were "certainly an indication of the very fine support that Mr. Hoover enjoys." Michaux departed headquarters at the close of the hour-long meeting, but not before he "reemphasized his sincere admiration and respect for the Director."[68]

The next day Hoover wrote a personal letter to Michaux, thanking him again. "I was pleased to learn of your visit with Assistant Director DeLoach yesterday," Hoover wrote. The director was thrilled to learn that Michaux had received letters that supported the G-men. "This response," Hoover asserted, "is most encouraging and is indicative of the straightforward manner in which you discussed this Bureau's role in the civil rights field." Hoover closed by saying, "You may be assured that I am indeed appreciative of your efforts in this regard."[69] The Bureau and Michaux sowed a sermonic seed that yielded a harvest of good will for the Bureau.

However, the Black press felt differently. Many African Americans viewed Michaux's public attack against King as nothing short of blasphemy. An editorial in the *Baltimore Afro-American* saw no value in Michaux's stance against King. There are "certain institutions," the region's leading Black paper noted, that one should never rush to attack, "motherhood, togetherness, Saturday night at the movies, and in some situations Martin Luther King." King was an "institution" representing the coordinated religious fight for Black equality. The weekly admitted that "Dr. King is not always right," but he was nonetheless the "spiritual leader" of the Civil Rights Movement and therefore untouchable. The *Afro-American* then was perplexed as to why the Elder, a fellow minister, would attack King. The only thing Michaux accomplished by siding with Hoover was "removing himself from the mainstream of thought" in the Black community. Even worse, Michaux publicly "indicated a division within the ranks" of Black Christian leadership. He committed the unpardonable sin.[70]

An editorial in the *Chicago Defender* followed suit. "Elder Michaux has been an effective force for good in the community," the national weekly admitted, "but we believe he is in error in these attacks on

Dr. King." The paper treaded lightly, "There is a danger in criticizing the action of any minister," however, the editorial pivoted, "this is a danger we must accept." The *Chicago Defender* maintained that the Elder's stance was "petty and ill-founded" even as it provided "aid and encouragement to our enemies." The missive concluded, "We believe that Elder Michaux, whatever his reasons, is hurting the civil rights movement, not helping it."[71] This was, after all, the Bureau's and the Elder's shared goal.

Letters to the editor were less diplomatic. E. B. Henderson of Michaux's native Virginia was flabbergasted. Michaux was uneducated and did not belong to any "organization of ministers" or civil rights groups such as the "SCLC, NAACP, or the Urban League." He had no right nor credentials to be a leader in the Black community, let alone criticize King. The Elder, Henderson wrote to the *Norfolk Journal and Guide*, was just like white fundamentalists Billy Hargis and Carl McIntire. Michaux may have a large following; however, "The Elder," Henderson wrote, "is no Moses."[72] Joan Arlington held no punches when she wrote to the *Chicago Defender*. "Rev. Michaux," she pronounced, "should excuse himself from our 20th Century society and join the old Ku Klux Klan organization."[73] To many African American citizens, the Elder's defense of the FBI and attacks on King made him a byword of backwardness in an era of racial progress.

Michaux and the Bureau nonetheless continued their sacred ambush. On Thursday, April 1, 1965, Elder Michaux and more than one hundred of his Church of God parishioners converged on Baltimore, Maryland, to launch an FBI-approved protest against King. King and the executive board of the SCLC were in the city, holding meetings inside the Lord Baltimore Hotel. SCLC was fresh from the triumphant voting rights march from Selma to Montgomery. They gathered at the Lord Baltimore to plan the Summer Community Organizing and Political Education (SCOPE) project. The campaign included a voter registration drive across the South and an economic boycott of the state of Alabama. SCOPE aimed to organize and register Black voters as well as galvanize support for the 1965 Voting Rights Act as it moved through Congress. SCOPE, King announced in a press release, would be "one of the most intensive attacks ever conceived to fight disfranchisement, educational deprivation, and poverty." The Bureau, Michaux, and his rambunctious followers were opposed to the plan and its advocates. The morning of the protest, Michaux told Agent DeLoach that the Nobel Prize winner was nothing but a "'fuss maker' instead of peace maker." Michaux blamed the civil rights minister for the deaths of many, including "Negroes." "Frankly," the Elder reportedly lobbied the Bureau, King was just "a selfish individual that was agitating for himself rather than for the good of the Negroes."[74] Agent DeLoach did not need to be convinced.

The Bureau clergyman and his Church of God faithful publicly registered this opposition in front of the entrance of the Lord Baltimore at 10am. Agent DeLoach dispatched FBI agents from Baltimore's Civil Rights Division to accompany Michaux and his protestors. The Bureau provided Michaux with the kind of protection the FBI continually and deliberately denied King and his civil rights protesters. Hoover had even crowed to a gaggle of reporters about it. "Mr. King . . . had the audacity to tell me he was going to Selma . . . and hoped FBI men would be there to keep him from harm." Hoover smirked, "I told Mr. King, I never addressed him as Reverend or Doctor, no FBI men would be there to protect him." Elder Michaux received very different treatment. The local G-men watched from afar and made certain that Michaux and crew were not arrested, hindered, nor removed by hotel security. The hovering agents jotted down, "approximately 100 to 125 Negroes dressed in burlap over their usual clothing and wearing burlap on their heads picketed the Lord Baltimore Hotel." The "singing, chanting, marching, and sackclothed" protestors were equipped with signs displaying various messages, including, "God Save America." The sacred musicality of their disdain signaled their deep abiding faith in God and the righteousness with which they pleaded their cause. Their coarse attire of "sackcloth" denoted mourning and the dire need for King and the SCLC to repent of their sins, lest God forsake the nation.[75]

Michaux joined the marchers' religious chorus as he distributed prepared remarks seemingly approved by the Bureau. A pack of startled white and Black journalists flipped through the boilerplate press packet as they hurled questions at the Elder: "Why are you picketing Dr. King?" Michaux told a reporter from the *New York Times* that a boycott against Alabama manufactured goods would "destroy the progress the Negro has made" and "throw thousands of Negroes in Alabama out of work and into breadlines." He then told the *Afro-American* columnist that a boycott "would bring about dissatisfaction among both white and colored people and would hurt the colored people of Alabama." As protesters paraded signs reading, "Russian Termites," Michaux announced that King's radical proposal made clear that the SCLC was riddled with "Communist infiltrators" who had turned their back on God. Like termites, the SCLC was bent on destroying America's Christian infrastructure from the inside. One journalist retorted, "Are you saying, sir, that Dr. King has turned his back on God?" Michaux boldly explained, "Well I say Dr. King has turned his back on the plans that God gave him to lead his people." True Christian leadership guided people to salvation, not politically motivated boycotts. "That's why," Michaux told the throng, King "is wrong and why the boycott cannot work." Scandalized white observers, a columnist noted, murmured about "all those colored people picketing Dr. King." Impervious, Michaux withdrew from the press to rejoin the marchers. The protestors pounded the pavement and bellowed the religious refrain: "I'm Praying for You."[76]

The religious protestors made quite a scene. SCLC, one of the foremost Black Christian protest organizations in the country, was being confronted with a Black Christian protest. Michaux and company left little doubt; King's discontent with America was not universally embraced within Black Protestantism. King's gospel was a ruse for something sinister and destructive. Divine presence and approval were not with King, the SCLC, nor their godless "communist" plans. God's anointing and favor resided with Michaux, his Church of God followers, and their colorblind gospel of personal conversion. In the eyes of many, divine approval was certainly debatable. However, FBI approval was not. Michaux marched in lockstep with the Bureau.

Michaux's Lord Baltimore Hotel protest coincided with a shift in the Bureau's campaign against King. Hoover continued to lambast King. Two weeks after the protests, the FBI director bragged to reporters

about how he "branded [King] a notorious liar." Nevertheless, the Bureau
was moving to a new strategy. The next week, the FBI terminated the
wiretap at King's home. The Bureau's documentation of its partnership
with Elder Michaux also concluded in the fall of the same year. They
had no need for him anymore because they found another minister to
take his place. By October 1965, the Atlanta FBI field office, after years
of failed recruitment, finally convinced Black itinerant minister and
SCLC accountant, James A. Harrison, to become a paid informant. Harrison, after much prayer, agreed to provide the FBI with personal information on King and the plans of SCLC. He did so, he claimed, out of
genuine concern. He wanted to get to the bottom of all of the communist rumors buzzing around King; ironically, he turned to the source of
the very rumors. Harrison was assured that his faithful service to God
and country would store up for him treasures in heaven. For good measure, he was also given earthly treasures: a monthly Bureau informant
salary ranging from $450 to $600 (a contemporary economic status of
about $4,000 to $8,000 a month). The Bureau's new strategy against King
was set. Labor and energy were moved away from Michaux's public
attacks, an SCLC outsider, to the devout Harrison, an inside mole.[77]
Michaux continued to preach over the radio and remained a favorite at
the Bureau. However, the G-men no longer called Michaux into "service" against King. He was a faithful "special correspondent," but his job
was done.

And it was a job well done. By early 1965, the Bureau's campaign
against King began to bear fruit. King felt it, and he knew the culprits.
He sent several ministers to FBIHQ on his behalf. Their task was simple:
vouch for his religious fidelity and convince the Bureau to cease its
"massive effort to discredit" him. Their attempts were futile. Every minister received the same script from the FBI. The Bureau repeatedly denied the existence of any crusade. Agent DeLoach even stonewalled
King's third emissary to the Bureau: Reverend Archibald Carey Jr., a
longtime friend of the Bureau. During his visit to FBIHQ on May 19,
1965, Reverend Carey told SA DeLoach that King had stayed with him
in Chicago the previous week. A beleaguered King told Reverend Carey
he knew the FBI was engaged in "a massive effort to discredit him."

Reverend Carey was not appalled by the effort, nor did he find it incredulous that the federal agency in charge of investigating civil rights violations was capable of such actions. Rather, he simply requested the "sympathies" of the Bureau to not let "any effort to discredit King occur." He laid out three reasons: "(1) Reverend King is a good man. (2) Reverend King stands as a 'symbol' to the Negro race today. (3) Reverend King is a 'safety valve' at the present time." King was the only thing standing between America and "more of the militant and violent Negroes from committing serious acts in the United States." SA DeLoach was not moved. He interrupted Reverend Carey. "[You] have known us for a long time," he scolded Reverend Carey, "[you know] in [your] own mind that the FBI ha[s] plenty to do without being responsible for a discrediting campaign against Reverend King." Reverend Carey quickly changed his tone, confessing he "did know [the FBI] better." He confessed he actually "doubted King's allegations from the very beginning." DeLoach was not satisfied with Carey's contrition. He offered the preacher a long list of the Bureau's dedicated work in the civil rights field. The FBI had actually tried to help King's Christian crusade. "The Director," he lectured, "[gave] Reverend King some very good advice insofar as [King's] moral responsibilities were concerned." It was a fine fiction. The Bureau publicly denied orchestrating a campaign against King, while it privately rejoiced over the same. Following the meeting, SA DeLoach satisfyingly noted, "It is obvious that King is becoming very disturbed and worried ... else he would not go to such great efforts to have people approach the FBI."[78]

King was rightly concerned. Reverend Carey, a man King counted as a close friend and ally, told him the Bureau campaign did not exist. He blamed King, advising the civil rights leader to "make a greater effort to praise the FBI for its excellent work in the civil rights field." King knew better. However, Reverend Carey was giving voice to popular opinion. A leading national public opinion poll showed that the public was increasingly siding with Hoover and the Bureau against King. The preacher was voted *Time* magazine's Man of the Year in early 1964. However, following his public spat with Hoover at the end of 1964, the foremost public opinion firm found that "a cross section of the American public" largely sided with Hoover over King. Harris and Associates, Inc., led by Louis Harris, the first presidential pollster, found in a 1965 survey that 50 percent of the public "sympathized" with Hoover, while only 16 percent identified with the Nobel Peace Prize winner. Overall, "three times as many people sided with the FBI head as did with the Negro civil rights leader." Reported in the *Washington Post*, the poll noted that despite Hoover's "civil rights controversies" and related criticisms by the likes of the internationally renowned King, the FBI chief maintained "the solid backing of nearly eight of ten Americans." Harris and Associates noted that King was increasingly viewed as a threat to national security, while the FBI Boss remained "a powerful symbol of law and order, a pillar of security in an uncertain nation and world." The poll reflected what Hoover already knew. An avalanche of support flowed into the director's office the day after his public attack on King. "I have been flooded today with telegrams from all sections of the country," Hoover gloated to Agent Sullivan, "and out of the many hundreds that have been received, there have only been two or three which have criticized me for what I *had* to say about Martin Luther King."[79]

Minister James (Jim) R. Hiskey was one of the many hundreds. The retired professional golfer turned area director for Campus Crusade for Christ assured Hoover, "I have been watching the paper closely concerning the remarks Dr. King has said . . . I am sure I am speaking for several hundred well-balanced Christians when I say that we are standing behind you . . . You will be remembered in our prayers."[80]

Hoover also had the prayers and well wishes of the editors of *Christianity Today*. In an editorial entitled "To Tell the Truth," the magazine called King's criticism of the FBI nothing more than a "slur," solely intended "to prod FBI Agents into the role of civil rights agitators." King's efforts, the magazine boasted, were rightly "met head on" by Hoover. *CT* lamented that criticisms of King and civil rights protests were always "dismissed as 'white backlash.'" King, they argued, warranted criticism. The magazine cited all the hearsay concerning the personal conduct of King and his associates. "Reports abound that certain developments might seriously impair the moral image of some civil rights crusaders and hence of the cause itself," *CT* confidently noted. The Bureau had, of course, provided the reports to friendly media and fanned the flames of such rumors. The magazine sent the editorial to ordained pastor turned G-man SA Stephen Sziarto, "even though he [did] not subscribe" to the magazine.[81] Subscription or not, CT always remained faithful to Hoover and his FBI, even to the point of helping to air and confirm the Bureau's counter-intelligence on King.

The efforts proved successful. As Baptist SA Milton Jones reflected years later, "Hoover publicly called [King] a liar and made it stick."[82] Indeed, leading ministers, flagship religious publications and organizations, as well as the broader public confirmed what the Bureau had been preaching: FBI Director J. Edgar Hoover was the virtuous prophet of a secure and righteous Christian America, with the power to determine who was godly or a godless enemy of the state. King was clearly deemed the latter.

Michaux aided this outcome. The evangelical preacher shrewdly employed his popular mass media empire and celebrity status to aid the Bureau's crusade to destroy King. Michaux—the purported "leading negro" in the nation's capital—utilized his status to illegally broadcast the Bureau's laundered intelligence to portray his fellow Black minister not as a clerical patriot or leading spokesman of Black discontent, but as a subversive con man determined to take the nation down the road to chaos and perdition. Such accusations only served to further justify the FBI's attack on King and the public's distrust of the civil rights leader.

In the process, Michaux articulated a Black public faith that not only dismissed King and his claims that racism was endemic to America, but also authenticated white evangelical commitments to the Bureau. America was a Christian state, they argued, where saved souls inevitably led to racial progress. The Elder assured his followers and listeners that the FBI not only guaranteed such advancements, but also made them possible. Michaux used his multi-media platform to continually laud Hoover and his Bureau as the "pillar" and protector of the nation's Christian soul. He heralded Hoover as a Christian statesman and his FBI as the legitimate Christian extension of the state. The Elder cooperated with the Bureau not only to reinforce this shared vision of white

Christian nationalism, but also to identify and defeat its enemies: people like Reverend Martin Luther King Jr.

———

Michaux and Hoover remained relatively close for the remaining three years of the Elder's life. Approximately a month after Michaux's Lord Baltimore protest, the FBI director nominated Michaux to serve on the President's Commission on Crime in the District of Columbia. The commission was charged with conducting hearings and investigations involving all aspects of the District's law enforcement, crime, criminal justice, and rehabilitation. On May 14, 1965, Hoover met with US Attorney General Nicholas Katzenbach and President Johnson to recommend Michaux, among others, for one of the prestigious spots on the president's committee. The president wanted a "blue ribbon" committee of professionals: attorneys, scholars, retired corporate executives, and experienced federal appointees. The Elder was none of these; but in Hoover's eyes he had the one necessary qualification: he was a Bureau clergyman.[83]

Hoover remained attentive to Michaux's personal life as well. The Elder was no longer working in concert with the FBI, but his status as a close and cherished partner was secure, no matter what was going on at the Bureau. When Mrs. Mary Michaux died on October 28, 1967, Hoover was busy implementing a black COINTELPRO, a nationwide routinization of the kind of service Michaux provided: to "expose, disrupt, misdirect, [and] discredit" Black freedom fighters. Nevertheless, FBIHQ found time to send the widowed preacher a personal note of sympathy. "My dear Elder," the Boss wrote, "I was indeed sorry to learn of the passing of your wife and want to express my heartfelt sympathy . . . May your fond memories of your life together bring you comfort in your sorrow. My thoughts are with you during your bereavement." The FBI consoled Michaux, while it tormented countless African American freedom fighters. The director's compassionate letter attempted to lift Michaux's spirit, while the Bureau was busy preventing the rise of what Hoover called a dreaded "black messiah."[84]

On April 4, 1968, an assassin's bullet ensured that King would not be that messiah. News that King had been shot spread like wildfire throughout FBIHQ. "Is he dead?" the director whispered to his personal clerk. The criminal violation was not the chief lawman's first concern. Rather, he was preoccupied with the potential historical significance of King's death. "I hope the son of a bitch doesn't die," the Boss said with scorching clarity. "If he does, they'll make a martyr out of him." Time would eventually prove Hoover to be a reluctant prophet.[85]

Special agents in the field were less circumspect. SA Arthur Murtaugh recalled seeing one agent "jump up and down with glee" when he heard King had been shot. The jolly G-man leaped for joy, yelling, "I'm glad they got 'em! I hope the son of a bitch is dead!" When he discovered his hope was fulfilled, he gave thanks, "I'm glad he's dead! I'm happy he's dead!"[86]

There was no joy at the Bureau when Elder Michaux died of natural causes six months later. His death was officially mourned by the FBI. A grieving Hoover wrote to the Elder's sister, "I was deeply saddened to learn of the passing of your brother and want to extend my heartfelt sympathy to you and your family. His *contributions* will never be forgotten, and I hope you will find solace in knowing his was a full and rewarding life. Sincerely yours, J. Edgar Hoover." Hoover's sympathetic and laudatory note was proclaimed from the pulpit during the funeral for all to hear and witness. In life and in death, the FBI made certain that everyone knew Elder Lightfoot Solomon Michaux was an anointed Bureau clergyman, an anti–civil rights crusader who enjoyed the approval and blessing of the almighty J. Edgar Hoover.[87]

EPILOGUE

Stained (Glass) Legacy

And just like that it was gone. In the spring of 1971, the J. Edgar Hoover stained glass window plaque disappeared like a thief in the night. The vanishing was very conspicuous, occurring days after the public revelation of the Bureau's sins. A group of eight white political activists—four Jews, three Protestants, and one Catholic—led in part by Temple University Religious Studies professor John Raines and his wife, Bonnie Raines, broke into the FBI resident agency in Media, Pennsylvania, and stole more than one thousand documents detailing the FBI's sins and illegal activities. The documents provided indisputable proof to what Americans knew all along: the Bureau was policing and shaping American religion and politics. Calling themselves the Citizens' Commission to Investigate the FBI, they sent the pilfered documents to Senator George McGovern (South Dakota) and Representative Parren Mitchell (Maryland) as well as three journalists: one from the *New York Times*, the *Los Angeles Times*, and the *Washington Post*, respectively. The congressmen and two journalists conceded to the federal government's demands to return the stolen government property. Betty Medsger at the *Washington Post* forged ahead. The former religion reporter's story revealed that the Bureau surveilled, harassed, and violated the civil rights of college students, professors, Black activist organizations, as well as white anti-war protesters. They were all FBI targets, not for crimes committed, but for their religious and political beliefs. Her story appeared on the front page of the *Washington Post* on March 24, 1971. Hoover's sacred plaque disappeared the next day.[1]

"Check and see if plaque has been stolen," an incredulous Hoover ordered his special agents. Surely news of the stolen tablet was mere rumor. Hoover's men immediately "made a discreet visit" to the church. The exterior plaque was indeed missing. The theft, the agents reported, "was not an easy job inasmuch as it had been initially placed with four large bolts." The new pastor of the church was the prime suspect. Reverend James Parker Archibald, they noted, was "quite liberal and has opened the church to moratorium marchers, civil rights groups, etc." The preacher welcomed the very groups the Bureau had harassed as enemies of the state. However, there was no evidence to connect the "liberal leaning" minister to the "crime." The sleuths warned that further investigation would prove difficult. There was no way to "diplomatically" use enhanced investigative practices without causing any more "publicity or embarrassment" to the Bureau. The agents were told to stand down. The case was closed.[2]

But all was not lost. The interior plaque was left intact, and it remains to this very day. The disappearance of the exterior plaque juxtaposed with the endurance of the interior plaque bears witness to Hoover's legacy in American religion and politics. From the outside, it appears Hoover's influence upon the FBI and white evangelicalism has been removed. However, Hoover's significance is clearly illuminated when history is told from the other side of J. Edgar Hoover's stained glass window. There it becomes clear: the FBI and white evangelicalism—hallmark entities in contemporary religion and politics—remain intertwined in the clutches of white Christian nationalism.[3]

Death

Following the *Washington Post*'s exposure of Hoover's sins, a public opinion poll revealed that the overwhelming majority of Americans continued to praise Hoover for doing a "first rate job of protecting the security of the United States." A month after Betty Medsger's revealing article, a national opinion poll revealed that the majority of Americans were still *not* convinced that the FBI spent "too much time spying on college students, politicians, and other civilians and too little time tracking down real criminals." Hoover enjoyed the most ardent support among a key demographic of grassroots evangelicals: working- and middle-class whites over the age of thirty in the Midwest and the South, who had obtained a high school diploma or less.[4] *Christianity Today* played a role in this. Editor Reverend Dr. Harold Lindsell was not fazed by the public disclosure of Hoover's career as the general of an immoral war against American citizens. The relentless pursuit of political power and recognition by white evangelicals fueled their ability and willingness to faithfully withstand, bless, or simply ignore hypocrisy. White evangelicals wanted a warrior priest, not a prom date for their teenagers. With no sense of irony, the editor of *CT* asked Hoover to address "the decline of morality" in American society for what would be the Boss's last *Christianity Today* article. Hoover and his team happily obliged. "A Morality for Violence" was a jeremiad on the rising moral justification for protests and lawlessness. The article appeared in the April 28, 1972, issue of *Christianity Today*. Hoover died four days later, leaving behind a witness and legacy for a morality of violence and extralegal politics in the name of white Christian nationalism.

James Crawford, Hoover's longtime African American driver, discovered the boss's body. On the morning of Tuesday May 2, 1972, Hoover was late to breakfast. The Boss was never late for anything. Concerned, Jimmy walked past the life-size oil painting and the bronze bust of Hoover that guarded the Boss's bedroom, and found the half-naked body lying lifeless on the floor. The man who was the heart of white Christian nationalism died of a heart attack.[5]

The funeral arrangements unfolded as expeditiously as Hoover lived his life. A small private viewing was held later that evening. The hair dye had been washed out of his hair and eyebrows, revealing the remains of a man who had aged and crumbled more considerably than most knew. It was the first of many blows that would wreck the façade Hoover spent his life erecting. The sight of his authentic grey hair and decaying body was too much for those who loved and idolized him. Helen Gandy ordered the casket closed. The next day, May 3, his body lay in state in the Capitol Rotunda. His $3,000 bronze coffin rested on the catafalque that was built to hold President Lincoln's casket. Only twenty-two men—all white elected statesmen and military officials—had received this honor. J. Edgar Hoover was the first civil servant to receive the honor. Chief Justice Warren Burger presided over the Rotunda service, reminding mourners that Hoover "was a man of high principle whose beliefs were based on Christian faith and he was steadfast in his beliefs throughout his entire life."[6]

More than twenty-five thousand admirers passed through the Rotunda to say goodbye, many waiting in the rain to pay their respects. President Nixon was not one of them. While he did see the death as a campaign opportunity, he elected to wait and hold court at the funeral, refusing to share the limelight with other public officials, men he dismissed as "those shit asses" on Capitol Hill. There were about five hundred anti-war protesters gathered outside the Capitol Building who also were not interested in mourning Hoover. Rumors swirled that they planned to desecrate Hoover's coffin. Nixon was not having it. No one had the right to disturb his attempt at being the nation's Comforter-in-Chief. He ordered a staged counterdemonstration, led by Roger Stone, the future Republican strategist and consigliere of President Trump. Assured of having God on their side, the young Stone and about twenty-five members of the College Republicans of DC protected the body and legacy of their fallen hero. Stone's crew assaulted the protesters with accusatory shouts of atheistic communism, followed by personal insults, culminating in fisticuffs. Stone, who would go on to be the founder of the white Christian nationalist organization "Stop the Steal," cut his political teeth, in part, by defending the resting place of white Christian nationalism in the nation's body politic.[7]

The funeral was held the next day, May 4, at Hoover's National Presbyterian Church. The location was finalized late in the game. The four thousand-seat National Cathedral was considered, but ultimately ruled out. The Bureau had long labeled the dean of the Cathedral, Reverend Sayre, "somewhat a liberal." Nixon was more candid in his veto, disqualifying Reverend Sayre as "a left-wing son of a bitch." Hoover's home church was deemed the place. More than 1,200 invited guests crammed into National Presbyterian Church, while all three national television stations beamed the live service into the nation's homes.[8]

President Nixon's eulogy was full of proper praise and platitudes. Nixon privately referred to Hoover as "that old cocksucker," but on this day, he had nothing but polite praise for the fallen hero. "Today is a day of sadness for the America people," he proclaimed. "America's pride has always been in its people . . . of great men and women in remarkable numbers, and once in a long while, of giants who stand head and shoulders above their countrymen, setting a high and noble standard for us all. J. Edgar Hoover was one of those giants." Nixon declared Hoover a standard-bearer, something white evangelicals knew all too well.[9] In his conclusion, the president accurately noted of Hoover, "In the Bible, the book which Edgar Hoover called his 'guide to daily life,' we find the words which best pronounce a benediction on his death. . . . 'Great peace have they which love thy law.' J. Edgar Hoover loved the law of *his* God."[10] It was the perfect description of Hoover's entire life: Hoover followed his God.

Next, Reverend Elson mounted the pulpit. After giving a final glance at Hoover's rented pew, he offered his pastoral tribute. He reflected on his pastoral visits to Hoover's home, reminding the nation of Hoover's call to the clergy. "There was a time in Mr. Hoover's young manhood when he struggled in the depth of his being over a call to enter the ministry of the church or to give his life to the legal profession," the faithful pastor noted. When Hoover chose the law, the church suffered the "loss of a clergyman," but the nation gained a saint. J. Edgar Hoover "believed that the moral law was given by God in the Ten Commandments and the Sermon on the Mount and that all other laws emanated from this premise. Thus," the pastor told America, "in serving the law," Hoover "was serving his God." He concluded the service with a prayer. "Almighty God . . . we thank thee for thy servant Edgar . . . Grant us a fresh dedication to honor Thee as he honored Thee." At the graveside, Special Agent Clyde Tolson received the flag that was draped over the faithful giant's coffin. No one was surprised.[11]

White evangelicals released statements, piling on the praise. *The Pentecostal Evangel* lauded Hoover's Christian witness. "Christians," the magazine decisively noted, "mourned" his passing.[12] *Christianity Today* extolled his "legendary stature." The magazine remained indifferent to

Hoover's revealed illegality and harassment of dissent. Taking the offensive, the magazine dismissed Hoover's critics as trafficking empty "partisan rhetoric." Instead, the editors exalted his decades of heroic service. "It seems difficult to believe that one man could serve in so high capacity, under both parties and in peace and war, for almost half a century, and harvest as little hostility as Hoover did." The editors acknowledged that although Hoover was "very reticent about making what evangelical Christians call a 'personal testimony,' he made no secret of his reverence for the Bible and his commitment to its precepts."[13] Hoover never admitted to being born again, a core principle for white evangelicals; but he was a white evangelical where it mattered most: his commitment to white Christian nationalism.

COINTELPRO

Everything changed when the COINTELPRO papers were released on December 6, 1973. Using documents pilfered by the Citizens' Commission to Investigate the FBI, NBC reporter Carl Stern made a FOIA request for all documents marked "COINTELPRO." More than twenty thousand documents were released. They detailed the full extent of the "FBI's covert action programs against American citizens," proving that COINTELPRO was not an anomaly, it was the Bureau's norm. Hoover took the law into his own hands for what he believed was "the greater good" of the nation. From 1956 to 1971 alone, the evangelical champion approved at least two thousand illegal direct actions targeting domestic civic organizations—clergy, students, advocates of civil rights, proponents of women's rights, and anti-war protestors were all subject to Hoover's evangelical wrath. The revelations led to the first congressional investigation into the nation's intelligence community and the permanent establishment of the Senate Select Committee on Intelligence.[14] The investigation showed that criticism of Hoover was not simply partisan rhetoric, as white evangelicals claimed throughout the years, but gospel truth. The FBI Boss, the once pious patriot, was transfigured into the nation's public enemy number one.

White evangelicals quickly distanced themselves from the villain, erasing their former icon from their history. Even the Chicago Bible Society removed J. Edgar Hoover and his 1956 award from their otherwise meticulous record of awardees. The historical and digital erasure seems necessary. Hoover became an embarrassment. Moreover, he was no longer useful. Anti-communism—a key to Hoover's appeal and power—was no longer the major issue motivating white evangelicals. New "existential" issues rallied white evangelicals—legalized abortion, the women's movement, school busing, and homosexuality. Such issues necessitated a new champion.

Legacy

Hoover was exorcised from white evangelical history; but not the soul of the movement. Hoover, and all that he represented, remain an enduring blueprint. He paved the way for white evangelical conservatism, authenticating it as the only religious and moral vision for a secure America. He eschewed the white Protestant nativism of his day, dismissing the prevalent distrust of Catholics. Instead, Hoover displayed how white Protestants and Catholics could work together as a force to save Christian America.[15] They remain a formidable coalition to this day.

White evangelicals embraced Hoover, and they held fast even as he failed to measure up to the professed theological and moral commitments of evangelical conservatism. A movement that was built upon theological and moral imperatives continues to willfully exchange it all for white Christian nationalist power.

Hoover was a political phenomenon, but he was not the cause of the phenomenon. He simply answered the call. Father Daniel Berrigan, SJ, the first priest on the FBI's Most Wanted List, told Hoover in a 1971 open letter, "One must admit that if you had not been available to the America of our century, American genius would have created someone like you." Someone who would garner the blessings of the church to lead crusades against all dissent and change, enabling the nation to be "a people of innocence, of conscience, of benevolence."[16] Hoover told white evangelicals they could be the people they longed to be: the new Israel, a white Christian nation. And they believed his every word.

Hoover was the first evangelical outsider to become the movement's political, theological, and moral champion; but he certainly was not the last. Once Hoover died, white evangelical ingenuity and the thirst for white power began looking for the next political hero, one who would pledge to lead them to the religious and political promised land of white Christian nationalism. Every generation turns to an ascendant white male politico of the era—Reagan, Trump, and so on—and, like John the Baptist, they ask, "Are you the one, or should we expect someone else?" Evangelical political ingenuity constantly searches and finds its political champion, by any means necessary. This pragmatic "ends justify the means" ethos is the very cunning creativity that led to the collaboration with J. Edgar Hoover and his FBI, and it remains a robust tradition within the movement. White evangelicals remain willing to compromise their stated morality and theology in exchange for the maintenance of whiteness and access to political power, all to bring America back to their God. As long as white evangelicals continue to ignore, forget, or refuse their history, they are doomed to repeat it.

———

The FBI has yet to learn this lesson. After Hoover's death, a few things changed: haircuts became longer, Hoover's weight program was relaxed, waistlines increased, and uniform standards loosened. But Hoover's white Christian nationalism lingers like a ghost. Two women joined the special agent ranks immediately after Hoover's death, but the trailblazers did not depart from Hoover's moral vision of white soldiers and ministers: Susan Roley Malone was a marine and Joanne Pierce Misko was a nun. It took the FBI four more years, and the appointment of forty more white women, to finally appoint Black women as special agents. SA Sylvia Elizabeth Mathis left the Bureau after three years, while SA Linda Berry endured the Bureau's gender bias and racism to carve out a decorated career of twenty-eight years, retiring in 2004. As of 2021, 37 percent of FBI special agents identify as women, but only 1 percent are Black women. As of 2022, the Bureau is facing two major crises involving gender discrimination. In 2019, seventeen women filed a class action lawsuit claiming systematic gender discrimination and sexual harassment. Two years later, the DOJ identified several senior bureau officials who avoided disciplinary actions after sexual misconduct charges were substantiated. The offenders were quietly transferred or allowed to retire with full benefits.[17] Patriarchy endures at the FBI.

The Bureau still remains overwhelmingly white, despite several lawsuits to right this wrong. In 1988, a federal judge ruled the FBI systematically discriminated against Latin@ special agents. Lead plaintiff Bernardo Perez testified that his complaints of discrimination led to retaliation and even demotion. The judge ruled that the Latin@ agents were refused promotions and raises, and were restricted to assignments derogatorily dubbed the "Taco Circuit." Three years later, Black agents, comprising 12 percent of special agents, also sued the FBI for systemic discrimination. The agents' attorney protested, "This goes all the way back to J. Edgar Hoover." A judge agreed, citing "statistical evidence of discrimination," ordering the FBI to institute a new personnel system, one guided by merit and fairness, not race. Nevertheless, the Bureau remained committed to whiteness. Black agents returned to court in 1998, winning again. The 2001 settlement required the FBI to pay the Black agents' legal fees, damages, and lost wages. The court also issued an unprecedented order: the FBI was required to bring in an outside mediator to assess discrimination complaints. But there was one caveat. The FBI director was given the authority to overrule the mediator's decisions. Since then, African Americans continue to apply to the FBI, but the percentage of Black special agents continues to decline: from 12% at the time of the lawsuit to just 4% in 2021.[18] Whiteness continues to reign at the FBI.

Efforts to address this trend continue to be short-circuited, in part, by white Christian nationalism within the ranks. White special agents across the country responded to the FBI's targeted recruitment of Black special agents by attempting to corral a class action lawsuit against the President Obama DOJ for discrimination. As the FBI held diversity recruitment events at historically Black colleges and universities

(HBCUs), a critical mass of white special agents demanded redress, proposing a national White History Month.[19]

All of this emanates from the Bureau's religious culture. The spiritual retreats and worship services have continued, albeit with a few changes. On advice from DOJ general counsel, the religious practices are no longer supported by federal appropriations. Funding now comes from employee donations. The respectable white evangelical ministers from established denominations have been replaced by the luminaries of televangelism and fundamentalism. Televangelist Pat Robertson was the featured preacher on two occasions in the 1980s, while clergy from Westboro Baptist Church—an anti-gay fundamentalist group—participated in the Bureau's training of new special agents in the early 2000s.[20]

The FBI continues to maintain relationships with highly visible Black evangelicals. In 2018, the Reverend Dr. Antipas Harris, president and dean of the TD Jakes Divinity School and associate pastor of the Texas megachurch The Potter's House, received the FBI Director's Community Leadership Award. Like Elder Michaux, the Bureau praised Reverend Harris for his commitment "to racial unity . . . and serving as a liaison between law enforcement and minority faith communities."[21]

Efforts to fill the Bureau with evangelicals continue. Special Agent Gwendolyn Hubbard, chief of the FBI Personnel Resources Unit, was clear about the mission. As the FBI's chief of recruitment during the early 2000s, she believed she had "a mandate . . . from God . . . to hire God-fearing people into the FBI because the demonic forces of evil could not be overcome with merely a badge and a gun. The FBI need[s] God-fearing people." Similar to Hoover, she believed working for the FBI was "a special calling." Special agents were "chosen by God" to "protect the nation."[22]

Building on the NAE Federal Seminars, today the FBI attends and formally recruits at evangelical and Pentecostal schools, churches, and large interracial conferences. International gatherings such as Reverend TD Jakes's "Man Power" and "Woman Thou Art Loose" have been favorites of the FBI's National Recruitment Team (NRT). The FBI has hosted a booth at both annual conferences where the more than ten thousand attendees can learn how to become a special agent. FBI SAs have even been allowed to address these gatherings from pulpits and stages, testifying to their experiences as evangelicals defending the soul of the nation. One well-known evangelist, documented as "Evangelist Paula" (likely Paula White, who would go on to become President Trump's spiritual advisor and prominent advocate of Christian nationalism), prayed for the NRT. During one 2007 event, she told them God was going to "open many doors" for the NRT because their recruitment efforts were not just about the FBI, "but had everything to do with the building up of God's Kingdom."[23] For many evangelicals, the FBI remains a vital tool in taking America back for God.

This force of white evangelical special agents remains the federal clearinghouse for "good" religion and politics and "bad" religion and politics, adjudicating and investigating the political commitments and activities of American citizens. The FBI is hypervigilant toward faith communities of color, while overlooking white Christian nationalist groups, despite the rise in white Christian nationalist violence. "There is no question," retired FBI SA Michael German admitted amidst the investigation of the January 6 insurrection, "the FBI and federal prosecutors have treated white supremacist and far-right violence far more leniently than Muslims they accuse of supporting terrorism." The former domestic extremist investigator noted that even nonviolent protestors opposing racism and police violence are treated more harshly than the perpetrators of violence in the name of white Christian nationalism. The Bureau maintains almost constant surveillance of American Muslims under the guise of preventing Muslim terrorist attacks, while such attacks have drastically decreased since 9/11. Closely related, the FBI Counterterrorism Division created a label for Black nationalist religious groups: "Black Identity Extremists." These groups, the Bureau argues, are prone to terrorist violence in response to "perceived racism and injustice." There is little evidence to support this claim. Yet, there is an abundance of evidence pointing to a significant increase in white Christian nationalist terrorism. White supremacists and other far-right extremists have killed far more people since 9/11 than any other category of domestic extremist. Since 2014, far-right violent attacks have increased 250 percent. This bloodshed has occured in houses of worship, schools, universities, and now on the steps and within the nation's Capitol. In 2020, the US Department of Homeland Security labeled white supremacist extremism the "most persistent and lethal threat" to domestic security. Yet, the Bureau has been slow to catch up to the threat because we have no national strategy to combat it. Such efforts are consistently blocked by white evangelicals on Capitol Hill. The US intelligence community has even received pleas for help from white pastors attempting to stop white supremacists from recruiting in their congregations. Their faith in the Bureau has largely proven misplaced.[24]

The Bureau struggles to identify and prevent white Christian nationalist terrorism, in part because white Christian nationalism has a home within the FBI. More diverse recruitment will help stem the tide of white Christian nationalism within the FBI, but as the decades and discrimination lawsuits have shown, it will not cure all that ails the Bureau. The FBI must look into the mirror of history and see itself clearly. This act of self-recognition can open the door to effective policy changes in FBI training. Since white supremacist extremism is the most pressing threat to our democracy, the first step to fixing the Bureau is obvious: a national strategy to root out federal law enforcement agents who have ties to white supremacist groups. A second step is an effective mandatory training course for special agents that names the FBI's religious and racial practices for what they have been, exposing the Bureau's past religious and racial sins, not as anomalies but as FBI norms. Then the Bureau must require religious studies courses for its domestic security corps to equip special agents to engage our ecumenical, diverse believing and non-believing nation. Such courses will constitute an effort toward rectifying the Bureau's own religious culture. Then and only then will the Bureau have a fighting chance to exorcise their own demons, the very demons that occupy so much of our religion and politics.

It will not be an easy fight. All of the FBI's activities emanate from an FBIHQ that remains anointed in Hoover's name. When the new $126.1 million FBIHQ was erected in 1975, Reverend Elson consecrated the edifice in Hoover's spirit as the J. Edgar Hoover Building. In his dedication, Hoover's pastor told the gathered throng that Hoover's faith had made him "a human instrument, finely tuned to public order and national security." He continued, "We are not likely soon to see his equal—a man precisely designed by his Creator for his job in his time." This unmatched "spirituality," he preached, "was projected into the FBI."[25] Truer words about the Bureau have never been spoken, for the spirit of J. Edgar Hoover remains in our FBI.

This spiritual monument rests on Pennsylvania Avenue, just a few blocks away from Hoover's stained glass window. The avenue, known as America's political thoroughfare, still bears witness to what lies at the heart of contemporary white evangelical religion and politics: the gospel of J. Edgar Hoover.

Acknowledgments

I could not have completed this book without the generous support of several fellowships and grants. Fellowships from the American Council of Learned Societies (ACLS) and the National Endowment for the Humanities (NEH) provided much needed time for research and drafting. A book grant from the Louisville Institute enabled me to make significant progress. The Institute for Citizens and Scholars (formerly The Woodrow Wilson National Fellowship Foundation), the Wabash Center for Teaching and Learning in Theology and Religion, and the Center for Humanities at Washington University in Saint Louis (WashU) supported visits to archives on both sides of the Atlantic. Finally, the support of the John C. Danforth Center on Religion and Politics at WashU helped me to acquire paper and digitized copies of thousands of FBI files I obtained under the Freedom of Information Act (FOIA). And finally, a sincere thanks to the retired FBI agents who shared their stories with me. I remain in awe of your integrity and service. The thousands of words contained in this book fall far short of expressing my sincere gratitude to all of you for your support, and your belief in me and this project. From the bottom of my heart, thank you.

Notes

Prologue: Suing the FBI

1. Statement by President Johnson Upon Signing Public Law 89-487, The Bill Revising Public Information Provisions of the Administrative Procedure Act, on July 4, 1966, https://www.justice.gov/oip/attorney-generals-memorandum-public-information-section-administrative-procedure-act, accessed August 8, 2021.

2. Tuan Samahon, "Fifty Years of FOIA in Operation, 1967–2017," *Villanova Law Review* 3, no. 5 (2018), 855–865. See, for example, Attorney General William P. Barr Delivers the 19th Annual Barbara K. Olson Memorial Lecture at the Federalist Society's 2019 National Lawyers Convention, Washington, DC, November 15, 2019, the US DOJ, https://www.justice.gov/opa/speech/attorney-general-william-p-barr-delivers-19th-annual-barbara-k-olson-memorial-lecture, accessed April 12, 2022.

3. Email, AUSA Molen to Tuan Samahon, July 29, 2021.

4. Settlement Agreement, *Martin v. United States Department of Justice, 2018,* Case Number 18-1885, October 26, 2021; Emma North-Best, "FBI's High Visibility Memoranda Document FOIA's Greatest Hits," *Muckrock*, June 27, 2018, https://www.muckrock.com/news/archives/2018/jun/27/FBI-high-visibility-memoranda/, accessed April 10, 2022.

Introduction: J. Edgar Hoover's Stained Glass Window

1. Capitol Hill Methodist Church Worship Bulletin June 26, 1966, in possession of author, emphasis in original. A special thank you to Capitol Hill United Methodist Church for providing me with a copy of the original worship bulletin; "The J. Edgar Hoover Window—Statesmanship Through the Christian Virtues," pamphlet in J. Edgar Hoover Personal Estate Collection, National Law Enforcement Museum, Washington, DC. See also Bureau File 94-55180-A; *Washington Post*, June 18, 1966, E11; June 25, 1966, E9; April 22, 2005, B06; *Washington Evening Star*, Sunday Magazine, November 6, 1966, 10. On economic cost, see Samuel H. Williamson, "Seven Ways to Compute the Relative Value of a U.S. Dollar Amount, 1774 to Present," *Measuring Worth*, 2015, www.measuringworth.com/uscompare/.

2. "The J. Edgar Hoover Window—Statesmanship Through the Christian Virtues"; Letterhead Memo, DeLoach to Tolson, "Rev. Edward B. Lewis, Capitol Hill Methodist Church, Washington, D.C.," January 11, 1966, Bureau File 94-55180-5; personal note, Hoover to Lewis, June 1, 1966, Bureau File 94-55180-6; *Washington Evening Star*, May 28, 1966, A10; Reverend

Lewis obituary, *Washington Post*, Friday, April 22, 2005, B06. On Elson, see *Washington Post and Times Herald*, July 4, 1959, B7.

3. Capitol Hill Methodist Church Worship Bulletin June 26, 1966.

4. Ibid.; Bureau File 94-55180-A; *Washington Evening Star*, Sunday Magazine, November 6, 1966, 10.

5. There are pioneering social histories of evangelical conservatism, racism, and Christian nationalism. A sample includes Robert T. Handy, *A Christian America: Protestant Hopes and Historical Realities* (New York: Oxford University Press, 1971); Leo P. Ribuffo, *The Old Christian Right: The Protestant Far Right from the Great Depression to the Cold War* (Philadelphia: Temple University Press, 1983); Mark A. Noll, Nathan O. Hatch, and George M. Marsden, *The Search for Christian America*, Expanded ed. (Colorado Springs, CO: Helmers & Howard, 1989); William C. Martin, *With God on Our Side: The Rise of the Religious Right in America*, 1st ed. (New York: Broadway Books, 1996); Anne C. Loveland, *American Evangelicals and the U.S. Military, 1942–1993* (Baton Rouge and London: Louisiana State University Press, 1996); Joel A. Carpenter, *Revive Us Again: The Reawakening of American Fundamentalism* (New York: Oxford University Press, 1997); Lisa McGirr, *Suburban Warriors: The Origins of the New American Right* (Princeton, NJ: Princeton University Press, 2002); Matthew Avery Sutton, *Aimee Semple McPherson and the Resurrection of Christian America* (Cambridge, MA: Harvard University Press, 2007); Mark A. Noll, *God and Race in American Politics: A Short History* (Princeton, NJ: Princeton University Press, 2008); Steven P. Miller, *Billy Graham and the Rise of the Republican South* (Philadelphia: University of Pennsylvania Press, 2009); Kim Phillips-Fein, *Invisible Hands: The Making of the Conservative Movement from the New Deal to Reagan*, 1st ed. (New York: W.W. Norton, 2009); Andrew S. Finstuen, *Original Sin and Everyday Protestants: The Theology of Reinhold Niebuhr, Billy Graham, and Paul Tillich in an Age of Anxiety*, 1st ed. (Chapel Hill: University of North Carolina Press, 2009); Darren Dochuk, *From Bible Belt to Sunbelt: Plain-Folk Religion, Grassroots Politics, and the Rise of Evangelical Conservatism*, 1st ed. (New York: W.W. Norton, 2011); Jonathan P. Herzog, *The Spiritual-Industrial Complex: America's Religious Battle against Communism in the Early Cold War* (New York: Oxford University Press, 2011); Daniel K. Williams, *God's Own Party: The Making of the Christian Right*, reprint ed. (New York; Oxford: Oxford University Press, 2012); Carolyn Renée Dupont, *Mississippi Praying: Southern White Evangelicals and the Civil Rights Movement, 1945–1975* (New York: New York University Press, 2013); Matthew Avery Sutton, *American Apocalypse: A History of Modern Evangelicalism* (Cambridge, MA: Belknap Press, 2014); Grant Wacker, *America's Pastor: Billy Graham and the Shaping of a Nation* (Cambridge, MA: Belknap Press, 2014); Kevin M. Kruse, *One Nation Under God: How Corporate America Invented Christian America* (New York: Basic Books, 2015); Sarah Ruth Hammond, *God's Businessmen: Entrepreneurial Evangelicals in Depression and War*, ed. Darren Dochuk (Chicago and London: University of Chicago Press, 2017); R. Marie Griffith, *Moral Combat: How Sex Divided American Christians and Fractured American Politics* (New York: Basic Books, 2017); Kathleen Belew, *Bring the War Home: The White Power Movement and Paramilitary America* (Cambridge, MA: Harvard University Press, 2018); John Fea, *Believe Me: The Evangelical Road to Donald Trump* (Grand Rapids, MI: William B. Eerdmans, 2018); Darren Dochuk, *Anointed with Oil: How Christianity and Crude Made Modern America* (New York: Basic Books, 2019); Kristin Kobes Du Mez, *Jesus and John Wayne: How White Evangelicals Corrupted a Faith*

and Fractured a Nation (New York: Liveright Publishing, 2020); Andrew L. Whitehead and Samuel L. Perry, *Taking America Back for God: Christian Nationalism in the United States* (New York: Oxford University Press, 2020); Randy Balmer, *Bad Faith: Race and the Rise of the Religious Right* (Grand Rapids, MI: William B. Eerdmans, 2021); John S. Huntington, *Far-Right Vanguard: The Radical Roots of Modern Conservatism* (Philadelphia: University of Pennsylvania Press, 2021); Jesse Curtis, *The Myth of Colorblind Christians: Evangelicals and White Supremacy in the Civil Rights Era* (New York; London: New York University Press, 2021); Anthea Butler, *White Evangelical Racism: The Politics of Morality in America* (Chapel Hill: University of North Carolina Press, 2021).

6. See David Bebbington, *Evangelicalism in Modern Britain: A History from the 1730s to the 1980s* (London: Routledge, 1989); "What Is an Evangelical," National Association of Evangelicals, https://www.nae.net/what-is-an-evangelical/, accessed July 16, 2021. One of the welcomed exceptions to this trend is Kobes Du Mez, *Jesus and John Wayne.*

7. On practice and Protestant religious identity, see Laurie F. Maffly-Kipp, Leigh Eric Schmidt, and Mark R. Valeri, *Practicing Protestants: Histories of Christian Life in America, 1630–1965 (Lived Religions)* (Baltimore, MD: Johns Hopkins University Press, 2006); on defining white evangelicalism and Christian nationalism, see Kobes Du Mez, *Jesus and John Wayne,* 5–7; Whitehead and Perry, *Taking America Back for God,* ix–21.

8. Letter, Reverend Carl Henry to Hoover, December 18, 1962, 94-51060-138.

9. On Hoover's early days of policing sexuality, gender, and race, see, for example, Theodore Kornweibel Jr., *Seeing Red: Federal Campaigns against Black Militancy, 1919–1925* (Bloomington: Indiana University Press, 1999); Jessica R. Pliley, *Policing Sexuality: The Mann Act and the Making of the FBI* (Cambridge, MA; London: Harvard University Press, 2014); Douglas M. Charles, *Hoover's War on Gays: Exposing the FBI's "Sex Deviates" Program* (Lawrence: University Press of Kansas, 2015). On conservative intellectual history, see George H. Nash, *The Conservative Intellectual Movement in America Since 1945* (New York: Basic Books, 1976); George F. Will, *Statecraft as Soulcraft: What Government Does* (New York: Simon & Schuster, 1983); Darren Dochuk, *From Bible Belt to Sunbelt: Plain-Folk Religion, Grassroots Politics, and the Rise of Evangelical Conservatism,* 1st ed. (New York: W.W. Norton, 2011); Nash, "The Conservative Intellectual Movement in America: Then and Now," *National Review,* April 26, 2016, https://www.nationalreview.com/2016/04/conservative-intellectuals-george-nash/, accessed December 20, 2021; Aaron Griffith, "Policing Is a Profession of the Heart: Evangelicalism and Modern American Policing," *Religions,* March 16, 2021; Hoover, "The Faith to Be Free," NBC Radio Network, December 7, 1961, reprinted in *Human Events,* February 24, 1962; see also Thomas C. Leonard, *Illiberal Reformers: Race, Eugenics & American Economics in the Progressive Era* (Princeton, NJ and Oxford: Princeton University Press, 2016).

10. *Washington Post,* June 26, 1949, B1; see, for example, Athan G. Theoharis and John Stuart Cox, *The Boss: J. Edgar Hoover and the Great American Inquisition* (Philadelphia: Temple University Press, 1988), 15.

11. On continuity in US political history, see Brent Cebul, Lily Geismer, and Mason B. Williams, eds., *Shaped by the State: Toward a New Political History of the 20th Century* (Chicago and London: University of Chicago Press, 2019); for an overview on religion, Cold War, and security, see William Inboden, *Religion and American Foreign Policy, 1945–1960: The Soul of*

Containment (Cambridge: Cambridge University Press, 2008). For a look at the CIA and its deployment of faith and clergy, see Matthew Avery Sutton, *Double Crossed: The Missionaries Who Spied for the United States During the Second World War* (New York: Basic Books, 2019); Michael Graziano, *Errand into the Wilderness of Mirrors: Religion and the History of the CIA* (Chicago: University of Chicago Press, 2021).

12. Hoover, "A Christmas Message," *The Investigator*, Christmas 1961, emphasis mine. *Men of the F.B.I.–Episode 9 1941*, *March of Time*, vol. 7, March of Time (HBO, 1941), https://video .alexanderstreet.com/watch/men-of-the-f-b-i-1941, accessed October 9, 2021.

13. Billy Graham, "A Christian America," *American Mercury*, March 1955; Whitehead and Perry, *Taking America Back for God*, 10.

14. Scholars are disrupting this narrative. See, for example, Kobes Du Mez, *Jesus and John Wayne*; Butler, *White Evangelical Racism*.

Chapter 1. Hoover's Faith

1. Unpublished notes, Reverend Elson, "J. Edgar Hoover," August 12, 1965, 94-39821-157 enclosure.

2. *The New Yorker*, "The Director, Part 2," October 2, 1937; James Phelan, "Hoover of the FBI," *Saturday Evening Post*, September 25, 1965, 28; Robert W. Lynn and Elliott Wright, *The Big Little School: Two Hundred Years of the Sunday School*, 2nd ed., rev. and enlarged (Birmingham, AL: Religious Education Press, 1980), 15; Richard Gid Powers, *Secrecy and Power: The Life of J. Edgar Hoover*, 1st ed. (New York: London: Free Press, 1987), 6, 16, 20, 28.

3. Hoover, "The American Ideal," *Vital Speeches of the Day*, March 15, 1957, 327–328; Hoover, "What American Means to Me," *This Week Magazine*, June 30, 1957.

4. Hoover, "Why I Go to Church," pamphlet, *Tidings: Materials for Christian Evangelism* (Nashville, TN, 1960).

5. Hoover, quoted in Hoover, "A Good Christian Is a Good Citizen," *The Lookout Magazine*, August 12, 1951, 5; *Congressional Record*, 97 Congress, House of Representatives, August 20, 1951, A5268; Hoover, "The American Ideal," *Vital Speeches of the Day*, March 15, 1957, 327–328; Hoover, "What American Means to Me," *This Week Magazine*, June 30, 1957; Hoover, "Why I Go to Church"; Hoover, *The Pentecostal Evangel*, June 27, 1965, 10–11. On Christian nationalism, see Andrew L. Whitehead and Samuel L. Perry, *Taking America Back for God: Christian Nationalism in the United States* (New York: Oxford University Press, 2020), ix–xi, 10; Kristin Kobes Du Mez, *Jesus and John Wayne: How White Evangelicals Corrupted a Faith and Fractured a Nation* (New York: Liveright Publishing, 2020), 11; Abram Van Engen, "Resident Aliens, a Response to Os Guinness," *Patheos*, August 20, 2020, https://www.patheos.com/blogs/anxiousbench/2020/08 /dangerous-christian-nationalism-a-conversation-between-abram-van-engen-and-os-guinness/, accessed August 29, 2020.

6. Whitehead and Perry, *Taking America Back for God*, ix–xi; Kobes Du Mez, *Jesus and John Wayne*, 11; Abram Van Engen, "Resident Aliens, a Response to Os Guinness," *Patheos*, August 20, 2020, https://www.patheos.com/blogs/anxiousbench/2020/08/dangerous-christian-nationalism -a-conversation-between-abram-van-engen-and-os-guinness/, accessed August 29, 2020.

7. Gid Powers, *Secrecy and Power*, 33; *Decision*, July 1971, 4.

8. *The New Yorker*, "The Director, Part 1," September 25, 1937; *The New Yorker*, "The Director, Part 2," October 2, 1937; Gid Powers, *Secrecy and Power*, 5–13; Richard Hack, *Puppetmaster: The Secret Life of J. Edgar Hoover* (Beverly Hills, CA: Phoenix Books, 2007), 29, 31, 43; Curt Gentry, *J. Edgar Hoover: The Man and the Secrets* (New York: W. W. Norton, 2001), 63.

9. Hoover's mother was also the granddaughter of John Hitz, the Swiss consul to the United States, the ranking Swiss diplomat in the United States. Later, her uncle replaced John Hitz, becoming the Swiss consul general. *The New Yorker*, "The Director, Part 1," September 25, 1937; *The New Yorker*, "The Director, Part 2," October 2, 1937.

10. Hoover, *The Pentecostal Evangel*, August 23, 1970, 24–25; Reverend Elson, "J. Edgar Hoover—Churchman," *Presbyterian Life*, November 27, 1948, 4–5; Gid Powers, *Secrecy and Power*, 5–13; Hack, *Puppetmaster*, 29, 31, 43; see Hoover, "J. Edgar Hoover's Last Farewell," *Family Weekly*, July 16, 1972; Gentry, *J. Edgar Hoover: The Man and the Secrets*, 63.

11. Hoover, "J. Edgar Hoover's Last Farewell."

12. Sydney E. Ahlstrom, ed., *Theology in America: The Major Protestant Voices from Puritanism to Neo-Orthodoxy* (Indianapolis; New York: Bobbs-Merrill Company, 1967), 317–318. On Christian nurture and evangelicalism, see also George M. Marsden, *Understanding Fundamentalism and Evangelicalism* (Grand Rapids, MI: W.B. Eerdmans, 1991), 34–35.

13. *Decision*, July 1971, 4.

14. Hoover, "J. Edgar Hoover's Last Farewell"; Hoover, *The Pentecostal Evangel*, 24–25; Gid Powers, *Secrecy and Power*, 5–10; Gentry, *J. Edgar Hoover: The Man and the Secrets*, 63; Hack, *Puppetmaster*, 32–33.

15. Letter, Hoover to Mrs. Viva C. Coleman, July 18, 1957, 100-HQ-413026-18; Hoover, "Crime and Sunday School," *Sunday School Times*, February 7, 1948.

16. *New York Times*, September 23, 1964, 40; see also *The Pentecostal Evangel*, October 4, 1970, 10–11.

17. Gid Powers, *Secrecy and Power*, 22–23, 33.

18. Hoover, *The Pentecostal Evangel*, August 23, 1970, 24–25, 22–23.

19. *Washington Herald*, June 17, 1913, 12; Hester O'Neil, "J. Edgar Hoover's School Days (Part 4)," *American Boy and Open Road* 36, no. 7 (September 1954): 8, 22–24; *The New Yorker*, "The Director, Part 2," October 2, 1937; Gid Powers, *Secrecy and Power*, 25–27, 498 n.56; Hack, *Puppetmaster*, 39–40, 46; Hoover, "J. Edgar Hoover's Last Farewell"; Hester O'Neil, "J. Edgar Hoover's School Days (Part 3)," *American Boy and Open Road* 36, no. 6 (July 1954): 8, 34–35.

20. Hoover, Personal Diary, Monday, September 27, 1909; Eugene L. Mayer, "Central High Gave Up Its Building Not Its Spirit," *Washington Post*, May 4, 2018; Hoover, "J. Edgar Hoover's Last Farewell"; O'Neil, "J. Edgar Hoover's School Days (Part 4)"; *The New Yorker*, "The Director, Part 2," October 2, 1937; Gid Powers, *Secrecy and Power*, 25–32; Hack, *Puppetmaster*, 39–41, 46.

21. *Washington Evening Star*, October 6, 1912, 7; *Washington Herald*, March 2, 1913, 11; O'Neil, "J. Edgar Hoover's School Days (Part 4)"; Gid Powers, *Secrecy and Power*, 29–30; Gentry, *J. Edgar Hoover: The Man and the Secrets*, 65.

22. *Washington Evening Star*, Oct. 6, 1912, 7; *Washington Herald*, March 2, 1913, 11; Hester O'Neil, "J. Edgar Hoover's School Days (Part 4)"; Gid Powers, *Secrecy and Power*, 29–30; Gentry, *J. Edgar Hoover: The Man and the Secrets*, 65.

23. Hoover, Personal Diary, Monday, September 27, 1909; Mayer, "Central High Gave Up Its Building Not Its Spirit"; Hoover, "J. Edgar Hoover's Last Farewell"; O'Neil, "J. Edgar Hoover's School Days (Part 4)"; *The New Yorker,* "The Director, Part 2," October 2, 1937; Gid Powers, *Secrecy and Power,* 25–32; Hack, *Puppetmaster,* 39–41, 46.

24. Hoover, "Why I Go to Church"; *The Pentecostal Evangel,* June 27, 1965, Digital Archive, Flower Pentecostal Heritage Center, Springfield, MO.

25. Hoover spent the remainder of his life at the church and its successor congregations. In 1947, the congregation was crowned the denomination's representative church and renamed the National Presbyterian Church. Booklet, *The National Presbyterian Church: The First 200 Years,* The Ervin N. Chapman Memorial Archives, The William Smith Culbertson Memorial Library, The National Presbyterian Church, Washington, DC; Gid Powers, *Secrecy and Power,* 15; Hack, *Puppetmaster,* 40.

26. *Washington Evening Star,* June 12, 1905, 3. Around 1907, Hoover followed his older brother Dick and joined the Church of the Reformation, the Lutheran congregation where Dick was married. See Hoover, Personal Diary, December 27, 1908; January 3, 1909; April 18, 1909, Folder: Hoover Original Dairy 1908, in J. Edgar Hoover Personal Estate Collection, National Law Enforcement Museum, Washington, DC; John S. Hart, *The Sunday-School Idea: An Exposition of the Principles Which Underlie the Sunday-School Cause, Setting Forth Its Objects, Organization, Methods, and Capabilities* (Philadelphia: J.C. Carrigues & Co., 1871), 41; *Decision,* July 1971, 4; Gentry, *J. Edgar Hoover: The Man and the Secrets,* 64.

27. Hoover, Personal Diary, December 27, 1908; January 3, 1909; April 18, 1909; Sunday, September 11, 1910, Folder: Hoover Original Dairy 1908, 1909, 1910, in J. Edgar Hoover Personal Estate Collection, National Law Enforcement Museum, Washington, DC; *First Presbyterian Church Registry,* October 17, 1909–March 10, 1912; Booklet, *The National Presbyterian Church: The First 200 Years,* both in the Ervin N. Chapman Memorial Archives, The William Smith Culbertson Memorial Library, The National Presbyterian Church, Washington, DC.

28. Hoover, "J. Edgar Hoover's Last Farewell"; *The New Yorker,* "The Director, Part 2," October 2, 1937; Booklet, *The National Presbyterian Church: The First 200 Years;* Gid Powers, *Secrecy and Power,* 15; Hack, *Puppetmaster,* 31.

29. Hart, *The Sunday-School Idea,* 127, 211–229.

30. Hoover, "What the Sunday School Has Done for Me," *Salt Lake Tribune,* November 8, 1942, 16; Hoover, "Crime and the Sunday School," *Sunday School Times,* February 7, 1948; Gid Powers, *Secrecy and Power,* 16.

31. Hoover, "Why I Believe in the Sunday School," *Baptist Leader,* September 1940, 6–7; Hart, *The Sunday-School Idea,* 14–17, 24–25, 44; Reverend Elson, "J. Edgar Hoover—Churchman," *Presbyterian Life,* November 27, 1948, 4–5; *The New Yorker,* "The Director, Part 2," October 2, 1937.

32. Hoover, "Why I Believe in the Sunday School," 6–7; Hoover's Diary, Sunday, August, 29, 30, 1910; Hart, *The Sunday-School Idea,* 14–17, 24–25, 44; Reverend Elson, "J. Edgar Hoover—Churchman," 4–5; Gid Powers, *Secrecy and Powers,* 16–20.

33. Hart, *The Sunday-School Idea,* 14–17, 138, 147, 167.

34. Lynn and Wright, *The Big Little School,* 93, 101–102, 109, 111, 114; Gid Powers, *Secrecy and Power,* 19.

35. Hoover Diary, August 29–30, 1910, J. Edgar Hoover Personal Estate Collection, National Law Enforcement Museum, Washington, DC; Edwin Wilbur Rice and James McConaughy, *Handbook on the Origin and History of the International Uniform Sunday-School Lessons from 1825 on and 1872–1924: With List of Lessons, 1872–1924, Arranged in Order of Their Sequence in the Bible, with the Date When Each Lesson Was Studied, and List of Lesson Committees, 1872–1922* (Philadelphia: American Sunday-School Union, 1922), 102; Martha Tarbell, *Tarbell's Teachers' Guide to the International Sunday-School Lessons for 1910* (New York: Fleming H. Revell Company, 1909), 338–345; Reverend David S. Warner and Reverend William B. Olmstead, eds., *Arnold's Practical Sabbath School Commentary on the International Lessons, 1910* (Philadelphia: American Baptist Publication Society, 1909), 160–163.

36. Hoover Diary, Sunday September 18, 1910.

37. Tarbell, *Tarbell's Teachers' Guide*, 359; Warner and Olmstead, eds., *Arnold's Practical Sabbath School Commentary on the International Lessons, 1910*, 170–171; Rice and McConaughy, *Handbook on the Origin and History of the International Uniform Sunday-School Lessons from 1825 on and 1872–1924*, 102.

38. Letter, Hoover to Mel Larson, December 15, 1952, 94-33052-55; Hack, *Puppetmaster*, 47–49; Gid Powers, *Secrecy and Power*, 41–42; Gentry, *J. Edgar Hoover: The Man and the Secrets*, 67–69.

39. *The New Yorker*, "The Director, Part 2," October 2, 1937; Gentry, *J. Edgar Hoover: The Man and the Secrets*, 69; Gid Powers, *Secrecy and Power*, 53–55.

40. Hoover quoted in Elson, "J. Edgar Hoover—Churchman," 4–5.

41. Gentry, *J. Edgar Hoover: The Man and the Secrets*, 69; Gid Powers, *Secrecy and Power*, 53–55.

42. *The New Yorker*, "The Director, Part 2," October 2, 1937; Hack, *Puppetmaster*, 51–74.

43. Mohr quoted in Ovid Demaris, *The Director: An Oral Biography of J. Edgar Hoover*, 1st ed. (New York: Harper's Magazine Press, 1975), 167; Hack, *Puppetmaster*, 101–103.

44. Elson, "J. Edgar Hoover—Churchman," 4–5; Reverend Elson, "The J. Edgar Hoover You Ought to Know, By His Pastor," *The Chaplain* 7, no. 5 (September–October 1950), 19–23; Unpublished notes, Reverend Elson, "J. Edgar Hoover," August 12, 1965, 94-39821-157 enclosure.

45. Elson, "J. Edgar Hoover—Churchman"; Elson, "The J. Edgar Hoover You Ought to Know, By His Pastor," 19–23; Letterhead memo, SA Jones to SA Bishop, May 11, 1971, 94-39821-illegible; Unpublished notes, Reverend Elson, "J. Edgar Hoover," August 12, 1965, 94-39821-157 enclosure; James Phelan, "Hoover of the FBI," *Saturday Evening Post*, September 25, 1965, 23–33; Gentry, *J. Edgar Hoover: The Man and the Secrets*, 66.

Part 1. Proselytizing Faith: The Religious Foundations of Hoover's FBI

1. Jack Anderson, "J. Edgar Hoover and His Alumni," *Parade*, June 20, 1971, 4–7; *Washington Post*, April 15, 1951, 22. M. Reverend Collier served in the Bureau from 1935 to 1951.

2. J. Edgar Hoover, *FBI Law Enforcement Bulletin* 6, no. 12 (December 1937), 1, emphasis mine. The pledge was reprinted in the *FBI Law Enforcement Bulletin* periodically until the 1950s.

3. J. Edgar Hoover, *FBI Law Enforcement Bulletin*; Reverend Elson quoted in Myron Jones, "The Nation's Watchdog—On Guard for America," *The Northern Light*, September 1971, 8–9;

Reverend Elson, "J. Edgar Hoover's FBI," NBC Radio Show *Second Sunday*, May 9, 1971, quoted in Letterhead Memo, SA Jones to SA Bishop, May 11, 1971, 94-39821-unserialized; "Retired Special Agent William Arthur Murtaugh FBI Interview," Transcript, May 7, 1980, 2, Jack Willis Collection, Library Department of Special Collections, Washington University in Saint Louis. On the early days of the Bureau and racist hiring practices, see Rhodri Jeffreys-Jones, *The F.B.I.: A History* (New Haven, CT; London: Yale University Press, 2007); Sarah Imhoff, "Hoover's Judeo-Christians: Jews, Religion, and Communism in the Cold War," in Sylvester A. Johnson and Steven Weitzman, eds., *The FBI and Religion: Faith and National Security before and after 9/11* (Berkeley: University of California Press, 2017). Following WWII, the ranks of special agent included a few Jewish men.

4. Report, Detective Inspector H. A. Leslie to Chief Inspector, Metropolitan Police Criminal Investigation Department, New Scotland Yard, September 20, 1938. Records of the Metropolitan Police Office, Office of the Commissioner: Correspondence and Papers, MEPO 2/2505, The National Archives of the United Kingdom (TNA) Kew, Richmond, England.

5. *The Manresan* 8, no. 5 (May 1943), 2, Special Collections, Woodstock Theological Library, Georgetown University, caps in original.

Chapter 2. Soldiers

1. G. Gordon Liddy quote found in his autobiography, *Will*, New York: St. Martin's Press, 1980, 173. League of Laymen's Retreats, Baltimore Section *Silver Jubilee 1938 Souvenir Program*, 32–41 in FBI File 94-1-9758; "Welcome to Manresa on Severn," undated promotional pamphlet, Box 8 Archives of the Maryland Province of the Society of Jesus, Georgetown University Special Collections; Richard H. Schmidt, *God Seekers: Twenty Centuries of Christian Spiritualities* (Grand Rapids, MI: W. B. Eerdmans, 2008), 159–160; William J. O'Malley, Joseph F. Downey, and James Martin SJ, *The Fifth Week*, 2nd ed. (Chicago: Loyola Press, 1998), 8; James Martin, SJ, *The Jesuit Guide to (Almost) Everything: A Spirituality for Real Life* (New York: Harper Collins, 2012), 1–2; League of Laymen's Retreats, Baltimore Section *Silver Jubilee 1938 Souvenir Program*, 23; Albert R. Jonsen and Stephen Toulmin, *The Abuse of Casuistry* (Berkeley: University of California Press, 1988), 147.

2. Hoover, "Law Enforcement as a Career," *The Tomahawk* (Worcester, MA: Holy Cross College), February 26, 1947, 4.

3. *The Manresan* 8, no. 5 (May 1943), 3; July 1943, 1–2, Special Collections, Woodstock Theological Library, Georgetown University.

4. On Protestant admiration of Roman Catholic figures, explorations, and evangelization, see Katherine D. Moran, *The Imperial Church: Catholic Founding Fathers and America's Civilizing Empire* (Ithaca, NY: Cornell University Press, 2020).

5. John T. McGreevy, *American Jesuits and the World: How an Embattled Religious Order Made Modern Catholicism Global* (Princeton, NJ: Princeton University Press, 2016), 13–18; John T. McGreevy, *Catholicism and American Freedom: A History*, 1st ed. (New York: W. W. Norton, 2003), 192–215; Donald F. Crosby, SJ, *God, Church, and Flag: Senator Joseph R. McCarthy and the Catholic Church, 1950–1957* (Chapel Hill: University of North Carolina Press, 1978), 3–25.

6. See Father Lloyd obituary in *Washington Post, Times Herald*, September 23, 1960, B9; *Washington Post, Times Herald*, "FBI Donated Plaque Honors Father Lloyd," April 24, 1965, B3;

The Manresan, May 1938, 2; February 1940, 2; May 1949, 4; October 1950, 2, Special Collections, Woodstock Theological Library, Georgetown University. FBI Memo, Hoover to Mr. Joseph, July 23, 1936, 94-4-3263-X2; Letterhead Memo, Special Agent MW Acers to Special Agent Nichols, July 26, 1939, 94-4-3263-2; Letter J. Edgar Hoover to Reverend Edward B. Rooney, SJ, July 3, 1950, 94-43263-142.

7. See Father Lloyd obituary in *Washington Post, Times Herald*, September 23, 1960, B9; *Washington Post, Times Herald*, "FBI Donated Plaque Honors Father Lloyd," April 24, 1965, B3; *The Manresan*, May 1938, 2; May 1949, 4; October 1950, 2, Special Collections Woodstock Theological Library, Georgetown University. FBI Memo, Hoover to Mr. Joseph, July 23, 1936, 94-4-3263-X2; Letter, Father Lloyd to Hoover, July 7, 1936, 94-4-3263-X; Letter, Father Lloyd to Tolson, July 14, 1936, 94-4-3263-XI; Letter, Reverend Lloyd, SJ to Hoover, June 14, 1939, 94-1-9758-13; enclosure 94-1-9758-83x1; Letter, Lloyd to Hoover, July 27, 1939, 94-4-3263-3; Letter, Alice Lloyd McVey to Hoover, August 20, 1939, 94-4-3263-no serial; Letter, Special Agent L. B. Nichols to Special Agent Tolson, June 29, 1950, 94-4-3263-141; Letterhead Memo, Special Agent MW Acers to Special Agent Nichols, July 26, 1939, 94-4-3263-2; Letter, Lloyd to Hoover, September 1, 1947, 94-4-3263-95.

8. See Father Lloyd obituary in *Washington Post, Times Herald*, September 23, 1960, B9; *Washington Post, Times Herald*, "FBI Donated Plaque Honors Father Lloyd," April 24, 1965, B3; *The Manresan*, May 1938, 2; February, 1940, 2; May 1949, 4; October 1950, 2, Special Collections, Woodstock Theological Library, Georgetown University. FBI Memo, Hoover to Mr. Joseph, July 23, 1936, 94-4-3263-X2; Letter, Father Lloyd to Hoover, July 7, 1936, 94-4-3263-X; Letter, Father Lloyd to Tolson, July 14, 1936, 94-4-3263-XI; Letter, Reverend Lloyd, SJ to Hoover, June 14, 1939, 94-1-9758-13; enclosure 94-1-9758-83x1; Letter, Lloyd to Hoover, July 27, 1939, 94-4-3263-3; Letter, Alice Lloyd McVey to Hoover, August 20, 1939, 94-4-3263-no serial; Letterhead Memo, Special Agent MW Acers to Special Agent Nichols, July 26, 1939, 94-4-3263-2; Letter, Lloyd to Hoover, September 1, 1947, 94-4-3263-95; Letter, J. Edgar Hoover to Reverend Edward B. Rooney, SJ, July 3, 1950, 94-43263-142. On Lloyd's addresses, see *The Manresan*, November 1936; August 1943.

9. Letter, Father Lloyd to Hoover, July 7, 1936, 94-4-3263-X; Letter, Father Lloyd to Tolson, July 14, 1936, 94-4-3263-XI; Western Union Telegram, Lloyd to Hoover, October 7, 1937, 94-4-3263-X5; Letter, Reverend Lloyd, SJ to Hoover, June 14, 1939, 94-1-9758-13; enclosure 94-1-9758-83x1; Letter, Lloyd to Hoover, July 27, 1939, 94-4-3263-3; Letter, Lloyd to Hoover, September 1, 1947, 94-4-3263-95; Letter, Hoover to Lloyd, August 24, 1940, 94-4-3263-14; Letter, Lloyd to Hoover, October 9, 1940, 94-4-3263-16; Letter, Hoover to Lloyd, January 16, 1941, 94-4-3263-17. See, for example, Personal and Confidential Letter, Director FBI to SAC St. Louis, May 25, 1948, 94-4-3263-106; Letter, Hoover to Lloyd, June 25, 1948, 94-4-3263-108; Letter, Lloyd to Hoover, August 4, 1948, 94-4-3263-110; Letterhead Memo, Special Agent N. P. Callahan to Special Agent Tolson, September 20, 1950, 94-4-3263-157-enclosure.

10. Letter, Father Lloyd to Hoover, July 7, 1936, 94-4-3263-X; Letter, Father Lloyd to Tolson, July 14, 1936, 94-4-3263-XI; Western Union Telegram, Lloyd to Hoover, October 7, 1937, 94-4-3263-X5; Letter, Reverend Lloyd, SJ to Hoover, June 14, 1939, 94-1-9758-13; enclosure 94-1-9758-83x1; Letter, Lloyd to Hoover, July 27, 1939, 94-4-3263-3; Letter, Lloyd to Hoover, September 1, 1947, 94-4-3263-95; Letter, Hoover to Lloyd, August 24, 1940, 94-4-3263-14; Letter, Lloyd to Hoover, October 9, 1940, 94-4-3263-16; Letter, Hoover to Lloyd, January 16, 1941, 94-4-3263-17.

See, for example, Personal and Confidential Letter, Director FBI to SAC St. Louis, May 25, 1948, 94-4-3263-106; Letter, Hoover to Lloyd, June 25, 1948, 94-4-3263-108; Letter, Lloyd to Hoover, August 4, 1948, 94-4-3263-110; Letterhead Memo, Special Agent N. P. Callahan to Special Agent Tolson, September 20, 1950, 94-4-3263-157-enclosure.

11. Letter, Reverend Lloyd, SJ to Hoover, June 14, 1939, 94-1-9758-13; enclosure 94-1-9758-83x1. See also Letter, Lloyd to Hoover, September 1, 1947, 94-4-3263-95; Handwritten Letter, Hoover to Reverend Lloyd, SJ, March 2, 1938, and Letterhead Personal Memo, Hoover to Father Lloyd, July 26, 1956, Stephen F. McNamee, SJ papers, Georgetown University Special Collections.

12. *The Catholic Review* (Baltimore, MD), "Manresans Hear Appeals to Guard United States from Its Internal Foes," January 27, 1939, 1; *Washington Post*, January 24, 1939, 15. In the summer of 1939, Washington, DC, was separated from the Archdiocese of Baltimore to form the new Archdiocese of Washington, DC. Curley remained the Archbishop of both until his death in 1947.

13. *The Catholic Review* (Baltimore, MD), January 27, 1939, 1–2; *Washington Post*, January 24, 1939, 15; *The Manresan*, January 1939, 1–2, enclosed in Bureau File 94-1-9758; Letter, Hoover to William J. Neale, January 19, 1939, 94-1-9758-2; Hoover's handwritten note on FBI Memo, Special Agent Tolson to Hoover, January 25, 1939, 94-1-9758-6; Letter, Hoover to Mr. Vincent Fitzpatrick, January 28, 1939, 94-1-9758-7XI. The event program is an enclosure in Bureau File 94-1-9758; *Washington Post*, "Archbishop Urges Ideals of Manresa," January 16, 1940, 15. Monetary calculations from Lawrence H. Officer and Samuel H. Williamson, "Measures of Worth," *MeasuringWorth*, 2019, www.measuringworth.com/worthmeasures.php.

14. *The Catholic Review* (Baltimore, MD), January 27, 1939, 1–2; *Washington Post*, January 24, 1939, 15; *The Manresan*, January 1939, 1–2, enclosed in Bureau File 94-1-9758; Letter, Hoover to William J. Neale, January 19, 1939, 94-1-9758-2; Hoover's handwritten note on FBI Memo, Special Agent Tolson to Hoover, January 25, 1939, 94-1-9758-6; Letter, Hoover to Mr. Vincent Fitzpatrick, January 28, 1939, 94-1-9758-7XI. The event program is an enclosure in Bureau File 94-1-9758.

15. *The Catholic Review* (Baltimore, MD), January 27, 1939, 1–2; *Washington Post*, January 24, 1939, 15; *The Manresan*, January 1939, 1–2, enclosed in Bureau File 94-1-9758; Letter, Hoover to William J. Neale, January 19, 1939, 94-1-9758-2; Hoover's handwritten note on FBI Memo, Special Agent Tolson to Hoover, January 25, 1939, 94-1-9758-6; Letter, Hoover to Mr. Vincent Fitzpatrick, January 28, 1939, 94-1-9758-7XI. The event program is an enclosure in Bureau File 94-1-9758.

16. *The Catholic Review* (Baltimore, MD), January 27, 1939, 1–2; *Washington Post*, January 24, 1939, 15; *The Manresan*, January, 1939, 1. The event program is an enclosure in Bureau File 94-1-9758.

17. *The Catholic Review* (Baltimore, MD), "Manresans Hear Appeals to Guard United States from Its Internal Foes," January 27, 1939, 1; *The Manresan*, January, 1939, 2.

18. *The Catholic Review* (Baltimore, MD), "Manresans Hear Appeals to Guard United States from Its Internal Foes," January 27, 1939, 1; *The Manresan*, January, 1939, 2.

19. *The Catholic Review* (Baltimore, MD), January 27, 1939, 1–2; *The Manresan*, January 1939, 2; *The Churchman*, "Hoover Presents Award to Jesuit, 'Our Chaplain,'" November 1, 1950,

Stephen F. McNamee, SJ papers, Georgetown University Special Collections; *The Jesuit Bulletin* (Chicago), "Jesuit World Front," January 1951, unpaginated back page. See also enclosure 94-1-9758-83x1.

20. Hoover "gave the necessary permission" for the retreats. See Letter, Father Lloyd to Hoover, March 24, 1958, 94-4-3263-215; Father Lloyd, SJ, was the spiritual director at Manresa until 1951, when he "suffered a stroke and partial paralysis." He died in September 1960. See Letterhead Memo, Special Agent M. A. Jones to Special Agent Mr. DeLoach, June 1, 1964, 94-1-9759-82x. Bureau files state that retreats exclusively for FBI employees began in 1941. See enclosure 94-1-9758-83x1 and Letter, Father Lloyd to Hoover, June 16, 1942, 94-4-3263-no serial.

21. See, for example, Letterhead Office Memo, Special Agent J. J. McGuire to Special Agent Mr. Tolson, May 14, 1945, 94-1-9758-illegible; on FBI retreat captains and sign-up sheet, see 94-1-9758-28 enclosure; on Special Agent Branigan, see his obituary in the *Washington Post*, "FBI Intelligence Agent William A. Branigan Dies," November 9, 1993; on Special Agent Wacks, see *Notre Dame Alumnus* 35, no. 2 (February–March 1957), 43; Special Agent Bellino and Lee, see *The Manresan*, 9, no. 5 (May 1944), 2; no. 7 (July 1944), 1; and *New York Times*, March 1, 1990, 26. Also see Lee's FBI personal file, available at https://archive.org/details/foia_Lee_Robert _E.-1/mode/2up, accessed February 1, 2020.

22. See *The Investigator*, 1932–1972. See also Athan G. Theoharis, *The FBI: A Comprehensive Reference Guide* (New York: Checkmark Books, 2000), 230; Paul Letersky and Gordon Dillow, *The Director: My Years Assisting J. Edgar Hoover* (New York; London: Scribner, 2021), 66–73.

23. Letter, J. Edgar Hoover to Mr. W. A. Dennick, Greyhound Terminal, Washington, DC, May 17, 1945, 94-1-9758-14X2; Official Memo, Special Agent J. J. McGuire to Special Agent Mr. Tolson, May 14, 1945, 94-1-9758-illegible; Letterhead Memo, Special Agent C. D. DeLoach to Special Agent Mohr, May 16, 1960, 94-1-9758-68. Greyhound only charged the Bureau "regular-roundtrip, [even though] the bus going out of its way," as "Chartering such [illegible] would have involved an unusual financial burden." See Memorandum, Special Agent F. T. Mc-Intyre to Special Agent E. A. Tamm, April 22, 1947, 94-9758-15.

24. Letterhead Office Memo, Special Agent J. J. McGuire to Special Agent Mr. Tolson, May 14, 1945, 94-1-9758-illegible; "Manresa: The Layman's House of Retreats, Manresa Station Annapolis, MD," undated pamphlet, Box 107, Folder 559A-559B, Archives of the Maryland Province of the Society of Jesus, Georgetown University Special Collections.

25. Ignatius, *The Spiritual Exercises of Saint Ignatius: A Translation and Commentary*, trans. George E. Ganns, SJ (Chicago: Loyola University Press, 1992), 21; Michael Ivens, *Understanding the Spiritual Exercises: Text and Commentary: A Handbook for Retreat Directors* (Leominster, Herefordshire: Gracewing, 1998), 1–2; Ignatius of Loyola and George E. Ganss, SJ, *Ignatius of Loyola: The Spiritual Exercises and Selected Works* (New York: Paulist Press, 1991), 11; McGreevy, *American Jesuits and the World*, 14; A New Fortress in the Struggle for the Minds of Men, no date, 94-1-9758-58 enclosure.

26. Ignatius, *The Spiritual Exercises of Saint Ignatius*, 28–29; Ivens, *Understanding the Spiritual Exercises*, 21; *Washington Post*, "Manresa-on-Severn Contemplates 25 Years as Jesuit Retreat," August 12, 1951, 16; Vincent J. Hart, S J, "The Baltimore League for Laymen's Retreats," Woodstock College (Woodstock, MD), Woodstock Letters, Vol. 57, 1928, 190–192, Jesuit Archives

Digital Collections and Resources, accessed July 4, 2019, https://jesuitarchives.omeka.net /items/show/878; *The Catholic Review*, "Manresa," April 30, 1986, Section B, 1, Archives of the Maryland Province of the Society of Jesus, Box 8, Georgetown University Special Collections; *The Manresan*, 2 no. 9 (September 1937), 1–2; Vol. 8, no. 5, May 1943, 3; May 1949, 2, Special Collections, Woodstock Theological Library, Georgetown University; *Washington Post*, May, 1, 1944; Archdiocese of Baltimore, "League of Laymen's Retreats: Golden Jubilee, 1915–1964," 47–50. Holy Bible, Matthew 3:3, New International Version.

27. Picture of Manresa Sign in Archives of the Maryland Province Archives Addenda Box 13, Folder: Buildings/Grounds, Georgetown University Special Collections.

28. Letter, Hoover to Father Lloyd, November 16, 1938, 94-1-9758-1; *The Manresan*, July 1951, 2 in Bureau File 94-1-9758; *The Manresan*, August, 1951, 3; *Washington Post*, "Manresa-on-Severn Contemplates 25 years as Jesuit Retreat," August 12, 1951, 16; *Washington Evening Star*, "Manresa Retreat House to Mark Anniversary," August 11, 1951. Extensive growth of the retreat movement in the area resulted in overcrowding at Manresa. Therefore, a new retreat house, Loyola Retreat House in Faulkner, Maryland, on the Potomac, was built to serve the Archdiocese of Washington, DC, and Richmond, VA, in 1958. FBI special agents from headquarters began making their annual retreats to Loyola in 1959. Agents were "very active in assisting in the fund campaign" to build Loyola, with the 1958 group of Bureau retreatants "pledg[ing] a considerable sum." See Office Memo, Deleted to Special Agent A. Rosen, January 12, 1959, 94-1-9758-58 and enclosures; Informal Memo, Special Agent G. A. Nease to Special Agent Tolson, January 16, 1959, 94-1-9758-59.

29. Vincent J. Hart, SJ, "The Baltimore League for Laymen's Retreats"; *The Catholic Review*, "Manresa," April 30, 1986, Section B, 1, Archives of the Maryland Province of the Society of Jesus, Box 8, Georgetown University Special Collections; *The Manresan*.2, no. 9 (September 1937), 1–2; Vol. 8, no. 5, May 1943, 3; May 1949, 2, Special Collections, Woodstock Theological Library, Georgetown University; *Washington Post*, May, 1, 1944; Archdiocese of Baltimore, "League of Laymen's Retreats: Golden Jubilee, 1915–1964," 47–50.

30. Vincent J. Hart, SJ, "The Baltimore League for Laymen's Retreats"; *The Catholic Review*, "Manresa," April 30, 1986, Section B, 1, Archives of the Maryland Province of the Society of Jesus, Box 8, Georgetown University Special Collections; *The Manresan*, 2 no. 9 (September 1937), 1–2; Vol. 8, no. 5, May 1943, 3; May 1949, 2, Special Collections, Woodstock Theological Library, Georgetown University; *Washington Post*, May, 1, 1944; *Washington Evening Star*, "Manresa Retreat House to Mark Anniversary," August 11, 1951; Archdiocese of Baltimore, "League of Laymen's Retreats: Golden Jubilee, 1915–1964," 47–50.

31. Vincent J. Hart, SJ, "The Baltimore League for Laymen's Retreats"; *The Catholic Review*, "Manresa," April 30, 1986, Section B, 1, Archives of the Maryland Province of the Society of Jesus, Box 8, Georgetown University Special Collections; *The Manresan* 2, no. 9 (September 1937), 1–2; Vol. 8, no. 5, May 1943, 3; May 1949, 2, Special Collections, Woodstock Theological Library, Georgetown University; *Washington Post*, May, 1, 1944; *Washington Evening Star*, "Manresa Retreat House to Mark Anniversary," August 11, 1951; Letter, Reverend Lloyd to Director J. Edgar Hoover, June 28, 1945, 94-4-3263-59x; Archdiocese of Baltimore, "League of Laymen's Retreats: Golden Jubilee, 1915–1964," 47–50.

32. Letter, Hoover to Lloyd, July 1, 1941, 94-4-3263; Letter, Lloyd to Hoover, July 10, 1941, 94-4-3263-22; Letter, Father Lloyd to Mr. Peter Wacks, Department of Justice, May 10, 1943,

94-1-9758-14X; *The Manresan* 8, no. 5 (May 1943), 1; July 1950, 2, Special Collections, Woodstock Theological Library, Georgetown University; Letter, Father Lloyd to Hoover, June 30, 1950, 94-4-3263-143; see also Letter, Hoover to Father Brew, March 25, 1958, 94-1-9758-57; Letterhead Memo, SA Lentz to Father Lloyd, July 14, 1950 and Letter, Archbishop of Baltimore to Father Lloyd, August 2, 1950; Father Stephen F. McNamee, SJ papers, Georgetown University Special Collections. The Catholic press praised the event while one man wrote to Reverend Lloyd requesting help in getting hired into the FBI. For example, see *The New York Catholic News*, August 5, 1950; *National Catholic Welfare Conference News Service* byline Washington, July 28; *National Catholic Welfare Conference News Service* (Domestic), August 2, 1950, 7; *Sunday Examiner* (Hong Kong), September 22, 1950; Letterhead Memo, Special Agent Nichols to Special Agent Tolson, August 11, 1950, 94-4-3263-155.

33. Letter, Father Lloyd to Mr. Peter Wacks, Department of Justice, May 10, 1943, 94-1-9758-14X; *The Manresan* 8, no. 5 (May 1943), 1; July 1950, 2, Special Collections, Woodstock Theological Library Georgetown University; "The Holy Sacrifice of the Mass Offered for Your Intentions," 94-1-9758-21 enclosure.

34. Letter, Father Lloyd to Mr. Peter Wacks, Department of Justice, May 10, 1943, 94-1-9758-14X; Letter, Father Lloyd to Hoover, July 5, 1943, 94-1-9758-14X1; *The Manresan 8*, no. 5 (July 1943), 1–2, Special Collections, Woodstock Theological Library, Georgetown University; Steven Rosswurm, *The F.B.I. and the Catholic Church, 1935–1962* (Amherst: University of Massachusetts Press, 2010), 97–107; Turner Publishing Company Staff, *Society of Former Special Agents of the FBI, Inc.* (Nashville, TN: Turner Publishing, 1996), 117.

35. League of Laymen's Retreats, Baltimore Section *Silver Jubilee 1938 Souvenir Program*, 32–41; *Washington Post, Times Herald*, September 23, 1960, B9; *The Manresan* 8, no. 5. (May 1943), 2, Special Collections, Woodstock Theological Library, Georgetown University. The retreat schedule was often reprinted in the *Manresan*, displaying the number of Bureau retreats; see, for example, *The Manresan*, February 1950, 3. On numbers see, for example, *The Manresan*, October 1950, 2; Letter, Father Lloyd to J. Edgar Hoover, July 5, 1943, 94-1-9758-14X1; Letterhead Office Memo, Special Agent J. J. McGuire to Special Agent Mr. Tolson, May 14, 1945, 94-1-9758-illegible; Father Lloyd to Hoover, May 13, 1946, 94-1-9758-14X5. See also Letterhead Office Memo, Redacted to Special Agent Mr. Tracy, April 11, 1949, 94-1-9758-17; Letterhead Office Memo, Special Agent D. M. Ladd to The Director, March 28, 1950, 94-1-9758-20.

36. Ignatius, *The Spiritual Exercises of Saint Ignatius*, [15], 25.

37. *The Manresan* 1, no. 3 (March 1936), 1, Special Collections, Woodstock Theological Library at Georgetown University.

38. The metaphor of transfiguration is used several times to describe a retreat at Manresa. The first time is in the inaugural edition of *The Manresan*, January 1936, 1. See also the retreat notes of FBI retreat master. Father M. V. Jarreau, SJ, Retreat Notes, no date, Box M. V. Jarreau, Folder: Martin Jarreau Retreat Notes, New Orleans Manuscript Collection, Jesuit Archives and Research Center, St. Louis, Missouri, July 2, 2019; *Manresa on Severn: The Archdiocesan Retreat House Under the Direction of the Jesuit Fathers*, undated pamphlet, Box 107, Folder 559A–559B, Archives of the Maryland Province of the Society of Jesus, Georgetown University Special Collections; "Welcome to Manresa on Severn," undated promotional pamphlet, Box 8 Archives of the Maryland Province of the Society of Jesus, Georgetown University Special Collections.

39. *The Manresan* 1, no. 3 (March 1936), 1–2; vol. 8, no. 5 (May 1943), 2, 4; November 1943, 4; July 1951, 4, Special Collections, Woodstock Theological Library at Georgetown University; *Washington Post*, "Manresa-on-Severn Contemplates 25 Years as Jesuit Retreat," August 12, 1951, 16.

40. Letter, James A. Martin, SJ, to Mr. J. Edgar Hoover, March 22, 1963, 94-1-9758-79; Letter, James A. Martin, SJ, to the Honorable J. Edgar Hoover, March 16, 1959, 94-1-9758-62; Letter, James A. Martin, SJ to Mr. J. Edgar Hoover, March 19, 1962, 94-1-9758-77; Letter, Father Lloyd to J. Edgar Hoover, July 5, 1943, 94-1-9758-14X1; Father Lloyd to Hoover, May 13, 1946, 94-1-9758-14X5.

41. *The Manresan* 1, no. 3 (March 1936), 1–2; vol. 8, no. 5 (May 1943), 2, 4; November 1943, 4; July 1951, 4, Special Collections, Woodstock Theological Library at Georgetown University; *Washington Post*, "Manresa-on-Severn Contemplates 25 Years as Jesuit Retreat," August 12, 1951, 16; Archdiocese of Baltimore, "League of Laymen's Retreats: Golden Jubilee, 1915–1964," 47–50.

42. *The Manresan* 1, no. 3 (March 1936), 1–2; vol. 8, no. 5 (May 1943), 2, 4; November 1943, 4; July 1951, 4, Special Collections, Woodstock Theological Library at Georgetown University; Letterhead Memo, Hoover to Father Lloyd, October 31, 1950, Stephen F. McNamee, SJ papers, Georgetown University Special Collections; *Washington Post*, "Manresa-on-Severn Contemplates 25 Years as Jesuit Retreat," August 12, 1951, 16.

43. Ignatius, *The Spiritual Exercises of Saint Ignatius*, [4], 22, 27–28; Ivens, *Understanding the Spiritual Exercises*, 5–6; Schmidt, *God Seekers*, 160–161; Philip Endean, "The Spiritual Exercises," in Thomas Worcester, ed., *The Cambridge Companion to the Jesuits* (Cambridge; New York: Cambridge University Press, 2008), 58–59. The exercises were a factor in the Counter-Reformation, the Catholic Reaction to the Protestant Reformation aimed at Catholic renewal and revival. See League of Laymen's Retreats, Baltimore Section *Silver Jubilee 1938 Souvenir Program*, 21 in FBI File 94-1-9758; on FBI leave, see Letterhead Office Memo, Special Agent L. B. Nichols to Assistant Director Special Agent Tolson, April 6, 1951, 94-1-9758-23.

44. Letter, Hoover to Reverend Robert S. Lloyd, July 13, 1943, 94-1-9758-14X1.

45. Ignatius, *The Spiritual Exercises of Saint Ignatius*, [4, 21], 22, 31; Ivens, *Understanding the Spiritual Exercises*, 2, 5; Schmidt, *God Seekers*, 160–161; Endean, "The Spiritual Exercises," 58–59; *Washington Post*, June 19, 1939, 1; *Washington Post*, "Manresa-on-Severn Contemplates 25 Years as Jesuit Retreat," August 12, 1951, 16; Father M. V. Jarreau, SJ, Retreat Notes, 15, Personal Sin, 3, Box M. V. Jarreau, Folder: Martin Jarreau Retreat Notes, New Orleans Manuscript Collection, Jesuit Archives and Research Center, St. Louis, Missouri, July 2, 2019.

46. Letter, Rev. Dennis J. Comey, SJ, to Mr. Hoover, May 31, 1945, 94-1-9458-14X4; Letterhead Office Memo, Special Agent J. J. McGuire to Special Agent Tolson, May 14, 1945, 94-1-9458-illegible; Letterhead Memo, SAC, Philadelphia to Director, FBI, May 26, 1955, 94-4628-43.

47. Letterhead Memo, Redacted to Special Agent Casper, May 9, 1966, 94-1-9458-106.

48. Letter, Hoover to Father Lloyd, SJ, April 23, 1947, 94-1-9458-15.

49. *Georgetown University presents J. Edgar Hoover with honorary law degree. Washington, D.C., June 5, 1939*, Harris and Ewing Collection, Prints and Photographs Division, Library of Congress, Washington, DC. Photo available at https://www.loc.gov/item/2016875750/.

50. Letterhead Memo, Redacted to Special Agent W. C. Sullivan, March 18, 1964, 94-9758-81.

51. Letterhead Memo, Special Agent W. A. Branigan to Special Agent Sullivan, March 23, 1965, 94-1-9758-88; on Special Branigan, see his obituary in the *Washington Post*, "FBI Intelligence Agent William A. Branigan Dies," November 9, 1993.

52. Letterhead Memo, Redacted to Special Agent W. A. Branigan, March 20, 1962, 94-1-9758-74; Letter, Father S. R. Pitts, SJ, to Mr. J. Edgar Hoover, March 25, 1962, 94-1-9758-78.

53. Father M. V. Jarreau, SJ, Retreat Notes Box M. V. Jarreau, Folder: Martin Jarreau Retreat Notes and Obituary, no date, Martin V. Jarreau Open File, New Orleans Manuscript Collection, Jesuit Archives and Research Center, St. Louis, Missouri; Letterhead Memo, Redacted to Special Agent Mr. Rosen, March 14, 1960, 94-1-9758-67.

54. James Martin, SJ, *The Jesuit Guide to (Almost) Everything: A Spirituality for Real Life* (New York: Harper Collins, 2012), 5–9; Schmidt, *God Seekers*, 161. On reformed tradition and work see, Barry Hankins, *Woodrow Wilson: Ruling Elder, Spiritual President*, 1st ed. (New York: Oxford University Press, 2016), 11.

55. Martin, SJ, *The Jesuit Guide to (Almost) Everything*, 5–9; Schmidt, *God Seekers*, 161.

56. See, for example, Hankins, *Woodrow Wilson*, 11; J. Edgar Hoover, *FBI Law Enforcement Bulletin* 6, no. 12 (December 1937), 1.

57. Letter, James A. Martin, SJ, to Mr. J. Edgar Hoover, March 17, 1960, 94-1-9758-66.

58. Ivens, *Understanding the Spiritual Exercises*, [172], 133. Martin, SJ, *The Jesuit Guide to (Almost) Everything*, 10; Schmidt, *God Seekers*, 161; Ignatius, *The Spiritual Exercises of Saint Ignatius*, [179], 77.

59. Letterhead Memo, Redacted to Special Agent Casper, January 24, 1967, 94-1-9758-110; Letterhead Memo, Special Agent M. A. Jones to Special Agent Mr. Bishop, January 19, 1971, 94-1-9758-125.

60. Letterhead Memo, Special Agent C. F. Downing to Special Agent Mr. Conrad, August 19, 1969, 94-4-6389-not recorded; Rosswurm, *The F.B.I and the Catholic Church, 1935–1962*, 82.

61. Letterhead Memo, Special Agent C. F. Downing to Special Agent Mr. Conrad, August 19, 1969, 94-4-6389-not recorded. On the relationship between Hoover and Sheen, see Sheen's FBI File, 94-4-6389, and on Fulton Sheen, see Thomas C. Reeves, *America's Bishop: The Life and Times of Fulton J. Sheen* (San Francisco, CA: Encounter Books, 2001).

62. Letterhead Memo, Special Agent C. F. Downing to Special Agent Mr. Conrad, August 19, 1969, 94-4-6389-not recorded; Letterhead Memo, Redacted to Special Agent Mr. Conrad, January 13, 1970, 94-1-9758-122; Sheen declined, Doctor's orders. See Special Agent J. P. Dunphy to Special Agent Callahan, January 21, 1970, 94-46287-113. On the June Mail program covering Elijah Muhammad, see 105-24822 June Mail.

63. Ignatius, *The Spiritual Exercises of Saint Ignatius*, [4], 22; Ivens, *Understanding the Spiritual Exercises*, 132; Schmidt, *God Seekers*, 160–161; Endean, "The Spiritual Exercises," 58–59; *Washington Post*, "Manresa-on-Severn Contemplates 25 Years as Jesuit Retreat," August 12, 1951, 16; *The Manresan* 1, no. 3, March 1936, 1–2; vol. 8, no. 5, May 1943, 2, 4, Special Collections, Woodstock Theological Library at Georgetown University; "Welcome to Manresa on Severn," undated promotional pamphlet, Box 8 Archives of the Maryland Province of the Society of Jesus Georgetown University Special Collections.

64. Martin, SJ, *The Jesuit Guide to (Almost) Everything*, 5–9; Schmidt, *God Seekers*, 161.

65. Endean, "The Spiritual Exercises," 64; Martin, SJ, *The Jesuit Guide to (Almost) Everything*, 8; Jonsen and Toulmin, *The Abuse of Casuistry*, 147; Schmidt, *God Seekers*, 160–161, emphasis in original.

66. Ignatius, *The Spiritual Exercises of Saint Ignatius*, [16, 175–188], 26, 76–79; Ivens, *Understanding the Spiritual Exercises*, 15–16, [135–145].

67. Ignatius, *The Spiritual Exercises of Saint Ignatius*, [16, 175–188], 26, 76–79; Ivens, *Understanding the Spiritual Exercises*, 15–16, [135–145]; Jonsen and Toulmin, *The Abuse of Casuistry*, 146–151, 304–332.

68. Transcript, "Interview of Honorable J. Edgar Hoover, Director of the Federal Bureau of Investigation, by Rep. Kenneth B. Keating, Sunday, July 22, 1956," Kenneth Barnard Keating Papers, A.K25, Rare Books, Special Collections, and Preservation, River Campus Libraries, University of Rochester. The transcript of the conversation does not include Hoover's "Moses" comment. Hoover ad-libbed "Moses" in the live interview at 10:40-11:15 of the video; see https://digitalcollections.lib.rochester.edu/ur/interview-honorable-j-edgar-hoover-director -federal-bureau-investigation-rep-kenneth-b-keating, accessed July 21, 2021.

69. "Retired Special Agent William Arthur Murtaugh FBI Interview, May 7, 1980," Transcript, n.d., 2–3, Jack Willis Collection, Library Department of Special Collections, Washington University in Saint Louis; Paul Letersky and Gordon Dillow, *The Director: My Years Assisting J. Edgar Hoover* (New York; London: Scribner, 2021), 121–122; Liddy, *Will*, 58–59.

70. Ivens, *Understanding the Spiritual Exercises*, 148–149.

71. Letter, Father Lloyd to Hoover, April 11, 1949, 94-1-9758-18, caps in original.

72. Father M. V. Jarreau, SJ, Retreat Notes, Last Summer 3, Box M. V. Jarreau, Folder: Martin Jarreau Retreat Notes, New Orleans Manuscript Collection, Jesuit Archives and Research Center, St. Louis, Missouri, July 2, 2019.

73. Father M. V. Jarreau, SJ, Retreat Notes, Last Summer 3, Box M. V. Jarreau, Folder: Martin Jarreau Retreat Notes, New Orleans Manuscript Collection, Jesuit Archives and Research Center, St. Louis, Missouri, July 2, 2019.

74. Letter, Father Lloyd to Hoover, April 11, 1949, 94-1-9758-18; Letter, Hoover to Father Brew, SJ January 10, 1957, 94-1-9758-50; Letter, Hoover to Lloyd, March 10, 1955, 94-4-3263-202.

75. Ivens, *Understanding the Spiritual Exercises*, 162–163.

76. Letterhead Office Memo, Special Agent J. J. McGuire to Special Agent Mr. Tolson, May 14, 1945, 94-1-9758-illegible; Letter, Hoover, Reverend Robert S. Lloyd, SJ, May 17, 1945, 94-1-9758-14X3. On McGuire, see Rosswurm, *The F.B.I and the Catholic Church, 1935–1962*, 10.

77. For an authoritative examination of the perceived connections between bodily and spiritual health in the twentieth-century United States, see R. Marie Griffith, *Born Again Bodies: Flesh and Spirit in American Christianity* (Berkeley: University of California Press, 2004), 7; *Manresan*, June 1950, 2, Special Collections, Woodstock Theological Library, Georgetown University; Archdiocese of Baltimore, "League of Laymen's Retreats: Golden Jubilee," 1915–1964, 53, Archives of the Maryland Province of the Society of Jesus, Box 8, Georgetown University Special Collections; Letter, Reverend Lloyd, SJ, to Hoover April 11, 1949, 94-9758-18.

78. Unpublished notes, Reverend Elson, "J. Edgar Hoover," August 12, 1965, 94-39821-157 enclosure.

79. Milton A. Jones, "The Story of My Life," Unpublished autobiography, 1981, 86–88. A very special thank you to Matthew Cecil for providing me with this unpublished yet priceless document. On Hoover's weight and the FBI program, see Gid Powers, *Secrecy and Power*, 28; Letersky

and Dillow, *The Director*, 75; M. Wesley Swearingen and Ward Churchill, *FBI Secrets: An Agent's Expose* (Boston, MA: South End Press, 1995), 48–49; Matthew Cecil, *Branding Hoover's FBI: How the Boss's PR Men Sold the Bureau to America* (Lawrence: University Press of Kansas, 2016), 14; James Phelan, "Hoover of the FBI," *Saturday Evening Post*, September 25, 1965; Robert Sisson and Jacob Hay, "The FBI: Public Friend Number One," *National Geographic Magazine* 119, no. 6 (June 1961), 886.

80. Jones, "The Story of My Life," 86–88; Letersky and Dillow, *The Director*, 75; Swearingen and Churchill, *FBI Secrets*, 48–49; Cecil, *Branding Hoover's FBI*, 14; Phelan, "Hoover of the FBI"; Sisson and Hay, "The FBI: Public Friend Number One," 886.

81. Letter, Director Hoover to Special Agent McGuire, April 26, 1941, Personal File 67-53404-1.

82. Letersky and Dillow, *The Director*, 186; Jones, "The Story of My Life," 87.

83. Letterhead memo, SA Adams to SA Callahan, February 14, 1966, 100-403320-138.

84. J. Edgar Hoover, *FBI Law Enforcement Bulletin* 6, no. 12 (December 1937), 1.

85. *The Manresan* 1, no. 3, March 1936, 2; May, 1943, 3; July 1951, 4, Special Collections, Woodstock Theological Library at Georgetown University.

86. Interview, Retired Special Agent Alan Ouimet, June 22, 2020, phone.

87. *The Manresan* 8, no. 5, May 1943, 2, Special Collections, Woodstock Theological Library, Georgetown University.

88. *Washington Post, Times Herald*, September 23, 1960, B9; *The Manresan* 8 no. 5, May 1943, 2, Special Collections, Woodstock Theological Library, Georgetown University.

89. On the practice and waywardness of the Eucharist, see Lauren Winner, *The Dangers of Christian Practice: On Wayward Gifts, Characteristic Damage, and Sin* (New Haven, CT; London: Yale University Press, 2018), 42–43.

90. Letter, Hoover to Reverend Lloyd, April 15, 1949, 94-1-9758-18; Letter, Hoover to Reverend Lloyd, November 23, 1945, 94-4-3263-72; Letter, Hoover to Reverend Lloyd, August 1, 1950, 940403263-150; Letter, Father Lloyd to Hoover, November 20, 1958, Stephen F. McNamee, SJ papers, Georgetown University Special Collections; Letter, Hoover to Father Lloyd, November 16, 1938, 94-1-9758-1; *The Manresan* (Annapolis, MD), July 1951, 2 in Bureau File 94-1-9758; Letter, Hoover to Lloyd, August 1, 1950, 94-4-3263-150.

91. Letter, Special Agent Sizoo to Director Kelley, February 14, 1974, 94-46707-77; Letterhead Memo, Office of the Director, Special Agent Bill Reed to Director, February 19, 1974, 94-46707-74; Letter, Director Clarence M. Kelley to Reverend William M. Driscoll, S., January 17, 1974, 94-1-9758-134.

Chapter 3. Ministers

1. Reverend Edward L. R. Elson, "The J. Edgar Hoover You Ought to Know, By His Pastor," *The Chaplain* 7, no. 5 (September–October 1950), 19–23.

2. Office of the Director, Letterhead Typed Manuscript, "Greetings to First Annual Communion Breakfast of FBI Employees, Sunday, May 7, 1950," 94-46287-7; Letterhead Memo, Special Agent L.B. Nichols to Special Agent Tolson, May 5, 1950, 94-46287-6 enclosure.

3. Letterhead Memo, SAC, Philadelphia to Director, FBI, May 26, 1955, 94-4628-43.

4. See SA Nichols to SA Tolson, April 28, 1942, 94-4-5283-2.

5. Hoover, "A Christmas Message," *The Investigator*, Christmas 1961.

6. Hoover, "Statement of the Director," April 7, 1957, 94-46287-54 enclosure; *Washington Post and Times Herald*, May 24, 1956, 25; Jonathan L. Walton, *Watch This! The Ethics and Aesthetics of Black Televangelism, Religion, Race, and Ethnicity* (New York: New York University Press, 2009), 171; Hoover, "A Good Christian Is a Good Citizen," *The Lookout*, August 12, 1951, 5, reprinted in *Congressional Record*, 97 Cong. Rec. A5268-A5269, 1951.

7. Letterhead Memo, Special Agent R. F. Cartwright to the Director, February 14, 1950, 94-46287-1; Hoover uses the phrase "sparked"; see handwritten note on Letterhead Memo, Special Agent Nichols to Special Agent Tolson, May 28, 1951, 94-HQ-46287-15.

8. Letterhead Memo, Special Agent H. H. Clegg to Special Agent Tolson, April 1, 1952, 94-HQ-46287-18; Letterhead Memo, Special Agent G. C. Gearty to Special Agent Tolson, January 7, 1953, 94-46287-23; Letterhead Memo, Special Agent N. P. Callahan to Special Agent Mohr, October 29, 1954, 94-46287-37; Letterhead Memo, Special Agent J. H. Gale to Special Agent DeLoach, May 22, 1967, 94-46287-98; 94-46287-140, enclosure.

9. 94-462870-96, enclosure. The service was held away from St. Matthew on a few occasions for reasons unspecified in Bureau files; Letterhead Memo, Special Agent J. H. Gale to Special Agent DeLoach, May 22, 1967, 94-46287-98 and enclosure; Personal email communication, Retired Special Agent Wayne Davis to Author, June 14, 2016.

10. Author Interview with Retired Special Agent in Charge Wayne Davis, Phone, October 6, 2015; Reverend Archibald Carey to Hoover, November 3, 1959, 77-59135-64; *Ebony*, October 1947; Letter, Reverend Carey to Alex Poinsett, *Ebony*, March 2, 1964, 161-2040-27; Personal Letter, SA William Sullivan to Hoover, October 6, 1971 in William C. Sullivan and Bill Brown, *The Bureau: My Thirty Years in Hoover's F.B.I.* (New York: W.W. Norton, 1979), 265–277; Ovid Demaris, *The Director: An Oral Biography of J. Edgar Hoover*, 1st ed. (New York: Harper's Magazine Press, 1975), 32–39. Jewish employees were treated similarly. SA Sullivan admitted that the Bureau deliberately avoided hiring significant numbers of Jewish agents. The Catholic special agent called it an "unwritten policy" in the FBI, one that mandated "always having one Jewish official up front for people to see" at FBIHQ. See Sullivan and Brown, *The Bureau.*

11. Author Interview with Retired Special Agent in Charge Wayne Davis, Phone, October 6, 2015 and November 4, 2016, Saint Louis, MO; Author Interview with Retired Special Agent Jesse House, Phone, March 10, 2017 and September 18, 2017, Atlanta, Georgia; *Ebony*, September 1962, 29–30, 32–-34; Phelan, "Hoover of the FBI"; Letterhead Memo, SA DeLoach to SA Mohr, June 2, 1960, 77-59135-82; Athan G. Theoharis, *The FBI & American Democracy: A Brief Critical History* (Lawrence: University Press of Kansas, 2004), 174.

12. Author Interview with Special Agent Allen "Al" Jordan, Phone, October 17, 2017. Jordan started as a clerk in 1968 and joined the ranks of special agent in 1974.

13. The Cathedral of St. Matthew the Apostle, https://www.stmatthewscathedral.org/about, accessed August 13, 2019; Pope Benedict XVI reflection on St. Matthew, Paul VI Audience Hall, Wednesday, 30 August 2006, http://w2.vatican.va/content/benedict-xvi/en/audiences/2006/documents/hf_ben-xvi_aud_20060830.html, accessed August 13, 2019.

14. The Cathedral of St. Matthew the Apostle, https://www.stmatthewscathedral.org/about, accessed August 13, 2019; Pope Benedict XVI reflection on St. Matthew, Paul VI Audience Hall,

Wednesday, 30 August 2006, http://w2.vatican.va/content/benedict-xvi/en/audiences/2006/documents/hf_ben-xvi_aud_20060830.html, accessed August 13, 2019; Matthew 28:18–20.

15. Report of the National Catholic Welfare Council, February 13, 1961, in Father John K. Cartwright Papers, Monsignor W. Ronald Jameson Cathedral Archive, Cathedral of St. Matthew the Apostle, Washington, DC. President Kennedy was eulogized at the church. The funeral is memorialized by a large marble plaque set in the floor where his casket rested before the altar.

16. Richard Schmidt and Claudia Rousseau, *Cathedral of St. Matthew the Apostle: Its History, Art, and Architecture* (Washington, DC: The Cathedral of St. Matthew the Apostle, 2008), 12; Tour of the Cathedral of St. Matthew the Apostle, https://www.stmatthewscathedral.org/tour/index.html, accessed August 23, 2019.

17. Schmidt and Rousseau, *Cathedral of St. Matthew the Apostle*, 12–25, 45; Tour of the Cathedral of St. Matthew the Apostle, https://www.stmatthewscathedral.org/tour/index.html, accessed August 23, 2019.

18. See, for example, Special Agent L. B. Nichols to Special Agent Tolson, March 29, 1954, 94-46287-36. Special Agent Tracy retired on May 31, 1954, see *FBI Law Enforcement Bulletin*, July 1954; Alan Belmont Personnel File, 67-94639-19. See Belmont obituary in *Washington Post*, August 2, 1977.

19. Letterhead Memo, Special Agent L. B. Nichols to Special Agent Tolson, April 11, 1956, 94-46287-48; *New York Times*, August 21, 1971, 8; February 1, 1997, 26; Demaris, *The Director*, 86. See Mohr's FBI personnel file at https://archive.org/details/foia_Mohr_John_P.-1/page/n45/mode/2up, accessed February 1, 2020; Letersky and Dillow, *The Director*, 116, 208, 242.

20. "The Priest and Communism," no date; Cartwright, "The False Paradise of Collectivism," Sunday Washington Catholic Radio Hour Sermon, April 18, 1937, both in Father John K. Cartwright Papers, Folder: "The Priest and Communism," Monsignor W. Ronald Jameson Cathedral Archive, Cathedral of St. Matthew the Apostle, Washington, DC; Reverend John K. Cartwright, Red Mass Sermon, January 31, 1954, St. Matthew's Cathedral, reprinted in the *Congressional Record*, February 4, 1954, in Sermons of Msgr. John K. Cartwright, Box 3 Folder: Sermons 1954–1955; Cartwright, Sermon delivered by Rt. Rev. John K. Cartwright, Rector, St. Matthew's Cathedral, Sunday 4, 1950, in Sermons of Msgr. John K. Cartwright, Box 2 Folder: Sermons 1950; Sermon manuscript, unnamed and undated, Sermons of Msgr. John K. Cartwright, Box 3 Folder: Sermons 1951–1953; Easter Sunday Sermon delivered by Rt. Rev. John K. Cartwright, March 25, 1951, in Sermons of Msgr. John K. Cartwright, Box 3 Folder: Sermons 1951–1953; "The Two Cities: Freedom and Vocation," Address by Rt. Rev. Monsignor John K. Cartwright, Meeting of Knights of Columbus, Mayflower Hotel, Washington, DC, no date, reprinted in *London Times*, March 22, 1952, in Sermons of Msgr. John K. Cartwright, Box 3 Folder: Sermons 1951–1953, all in Rhoads Memorial Archives, Mount St. Mary's University, Emmitsburg, MD.

21. Cartwright, "Sermon delivered by the Right Reverend John K. Cartwright at the Requiem Mass for the repose of the soul of the Honorable Joseph R. McCarthy, May 6, 1957, St. Matthew's Cathedral, Washington D.C.," Box 3 Sermons, Msgr. John K. Cartwright, Folder: Cartwright Sermons, 1956–1959, Monsignor W. Ronald Jameson Cathedral Archive, Cathedral of St. Matthew the Apostle, Washington, DC; Cartwright, "The Priest and Communism," no date; Cartwright, "The False Paradise of Collectivism," Sunday Washington Catholic Radio Hour Sermon, April 18, 1937, Father John K. Cartwright Papers, Folder: "The Priest and

Communism," Monsignor W. Ronald Jameson Cathedral Archive, Cathedral of St. Matthew the Apostle, Washington, DC.

22. *Washington Times-Herald*, "Did You Happen to See: Father John K. Cartwright," March 14, 1944; *The Sunday Star* (Washington, DC), "Msgr. John Cartwright, Catholic Leader, Dies," January 16, 1972; *Washington Post*, "Cathedral's Msgr. John K. Cartwright," no date, and "The Cartwright Years," undated manuscript in Father John K. Cartwright Papers, Monsignor W. Ronald Jameson Cathedral Archive, Cathedral of St. Matthew the Apostle, Washington, DC; Letterhead Memo, Special Agent R. F. Cartwright to The Director, February 14, 1950, 94-46287-1; Letterhead Memo, Special Agent Nichols to Special Agent Tolson, March 22, 1950, 94-46287-2; Letterhead Memo, Special Agent Nichols to Special Agent Tolson, January 15, 1951, 94-46287-10.

23. Letterhead Memo, Special Agent Nichols to Special Agent Tolson, May 8, 1950, 94-46287-7; Letterhead Memo, Special Agent Nichols to Special Agent Tolson, January 15, 1951, 94-46287-10; Letterhead Memo, Special Agent Nichols to Special Agent Tolson, May 28, 1951, 94-46287-15; "The Two Cities: Freedom and Vocation," Address by Rt. Rev. Monsignor John K. Cartwright, Meeting of Knights of Columbus, Mayflower Hotel, Washington, DC, no date, reprinted in *London Times*, March 22, 1952, and Rev. John K. Cartwright, Sermon, Franciscan Monastery, Washington, DC, October 23, 1956, in Sermons of Msgr. John K. Cartwright, Box 3 Folder: Sermons 1956–1959, Rhoads Memorial Archives, Mount St. Mary's University, Emmitsburg, MD. On SA O'Bierne, see obituary in *New York Times*, September 9, 1990; *Washington Post*, September 7, 1990; Letterhead Memo, Special Agent L. B. Nichols to Special Agent Tolson, March 29, 1954, 94-46287-36.

24. "Instructions on the Liturgy, Archdiocese of Washington," undated pamphlet in Father John K. Cartwright Papers, Monsignor W. Ronald Jameson Cathedral Archive, Cathedral of St. Matthew the Apostle, Washington, DC.

25. Letter, J. Edgar Hoover to Right Reverend Monsignor Cartwright, May 20, 1951, 94-46287-14.

26. Letterhead Memo, Special Agent H. H. Clegg to Special Agent Tolson, April 1, 1952, 94-HQ-46287-18.

27. Letterhead Memo, Special Agent Nichols to Special Agent Tolson, May 8, 1950, 94-46287-7; Letterhead Memo, Special Agent Nichols to Special Agent Tolson, January 15, 1951, 94-46287-10.

28. Letterhead Memo, Special Agent H. H. Clegg to Special Agent Tolson, April 1, 1952, 94-HQ-46287-18.

29. Letterhead Memo, Special Agent A. H. Belmont to The Director, January 8, 1956, 94-46287-51; Alan Belmont Personnel File, 67-94639-19.

30. Letterhead Memo, Special Agent J. H. Gale to Special Agent DeLoach, May 22, 1967, 94-46287-98 and enclosure.

31. Letterhead Memo, Special Agent H. L. Edwards to Special Agent DeLoach, June 12, 1959, 94-46287-70; Letterhead Memo, Special Agent D. J. Brennan to Special Agent W. C. Sullivan, May 2, 1963, 94-46287-84; Letterhead Memo, Special Agent N. P. Callahan to Special Agent Mohr, April 10, 1964, 94-46287-82; Letterhead Memo, Special Agent McAndrews to Special Agent J. H. Gale, March 16, 1967, 94-46287-95; Letterhead Memo, Special Agent J. H. Gale to

Special Agent DeLoach, May 22, 1967, 94-46287-98; Letterhead Memo, Special Agent J. J. Mc-Dermott to Special Agent N. P. Callahan, March 12, 1969, 94-46287-108; Letter, Special Agent J. P. Dunphy to Corneal J. Mack, May 29, 1970, 94-46287-120.

32. Letterhead Memo, Special Agent J. H. Gale to Special Agent DeLoach, May 22, 1967, 94-46287-98; Letter, Special Agent N. P. Callahan to Reverend James Keller November 1, 1954, 94-46287-37.

33. 94-46287-134 enclosure; Letterhead Memo, Special Agent H. L. Edwards to Special Agent DeLoach, June 12, 1959, 94-46287-70; Letterhead Memo, Special Agent D. J. Brennan to Special Agent W. C. Sullivan, May 2, 1963, 94-46287-84; Letterhead Memo, Special Agent DeLoach to Special Agent Tolson, May 18, 1959, 94-46287-68; Letter, Hoover to Miss Constance Howe, May 26, 1960, 94-46287-74; Letter, Director to Mr. Mack, May 18, 1959, 94-46287-65; Letterhead Memo, Special Agent J. J. McDermott to Special Agent N. P. Callahan, March 12, 1969, 94-46287-108. Letterhead Memo, Special Agent N. P/ Callahan to Special Agent Mohr, April 10, 1964, 94-46287-82; Letterhead Memo, Special Agent McAndrews to Special Agent J. H. Gale, March 16, 1967, 94-46287-95; Letterhead Memo, Special Agent J. H. Gale to Special Agent DeLoach, May 22, 1967, 94-46287-98; Letterhead Memo, Special Agent J. J. McDermott to Special Agent N. P. Callahan, March 12, 1969, 94-46287-108; Letter, Special Agent J. P. Dunphy to Corneal J. Mack, May 29, 1970, 94-46287-120; Letterhead Memo, Special Agent James R. Maller to The Director, May 26, 1960, 94-46287-73; Letter, Director Kelley to Mr. Frank E. Glaine, Catering Sales Manager, November 16, 1973, 94-4628-not recorded; Seating chart, 94-46287-140 enclsure; History of The Mayflower Hotel, http://www.themayflowerhotel.com/history/, accessed August 13, 2019; Letterhead Memo, Special Agent McGowan to Special Agent Bates, June 2, 1972, 94-4628-131.

34. See, for example, Letterhead Memo, Special Agent Nichols to Special Agent Tolson, May 5, 1950, 94-46287-6; Letterhead Memo, Special Agent Nichols to Special Agent Tolson, January 15, 1951, 94-46287-10; Memo, Special Agent Nichols to Special Agent Tolson, May 5, 1951, 94-46287-11; Special Agent Jones to Special Agent Nichols, March 23, 1954, 94-46287-32. On Hoover's preferred Sunday activities, see Demaris, *The Director*.

35. Milton A. Jones, "The Story of My Life." A special thanks to Matthew Cecil for providing me with this priceless autobiography. See also Jones's personnel file, 67-109106-29, https://archive.org/details/MiltonA.Jones/page/n39, accessed December 1, 2019; Obituary in the *Washington Post*, April 28, 1994. On Jones and Crime Research Section, see Cecil, *Branding Hoover's FBI*, 110–112.

36. Hoover's note on Letterhead Memo, Special Agent M. A. Jones to Special Agent Nease, April 17, 1958, 94-46287-58; Letterhead Memo, Special Agent Jones to Special Agent Mr. De-Loach, April 21, 1964, 94-46287-83; Letterhead Memo, Special Agent Nichols to Special Agent Tolson, May 5, 1950, 94-46287-6; Letterhead Memo, Special Agent Nichols to Special Agent Tolson, January 15, 1951, 94-46287-10; Memo, Special Agent Nichols to Special Agent Tolson, May 5, 1951, 94-46287-11; Special Agent Jones to Special Agent Nichols, March 23, 1954, 94-46287-32.

37. Hoover, "Statement of the Director," April 7, 1957, 94-46287-54 enclosure.

38. Hoover, "Statement of the Director," April 7, 1957, 94-46287-54 enclosure.

39. Special Agent Jones to Special Agent Nichols, March 23, 1954, 94-46287-32 enclosure.

40. Statement of Director, May 17, 1964, 94-46287-83 enclosure.

41. Letterhead Memo, Special Agent Nichols to Special Agent Tolson, May 8, 1950, 94-46287-7.

42. Letterhead Memo, Special Agent H. H. Clegg to Special Agent Tolson, April 1, 1952, 94-HQ-46287-18; Letterhead Memo, Special Agent G. C. Gearty to Special Agent Tolson, January 7, 1953, 94-46287-23; Letterhead Memo, Special Agent N. P. Callahan to Special Agent Mohr, October 29, 1954, 94-46287-37; Letterhead Memo, Special Agent J. H. Gale to Special Agent DeLoach, May 22, 1967, 94-46287-98; Enclosure 94-46287-140.

43. Letterhead Memo, Special Agent Callan to Special Agent Rosen, February 8, 1954, 94-46287-31x1; https://laetare.nd.edu, accessed September 9, 2019.

44. Letter, Special Agent DeLoach to Senator George L. Murphy, Janaury 26, 1967, 94-4628-90x; Letter, Special Agent McAndrews to Special Agent Gale, March 4, 1967, 94-4628-91.

45. Letterhead Memo, Special Agent Nichols to Special Agent Tolson, May 8, 1950, 94-46287-7.

46. 94-46287 Sub A enclosure, *The Catholic Standard*, Washington, DC, April 2, 1954.

47. Letterhead Memo, Special Agent James R. Maller to The Director, May 23, 1960, 94-46287-72 and enclosure.

48. Letterhead Memo, Special Agent McDermott to Special Agent Callahan, February 12, and March 12, 1969, 94-46287-109 and 108; Special Agent Dunphy to Special Agent Callahan, April 2, 1970, 94-46287-117; Letter, Hoover to Lombardi, May 7, 1969, 94-46287-107.

49. Letterhead Memo, Special Agent Dunphy to Special Agent Callahan, October 19, 1970, 94-46287-123 and enclosure; Hoover, "How J. Edgar Hoover Felt About TV's 'The FBI,'" *TV Guide*, May 20, 1972; *Washington Post, Times Herald*, August 1, 1971, 9.

50. Letterhead Memo, Special Agent Callahan to Special Agent Mohr, October 29, 1954, 94-46287-37; Letterhead Memo, Special Agent Nichols to Special Agent Tolson, May 5, 1955, 94-37152-58; Father James Keller, *Government Is Your Business* (Garden City, NY: Doubleday, 1951), 318–319; Father James Keller, *All God's Children: What Your Schools Can Do for Them* (Garden City, NY: Hanover House, 1953), vii; *Washington Post and Times Herald*, April 2, 1955, 2; April 4, 1955, 21; Hoover's statement, July 6, 1953, 94-37152-illegible; Letterhead Memo, Special Agent Nichols to Special Agent Tolson, May 5, 1955, 94-37152-58; Letter, Hoover to Father Keller, April 4, 1955, 94-37152-57; Letterhead Memo, Special Agent Jones to Special Agent Nichols, April 4, 1955, 94-46287-40; Letter, Father Keller to Hoover, October 11, 1955, 94-37152-illegible; 94-46287, Sub A enclosure, *Washington Post and Times Herald*, April 4, 1955.

51. Letterhead Memo, Special Agent Callan to Special Agent Rosen, December 12, 1953, 94-46287-29; Rosswurm, *The F.B.I. and the Catholic Church, 1935–1962*, 82

52. Letterhead Memo, Special Agent L. B. Nichols to Special Agent Tolson, April 11, 1956, 94-46287-48; Letterhead Memo, Special Agent L. B. Nichols to Special Agent Tolson, April 9, 1956, 94-46287-49. Sheen was invited back in 1970. He originally accepted only to later decline on doctor's orders.

53. *Washington Post and Times Herald*, April 9, 1956, 22.

54. *Washington Post and Times Herald*, April 9, 1956, 22.

55. Letterhead Memo, Special Agent W. C. Sullivan to Special Agent A. H. Belmont, March 23, 1962, 94-46287-78; Letterhead Memo, Special Agent W. C. Sullivan to Special Agent A. H. Belmont, January 27, 1965, 94-46287-85.

56. Letterhead Memo, Special Agent W. C. Sullivan to Special Agent A. H. Belmont, January 27, 1965, 94-46287-85; James F. Findlay, Jr., *Church People in the Struggle: The National Council of Churches and the Black Freedom Movement, 1950–1970*, paperback ed. (New York: Oxford University Press, 1997), 87–88.

57. Letterhead Memo, Special Agent W. C. Sullivan to Special Agent A. H. Belmont, January 27, 1965, 94-46287-85; Letterhead Memo, Special Agent Belmont to Special Agent Parsons, March 25, 1960, 100-403529-112 enclosure; Sullivan quoted in Louis Cassels, "The Rightist Crisis in Our Churches," *Look*, April 24, 1962, 44; 62-44136-10 enclosure.

58. Letterhead Memo, Special Agent W. C. Sullivan to Special Agent A. H. Belmont, January 27, 1965, 94-46287-85; *New York Times*, January 18, 1993, B6; Letersky and Dillow, *The Director*, 119.

59. Letter, Mrs. K. J. Hopkins to Hoover, May 10, 1961, 94-51060-94.

60. Letterhead Memo, Special Agent W. C. Sullivan to Special Agent A. H. Belmont, January 27, 1965, 94-46287-85; Letterhead Memo, Special Agent Callahan to Special Agent Mohr, April 27, 1965, 94-46287-87; Letersky and Dillow, *The Director*, 119.

61. Letterhead Memo, Special Agent W. C. Sullivan to Special Agent A. H. Belmont, January 27, 1965, 94-46287-85; Letterhead Memo, Special Agent Callahan to Special Agent Mohr, April 27, 1965, 94-46287-87. On Special Agent Joseph M. Sizoo, see Obituary in *The Williamsburg Yorktown Daily*, October 21, 2015, https://wydaily.com/obits/2015/10/21/obits-joseph-m -sizoo-95-25-year-fbi-special-agent-who-researched-prepared-internal-documents/, accessed September 17, 2019; on Special Agent Joseph A. Sizoo, see Obituary in the *Washington Post*, September 1, 1995, https://www.washingtonpost.com/archive/local/1995/09/01/joseph-sizoo -fbi-official-dies-at-age-85/4af12c3b-458f-494a-ae1b-6355a76d79d0/?noredirect=on, accessed September 17, 2019; see also Letterhead Memo, Special Agent W. S. Tavel to Special Agent Mohr, March 26, 1958, 94-46705-10.

62. Catholic publications quoted in Rosswurm, *The F.B.I. and the Catholic Church, 1935–1962*, 1; Gunther quoted in Reverend Edward L. R. Elson, "The J. Edgar Hoover You Ought to Know, By His Pastor," *The Chaplain*, Vol. 7 No. 5, September-October 1950, 19–23.

63. "Biography," Donald Grey Barnhouse Papers, RG 480, Presbyterian Historical Society, Philadelphia, Pennsylvania; *Eternity*, March 1954, 8–9, 54--58; *Eternity*, "Letters to the Editors," May 1954.

64. Letter, Hoover to Reverend Elson, March 22, 1954, 94-39821-58; *The Pentecostal Evangel*, "J. Edgar Hoover Refutes Charge," May 2, 1954, 16.

65. Denominational Letterhead, Reverend Blake to Hoover, April 6, 1954, 94-39821-59.

66. James DeForest Murch, *Cooperation Without Compromise: A History of the National Association of Evangelicals* (Grand Rapids, MI: W. B. Eerdmans, 1956), 46–47.

67. "Clyde Taylor: 'Mr. NAE,'" *Christianity Today*, July 15, 1988; "Biography," Papers of Clyde Willis Taylor, Billy Graham Center Archives, Wheaton College, Wheaton, IL; Letter, Rev. John Kelly to Hoover, November 5, 1956, 62-103627-1.

68. Personal and Confidential Letter, Hoover to Reverend Taylor, November 13, 1956, 62-103627-4.

69. Personal and Confidential Letter, Hoover to Reverend Taylor, November 13, 1956, 62-103627-4; Hoover's handwritten note on Letterhead Memo, November 29, 1956, 62-103627-4;

Letterhead Memo, SA Nichols to SA Tolson, November 30, 1956, 62-103627-4; Hoover's hand-written diatribe on Letterhead Memo, SA Nichols to SA Tolson, January 9, 1957, 62-103627-not recorded; SA Wick FBI Personnel File is available at https://archive.org/details/foia_Wick _Robert_E.-3/page/n83/mode/2up/search/Church, accessed February 1, 2020.

70. Quotes from Avro Manhattan, *The Dollar and the Vatican* (London: Pioneer Press, 1957), 248; Avro Manhattan, *Catholic Power Today* (New York: L. Stuart, 1967), 129.

71. Letter, Hoover to Reverend Blake, April 8, 1954, 94-39821-59; *Eternity*, "Letters to the Editors," May 1954.

72. *Eternity*, "Letters to the Editors," May 1954.

73. Letterhead Memo, SA M. A. Jones to SA Wick, May 15, 1967, 94-46705-49; Reverend Edward R. L. Elson Diary #1 May 23, 1954, Record Group 253 Box 10, Folder 12, Reverend Edward L. R. Elson Papers, 1924-1988, Presbyterian Historical Society Archives, Philadelphia, PA.

74. Letterhead Memo, Special Agent Cleveland to Special Agent Gale, March 26, 1965, 94-46705-illegible.

75. Letter, Hoover to Reverend Harris, April 19, 1967, 94-HQ-45253-32; Letter, Hoover to Reverend Elson, April 27, 1971, 94-39821-illegible.

76. Hoover, "Why I Go to Church," pamphlet, *Tidings: Materials for Christian Evangelism* (Nashville, TN, 1960).

77. Letterhead Memo, Special Agent C. R. Davidson to Special Agent Callahan, April 27, 1964, 94-46705-32; Letterhead Memo, Special Agent M. A. Jones to Special Agent Bishop, March 10, 1970, 94-46705-67; Private email communication, Retired Special Agent to Author, June 14, 2016.

78. "The National Presbyterian Church: The First 200 Years, 1795–1995," Booklet, no author, no date, The Ervin N. Chapman Memorial Archives, The William Smith Culbertson Memorial Library, The National Presbyterian Church, Washington, DC; *Religion News Service*, "FBI Employees Attend Protestant Vesper Service," May 28, 1954 in Bureau File 94-46705-3 enclosure; Caspar Nannes, "The President and His Pastor," *Collier's*, November 11, 1955.

79. Airmail, Hoover to Dr. Harry Clayton Rogers, October 7, 1952, 94-39821-illegible; Membership profile, "John Edgar Hoover"; *National Presbyterian Church Trustees' Minutes*, Vol. 1, 1947–1951, Vol. 2, 1952–1960, The Ervin N. Chapman Memorial Archives, The William Smith Culbertson Memorial Library, The National Presbyterian Church, Washington, DC; see also *The Book of Order*; Church Letterhead, Reverend Elson to Hoover, October 3, 1957, 94-39821-illegible; FBI Letterhead, Hoover to Reverend Elson, April 22, 1948, Record Group 253 Box 1, Folder 10, Reverend Edward L. R. Elson Papers, 1924–1988, Presbyterian Historical Society Archives, Philadelphia, PA; Letterhead Memo, SA Jones to SA DeLoach, August 12, 1965, 94-39821-157.

80. "The National Presbyterian Church: The First 200 Years, 1795–1995"; *Religion News Service*, "FBI Employees Attend Protestant Vesper Service," May 28, 1954 in Bureau File 94-46705-3 enclosure; Caspar Nannes, "The President and His Pastor," *Collier's*, November 11, 1955.

81. "The National Presbyterian Church: The First 200 Years, 1795–1995," Booklet, no author, no date; "FBI Vesper Service Worship Bulletin at The National Presbyterian Church, Washington DC," both in The Ervin N. Chapman Memorial Archives, The William Smith Culbertson Memorial Library, The National Presbyterian Church, Washington DC; *Religion News Service*

"FBI Employees Attend Protestant Vesper Service," May 28, 1954 in Bureau File 94-46705-3 enclosure.

82. *Religion News Service*, "FBI Employees Attend Protestant Vesper Service," May 28, 1954, in Bureau File 94-46705-3 enclosure; Letterhead Memo, Special Agent Jones to Special Agent DeLoach, March 6, 1963, 94-46705-illegible; Caspar Nannes, "The President and His Pastor," *Collier's*, November 11, 1955.

83. FBI Vesper Service Worship Bulletin at The National Presbyterian Church, Washington, DC. The Ervin N. Chapman Memorial Archives, The William Smith Culbertson Memorial Library, The National Presbyterian Church, Washington, DC.

84. *Washington Post*, July 4, 1959, B7.

85. Reverend Elson, "J. Edgar Hoover—Churchman," *Presbyterian Life*, November 27, 1948, 4–5; Reverend Elson, "How I Pray for My People," *New Christian Advocate*, July 1959, 19; *Washington Post*, July 4, 1959, B7; Letterhead Memo, SA Jones to SA DeLoach, August 12, 1965, 94-39821-157; Unpublished notes, Reverend Elson, "J. Edgar Hoover," August 12, 1965, 94-39821-157 enclosure.

86. *Washington Post and Times Herald*, April 30, 1955, 8; Caspar Nannes, "The President and His Pastor," *Collier's*, November 11, 1955; FBI Letterhead, Hoover to Elson, January 2, 1952; Reverend Elson Diary #1 January 1, 1952, Record Group 253 Box 10, Folder 12; FBI Letterhead, Hoover to Elson, January 4, 1967; "Strictly Personal" Letter, Elson to Hoover, April 29, 1968, Record Group 253 Box 1, Folder 10; Reverend Elson, Undated notes, Record Group 253 Box 10, Folder 4, Reverend Edward L.R. Elson Papers, 1924-1988, Presbyterian Historical Society Archives, Philadelphia, PA; Letter, Hoover to SA Tolson, March 14, 1956, 94-39821-87; Unpublished notes, Reverend Elson, "J. Edgar Hoover," August 12, 1965, 94-39821-157 enclosure.

87. FBI Letterhead, Hoover to Elson, December 21, 1951, Record Group 253 Box 1, Folder 10, Reverend Edward L. R. Elson Papers, 1924–1988, Presbyterian Historical Society Archives, Philadelphia, PA; *Washington Post*, August 1, 1970, D10; Unpublished notes, Reverend Elson, "J. Edgar Hoover," August 12, 1965, 94-39821-157 enclosure; Reverend Elson Diary #1 January 1, 1952, Record Group 253 Box 10, Folder 12, Reverend Edward L. R. Elson Papers, 1924–1988, Presbyterian Historical Society Archives, Philadelphia, PA; Letter, Hoover to Reverend Elson, April 10, 1955, 94-39821-83; see, for example, Letter, Hoover to Reverend Elson, January 10, 1949, 94-39821-illegible; Letter, Reverend Elson to Hoover, August 3, 1954, 94-39821-illegible; Hoover autographed self-portrait to Elson, July, 3, 1950, Record Group 253 Box 13, Folder 42, Reverend Edward L. R. Elson Papers, 1924–1988, Presbyterian Historical Society Archives, Philadelphia, PA. Hoover autographed self-portrait to Elson, July, 3, 1950, Record Group 253 Box 13, Folder 42; Letter, Reverend Elson to Hoover, April 8, 1964; "Strictly Personal" Letter, Elson to Hoover, April 29, 1968, Record Group 253 Box 1, Folder 10, Reverend Edward L. R. Elson Papers, 1924–1988, Presbyterian Historical Society Archives, Philadelphia, PA.

88. "Biographical Note;" "Reverend Elson Diary #1," November 22, 1953; "Unpublished biography," all in Record Group 253 Box 10, Folder 12, Reverend Edward L. R. Elson Papers, 1924–1988, Presbyterian Historical Society Archives, Philadelphia, PA; *Washington Post*, August 1, 1970, D10; Edward L. R. Elson, *Wide Was His Parish: An Autobiography* (Wheaton, IL: Tyndale House Publishers, 1986), 125; Special Agent Nichols to Special Agent Tolson,

May 24, 1954, 94-46705-2; Memo, Hoover to SA Tolson and SA Nichols, February 11, 1954, 94-39821-illegible; Letter, Frank S. Mead, Editor Revell Publishing to Hoover, no date, 94-39821-53 enclosure; Letterhead Memo, SA Jones to SA Nichols, February 23, 1954, 94-39821-54; Edward L. R. Elson and Introduction by J. Edgar Hoover, *America's Spiritual Recovery* (F. H. Revell Co, 1954), 9–11, 113–124; Church Letterhead, Reverend Elson to Hoover, March 11, 1954, 94-39821-55; Letter, Frank S. Mead to Hoover, March 9, 1954, 94-39821-55; *Washington Post and Times Herald*, April 30, 1955, 8; Caspar Nannes, "The President and His Pastor," *Collier's*, November 11, 1955; Elson Edward L. R. Elson, "Memorable Years in a Washington Pulpit," *Christianity Today*, March 30, 1973.

89. Caspar Nannes, "The President and His Pastor," *Collier's*, November 11, 1955; *Washington Post and Times Herald*, April 30, 1955, 8; August 8, 1959, C17; August 1, 1970, D10; Special Agent Nichols to Special Agent Tolson, May 24, 1954, 94-46705-2; Elson and Introduction by J. Edgar Hoover, *America's Spiritual Recovery*, 113–124.

90. FBI Vesper Service Worship Bulletin at The National Presbyterian Church, Washington, DC. The Ervin N. Chapman Memorial Archives, The William Smith Culbertson Memorial Library, The National Presbyterian Church, Washington, DC.

91. Special Agent Nichols to Special Agent Tolson, May 24, 1954, 94-46705-2; Edward R. Elson Diary #1 May 23, 1954, Record Group 253 Box 10, Folder 12, Reverend Edward L. R. Elson Papers, 1924–1988, Presbyterian Historical Society Archives, Philadelphia, PA; *Religion News Service*, "FBI Employees Attend Protestant Vesper Service," May 28, 1954 in Bureau File 94-46705-3.

92. Hoover to Reverend Elson, September 12, 1958, 94-46705-illegible.

93. Letterhead Memo, Special Agent J. A. Sizoo to Special Agent Tolson, May 2, 1955, 94-46705-4; 62-101087-3 enclosure; Jeremiah 20:9 NKJV; Hoover to Rev. Hastings, May 2, 1955, 94-46705-5.

94. Letterhead Memo, Special Agent J. A. Sizoo to Special Agent Tolson, May 2, 1955, 94-46705-4; 62-101087-3 enclosure; Jeremiah 20:9 NKJV; Hoover to Rev. Hastings, May 2, 1955, 94-46705-5.

95. Letterhead Memo, SA Cleveland to SA Gale, May 17, 1968, 94-46705-illegible; Letter, Hoover to Reverend Davis, May 27, 1968, 94-46705-illegible; *Congressional Record*, 114, August 1, 1968, 24843-24844; Letter, SA JM Sizoo to Director Kelley, Feb 14, 1974, 94-46287-77.

96. *Congressional Record*, 114, August 1, 1968, 24843-24844.

97. *Congressional Record*, 114, August 1, 1968, 24843-24844.

98. Letterhead Memo, SA Cleveland to SA Gale, May 17, 1968, 94-46705-illegible; Letter, Hoover to Reverend Davis, May 27, 1968, 94-46705-illegible; *Congressional Record*, 114, August 1, 1968, 24843-24844; Letter, SA JM Sizoo to Director Kelley, February 14, 1974, 94-46287-77.

99. Airtel Memo, FBI Director to SAC Detroit, May 7, 1957, 62-101087-221; Memo, FBI Director to FBI Executives, May 10, 1957, 62-101087-246; Airtel Memo, SAC Washington Field Office to FBI Director, May 17, 1957, 62-101087-267 enclosure; Letterhead Memo, Special Agent A. E. Leonard to Special Agent Mohr, January 30, 1959, 94-46705-14.

100. Letterhead Memo, Special Agent A. E. Leonard to Special Agent Mohr, January 30, 1959, 94-46705-14; Letterhead Memo, Special Agent A. E. Leonard to Special Agent Mohr, March 3, 1959, 94-46705-illegible.

101. Letterhead Memo, Special Agent A. E. Leonard to Special Agent Mohr, January 30, 1959, 94-46705-14; Letterhead Memo, Special Agent A. E. Leonard to Special Agent Mohr, February 18, 1959, 94-46705-illegible; *Time Magazine*, "The New Lutheran," April 7, 1958; *New York Times*, June 7, 1968, 36.

102. Letterhead Memo, Special Agent A. E. Leonard to Special Agent DeLoach, March 12, 1959, 94-46705-illegible; *Time Magazine*, "The New Lutheran," April 7, 1958; *Northern Virginia Sun* (Arlington, Virginia), "6th Annual FBI Vesper Service Sunday Afternoon," May 9, 1959, in 94-46705 enclosure.

103. See Letterhead Memo, Special Agent C. R. Davidson to Special Agent Callahan, March 8, 1960, 94-46705-illegible.

104. "It subsequently developed that the officers of the American Civil Liberties Union would not release such a membership list." See Letterhead Memo, Special Agent C. R. Davidson to Special Agent Callahan, March 8, 1960, 94-46705-illegible; see Sziarto Obituary in *Washington Post, Times Herald*, April, 18, 1998, https://www.washingtonpost.com/archive/local/1998/04/11/john-l-nemes-78-dies/7bf4017a-5058-468f-9784-296271385b3c/, accessed October 22, 2019.

105. Letterhead Memo, Special Agent C. R. Davidson to Special Agent Callahan, May 17, 1960, 94-46287-illegible; *Washington Post, Times Herald*, May 14, 1960, B9.

106. Letter, Hoover to Assistant Attorney General Olney, May 24, 1954, 62-101087-4; Letterhead Memo, Assistant Attorney General Olney to Hoover, illegible, 62-101087-illegible; Letterhead Memo, SA Price to SA Rosen, September 12, 1955, 62-101087-46; Cecil, *Branding Hoover's FBI*, 48.

107. Letterhead memo, SA Rogers to SA Clegg, December 1, 1952, 94-HQ-45253-1 enclosure; Letter, Hoover to Walter G. Keim, Lay Leader, Foundry Church, October 26, 1954, 94-HQ-45253-2; FBI Internal memo to Office of Director, September 9, 1955, 94-HQ-45253-3; Truman Diary, February 8, 1948, in Robert H. Ferrell, ed., *Off the Record: The Private Papers of Harry S. Truman* (New York: Penguin Books, 1982), 123; Dr. Frederick Brown Harris, "Spires of the Spirit: Who Speaks for the Church?" *Washington Evening Star*, March 28, 1965; Hoover's handwritten note on sermon clipping "The Heel of Achilles," *Washington Star*, January 13, 1957, 94-HQ-45253-5 enclosure; *Washington Star*, February 28, 1960, 94-HQ-45253-A enclosure; United States Senate Letterhead, Reverend Harris to Hoover, April 21, 1959, 94-HQ-45253-13; Letter, Hoover to Harris, January 25, 1961, 94-HQ-45253-illegible.

108. Letterhead memo, SA Price to SA Rosen, April 30, 1956, 94-46705-7; Letterhead Memo, Special Agent Baumgardner to Special Agent Sullivan, April 10, 1964, 94-46705-illegible; *Washington Post*, "A Blessed Ministry Winds Down," June 20, 1992.

109. Mount Vernon Place Methodist Church Worship Bulletin, May 25, 1941, 94-1-10300 enclosure; Letter, Reverend John W. Rustin to Hoover, March 25, 1947, 94-1-10300-illegible; Mount Vernon Place United Methodist Church, "We Repent," 2017, http://mvpumc.org/we-repent/, accessed October 22, 2019; Letterhead Memo, SA Cleveland to SA Gale, September 24, 1965, 94-46705-illegible; Letter, Reverend Albert P. Shirkey to Hoover, November 15, 1965, 94-46705-illegible; *Washington Post*, February 10, 1962, D6, February 21, 1970, B9.

110. Mount Vernon Place Methodist Church FBI File 94-1-10300; Mount Vernon Place Methodist Church Worship Bulletin, May 25, 1941, 94-1-10300 enclosure; Letter, Reverend

John W. Rustin to Hoover, March 25, 1947, 94-1-10300-illegible; Mount Vernon Place United Methodist Church, "We Repent," 2017, http://mvpumc.org/we-repent/, accessed October 22, 2019; Letterhead Memo, SA Cleveland to SA Gale, September 24, 1965, 94-46705-illegible; Letter, Reverend Albert P. Shirkey to Hoover, November 15, 1965, 94-46705-illegible; Letterhead Memo, SA Sullivan to SA DeLoach, May 10, 1967, 94-1-10300-35 enclosure; Letter, Reverend Dr. Edward Lewis to Hoover, April 29, 1979, 94-1-10300-39; Letter, Hoover to Reverend Dr. Edward Lewis, May 6, 1970, 94-1-10300-39. The church began participating in "Race Relations Sunday" during the 1960s. Once a year the church hosted a prominent Black preacher, usually the Dean of Howard University Divinity School, in their pulpit. See *Washington Post*, February 10, 1962, D6, February 21, 1970, B9.

111. Memo, SA Fletcher D. Thompson to Bureau Heads, March 22, 1967, 94-46705-50; Letter, Hoover to Reverend Harris, May 22, 1967, 94-HQ-45253-33.

112. Letterhead Memo, SA Tavel to SA Mohr, March 26, 1958, 94-46705-illegible; *Washington Post*, October 11, 1958, C10; November 18, 1965, D25; June 2, 1967, B1; June 19, 1967,C1; see obituary in November 3, 2000, https://www.washingtonpost.com/archive/local/2000/11/03/merrill-w-drennan-dies/8e9138ee-6dbc-4942-bae8-5025d3e8f6ee/, accessed October 24, 2019; *The History of National UMC*, https://nationalchurch.org/history, accessed October 24, 2019; Letterhead Memo, SA Marshall to SA Tavel, April 13, 1970, 94-46705-illegible.

113. Letterhead Memo, SA Eames to SA Nichols, May 21, 1957, 94-46705-8; Dr. Cranford Obituary, *Washington Post*, October 26, 1983, https://www.washingtonpost.com/archive/local/1983/10/26/cw-cranford-baptist-minister-dies-of-cancer/26d15f25-f4b2-4a73-879e-6fab79cd989e/, accessed October 25, 2019; *Faith and Leadership*, "Love God, Love your Neighbor," December 21, 2009, https://faithandleadership.com/love-god-love-your-neighbor, accessed October 25, 2019; *Time Magazine*, "The Southern Manifesto," March 26, 1956; *Milwaukee Sentinel*, July 26, 1957, 5.

114. Letterhead Memo, SA Eames to SA Nichols, May 21, 1957, 94-46705-8; *Lewiston Evening Journal*, March 10, 1967, 10; Dr. Cranford Obituary, *Washington Post*, October 26, 1983, https://www.washingtonpost.com/archive/local/1983/10/26/cw-cranford-baptist-minister-dies-of-cancer/26d15f25-f4b2-4a73-879e-6fab79cd989e/, accessed October 25, 2019.

115. *Decision*, July 1971, 4.

116. Letter, Hoover to Reverend Merrill Drennan, April 14, 1970, 94-46287-68.

117. Letterhead Memo, Special Agent Jones to Special Agent Nease, April 21, 1958, 94-46287-59.

Part 2. Promoting Faith: The FBI and White Evangelicals

1. "Address of J. Edgar Hoover," *America Fights for God-Given Rights*, Nation-Wide Radio Program, NBC, Presented by Fourth Degree, Knights of Columbus, March 22, 1942, 13–14. Francis Cardinal Spellman Collection (S), box A-20, folder 11, Archives of the Archdiocese of New York (AANY).

2. J. Edgar Hoover, *Masters of Deceit: The Story of Communism in America and How to Fight It* (New York: Henry Holt and Co., 1958), vi; Jonathan P. Herzog, *The Spiritual-Industrial

Complex: America's Religious Battle against Communism in the Early Cold War (New York: Oxford University Press, 2011), 6.

3. My discussion of the jeremiad relies on Andrew Murphy, *Prodigal Nation: Moral Decline and Divine Punishment from New England to 9/11* (New York; London: Oxford University Press, 2009). Here I am using Murphy's definition of "traditional jeremiad." He also considers "progressive jeremiad," which looks to the past not for concrete examples but for the fundamental principles that sit at the heart of American democratic ideals.

4. Hoover, "What Faith in God Has Meant to Me," *These Times*, August 1960.

5. Hoover, quoted in *Sunday School Times*, February 7, 1948; *Christianity Today*, September 11, 1964.

6. Richard Gid Powers, *Secrecy and Power: The Life of J. Edgar Hoover*, 1st ed. (New York: London: Free Press, 1987), 93–129; Richard Hack, *Puppetmaster: The Secret Life of J. Edgar Hoover* (Beverly Hills, CA: Phoenix Books, 2007), 73.

7. On conservative media and postwar politics, see Nicole Hemmer, *Messengers of the Right: Conservative Media and the Transformation of American Politics* (Philadelphia: University of Pennsylvania Press, 2016).

Chapter 4. *Christianity Today*

1. *Christianity Today* Letterhead Memo, Reverend Carl Henry to J. Edgar Hoover, December 18, 1962, 94-51060-138.

2. Jonathan P. Herzog, *The Spiritual-Industrial Complex: America's Religious Battle against Communism in the Early Cold War* (New York: Oxford University Press, 2011), 178.

3. FBI "Brief on Communism and Religion," March 25, 1960, 100-403429-112 enclosure; Letterhead Memo, SA DeLoach to SA Mohr, February 19, 1960, 97-3475-12; *New York Times*, December 1, 1962, 8; Unpublished article, Reverend Elson, "J. Edgar Hoover," August 12, 1965, 94-39821-157 enclosure.

4. Letterhead Memo, SA Nichols to SA Tolson, April 28, 1942, 94-4-5283-2; Letterhead Memo, SA DeLoach to SA Mohr, February 19, 1960, 97-3475-12; *New York Times*, December 1, 1962, 8; Leo P. Ribuffo, *The Old Christian Right: The Protestant Far Right from the Great Depression to the Cold War* (Philadelphia: Temple University Press, 1983), 260.

5. Grant Wacker, *America's Pastor: Billy Graham and the Shaping of a Nation* (Cambridge, Massachusetts: Belknap Press, 2014), 164–170. On conservative intellectual print culture, see Lisa McGirr, *Suburban Warriors: The Origins of the New American Right* (Princeton, NJ: Princeton University Press, 2002), 95; Darren Dochuk, *From Bible Belt to Sunbelt: Plain-Folk Religion, Grassroots Politics, and the Rise of Evangelical Conservatism*, 1st ed. (New York: W.W. Norton, 2011), 141–166.

6. Wacker, *America's Pastor*, 164–170. In 1965, its tenth year of operation, *National Review* reached its highest print circulation to date, approximately 85,000. See *New York Times*, March 14, 1965, 70.

7. Letterhead Memo, SA Nichols to SA Tolson, October 23, 1957, 67-308185-145. For more on Stukenbroeker, *Masters of Deceit*, as well as his broader Bureau ghostwriting, see Cecil, *Branding Hoover's FBI*, 120–134; Stukenbroeker FBI Employee File, 67-308185, available at https://archive.org/details/FernC.Stukenbroeker/page/n4/mode/2up.

8. Stukenbroeker FBI Employee File, 67-308185.

9. Letterhead Memo, SA Feeney to SA Callahan, December 5, 1972, Permanent Brief of SA Fern Stukenbroeker, 67-308185-unrecorded.

10. Letterhead Memo, SA Feeney to SA Callahan, December 5, 1972, Permanent Brief of SA Fern Stukenbroeker, 67-308185-unrecorded; SA H. L. Edwards to SA Mohr, June 9, 1958, 67-308185-150. Stukenbroeker wanted to be promoted to Special Agent in Charge of an FBI field office. However, due to his unique skill set, the Bureau continually denied him, as one supervisor noted in a March 31, 1958, performance review, "This Special Agent is interested in advancement in the Bureau's service. He is, however, an expert in the research field and it is felt that in view of this situation it would be to the Bureau's advantage for his advancement to be confined to the Seat of Government at the present time." See Stukenbroeker FBI Employee File, 67-308185.

11. Obituary, *Washington Post*, February 11, 2006; Letterhead Memo, SA Feeney to SA Callahan, December 5, 1972, Permanent Brief of SA Fern Stukenbroeker, 67-308185-unrecorded; Fern C. Stukenbroeker, *A Watermelon for God: A History of Trinity United Methodist Church, Alexandria, Virginia, 1774–1974* (Alexandria, VA: Stukenbroeker, 1974). Letterhead Memo, SA Jones to SA Tolson, October 21, 1957, 67-308185-142; Letterhead Memo, SA Nease to SA Tolson, September 9, 1957, 67-308185-141.

12. Ovid Demaris, *The Director: An Oral Biography of J. Edgar Hoover*, 1st ed. (New York: Harper's Magazine Press, 1975), 88–90; Matthew Cecil, *Branding Hoover's FBI: How the Boss's PR Men Sold the Bureau to America* (Lawrence: University Press of Kansas, 2016), 125.

13. Hoover, *Masters of Deceit*, 334, 337.

14. Hoover, *Masters of Deceit*, 334, 337, italics in original.

15. Hoover, *Masters of Deceit*, 319, 333, 336–337, italics in original.

16. See Hawes Publications, http://www.hawes.com/1958/1958.htm, accessed January 11, 2020. The book stayed on the list for approximately 31 weeks. On required reading, see Paul Letersky and Gordon Dillow, *The Director: My Years Assisting J. Edgar Hoover* (New York; London: Scribner, 2021), 27.

17. Demaris, *The Director*, 88; Richard A. Schwartz, *The 1950s, Eyewitness History* (New York: Facts on File, 2002), 363–364; Cecil, *Branding Hoover's FBI*, 125–127.

18. Schwartz, *The 1950s*, 363–364; Cecil, *Branding Hoover's FBI*, 125–127.

19. Reverend Harris, "Spires of the Spirit: Who Speaks for the Church," *Washington Star*, March 28, 1965.

20. Letterhead Memo, Letterhead Memo, SA Jones to SA Nease, February 21, 1958, 94-51006-3.

21. Letterhead Memo, SA Jones to SA Nease, February 14, 1958, 94-51060-2.

22. Wacker, *America's Pastor*, 164–167.

23. *Christianity Today*, "Why 'Christianity Today'" 1, no. 1, October 15, 1956; Billy Graham, *Just As I Am: The Autobiography of Billy Graham* (New York: HarperOne, 1997). Excerpted at *Christianity Today*, "Envisioning *Christianity Today*," https://www.christianitytoday.org/who-we-are/our-history/envisioningct.html, accessed January 13, 2020; Wacker, *America's Pastor*, 164; Harold J. Ockenga, "Resurgent Evangelical Leadership," *Christianity Today*, October 10, 1960; *Washington Post*, May 4, 1956, 28; Daniel Silliman, "An Evangelical Is Anyone Who Likes Billy Graham: Defining Evangelicalism with Carl Henry, Networks, and a Joke George Marsden

Told," *Church History* (n.d.); Darren Grem, "'Christianity Today,' J. Howard Pew, and the Business of Conservative Evangelicalism," *Enterprise & Society* 15, no. 2 (June 2014): 353, 357; George M. Marsden, *Understanding Fundamentalism and Evangelicalism* (Grand Rapids, MI: W.B. Eerdmans, 1991), 1–5.

24. Harold J. Ockenga, "Resurgent Evangelical Leadership," *Christianity Today*, October 10, 1960; Darren Grem, "'Christianity Today,' J. Howard Pew, and the Business of Conservative Evangelicalism," 349.

25. *Christianity Today*, "Why 'Christianity Today'" 1, no. 1, October 15, 1956; Billy Graham, *Just As I Am: The Autobiography of Billy Graham* (New York: HarperOne, 1997). Excerpted at *Christianity Today*, "Envisioning *Christianity Today*," https://www.christianitytoday.org/who -we-are/our-history/envisioningct.html, accessed January 13, 2020; Wacker, *America's Pastor*, 164; Harold J. Ockenga, "Resurgent Evangelical Leadership," *Christianity Today*, October 10, 1960; *Washington Post*, May 4, 1956, 28; Daniel Silliman, "An Evangelical Is Anyone Who Likes Billy Graham: Defining Evangelicalism with Carl Henry, Networks, and a Joke George Marsden Told," *Church History* (n.d.); Darren Grem, "'Christianity Today,' J. Howard Pew, and the Business of Conservative Evangelicalism," *Enterprise & Society* 15, no. 2 (June 2014): 350, 353, 357; Marsden, *Understanding Fundamentalism and Evangelicalism*, 1–5.

26. Ockenga, "Resurgent Evangelical Leadership."

27. Silliman, "An Evangelical Is Anyone Who Likes Billy Graham." On Whiteness as an unmarked category, see, for example, George Lipsitz, "The Possessive Investment in Whiteness: Racialized Social Democracy and the 'White' Problem in American Studies," *American Quarterly* 47, no. 3 (September 1995): 369–387.

28. *Christianity Today*, "Why 'Christianity Today'"; Graham, *Just As I Am*. Excerpted at *Christianity Today*, "Envisioning Christianity Today," https://www.christianitytoday.org/who -we-are/our-history/envisioningct.html, accessed January 13, 2020; *Washington Post*, May 4, 1956, 28; Silliman, "An Evangelical Is Anyone Who Likes Billy Graham." On white evangelicalism and masculinity, see Kristin Kobes Du Mez, *Jesus and John Wayne: How White Evangelicals Corrupted a Faith and Fractured a Nation* (New York: Liveright Publishing, 2020).

29. Curtis Evans, "White Evangelical Protestant Responses to the Civil Rights Movement," *Harvard Theological Review* 102, no. 2 (April 2009): 261, 265.

30. *Christianity Today*, "Why 'Christianity Today.'"

31. Letterhead Memo, SA Jones to SA Nease, Feburary 13, 1958, 94-51060-4.

32. Letterhead Memo, SA Jones to SA Nease, Feburary 27, 1958, 94-51060-5. On white evangelicals and Catholics, see, for example, Wacker, *America's Pastor*, 189–192.

33. Letter, Dr. Reverend Henry to Hoover, February 24, 1958, 94-51060-6.

34. SA Jones to SA Nease, April 17, 1958, 94-51060-9 and enclosure.

35. SA Jones to SA Nease, April 17, 1958, 94-51060-9 and enclosure; Luther A. Huston, *The Department of Justice*, Praeger Library of US Government Departments and Agencies (New York; London: Frederick A. Praeger, 1967), 56; Luther Huston obituary, *New York Times*, November 27, 1975, 36; Luther Huston FBI File, 62-104375; Jack Keith Jr. obituary, *San Diego Union Tribune*, September 8, 2010.

36. *CT* Letterhead, Reverend Henry to Hoover, May 23, 1958, 94-51060-15; *Christianity Today*, May 26, 1958, 4.

37. *CT* Letterhead, Dr. Reverend Henry to Hoover, June 7, 1958, 94-51060-13 and enclosure; *Congressional Record–Appendix*, June 4, 1958, A5124.

38. *CT* Letterhead, Reverend Henry to Hoover, February 10, 1959, 94-51060-18.

39. Letter, Hoover to Reverend Carl Henry, June 17, 1958, 94-51060-14; *CT* Letterhead, L. Nelson Bell to Hoover, June 18, 1958, 94-51060-16.

40. Letterhead Memo, SA Jones to SA DeLoach, February 11, 1959, 94-51060-22; Letterhead Memo, SA Jones to SA DeLoach, April 20, 1959, 94-5106-24; Letterhead Memo, SA Jones to SA DeLoach, August 30, 1963, 94-51060-144.

41. Letterhead Memo, SA Jones to SA DeLoach, February 11, 1959, 94-51060-22; Letterhead Memo, SA Jones to SA DeLoach, April 20, 1959, 94-5106-24; Letterhead Memo, SA Jones to SA DeLoach, August 30, 1963, 94-51060-144.

42. *CT* Letterhead, Reverend Henry to Hoover, February 10, 1959, 94-51060-18; Fred J. Cook, "The FBI," *The Nation*, October 18, 1958. The articles were later expanded into the book *The F.B.I. Nobody Knows*, in 1964; Fred Cook Obituary, *New York Times*, May 4, 2003, 54.

43. Letterhead Memo, SA Nease to SA Tolson, December 9, 1958, 67-8?004-802-36; Cecil, *Branding Hoover's FBI*, 118; Letterhead Memo, SA Jones to SA DeLoach, February 13, 1959, 94-51060-19; Letterhead Memo, SA Jones to SA Nease, December 17, 1958, 94-51060-21; Letterhead Memo, SA Jones to SA DeLoach, February 11, 1959, 94-51060-22; *CT* Letterhead, Reverend Henry to Hoover, February 10, 1959, 94-51060-18.

44. *CT* Letterhead, Reverend Henry to Hoover, February 10, 1959, 94-51060-18; Letterhead Memo, SA Nease to SA Tolson, December 9, 1958, 67-8?004-802-36; Letterhead Memo, SA Jones to SA DeLoach, February 13, 1959, 94-51060-19; Letterhead Memo, SA Jones to SA Nease, December 17, 1958, 94-51060-21; Letterhead Memo, SA Jones to SA DeLoach, February 11, 1959, 94-51060-22.

45. Letter, Hoover to Reverend Henry, February 16, 1959, 94-51060-18.

46. *CT* Letterhead, Reverend Henry to Hoover, Feb. 17, 1959, 94-51060-20.

47. Letterhead Memo, SA Jones to SA DeLoach, April 20, 1959, 94-51060-24 and enclosure; on editorial policy, see Darren Grem, "'Christianity Today,' J. Howard Pew, and the Business of Conservative Evangelicalism."

48. *CT* Letterhead, Reverend Henry to Hoover, June 18, 1959, 94-51060-26; David E. Kucharsky, News Editor, *Christianity Today* News Release, 94-51060-25 enclosure; *Washington Post and Times Herald*, June 20, 1959, D6.

49. Letterhead Memo, SA Jones to SA DeLoach, August 26, 1959, 94-51060-32 and enclosure. Caps in original.

50. Freedoms Foundation National Awards, https://www.freedomsfoundation.org/awards/national-awards/, accessed February 6, 2020; Demaris, *The Director*, 97; *CT* Letterhead, Reverend Henry to Hoover, February 16, 1960, 94-51060-34; *CT* Letterhead, Reverend Henry to SA Keith, February 29, 1960, 94-51060-39 and enclosure; Letterhead memo, Unnamed to Office of Director, February 15, 1960, 94-51060-37; Letterhead Memo, SA Jones to SA DeLoach, February 12, 1960, 94-51060-38; *Christianity Today*, February 29, 1960, 33.

51. *CT* Letterhead, Reverend Henry to Hoover, October 19, 1959, 94-51060-33; Letter, Hoover to Reverend Henry, October 23, 1959, 94-51060-33. On circulation, *New York Times*, March 14, 1965, 70.

52. Letterhead Memo, SA Jones to SA DeLoach, July 25, 1960, 94-51060-40; Letter, SA Jack Keith, Jr. to SA DeLoach, October 31, 1960, 94-51060-59.

53. Letterhead Memo, SAC Cincinnati to Director, July 29, 1960, 94-51060-41; see also, Letter, J. Howard Pew to Hoover, June 23, 1961, 62-44136-11. For more on Pew's relationship to white evangelicalism, see Darren E. Grem, *The Blessings of Business: How Corporations Shaped Conservative Christianity*, 1st ed. (New York: Oxford University Press, 2016); Darren Grem, "'Christianity Today,' J. Howard Pew, and the Business of Conservative Evangelicalism"; Darren Dochuk, *Anointed with Oil: How Christianity and Crude Made Modern America* (New York: Basic Books, 2019).

54. Letterhead Memo, SA Jones to SA DeLoach, November 21, 1960, 67-264895-115.

55. Letterhead Memo, SA Jones to SA DeLoach, August 1, 1960, 94-51060-44, enclosure; Hoover, "The Communist Menace: Red Goals and Christian Ideals," *Christianity Today*, October 10, 1960.

56. Letterhead Memo, SA Jones to SA DeLoach, August 1, 1960, 94-51060-44, enclosure.

57. 94-51060-45 enclosure; Hoover, "Communist Propaganda and the Christian Pulpit," *Christianity Today*, October 24, 1960, emphasis in original.

58. Letterhead Memo, SA Jones to SA DeLoach, August 26, 1960, 94-51060-43, enclosure.

59. Letterhead Memo, SA Jones to SA DeLoach, August 1, 1960, 94-51060-44, enclosure; Letterhead Memo, SA Jones to SA DeLoach, August 26, 1960, 94-51060-43, enclosure; Letter, SA Jack Keith Jr. to SA DeLoach, October 31, 1960, 94-51060-59.

60. Letter, Reverend Henry to Hoover, November 1, 1960, 94-51060-65; Letterhead Memo, SA Jones to SA DeLoach, November 21, 1960, 94-51060-136.

61. *Christianity Today* 1961 Christmas Subscription newsletter, 94-51060-119 enclosure.

62. Personal Letter, Hoover to SA Stukenbroeker, November 25, 1960, 67-308185-183.

63. Letter, Reverend Henry to Hoover, January 17, 1961, 94-51060-72; 94-51060-A. On Louis Cassels, see *New York Times*, January 24, 1974, 40.

64. Reverend V. C. Frank to Hoover, January 19, 1961, 94-51060-73.

65. 107 *Congressional Record*, January 9, 1961, A118-A119; January 10, 1961, A164.

66. Letterhead Memo, SA Callahan to Director, February 27, 1961, 94-51060-not recorded; 107 *Congressional Record*, Friday, February 24, 1961, 2644.

67. Letterhead Memo, SA DeLoach to SA Mohr, May 23, 1961, 94-51060-97.

68. Letter, Hoover to Reverend Henry, February 27, 1961, 94-51607-79; Freedoms Foundation National Awards, https://www.freedomsfoundation.org/awards/national-awards/, accessed February 6, 2020; 94-51060-94 enclosure; *Washington Evening Star*, February 13, 1961, A8, 62-44136-8 enclosure; Letter, J. Howard Pew to Hoover, March 30, 1961, 62-44136-9.

69. Letter, Reverend Henry to Hoover, November 21, 1960, 94-51060-136, enclosure; *Christianity Today*, "Eutychus and His Kin," December 19, 1960; Letter, Reverend Henry to Hoover, November 1, 1960, 94-51060-65; Letterhead Memo, SA Jones to SA DeLoach, November 21, 1960, 67-264895-115.

70. Gospel Light, https://www.gospellight.com/inside-gospel-light/, accessed March 16, 2020; Jennifer Woodruff Tait, "Ambitious for God," *Christianity Today*, no. 92, Fall 2006, 30–32; Wendy Zoba, "The Grandmother of Us All," *Christianity Today*, September 16, 1996, 44–46; Letter, Fritz Ridenour to Hoover, November 21, 1960, 94-51060-55; Timothy Larsen, David W. Bebbington, and Mark A. Noll, eds., "Henrietta C. Mears," in *Biographical Dictionary of Evangelicals* (Westmont, IL: Intervarsity Press, 2003), 419–421; see also Arlin C. Migliazzo, *Mother of American Evangelicalism: The Life and Legacy of Henrietta Mears* (Grand Rapids, mi: W.B.

Eerdmans, 2020), 141–143, 198; 244–246. On Bill Bright and Campus Crusade for Christ, see Pamphlet, Campus Crusade for Christ, "Where Are You Going for Christ" (Arrowhead Springs, CA, n.d.), 94-HQ-50997-28 enclosure.

71. Gospel Light Publications Letterhead, Editorial Director Eleanor Doan to Hoover, September 26, 1958, 94-38111-67; Gospel Light Publications Letterhead, Fritz Ridenour to Hoover, November 21, 1960, 94-51060-55; Letterhead Memo, Hoover to Ridenour, November 29, 1960, 94-51060-55. On "evangelical Sunday School," see *Teach* 2, No. 2, Winter 1961, 7; see also Hoover's issue, *Teach* 2, No. 4, Summer 1961.

72. Campus Crusade for Christ Letterhead, Bill Bright to Hoover, January 24, 1958, 94-HQ-50997-1; Letterhead Memo, SA Jones to SA Nease, January 30, 1958, 94-HQ-50997-2; Campus Crusade for Christ Letterhead, Bill Bright to Hoover, December 19, 1961, 94-HQ-50997-8; Campus Crusade for Christ Letterhead, Bill Bright to Hoover, June, 5 1962, 94-HQ-50997-19; Pamphlet, Campus Crusade for Christ, "Where Are You Going for Christ" (Arrowhead Springs, CA, n.d.), 94-HQ-50997-28, enclosure; *New York Times*, July 22, 2003, Section A, p. 17,

73. Campus Crusade for Christ Letterhead, Bill Bright to Hoover, December 19, 1961, 94-HQ-50997-8; Airtel, Director to SAC Minneapolis, January 1, 1962, 94-HQ-50997-illegible; Campus Crusade for Christ Letterhead, Bill Bright to Hoover, February 23, 1962, 94-HQ-50997-illegible; Letterhead Memo, SA Jones to SA DeLoach, March 1, 1962, 94-HQ-50997-illegible; Pamphlet, Campus Crusade for Christ, "Where Are You Going for Christ" (Arrowhead Springs, CA, n.d.), 94-HQ-50997-28, enclosure.

74. Daniel Vaca, *Evangelicals Incorporated: Books and the Business of Religion in America* (Cambridge, MA; London: Harvard University Press, 2019), 59–96.

75. Larry ten Harmsel and Reinder Van Til, *An Eerdmans Century* (Grand Rapids, MI: Eerdmans, 2011), 113–116; Letter, Hoover to Calvin Bulthuis, December 2, 1960, 94-51060-58.

76. Letter, Reverend Carl Henry to Hoover, June 8, 1965, 94-51060-163, enclosure; Wheaton History, A to Z, http://a2z.my.wheaton.edu/faculty/s-ritchey-kamm, accessed January 29, 2020; Harold J. Ockenga, "Resurgent Evangelical Leadership," *Christianity Today*, October 10, 1960. Letter, Hoover to Reverend Carl Henry, June 11, 1965, 94-51060-163 enclosure.

77. *Christianity Today* 1961 Christmas Subscription newsletter, 94-51060-119 enclosure.

Chapter 5. Message to the White Evangelical Grassroots

1. Handwritten Letter, Reverend Clinton Criswell to Hoover, September 17, 1964, 94-51060-157.

2. See, for example, Letterhead Memo, SA Jones to SA Wick, June 7, 1967, 94-51060-168; Letterhead Memo, SA Jones to SA Bishop, August 10, 1967, 94-51060-171.

3. Letter, Hoover to Reverend Carl Henry, August 10, 1967, 94-51060-172; SAC Letter, Hoover to SACs, August 24, 1967, 94-51060-173; Letter, Hoover to Mrs. Getty, March 14, 1969, 94-51060-191; Letter, Hoover to Dr. Harold Lindsell, March 27, 1969, 94-51060-190.

4. Letter, Miss Irma E. Peterson, Secretary to Reverend Carl Henry to Miss Helen Gandy, Secretary to Mr. Hoover, August 23, 1965, 94-51060-164; Vaca, *Evangelicals Incorporated*, 102. On the financial woes of *CT*, see Grem, "'Christianity Today.'"

5. Letter, SA Jack Keith Jr. to SA DeLoach, October 31, 1960, 94-51060-59; Hoover to Reverend Dennison, December 5, 1960, 94-51060-60; Letterhead Memo, SA Jones to SA DeLoach, December 7, 1960, 94-51060-64.

6. FBI US DOJ Report of Performance Rating for SA Fern C. Stukenbroeker, March 31, 1961, 67-308185-187.

7. Graham preached the sermon on at least two occasions, once during the LA crusade and another during the Chicago Crusade. See Sermon outline, "The Lost Frontier," Sermon Number 613, Box 24 Folder 128, Billy Graham Papers, Collection 285, Part III: File Cabinet Sermons 1951, 1953–2006, Billy Graham Evangelistic Association, Montreat, NC, Office, Billy Graham Center Archives, Wheaton College, Wheaton, IL; Sermon Outline, Billy Graham, "Siren Songs," September 4, 1968. Sermon Number 831, Box 12, Folder 46, Billy Graham Papers, Collection 285, Part I: Crusade Sermon Notebooks 1954, 1957, 1969–2005, Records of the Billy Graham Evangelistic Association (BGEA), Montreat, NC, Office, Billy Graham Center Archives, Wheaton College, Wheaton, IL. The sermon was repeated in countless other locations as well. See also Sermon Outline, "Kiwanis Club Banquet," Minneapolis, Minnesota, December 6, 1968, Sermon Number 581, Box 24 Folder 80, Billy Graham Papers, Collection 285 Part III: File Cabinet Sermons 1951, 1953-2006; see also the Finding Aid of the Records of the BGEA, Billy Graham Sermons Collection 265, Billy Graham Center Archives, Wheaton College, Wheaton, IL.

8. Billy Graham, "Rioting or Righteousness," *Hour of Decision*, Tract Number 173 (Minneapolis, MN: The Billy Graham Evangelistic Association, 1967). On *Hour of Decision*, see Wacker, *America's Pastor*, 21.

9. Letterhead Memo, SAC, Pittsburgh to Director, November 25, 1960, 94-51060-57; Letter, Hoover to Dr. Illingworth, December 1, 1960, 94-51060-57.

10. On the Sunbelt and suburbanization and the rise of white evangelical conservatism, see McGirr, *Suburban Warriors*; Kevin Michael Kruse, *White Flight: Atlanta and the Making of Modern Conservatism* (Princeton, NJ: Princeton University Press, 2005); Matthew Lassiter, *The Silent Majority: Suburban Politics in the Sunbelt South* (Princeton, NJ: Princeton University Press, 2007); Dochuk, *From Bible Belt to Sunbelt: Plain-Folk Religion, Grassroots Politics, and the Rise of Evangelical Conservatism*.

11. Letter, Pastor Arnold Barnum Hawkes to Hoover, July 2, 1962, 94-51060-127 enclosure; Hoover, "Spiritual Priorities: Guidelines for a Civilization in Peril," *Christianity Today*, June 22, 1962, 3–4.

12. Ibid.

13. Letter, Robert S. Neuenschwander, MD, to Reverend Carl Henry, September 22, 1961, 94-51060-117.

14. Letter, Reverend W. M. Dennison to Hoover, November 29, 1960, 94-51060-60; Hoover to Reverend Dennison, December 5, 1960, 94-51060-60.

15. Letter, Reverend Al Casebeer to Hoover, August 31, 1967, 94-51060-179.

16. Handwritten Letter, Creola L. Paradise to Hoover, January 21, 1971, 94-51060-208.

17. Handwritten Letter, Mrs. Wallace K. Dyer to Hoover June 1, 1961, 94-51060-99; Registered Mail, Hoover to Mrs. Dyer, June 8, 1961, 94-51060-99; Letter, Mrs. Wallace K. Dyer to Hoover June 22, 1961, 94-51060-106.

18. Letter, Mrs. David W. Smith to Hoover, June 10, 1961; Hoover to Mrs. Smith, June 16, 1961, 94-51060-102.

19. Letter, Mrs. D. A. Kemp to Hoover, December 28, 1960, 94-51060-67; Letter, Hoover to Kemp, January 9, 1961, 94-51060-67.

20. On kitchen-table activists, see McGirr, *Suburban Warriors*, 6, 97–110; Michelle Nickerson, *Mothers of Conservatism: Women and the Postwar Right* (Princeton, NJ and Oxford: Princeton University Press, 2012), 32–68.

21. Handwritten Letter, Regina Olbertz to Hoover, 94-51060-81; Letter, Hoover to Regina Olbertz, March 31, 1961, 94-51060-81.

22. Letter, Mrs. McDaniel to Hoover, August 10, 1961, 94-51060-113.

23. Handwritten Letter, Mrs. Fran A. Smith to Hoover, August 24, 1961, 94-51060-116.

24. Letter, Mrs. E. R. Katzorke to Hoover, May 22, 1962; Hoover to Mrs. Katzorke, May 31, 1962, 94-51060-125.

25. Letter, Floyd Suder Jr. to Hoover, December 20, 1960, 94-51060-66; Hoover to Suder, December 30, 1960, 94-51060-66.

26. Letter, Robert Null, MD, to Hoover, January 5, 1961, 94-51060-68; Letter, Hoover to Null, MD, January 12, 94-51060-68.

27. Card, Clarence Brueggeman to Hoover, January 6, 1961, 94-51060-69; Letter, Hoover to Clarence Brueggeman, January 13, 1961, 94-51060-69.

28. Letter, Sgt. R. G. Dehn to Hoover, January 14, 1961, 94-51060-71.

29. Handwritten Letter, Captain W. G. Cook to Hoover, 94-51060-80.

30. Letter, Gene Darnall to Hoover, November 18, 1961, 94051969-118.

31. FBI Airtel, Hoover to SAC, Los Angeles, July 10, 1961, 94051969-108.

32. Letter, Mrs. Nicholas D. Davis to Hoover, May 11, 1961, 94-51060-96; Letterhead memo, SA Morrell to SA DeLoach, May 18, 1961, 94-51060-95; Letter, Hoover to Mrs. Davis, May 18, 1961, 94-51060-96; James Phelan, "Hoover of the FBI," *Saturday Evening Post*, September 25, 196; McGirr, *Suburban Warriors*, 77–79; Ribuffo, *The Old Christian Right*, 261.

33. Letter, Mrs. Lorna T. Wood and Mr. William T. Wood to Hoover, July 10, 1961, 94-51060-107; FBI Airtel, Hoover to SAC, Los Angeles, July 10, 1961, 94051969-108; FBI Airtel, SAC Los Angeles to Director, July 13, 1961, 94-51060-109; Hoover to Mrs. William T. Wood, July 16, 1961, 94-51060-109.

34. Handwritten Letter, James F. Davis Jr. to Hoover, April 27, 1961; Airtel, Director to SAC Dallas, May 5, 1961, 94-51060-90, enclosure; Airtel, SAC, Dallas to Director, May 9, 1961; Helen Gandy to James Davis Jr., May 11, 1961, 94-51060-91.

35. Letter, Wilbur Benedict to Hoover, August 21, 1967, 94-51060-175, enclosure; Letterhead Memo, SA Jones to SA Bishop, August 24, 1967, 94-51060-176; Airtel, SAC, Los Angeles to Director, August 28, 1967, 94-51060-177; Letterhead Memo, SA Jones to SA Bishop, September 1, 1967, 94-51060-178

36. Letter, Irvin Andres to Hoover, November 17, 1960, 94-51060-54.

37. *Christianity Today*, "Eutychus and His Kin," January 30, 1970.

38. *Christianity Today*, "Eutychus and His Kin," August 31, 1959.

39. *Christianity Today*, "Eutychus and His Kin," October 9, 1964.

40. *Christianity Today*, "Eutychus and His Kin," January 16, 1970.

41. *Christianity Today*, "Eutychus and His Kin," May 26, 1972.

42. Letter, Mark F. Bartling to Hoover, September 13, 1962, 94-51060-132.

43. Letter, Duane H. Anderson, January 7, 1970, 94-51060-204.

44. Letterhead Memo, SA Jones to SA Nease, February 14, 1958, 94-51060-2.

45. Letter, Reverend Carl Henry to Hoover, December 18, 1962, 94-51060-138.

Part 3. Policing Faith: Hoover, the Adjudicator of White Evangelicalism

1. Letter, Mrs. Joyce Carter to Hoover, August 10, 1962, 100-413026-38.

2. I am indebted to Grant Wacker's framing of Billy Graham as "America's Pastor." See Wacker, *America's Pastor*, 248–282.

3. Ibid., 29, 267.

Chapter 6. Bishop

1. On Truman and Catholicism, see William Inboden, *Religion and American Foreign Policy, 1945–1960: The Soul of Containment* (New York City: Cambridge University Press, 2008), 110–111; Curt Gentry, *J. Edgar Hoover: The Man and the Secrets* (New York: W. W. Norton, 2001), 395.

2. Gentry, *J. Edgar Hoover: The Man and the Secrets*, 395; Reverend Elson Diary #1 January 1, 1952, Record Group 253 Box 10, Folder 12, Reverend Edward L. R. Elson Papers, 1924–1988, Presbyterian Historical Society Archives, Philadelphia, PA; Paul Letersky and Gordon Dillow, *The Director: My Years Assisting J. Edgar Hoover* (New York & London: Scribner, 2021), 127.

3. FBI File 100-HQ-413026; Peter J. Thuesen, *In Discordance with the Scriptures: American Protestant Battles Over Translating the Bible* (London; New York: Oxford University Press, 1999), 72–75, 90–91.

4. 100-HQ-413026; Carl McIntire, *The New Bible: Why Christians Should Not Accept It* (Collingswood, NJ: Christian Beacon, ND) in Bureau File 94-37990-10 enclosure.

5. McIntire, *The New Bible*, emphasis in original.

6. Thuesen, *In Discordance with the Scriptures*, 94–98.

7. Summaries of the Bureau's position on McIntire are found in numerous places, including Letter, Hoover to McIntire, July 11, 1951, 94-36904-3; Letterhead Memo, SA Morrell to SA DeLoach, May 18, 1962, 94-37990-56; Letter, Hoover to Deleted, December 4, 1963, 94-37990-73; Letterhead Memo, SA Jones to SA DeLoach, December 12, 1963, 94-37990-74.

8. Note on Letter, Hoover to Reverend Pierce, February 13, 1953, 100-HQ-413026-1; Note on Letter, Hoover to Miss Myrtle Duncan, April 8, 1954, 100-HQ-413026-9.

9. Note on Letter, SAC E. D. Mason to Mr. Claude Maddox Postal Inspector in Charge, Cincinnati, Ohio, May 6, 1960, 100-HQ-413026-23; the identity of Homer H. Hyde was revealed during a congressional debate. See *Congressional Record*, 86th Congress, 2nd ses., House of Representatives, March 3, 1960, 4404–4407.

10. *Congressional Record*, 86th Congress, 2nd sess., House of Representatives, March 3, 1960, 4404–4407.

11. See, for example, Letter, Deleted to Hoover, March 15, 1963, 94-37990-67; Letter, W. E. Baker to Hoover, August 3, 1954, 100-HQ-413026; Billy Graham received similar bare-bones envelopes. See Wacker, *America's Pastor*, 280.

12. Handwritten Letter, Reverend Pierce to Hoover January 5, 1953, 100-HQ-413026-1.

13. Letter, Reverend Newman to Hoover, September 19, 1960, 100-HQ-413026-not recorded.

14. Letter, Reverend Carl Yoder to Hoover, no date, 100-413026-27.

15. Letter, Reverend Billy Gaither to Hoover, March 22, 1964, 100-413026-42.

16. Handwritten Letter, Mrs. Ryckman to Hoover, February 13, 1953, 100-HQ-413026-5.

17. Letter, Ted Miller to FBI, March 15, 1953, 94-37990-11.

18. Letter, Harold E. Owings to Hoover, December 14, 1960, 100-413026-30.

19. Letter, Francis K. Ludwick to Hoover, January 14, 1961, 100-413026-31.

20. Letter, George Hieb to Hoover, September 28, 1960, 100-413026-26.

21. Letter, Mrs Ellen L. Forson to Hoover, January 30, 1961, 100-413026-32.

22. Letter, Mrs. Merrill M. Abernathy to Hoover, September 27, 1967, 100-413026-43.

23. For example, see Letter, Hoover to George Hieb, October 10, 1960, 100-413026-26; Letter, Hoover to Reverend Carl Yoder, November 2, 1960, 100-413026-27; Letter, Hoover to Harold Owings, December 28, 1960, 100-413026-30; Oswald T. Allis, "RSV Appraisal: Old Testament," *Christianity Today*, July 8, 1957; Harold J. Ockenga, "Resurgent Evangelical Leadership," *Christianity Today*, October 10, 1960.

24. Reverend Elson, Undated notes, Record Group 253 Box 10, Folder 4, Reverend Edward L. R. Elson Papers, 1924–1988, Presbyterian Historical Society Archives, Philadelphia, PA; Letter, Reverend Elson to Hoover, March 19, 1952, 94-39821-28.

25. Edward L. R. Elson, *Wide Was His Parish: An Autobiography* (Wheaton, IL: Tyndale House Publishers, 1986), 124–125.

26. Letter, Reverend Humerickhouse to Hoover, March 24, 1960, 94-46796-14.

27. Letter, Reverend Karl E. Blake to Hoover, December 20, 1969, 94-51060-195.

28. Letter, Reverend Tyler Terry to Hoover, May 17, 1968, 94-58567-9.

29. Letter, Deleted to Hoover, April 17, 1962 94-37990-53. The name is redacted from the Bureau files, but the Bureau noted the correspondent "is described in Bufiles as a young man with liberal views."

30. Letter, Reverend John C. Calhoun to Hoover, November 11, 1966, 94-55180-11.

31. Letter, Deleted to Hoover, March 7, 1961, 94-37990-32.

32. Letter, Redacted to Hoover, October 10, 1962, 62-105577-6.

33. Letter, Paul Hamer to FBI, September 7, 1962, 94-36904-13.

34. Letter, Deleted to Hoover, March 19, 1963, 94-37990-68.

35. Letter, Miss Martha Wald to Hoover, January 6, 1966, 94-HQ-50997-illegible.

36. Church Letterhead, J. Robert Ashton to FBI, April 26, 1971, 94-HQ-50997-illegible.

37. Letter, Mr. and Mrs. R. B. Paine to Hoover, October 4, 1962, 94-HQ-50997-illegible.

38. Church Letterhead, Reverend O'Connell to FBI, April 7, 1967, 94-HQ-50997-32.

39. See, for example, Letter, Hoover to Mr. and Mrs. R. B. Paine, October 10, 1962, 94-HQ-50997-illegible; *The Collegiate Challenge*, May–June 1962.

40. Letter, A. B. Cowen to Hoover, February 28, 1960, 94-46796-13.

41. Letter, Mrs. J. R. Whisman to Hoover, March 2, 1964, 94-46796-26.

42. Letter, Ruth B. Tanner to Hoover, October 19, 1966, 94-46796-28.

43. Letter, Mrs. Barry to Hoover, October 12, 1959, 94-37990-23.

44. Letter, Deleted to Hoover, October 27, 1961, 94-37990-44x.

45. Letter, Deleted to Hoover, July 18, 1961, 94-37990-37.

Chapter 7. Champion

1. Chicago Bible Society, http://chicagobiblesociety.org/programs/gutenberg/the-gutenberg-award, accessed December 31, 2019. J. Edgar Hoover and the 1956 award slot have been removed from the website. Billy Graham did not receive the award until 1962, while Archbishop Fulton Sheen received the honor in 1974. On the ABS, see John Fea, *The Bible Cause: A History of the American Bible Society* (New York: Oxford University Press, 2016), 3.

2. The Chicago Bible Society Gutenberg Award for the Year 1956, "Awards," J. Edgar Hoover Personal Estate Collection, National Law Enforcement Museum, Washington, DC, caps in original.

3. Tona J. Hangen, *Redeeming the Dial: Radio, Religion, & Popular Culture in America* (Chapel Hill: University of North Carolina Press), 149.

4. Ibid., 123–124, 134; "Biography," Papers of Eugene Rudolph Bertermann, Billy Graham Center Archives, Wheaton, IL; Lutheran Hour Letterhead Memo, Reverend Walter A. Maier to Hoover, August 18, 1947, 100-7092-20; Lutheran Hour Letterhead Memo, Bertermann to Hoover, August 20, 1951, 100-7092-21 enclosure. For 1947 congressional testimony, see Bertermann, "Plea for More Time for Gospel Radio Broadcasts, *United Evangelical Action*, August 15, 1947, 5-6.

5. Lutheran Hour Letterhead Memo, Reverend Walter A. Maier to Hoover, August 18, 1947, 100-7092-20; Lutheran Hour Letterhead Memo, Bertermann to Hoover, August 20, 1951, 100-7092-21; Letter, Hoover to Bertermann, August 29, 1951, 100-7092-21 enclosure.

6. Telegram, Western Union, from Dr. Eugene R. Bertermann to Hoover, November 17, 1961, 94-56355-2, enclosure; NRB Letterhead, Dr. Eugene Bertermann to Hoover, November 17, 1961, 94-56355-2.

7. NRB Letterhead Memo, Dr. Eugene Bertermann to Hoover, November 17, 1961, 94-56355-2.

8. Letter, Helen Gandy to Bertermann, November 21, 1961, 94-56355-1.

9. Airtel, Hoover to SAC, St. Louis, November 21, 1961, 94-56355-3.

10. Airtel, SAC, St. Louis to Hoover, November 25, 1961, 94-56355-4.

11. Letter, Hoover to Bertermann, November 28, 1961, 94-56355-4; Letterhead Memo, SA Jones to SA DeLoach, January 12, 1962, 94-56355-5.

12. Airmail, NRB Letterhead Memo, Bertermann to Hoover, December 5, 1961, 94-56355-14.

13. Letterhead Memo, SA Jones to SA DeLoach, January 12, 1962, 94-56355-5; NRB Letterhead, Bertermann to SA DeLoach, January 4, 1962, 94-56355-11; Letter, Hoover to Earl Paulk, January 31, 1962, 94-56355-8; "Biographical Note," James DeForest Murch Papers, Collection C0001, The Holloway Archives at Milligan College, Milligan College, TN.

14. NRB Letterhead, Bertermann to Hoover, January 16, 1962, 94-56355-15; *The Pentecostal Evangel*, March 18, 1962, 13; "Historical Background," Papers of Walter F. Bennet and Company, Billy Graham Center Archives, Wheaton, IL; *The Investigator*, March 1962, 39.

15. Copy of plaque in FBI File 94-56355-19 enclosure.

16. 94-56355-5 enclosure; *The Pentecostal Evangel*, March 25, 1962, 22.

17. Letterhead Memo, SA DeLoach to SA Mohr, January 24, 1962, 94-56355-19.

18. Letterhead Memo, "Address of Assistant Director C. D. DeLoach Federal Bureau of Investigation at the 19th Annual Convention of the National Religious Broadcasters, Inc., in Washington D.C. January 24, 1962," 94-56355-17 enclosure.

19. Letter sent by special messenger, Hoover to Bertermann, January 24, 1962, 94-56355-6; NRB Letterhead, Bertermann to Hoover, January 30, 1962, 94-56355-9; NRB Letterhead, Bertermann to Hoover, September 24, 1962, 94-56355-22.

20. Church of God Letterhead, Paulk to Hoover, January 26, 1962, 94-56355-7.

21. Church of God Letterhead, Paulk to SA DeLoach, January 26, 1962, 94-56355-8.

22. Letter, Hammond to SA DeLoach, February 1, 1962, 94-56355-8; Letter, Hoover to Hammond, February 7, 1962, 94-56355-10.

23. NRB Letterhead memo, Willingham to Hoover, February 16, 1962, 94-56355-20; Letter, Hoover to Willingham, February 23, 1962, 94-56355-20.

24. *New York Times*, September 23, 1964, 40; November 25, 1964, 74.

25. *Chicago Tribune*, November 22, 1964, 12.

26. *Sword of Loyola* Program, November 24, 1964 in J. Edgar Hoover Personal Estate Collection, National Law Enforcement Museum, Washington, DC; "Hoover's Sword of Loyola, 1964," Loyola University Chicago Digital Special Collections, accessed December 18, 2014, http://www.lib.luc.edu/specialcollections/exhibits/show/loyola-traditions/item/320; *New York Times*, November 25, 1964, 74.

27. Speech reprinted in *Congressional Record Appendix*, February 4, 1965. 111th Congress, Record A511.

28. *Congressional Record Appendix*, February 4, 1965. 111th Congress, Record A511; The Associated Press Archive has footage of the event, available at https://www.youtube.com/watch?v=eYYfasm-l2M, accessed May 6, 2020.

29. *Congressional Record*, February 4, 1965,111[th] Congress, Record A511.

30. Ibid.

31. On Campus Crusade for Christ, see *Where Are You Going For Christ*, a booklet "which describes the ministry of Campus Crusade for Christ," and Bill Bright to Hoover, personal letter, December 22, 1964, both in 94-HQ-50997-illegible.

32. *The Pentecostal Evangel*, June 27, 1965, 10–11.

33. Iain MacRobert, *The Black Roots and White Racism of Early Pentecostalism in the USA* (Basingstoke: Macmillan, 1988), 64.

34. Wacker, *America's Pastor*, 169; Benjamin A. Wagner, "'Full Gospel' Radio: Revivaltime and the Pentecostal Uses of Mass Media, 1950–1979," *Fides et Historia* 35, no. 1 (2003): 107–122.

35. Memo, Acting National Director Division of Communications Lee Schultz to Executive Presbyters, "Special Report on *The Pentecostal Evangel*," August 8, 1973, Location 21/3/6, Record Group 15-60, Flower Pentecostal Heritage Center; Ken Horn, "The Centennial of the Pentecostal Evangel," *Assemblies of God Heritage Magazine* 33, 2013, 5–15; *The Pentecostal Evangel*, April 1, 1950, 6.

36. *The Pentecostal Evangel*, June 27, 1965, 10–11.

37. *The Pentecostal Evangel*, June 27, 1965, 10–11.

38. *The Pentecostal Evangel*, April 1, 1950, cover page; July 29, 1950, 13; April 22, 1951, 3; November 15, 1953, 8–9, 11; October 3, 1954, 8–9; December 16, 1956, 16–17; December 8, 1957, 18; Benjamin A. Wagner, "C. M. Ward: The Voice of Revivaltime, 1953–1976," *Assemblies of God Heritage Magazine* 33, 2013, 17–25; Benjamin A. Wagner, "'Full Gospel' Radio: Revivaltime and the Pentecostal Uses of Mass Media, 1950–1979."

39. *The Pentecostal Evangel*, April 1, 1950, cover page; July 29, 1950, 13; April 22, 1951, 3; November 15, 1953, 8–9, 11; October 3, 1954, 8–9; December 16, 1956, 16–17; December 8, 1957, 18; Benjamin A. Wagner, "C. M. Ward: The Voice of Revivaltime, 1953–1976," *Assemblies of God Heritage Magazine* 33, 2013, 17–25; Benjamin A. Wagner, "'Full Gospel' Radio: Revivaltime and the Pentecostal Uses of Mass Media, 1950–1979."

40. Ibid., The NRB Hall of Fame, http://nrb.org/membership/media-awards/nrb_hall_of _fame/, accessed May 14, 2020.

41. *The Pentecostal Evangel*, July 28, 1968; August, 31, 1969, 13.

42. *The Pentecostal Evangel*, August 23, 1970, 24–25; September 13, 1970, 24, italics in original.

43. Reverend C. M. Ward, *Revivaltime Tracts: J. Edgar Hoover Testifies*, Springfield, MO: Assemblies of God, 1970, Archive ID: 23984, Location: 1/6/8 Mini-tracts, Flower Pentecostal Heritage Center, Springfield, MO.

44. *The Pentecostal Evangel*, October, 1970, 11; December 20, 1970, 29; December 12, 1971, 31.

45. Reverend C. M. Ward, *Revivaltime Tracts: J. Edgar Hoover Testifies*, Springfield, MO: Assemblies of God, 1970, Archive ID: 23984, Location: 1/6/8 Mini-tracts, Flower Pentecostal Heritage Center, Springfield, MO.

46. Wacker, *America's Pastor*, 15, 22, 64; Advertisement for *Decision* Magazine in "Rioting or Righteousness," Hour of Decision Tract, Number 173, Box 6, Folder 4, Ephemera of Billy Graham, Collection 74, Billy Graham Center Archives, Wheaton College, Wheaton, IL.

47. Wacker, *America's Pastor*, 15, 164.

48. Ibid., 164.

49. Photo of Billy Graham with Hoover, FBI Headquarters May 1, 1969, Record Group 065, Photos of FBI Personnel and Activities, 1935–1972, Photo HN-9005, National Archives and Record Administration, College Park, MD; Graham and Hoover Photo, BGEA Crusade Activities Collection 17, Records of the Billy Graham Evangelistic Association, Billy Graham Center Archives, Wheaton College, Wheaton, IL.

50. *Decision*, July 1971, 4.

51. Ibid.

52. Ibid.

Chapter 8. Crusader

A version of chapter 8 appeared previously in L. Martin, "Bureau Clergyman: How the FBI Colluded with an African American Televangelist to Destroy Dr. Martin Luther King, Jr.," *Religion and American Culture: A Journal of Interpretation* 28, no. 1 (2018): 1–51.

1. Hoover, "Off the Record Remarks of J. Edgar Hoover, Director, FBI at Informal FBI Reception for Editors of Georgia and Michigan Newspapers Thursday, April 15, 1965," Kenneth

O'Reilly Research Materials, 1922–1991, Series 90, FBI Investigation and Surveillance Records, Special Collections and University Archives, Marquette University.

2. Hoover, "Off the Record Remarks of J. Edgar Hoover."

3. On white supremacy, religion, and conservative opposition to interracial marriage, see R. Marie Griffith, *Moral Combat: How Sex Divided American Christians and Fractured American Politics* (New York: Basic Books, 2017), 83–120; Jane Dailey, "Sex, Segregation, and the Sacred after Brown," *Journal of American History* 91, no. 1 (June 2004): 119–144.

4. *Christianity Today*, "Segregation and the Kingdom of God," March 18, 1957, 6–9; *Christianity Today*, January 19, 1959, 20–23; Curtis Evans, "White Evangelical Protestant Responses to the Civil Rights Movement," *Harvard Theological Review* 102, no. 2 (April 2009): 263.

5. *Christianity Today*, "Segregation and the Kingdom of God," March 18, 1957, 6-9; *Christianity Today*, January 19, 1959, 20-23; Curtis Evans, "White Evangelical Protestant Responses to the Civil Rights Movement," 263.

6. Daniel Silliman, "An Evangelical Is Anyone Who Likes Billy Graham"; *Christianity Today*, "Why 'Christianity Today'" 1, no. 1, October 15, 1956; Billy Graham, *Just As I Am: The Autobiography of Billy Graham*. Excerpted at *Christianity Today*, "Envisioning *Christianity Today*," https://www.christianitytoday.org/who-we-are/our-history/envisioningct.html, accessed January 13, 2020; *Washington Post*, May 4, 1956, 28; Darren Grem, "'Christianity Today,' J. Howard Pew, and the Business of Conservative Evangelicalism," 339–340, 364–365; Wacker, *America's Pastor*, 131; Curtis Evans, "White Evangelical Protestant Responses to the Civil Rights Movement," 263.

7. James DeForest Murch, *Cooperation Without Compromise: A History of the National Association of Evangelicals* (Grand Rapids, MI: W. B. Eerdmans, 1956), 135–152; Axel R. Schafer, *Piety and Public Funding: Evangelicals and the State in Modern America* (Philadelphia: University of Pennsylvania Press, 2012), 10, 66–67, 70.

8. Letterhead Memo, SA Nichols to SA Tolson, January 4, 1957, 62-103627-5; OPA Letterhead Memo, Reverend Taylor to SA Nichols, January 8, 1957, 62-HQ-103627-not recorded; Axel R. Schafer, *Piety and Public Funding*, 68.

9. NAE Letterhead, Reverend Clyde Taylor to SA Nichol [*sic*], January 8, 1957, 62-103627-not recorded; Letter, NAE Letterhead, Redacted to Hoover, January 24, 1966, 67-308185-not recorded; Letter, Hoover to Redacted at NAE Offices, January 27, 1966, 67-308185-not recorded. The NAE made similar overtures concerning careers in the federal government to the State Department, Civil Service, and the Department of Defense. See NAE Letterhead, Reverend Clyde Taylor to SA Nichol [*sic*], January 8, 1957, 62-103627-not recorded.

10. Letter, Hoover to Redacted at NAE Offices, January 27, 1966, 67-308185-not recorded; NAE Letterhead, Rev. Taylor to SA Stukenbroeker, Feb. 25, 1964, 67-308185-not recorded; NAE Letterhead, Redacted to Hoover, January 24, 1966, 67-308185-not recorded; Letter, Rev. Taylor to Hoover, January 26, 1967, 67-308185-not recorded; Letter, Rev. Taylor to Hoover, March 7, 1972, 67-308185-not recorded.

11. On white evangelicals and colorblindness, see Jesse Curtis, *The Myth of Colorblind Christians: Evangelicals and White Supremacy in the Civil Rights Era* (New York; London: New York University Press, 2021).

12. Michaux quoted in *Associated Negro Press* Release, "Is the Negro Treated Right in America," June 4, 1958, in Chicago Historical Society, The Claude A. Barnett Papers. Some have

referred to Michaux as "Solomon Lightfoot Michaux"; however, I am using the name Lightfoot Solomon Michaux according to US Census notes and Church of God histories. See 1910 US Census, Newport, Warick, Virginia, Roll/ T624_1650, Page 6A. Enumeration District 0120 FHL microfilm/1375663; The Church of God at Williamsburg, "Who We Are," http://www.thechurchofgodatwilliamsburg.org, accessed August 21, 2015. Michaux based his views on religion, law, and race on Romans 13:1–7. See "Elder Michaux's View on Church and State. . . ." No date, Archive, The Church of God at Williamsburg, "Who We Are," http://www.thechurchofgodatwilliamsburg.org, accessed August 21, 2015. On early years, see *Radio Guide*, May 5, 1934, May 12, 1934; *Washington Evening Star*, July 10, 1938, 3A; *Washington Evening Star*, July 10, 1938, 3A; July 11, 1938; *Pittsburgh Courier*, January 6, 1934, A3; Williams, "The Socio-Economic Significance of the Store-Front Church Movement in the United States Since 1920," Doctoral Dissertation, The American University Washington, D.C., 1949, 51–57, 86–87.

13. US Department of Justice Memo, L. B. Nichols to Mr. Tolson, "Memorandum for Mr. Tolson," September 16, 1941, 94-4-2848-2; Memo, Nichols to Tolson, June 27, 1943, 94-4-2848-4, emphasis mine.

14. CBS dropped Michaux from many of its stations by the outbreak of war in Europe as a result of the ministry being dogged by accusations of financial mismanagement. The Mutual Network picked up Michaux's show on their national network. On CBS stations, see E. Nelson Palmer, "Elder Michaux and His Church of God: A Sociological Interpretation" (Fisk University Charles S. Johnson Papers, Social Sciences Documents, Section 3 Row 6 Box 6 Folder 5, 1944–1947), 11. On Mutual, see Associated Negro Press Release, Church News: Washington, "Thousands Pay Tribute to 'Happy Am I' Preacher at Griffith Stadium," October 3, 1951, in Chicago Historical Society, The Claude A. Barnett Papers; *The Radio Guide*, May 5, 1934, 5, 34; May 12, 1934, 5, 34; *The Billboard*, June 26, 1937, 11. On acting career, see unpublished paper, Palmer, "Elder Michaux and His Church of God, 37. Palmer uses the term "'end man' in a minstrel show." Special thanks to Jamil Drake for bringing this unpublished piece to my attention; *Afro-American*, April 9, 1932, 13.

15. Many scholars of religion in America have long held the consensus that Rex Humbard became the first minister/evangelist to host his own weekly television show in 1952. See, for example, *God in America*, http://www.pbs.org/wgbh/pages/frontline/godinamerica/timeline/, accessed January 31, 2017. However, Michaux's weekly show was launched four years before Humbard's series. Michaux's local run outlasted its national broadcast. After four total years on the air, the show folded in 1951 when the DuMont network began broadcasting the television show of another Bureau clergyman: Bishop Fulton Sheen. On Michaux's show, see *The Billboard*, November 27, 1948, 10; December 27, 1948, 12; David Weinstein, "Du Mont in Washington, D.C.: Out on a Limb," *Quarterly Review of Film and Video* 16, no. 3–4 (1997), 379–381; Hal Erickson, *Religious Radio and Television in the United States, 1921–1991: The Programs and Personalities* (Jefferson, NC: McFarland, 1992), 71. For more on the DuMont Television Network, see David Weinstein, *The Forgotten Network: DuMont and the Birth of American Television* (Philadelphia: Temple University Press, 2006).

16. *The Billboard*, November 27, 1948, 10; December 18, 1948, 12; December 27, 1948, 12; December, 3, 1949, 10; David Weinstein, "Du Mont in Washington, D.C.: Out on a Limb," 379–381.

17. *The Billboard*, November 27, 1948, 10; December 27, 1948, 12; David Weinstein, "Du Mont in Washington, D.C.: Out on a Limb," 381.

18. Letter, Hoover to Michaux, 94-HQ-4-2848-7.

19. In addition to remarks from Hoover, Eisenhower, and McGrath, Michaux also received well wishes from Federal Security Administrator Oscar R. Ewing (who also attended the event), CBS Vice President Earl H. Gammons, as well as Clark Griffith, who was the owner of the Washington Senators baseball team. Fellow CBS radio personalities from the *Jack Benny* show and the *Amos 'n' Andy* show also sent along congratulatory notes. Western Union Telegram, Hoover to Michaux's home at 1712 R. Street N.W. Washington DC, CC to Agent Jones, 6:47pm, September 20, 1951, 94-4-2848-10. On contemporary cost, see Lawrence H. Officer and Samuel H. Williamson, "Measures of Worth," MeasuringWorth, 2012, www.measuringworth.com /worthmeasures.php, accessed January 26, 2017. On other congratulatory notes, see Office Memo, Jones to Nichols, September 24, 1951, 94-4-2848-9; *Washington Post*, September 22, 1951, 7; *The Chicago Defender*, October 6, 1951, 2; Associated Negro Press Release, Church News: Washington, "Thousands Pay Tribute to 'Happy Am I' Preacher at Griffith Stadium," October 3, 1951 in Chicago Historical Society, The Claude A. Barnett Papers: The Associated Negro Press, 1918–1967, File, "Radio Church of God, Elder Lightfoot Solomon Michaux, Jul 13, 1934–Sep 16, 1956." The Associated Negro Press, interestingly, omitted Hoover's name from their catalogue of well-wishers.

20. All FBI documents obtained through the Freedom of Information and Privacy Act, Office Memo, L. B. Nichols to Mr. Tolson, CC-Mr. Holloman, Mr. Jones, "Elder Lightfoot Solomon Michaux," January 23, 1956, 94-4-2848-illegible. Original copy filed in 62-66723-4; US Department of Justice Memo, L. B. Nichols to Mr. Tolson, "Memorandum for Mr. Tolson," September 16, 1941, no file number; Office Memo, Nichols to Tolson, September 20, 1951, 94-4-2848-8; Letter, Nichols to [deleted] The Methodist Church, July 9, 1948, 100-15139-44. On Nichols, see his obituary in *Washington Post*, "Louis Nichols Dies, Was No. 3 at FBI," June 10, 1977, and his interview in Demaris, *The Director*, 65–76; Cecil, *Branding Hoover's FBI*, 27. On YMCA and YWCA racial segregation, see Susan Kerr Chandler, "'Almost a Partnership': African-Americans, Segregation, and the Young Men's Christian Association," *Journal of Sociology & Social Welfare*, 21, no. 1 (March 1994); Judith Weisenfeld, *African American Women and Christian Activism: New York's Black Y.W.C.A, 1905–1945* (Cambridge, MA: Harvard University Press, 1997).

21. Office Memo, Special Agent Nichols to Special Agent Tolson, February 14, 1956, 62-101087-79; Letterhead Memo, L. B. Nichols to Mr. Tolson, CC-Mr. Holloman, Mr. Jones, "Elder Lightfoot Solomon Michaux," January 23, 1956, 94-4-2848-illegible. Original copy filed in 62-66723-4; Teletype Telegram, Michaux to Hoover, April 15, 1956, Bureau File, 94-4-2848-22.

22. Office Memo, L. B. Nichols to Mr. Tolson, CC-Mr. Holloman, Mr. Jones, "Elder Lightfoot Solomon Michaux," January 23, 1956, 94-4-2848-illegible. Original copy filed in 62-66723-4; Teletype Telegram, Michaux to Hoover, April 15, 1956, Bureau File, 94-4-2848-22. On number of FBI agents, see Athan G. Theoharis, *The FBI & American Democracy: A Brief Critical History* (Lawrence: University Press of Kansas, 2004), 174. On Cold War ideas of political and domestic "containment," "spiritual mobilization," "spiritual insolvency," and religious "anxiety," see respectively, Elaine Tyler May, *Homeward Bound: American Families in the Cold War Era*, fully rev. and

updated 20th anniversary ed. (New York: Basic Books, 2008), 16–17; Jonathan P. Herzog, *The Spiritual-Industrial Complex: America's Religious Battle against Communism in the Early Cold War* (New York: Oxford University Press, 2011), 15–16; Andrew S. Finstuen, *Original Sin and Everyday Protestants: The Theology of Reinhold Niebuhr, Billy Graham, and Paul Tillich in an Age of Anxiety*, 1st ed. (Chapel Hill: University of North Carolina Press, 2009).

23. Michaux's first visit to the FBI was in 1941. During WWII, he worked with the G-men to extol the FBI as a paragon of Christianity, patriotism, and racial progress; while discrediting and slandering a number of "subversive" Black civil rights advocates from the National Negro Congress and the Regional Council of Negro Leadership. The FBI credited the preacher with being "instrumental on more than one occasion in rendering us a real service." See, for example, US Department of Justice Memo, L. B. Nichols to Mr. Tolson, "Memorandum for Mr. Tolson," September 16, 1941, no file number. Memo, Nichols to Tolson, September 20, 1951, 94-4-2848-8; Office Memo, Nichols to Tolson, September 20, 1951, 94-4-2848-8; Office Memo, L. B. Nichols to Mr. Tolson, CC-Mr. Holloman, Mr. Jones, "Elder Lightfoot Solomon Michaux," January 23, 1956, 94-4-2848-illegible. Original copy filed in 62-66723-4, emphasis mine.

24. Reprinted in *Congressional Record Appendix*, 109 Congress, August 5, 1963, A4978-A4979.

25. Hoover, "A Christmas Message," *The Investigator*, Christmas 1961, emphasis mine.

26. Hoover, "Message from the Director to all Law Enforcement Officials," *FBI Law Enforcement Bulletin*, November 1964.

27. J. Edgar Hoover, "Wholly Loyal," *Crusader*, June 1961, 15.

28. *Report of the Department of Justice Task Force to Review the FBI Martin Luther King, Jr., Security and Assassination Investigations*, January 11, 1977, 113–114, found in Martin Luther King Jr. Main File, 100-106670 Section 103; Cartha D. DeLoach, *Hoover's FBI: The Inside Story by Hoover's Trusted Lieutenant* (Washington, DC: Regnery Publishing, 1997), 202; see also FBI Secret Monograph, *The Communist Party and the Negro, 1953–1956*, October 1956; David J. Garrow, *The F.B.I. and Martin Luther King Jr: From Solo to Memphis* (New York: W.W. Norton, 1981).

29. Alexander Charns, *Cloak and Gavel: FBI Wiretaps, Bugs, Informers, and the Supreme Court* (Urbana and Chicago: University of Illinois Press, 1992), xii–xiii; *Report of the Department of Justice Task Force to Review the FBI Martin Luther King, Jr., Security and Assassination Investigations*, 116–118; US Senate Select Committee to Study Governmental Operations with Respect to Intelligence Activities, *Final Report of the Senate Select Committee to Study Governmental Operations with Respect to Intelligence Activities, Supplementary Detailed Staff Reports on Intelligence Activities and the Rights of Americans, Book 3*, 104–107; Paul Letersky and Gordon Dillow, *The Director: My Years Assisting J. Edgar Hoover* (New York; London: Scribner, 2021), 117–121.

30. Dean Fischer, "J. Edgar Hoover Speaks Out with Vigor"; Cartha D. DeLoach, *Hoover's FBI*, 200.

31. Memo, William C. Sullivan to Alan H. Belmont, "Communist Party, USA, Negro Question; IS-C," August 30, 1963, and Unofficial Memo, William C. Sullivan to Alan H. Belmont, "Communist Party, USA, Negro Question; Communist Influence in Racial Matters," September 25, 1963, 100-106670 in *Report of the Department of Justice Task Force to Review the FBI Martin Luther King, Jr., Security and Assassination Investigations*; US Senate Select Committee to Study Governmental Operations with Respect to Intelligence Activities, *Final Report of the Senate*

Select Committee to Study Governmental Operations with Respect to Intelligence Activities, Supplementary Detailed Staff Reports on Intelligence Activities and the Rights of Americans, Book 3, 104–107, 134–135; Memo, William C. Sullivan to Alan H. Belmont, "Samuel Riley Pierce, Jr.," January 8, 1964, reprinted in full in Victor Navasky, "The FBI's Wildest Dream," *Nation* 226, no. 23 (June 17, 1978): 716–718.

32. See Hoover's handwritten comments on Memo, William C. Sullivan to Alan H. Belmont, "Samuel Riley Pierce, Jr.," January 8, 1964, reprinted in full in Navasky, "The FBI's Wildest Dream." See also Garrow, *The F.B.I. and Martin Luther King Jr: From Solo to Memphis*, 68.

33. US Senate Select Committee to Study Governmental Operations with Respect to Intelligence Activities, *Final Report of the Senate Select Committee to Study Governmental Operations with Respect to Intelligence Activities, Supplementary Detailed Staff Reports on Intelligence Activities and the Rights of Americans, Book 3*, 81–82, 108; Memo, William C. Sullivan to Alan H. Belmont, "Samuel Riley Pierce, Jr.," January 8, 1964. For a periodization of the Bureau's campaign against King, see Garrow, *The F.B.I. and Martin Luther King Jr: From Solo to Memphis*, 100.

34. Unofficial Memo, William C. Sullivan to Alan H. Belmont, "Communist Party, USA, Negro Question; Communist Influence in Racial Matters," September 25, 1963, 100-106670 in *Report of the Department of Justice Task Force to Review the FBI Martin Luther King, Jr., Security and Assassination Investigations*.

35. "Sunday Radio Logs," 1963–1967, *Washington Post, Times Herald*; Transcript of Michaux's sermon in *John F. Kennedy Presidential Library: The White House Central Files, Series, Human Rights—Equality of the Races: Federal Government—Organizations, March on Washington, Folder: Gen Hu 2/Fg*. Several white evangelicals including Billy Graham joined Michaux in this view. See, for example, Steven P. Miller, *Billy Graham and the Rise of the Republican South* (Philadelphia: University of Pennsylvania Press, 2009); Curtis Evans, "White Evangelical Protestant Responses to the Civil Rights Movement."

36. The transcript of King's speech is available at the King Center archives; see http://www.thekingcenter.org/archive/document/mlk-addresses-national-association-radio-announcers#. See also Martin Luther King Jr., "Transcript: Transforming a Neighborhood into a Brotherhood, Recorded Live by R.C.A. Records at the National Association of Television and Radio Announcers Convention–R.C.A. Dinner, Atlanta, Friday August 11, 1967," *Jack the Rapper* 13, no. 666 (January 11, 1989). Only CBS carried live television coverage of the MOW, but only the speeches were televised live; not even the musical performance of Bob Dylan made the live broadcast. Later, NBC and ABC televised heavily edited recaps of the MOW. King's speech gradually grew in cultural significance. On the importance of radio during the Civil Rights Movement, see Brian Ward, *Radio and the Struggle for Civil Rights in the South* (Gainesville: University Press of Florida, 2004).

37. Letter from Michaux, Washington DC, to President John F. Kennedy, The White House, September 25, 1963, in *John F. Kennedy Presidential Library: The White House Central Files, Series, Human Rights—Equality of the Races: Federal Government—Organizations, March on Washington, Folder: Gen Hu 2/Fg*.

38. Transcript, "Louis Martin Oral History Interview I," 5/14/69, by David G. McComb; Transcript, "Louis Martin Oral History Interview II," 6/12/86, by Michael L. Gillette, Electronic Copies LBJ Library; *New York Times*, "Louis E. Martin, 84, Aide to 3 Democratic Presidents,"

January 30, 1997; Simeon Booker, "New Negro Power Structure in D.C.," *Jet* 27, no. 17 (February 1965), 21. Memo, Louis Martin, Deputy Chairman, Democratic National Committee to Lee C. White, December 4, 1963, *John F. Kennedy Presidential Library: The White House Central Files, Series, Human Rights—Equality of the Races: Federal Government—Organizations, March on Washington, Folder: Gen Hu 2/Fg.* Martin successfully advised Johnson to nominate Robert Weaver as the first African American to hold a cabinet level position in the White House (the first Secretary of Housing and Urban Development), Thurgood Marshall as the first Black Supreme Court justice, and St. Louis native Frankie Freeman as the first Black woman appointed to the US Commission on Civil Rights. For more on Freeman see her autobiography, Frankie Muse Freeman and Candace O'Connor, *A Song of Faith and Hope: The Life of Frankie Muse Freeman* (St. Louis: Missouri Historical Society Press: Distributed by University of Missouri Press, 2003).

39. On wiretaps and bugs, see US Senate Select Committee to Study Governmental Operations with Respect to Intelligence Activities, *Final Report of the Senate Select Committee to Study Governmental Operations with Respect to Intelligence Activities, Supplementary Detailed Staff Reports on Intelligence Activities and the Rights of Americans, Book 3,* 115–123.

40. On Special Agent Joseph A. Sizoo, see Obituary in *Washington Post,* September 1, 1995, https://www.washingtonpost.com/archive/local/1995/09/01/joseph-sizoo-fbi-official-dies -at-age-85/4af12c3b-458f-494a-ae1b-6355a76d79d0/?noredirect=on, accessed September 17, 2019; FBI Memo, "Questions to be explored at Conference 12/23/1963 Re: Communist influence in racial matters," Undated, not-recorded in 100-3-116; Letterhead Memo, SA Sullivan to SA Belmont, December 24, 1963, 100-3-116-684.

41. *New York Times,* November 19, 1962, 21; Transcript, Cartha D. "Deke" DeLoach Oral History Interview I, 1/11/91, Michael L. Gillette, Electronic Copy, *LBJ Library.* See also *Washington Post, Times Herald,* November 19, 1964, A1; Garrow, *The F.B.I. and Martin Luther King Jr: From Solo to Memphis,* 54–55, 122–127; James Phelan, "Hoover of the FBI," *Saturday Evening Post,* September 25, 1965, 23–33.

42. For one example of Hoover's indirect rebukes of King, see J. Edgar Hoover, "The Role of the F.B.I. in Civil Rights Disputes," *Yale Political,* no. 2 (August 1963): 12, 31–32; *New York Times,* September 23, 1964, 40.

43. Transcript, Cartha D. "Deke" DeLoach Oral History Interview I, 1/11/91, Michael L. Gillette, Electronic Copy, *LBJ Library;* Nicholas deB. Katzenbach, testimony, "Hearings Before the Senate Select Committee to Study Governmental Operations with Respect to Intelligence Activities of US Senate 94th Congress, Vol. 6," 1975, 209; William C. Sullivan and Bill Brown, *The Bureau: My Thirty Years in Hoover's F.B.I.* (New York: W.W. Norton, 1979), 139; Paul Letersky and Gordon Dillow, *The Director: My Years Assisting J. Edgar Hoover* (New York and London: Scribner, 2021), 220; Hoover to Sullivan, Personal Letter, November 19, 1964, published in *Washington Post,* December 13, 2017, https://www.washingtonpost.com/amphtml/news/retropolis /wp/2017/12/13/an-old-letter-sheds-light-on-fbis-malice-toward-martin-luther-king-jr/ ?noredirect=on, accessed July 10, 2018; Hoover, "Off the Record Remarks at Informal FBI Reception for Editors Georgia and Michigan Newspapers Thursday April 15, 1965," Office of Congressional and Public Affairs, Kenneth O'Reilly Research Materials 1922–1991, Series 90, FBI Investigation and Surveillance Records, Special Collections and University Archives, Marquette

University; Milton A. Jones, "The Story of My Life," 88; Cartha D. DeLoach, *Hoover's FBI*, 206. See also *Washington Post, Times Herald*, November 19, 1964, A1; Garrow, *The F.B.I. and Martin Luther King Jr: From Solo to Memphis*, 122–127; Liddy, *Will*, 96; on Hoover's penchant for holding grudges and his obsession with winning any and all debates, see his biographer, Richard Gid Powers, *Secrecy and Power*. King also publicly criticized Hoover in May 1964. See, for example, *Norfolk Journal and Guide*, May 2, 1964, 10.

44. "Statement re: J. Edgar Hoover," Records of the Southern Christian Leadership Conference, 1954–1970, Records of the President's Office, Folder 27:41 November 1964, King Library and Archive at the Martin Luther King, Jr. Center for Non-Violent Social Change in Atlanta, Georgia; also reprinted in King to J. Edgar Hoover, Western Union Telegram, November 19, 1964, in Michael Friedly, *Martin Luther King, Jr.: The FBI File*, ed. David Gallen, 1st ed. (New York: Carroll & Graf, 1993), 272; *Washington Post, Times Herald*, November 20, 1964, A2; *U.S. News and World Report*, "Martin Luther King's Reaction," November 30, 1964, 58.

45. US Senate Select Committee to Study Governmental Operations with Respect to Intelligence Activities, *Final Report of the Senate Select Committee to Study Governmental Operations with Respect to Intelligence Activities, Supplementary Detailed Staff Reports on Intelligence Activities and the Rights of Americans, Book 3*, 160–161; Sullivan and Brown, *The Bureau*, 142; Garrow, *The F.B.I. and Martin Luther King Jr: From Solo to Memphis*, 124–126; Ward Churchill and Jim Vander Wall, *The Cointelpro Papers: Documents from the F.B.I.'s Secret Wars Against Domestic Dissent* (Boston, MA: South End Press, 1990), 97. For the story of one of King's purported paramours, see Georgia Davis Powers, *I Shared the Dream*, 1st ed. (Far Hills, NJ: New Horizon Press, 1995). The entirety of the FBI's letter to King was recently discovered by Beverly Gage and reprinted in *The New York Times Sunday Magazine*: Beverly Gage, "What an Uncensored Letter to M.L.K. Reveals," *New York Times*, November 11, 2014, sec. Magazine, accessed November, 16 2014, https://www.nytimes.com/2014/11/16/magazine/what-an-uncensored-letter-to -mlk-reveals.html.

46. FBI Memo, December 1, 1964, in Friedly, *Martin Luther King, Jr.*, 280–283; Sullivan and Brown, *The Bureau*, 142; Garrow, *The F.B.I. and Martin Luther King Jr: From Solo to Memphis*, 124–126. The Southern Regional Council did indeed release a statement supporting King; see the front page of the *Norfolk Journal and Guide*, November 28, 1964. A. Phillip Randolph, Whitney Young of the Urban League, Dorothy Height of the NCNW, NAACP head Roy Wilkins, and CORE's James Farmer also publicly expressed their support of King and also met with President Johnson. See *Norfolk Journal and Guide*, November 21, 1964, C1. Soon after, however, Wilkins appeared on CBS's *Face the Nation*, and called Hoover "a good public servant" and that a call for his dismissal was unnecessary because Hoover had enjoyed a "long and distinguished career." See *Washington Post, Times Herald*, November 23, 1964, A8; *The Hartford Courant*, November 26, 1964, 26. Noted Mississippi minister Ed King led a "bi-racial" coalition supporting King and calling for Hoover's resignation. See *Norfolk Journal and Guide*, November 28, 1964, A17.

47. Memorandum, C. D. DeLoach, Washington, DC, to Mr. Mohr, Washington, DC, November 23, 1964, Elder L. S. Michaux, Bureau File 94-HQ-4-2848-27; Memo, M. A. Jones to Mr. DeLoach, February 24, 1965, Elder Michaux Negro Religious Leader, Washington, DC, Bureau File 94-HQ-4-2848-32.

48. Memo, Jones to DeLoach, "Elder Michaux Negro Religious Leader Washington D.C.," February 2, 1965, 94-4-2848-32; Transcript, Cartha D. "Deke" DeLoach Oral History Interview I, 1/11/91, Michael L. Gillette, Electronic Copy, *LBJ Library*; Transcript, Lee C. White Oral History Interview II, 2/18/1971, by Joe B. Frantz, Electronic Copy, *LBJ Library*; Transcript, Interview of Former Deputy Director of the FBI Cartha D. "Deke" DeLoach, by David G. Binney, May 1, 2007, Electronic Copy, Society of Former Special Agents of the FBI, Inc. Oral History Program; Sullivan and Brown, *The Bureau*, 61–70; Will Haygood, "The Man From Jet," *Washington Post*, July 15, 2007, sec. *Washington Post Magazine*. On Crime Records Division, see Ann Mari Buitrago and Leon Andrew Immerman, *Are You Now or Have You Ever Been in the F.B.I Files? How to Secure and Interpret Your F.B.I. Files* (New York: Grove Press, 1981), 171.

49. See US Senate Select Committee to Study Governmental Operations with Respect to Intelligence Activities, *Final Report of the Senate Select Committee to Study Governmental Operations with Respect to Intelligence Activities, Supplementary Detailed Staff Reports on Intelligence Activities and the Rights of Americans, Book 3*, 152; Garrow, *The F.B.I. and Martin Luther King Jr: From Solo to Memphis*, 124–126; Howard Bray, *The Pillars of the Post: The Making of a News Empire in Washington* (New York: W. W. Norton, 1984), 109–110; James F. Findlay, Jr., *Church People in the Struggle: The National Council of Churches and the Black Freedom Movement, 1950–1970*, paperback ed. (New York: Oxford University Press, 1997), 87–88.

50. Memo, CD DeLoach to Mr. Mohr, "Elder L.S. Michaux," November 23, 1964. Bureau File, 94-HQ-4-2848-27.

51. *Sword of Loyola* Program, November 24, 1964 in J. Edgar Hoover Personal Estate Collection, National Law Enforcement Museum, Washington, DC; "Hoover's Sword of Loyola, 1964," *Loyola University Chicago Digital Special Collections*, accessed December 18, 2014, http://www .lib.luc.edu/specialcollections/exhibits/show/loyola-traditions/item/320; *New York Times*, September 23, 1964, 40; November 25, 1964, 74; *Chicago Daily Defender*, November 25, 1964, 3.

52. Speech reprinted in *Congressional Record Appendix*, February 4, 1965. 111th Congress, Record A511.

53. On Reverend Archibald Carey, see, Dickerson, *African American Preachers and Politics*. See the similar accounts of the meeting in United States Senate Select Committee to Study Governmental Operations with Respect to Intelligence Activities, 164-168; Letterhead Memo, DeLoach to Mohr, "Martin Luther King Appointment with Director 3:35pm, 12-1-64," December 2, 1964, and Letter, J. Edgar Hoover to President Johnson, December 2, 1964, both in Friedly, *Martin Luther King, Jr.*, 294–307; Transcript, Andrew J. Young, Jr., Oral History Interview I, 6/18/70, by Thomas H. Baker, Electronic Copy, LBJ Library; Transcript, Cartha D. "Deke" DeLoach Oral History Interview I, 1/11/91, Michael L. Gillette, Electronic Copy, LBJ Library; Cartha D. DeLoach, *Hoover's FBI*, 210; Sullivan and Brown, *The Bureau*, 101, 140; *Washington Post, Times Herald*, December 2, 1964, A1 and December 5, 1964, E15; James Phelan, "Hoover of the FBI," *Saturday Evening Post*, September 25, 1965, 23–33. See also Garrow, *The F.B.I. and Martin Luther King Jr: From Solo to Memphis*, 122–124, 129–130, 271.

54. Letterhead Memo, DeLoach to Mohr, "Martin Luther King Appointment with Director 3:35pm, 12-1-64," December 2, 1964, and Letter, J. Edgar Hoover to President Johnson, December 2, 1964, both in Friedly, *Martin Luther King, Jr.*, 294–307; Hoover, "Off the Record Remarks at Informal FBI Reception for Editors Georgia and Michigan Newspapers Thursday April 15,

1965," Office of Congressional and Public Affairs, Kenneth O'Reilly Research Materials 1922–1991, Series 90, FBI Investigation and Surveillance Records, Special Collections and University Archives, Marquette University; Letersky and Dillow, *The Director*, 41; Dean Fischer, "J. Edgar Hoover Speaks Out with Vigor." FBI phone taps revealed that King said of his meeting with Hoover, "the old man talks too much." See Sullivan and Brown, *The Bureau*, 140–141. On Hoover's flags, see *The New Yorker*, "The Director, Part 1," September 25, 1937. On Hoover's Bible, see Gentry, *J. Edgar Hoover: The Man and the Secrets*, 384. On Hoover's monologues, see, for example, James Phelan, "Hoover of the FBI," *Saturday Evening Post*, September 25, 1965, 23–33.

55. Letterhead Memo, DeLoach to Mohr, "Martin Luther King Appointment with Director 3:35pm, 12-1-64," December 2, 1964 and Letter, J. Edgar Hoover to President Johnson, December 2, 1964, both in Friedly, *Martin Luther King, Jr.*, 294–307; Dean Fischer, "J. Edgar Hoover Speaks Out with Vigor"; Sullivan and Brown, *The Bureau*, 140–141; Gentry, *J. Edgar Hoover: The Man and the Secrets*, 384; James Phelan, "Hoover of the FBI," *Saturday Evening Post*, September 25, 1965, 23–33. See King's *Letter from Birmingham Jail*, April 16, 1963.

56. *Washington Post, Times Herald*, December 2, 1964, A1 and December 5, 1964, E15; also in Friedly, *Martin Luther King, Jr.*, 291. On McCartney, see Garrow, *The F.B.I. and Martin Luther King Jr: From Solo to Memphis*, 130.

57. US Senate Select Committee to Study Governmental Operations with Respect to Intelligence Activities, 82.

58. Memo, CD DeLoach to Mr. Mohr, "Elder Michaux Negro Religious Leader," December 9, 1964. Bureau File 94-HQ-4-2848.

59. Some newspapers did mention the letter, but no major paper published it in full. See, for example, the front page of the *Norfolk Journal and Guide*, January 9, 1965, 1 and *Washington Post, Times Herald*, December 23, 1964, C1. The full letter is contained in Bureau File 94-HQ-2848-29. On Bureau report, see Garrow, *The F.B.I. and Martin Luther King Jr: From Solo to Memphis*, 133.

60. Letter, Michaux to Martin Luther King, December 22, 1964, Bureau File 94-HQ-2848-29.

61. Letter, Michaux to Martin Luther King, December 22, 1964, Bureau File 94-HQ-2848-29; James Phelan, "Hoover of the FBI," *Saturday Evening Post*, September 25, 1965.

62. Letter, Michaux to Martin Luther King, December 22, 1964, Bureau File 94-HQ-2848-29.

63. Letter, Michaux to Martin Luther King, December 22, 1964, Bureau File 94-HQ-2848-29.

64. Memo, CD DeLoach to Mr. Mohr, "Elder L. S. Michaux," November 23, 1964. Bureau File, 94-HQ-4-2848-27; see also FBIHQ 105-340953. In addition to the FBI's civil rights activities, DeLoach also provided Michaux with the "current home address" of his old friend and ally, Special Agent Louis Nichols. See Letter, CD DeLoach to Elder Lightfoot Solomon Michaux, November 30, 1964, Bureau File 94-HQ-42848-26; Letter, Michaux to Martin Luther King, December 22, 1964, Bureau File 94-HQ-2848-29; Letter, J. Edgar Hoover to Michaux, January 4, 1965, Bureau File 94-HQ-42848-30.

65. Memo, CD De Loach to Mr. Hoover, December 23, 1964, Bureau File 94-HQ-4-2848-29.

66. *Washington Post, Times Herald*, January 4, 1965, A-20; also in Bureau File 94-4-2848-30.

67. Letter, J. Edgar Hoover to Elder Lightfoot Solomon Michaux, January 4, 1965, Bureau File 94-4-2848-30.

68. Memo, M. A. Jones to Mr. DeLoach, Feburary 24, 1965, Elder Michaux Negro Religious Leader Washington DC, Bureau File 94-HQ-4-2848-32; US Senate Select Committee to Study Governmental Operations with Respect to Intelligence Activities, *Final Report of the Senate Select Committee to Study Governmental Operations with Respect to Intelligence Activities, Supplementary Detailed Staff Reports on Intelligence Activities and the Rights of Americans, Book 3*, 120. On Michaux's admittance to receiving letters that "applauded King," see Parke Rouse Jr., "Happy Am I!," *The Commonwealth* (July 1965), 30–33.

69. Letter, J. Edgar Hoover to Elder Lightfoot Solomon Michaux, February 24, 1965, Bureau File 94-4-2848-31.

70. *Afro-American*, February 6, 1965, 5.

71. *The Chicago Defender*, May 1, 1965, 8.

72. *Norfolk Journal and Guide*, March 13, 1965, 9.

73. *The Chicago Defender*, January 2, 1965, 9.

74. *New York Times*, April 2, 1965, 24; *Los Angeles Times*, April 2, 1965, 2; Martin Luther King Jr., "Let My People Vote," and in "Records of the Southern Christian Leadership Conference, 1954-1970, Part 1: Records of the President's Office, Folder: 27:35, May 1964—School Desegregation, a Few Years After. King Library and Archive at the Martin Luther King, Jr. Center for Nonviolent Social Change in Atlanta, Georgia."

75. *New York Times*, April 2, 1965, 24; *Afro-American*, April 10, 1965, 1; Internal Security Memo, US Department of Justice, FBI Baltimore, Maryland, April 5, 1965, Reverend Lightfoot Solomon Michaux, Bureau File 100-442529896; Hoover, "Off the Record Remarks at Informal FBI Reception for Editors Georgia and Michigan Newspapers Thursday April 15, 1965," Office of Congressional and Public Affairs, Kenneth O'Reilly Research Materials 1922–1991, Series 90, FBI Investigation and Surveillance Records, Special Collections and University Archives, Marquette University. The *Afro-American* stated the protest was smaller than one hundred. I have chosen to go with the estimates of the *New York Times* and the FBI field report, as their estimates agree.

76. *New York Times*, April 2, 1965, 24, emphasis mine. Internal Security Memo, US Department of Justice, FBI Baltimore, Maryland, April 5, 1965, Reverend Lightfoot Solomon Michaux, Bureau File 100-442529896; Afro-American, April 10, 1965, 1.

77. Hoover, "Off the Record Remarks at Informal FBI Reception for Editors Georgia and Michigan Newspapers Thursday April 15, 1965," Office of Congressional and Public Affairs, Kenneth O'Reilly Research Materials 1922–1991, Series 90, FBI Investigation and Surveillance Records, Special Collections and University Archives, Marquette University. On wiretaps and the Bureau's shift in focus, see US Senate Select Committee to Study Governmental Operations with Respect to Intelligence Activities, *Final Report of the Senate Select Committee to Study Governmental Operations with Respect to Intelligence Activities, Supplementary Detailed Staff Reports on Intelligence Activities and the Rights of Americans, Book 3*, 116, 121. On James Harrison, see Paul Good, "An Uneasy Life for Man who Spied on King," *Atlanta Journal-Constitution*, November 16, 1980, 1A, 16A; Garrow, *The F.B.I. and Martin Luther King Jr: From Solo to Memphis*, 174–175, 286 n.2.

78. Letterhead Memo, SA DeLoach to SA Mohr, May 19, 1965, 161-2040-30.

79. *Washington Post, Times Herald,* Feb 17, 1965, A8. 21% were not sure, while 13% agreed with neither. Hoover to Sullivan, Personal Letter, November 19, 1964, published in *Washington Post,* December 13, 2017, https://www.washingtonpost.com/amphtml/news/retropolis /wp/2017/12/13/an-old-letter-sheds-light-on-fbis-malice-toward-martin-luther-king-jr/ ?noredirect=on, accessed July 10, 2018. King's overall public approval rating continued to decline. It dipped tremendously when he publicly condemned America's involvement in the Vietnam War. At the SCLC Convention on August 12, 1965, King made a conciliatory and tepid statement calling for an end to war in Vietnam, noting there was no "blame" to be had. However, he infamously indicted US involvement in Vietnam at New York's Riverside Church on April 4, 1967. See 1965 statement at http://kingencyclopedia.stanford.edu/encyclopedia /documentsentry/statement_by_king_at_the_sclc_convention.1.html. See 1967 sermon at: http://kingencyclopedia.stanford.edu/kingweb/publications/speeches/Beyond _Vietnam.pdf.

80. Personal Letter, Jim Hiskey to Hoover, November 22, 1964, 94-HQ-50997-illegible. Hiskey went on to work with the National Prayer Breakfast as well as the PGA Tour Fellowship and its Christian testimonial, the *Links Letter,* as well as the C. S. Lewis Institute.

81. *Christianity Today,* December 4, 1964; 94-51060-158, enclosure. SA Jones to SA Wick, June 7, 1967, 94-51060-168.

82. Milton A. Jones, "The Story of My Life," 88.

83. Memo, Jones to DeLoach, "District of Columbia Crime Commission," May 13, 1965, 62-110232-6; Hoover to Attorney General, "District of Columbia Crime Commission Suggested List of Names," May 14, 1965, 62-110232-3; *Washington Post, Times Herald,* July 17, 1965, A1, A5. Johnson, despite Hoover's recommendation, did not choose the preacher.

84. On Black COINTELPRO, see Director to SAC Albany, Counter-Intelligence Program Black Nationalist-Hate Groups Internal Security, August 25, 1967, 100-448006-1, and Airtel Memo, Director to SAC Albany, "Counter-Intelligence Program Black Nationalist-Hate Groups Racial Intelligence," March 4, 1968, 100-448006-17, both in Churchill and Vander Wall, *The Cointelpro Papers: Documents from the F.B.I's Secret Wars against Domestic Dissent,* 92, 108–11. On the Bureau's renewed effort to recruit "racial informants," see FBI Internal Monograph, *Development of Racial Informants,* September 1967. On the death of Mrs. Michaux, see *Washington Post, Times Herald,* October 29, 1967, D4; Letter, J. Edgar Hoover to Michaux, Washington, DC, October 30, 1967. Elder Lightfoot Solomon Michaux File, Bureau File 94-4-2848-34.

85. Letersky and Dillow, *The Director,* 84.

86. "Retired Special Agent William Arthur Murtaugh FBI Interview," Transcript, May 7, 1980, 2, Jack Willis Collection, Library Department of Special Collections, Washington University in Saint Louis; Television interview, Retired SA Arthur Murtaugh. *ABC Thursday Night Special: Who Killed Martin Luther King,"* 1977, https://www.youtube.com/watch?v=NmwiQq5L -0M, accessed May 10, 2021.

87. *Afro-American,* September 7, 1968, A1; *Washington Post, Times Herald,* October 21, 1968, A1; October 22, 1968, B4; October 28, 1968, B8; *Journal and Guide,* November 2, 1968, B27; Airtel Memo, Director to SAC Albany, "Counter-Intelligence Program Black Nationalist-Hate Groups Racial Intelligence," March 4, 1968, 100-448006-17 in Churchill and Vander Wall, *The Cointelpro*

Papers: Documents from the F.B.I.'s Secret Wars against Domestic Dissent, 108–111; Letter, J. Edgar Hoover to Ruth Michaux, Washington, DC, October 21, 1968. Elder Lightfoot Solomon Michaux File, Bureau File 94-4-2848-35, emphasis mine. *Journal and Guide*, Nov 2, 1968, B27.

Epilogue: Stained (Glass) Legacy

1. *The Temple News*, November 14, 2017, https://temple-news.com/former-religion-professor
-activist-john-raines-dies-at-84/, accessed June 24, 2020; *Washington Post*, March 24, 1971, A1;
Capitol Hill Spectator, March 25, 1971 enclosed in Bureau File, 94-55180-13. For a fuller look at
the break-in, see Betty Medsger, *The Burglary: The Discovery of J. Edgar Hoover's Secret FBI* (New
York: Knopf, 2014); see also the documentary film, Johanna Hamilton, *1971*, 2014, https://www
.1971film.com. Betty Medsger's bio and career timeline can be found at https://investigatingpower
.org/betty-medsger/, accessed June 29, 2020.

2. Hoover note on Bureau File, 94-55180-13; Letterhead Memorandum, SA Jones to SA
Bishop, March 30, 1971, 94-55180-14.

3. Letterhead Memorandum, SA Jones to SA Bishop, March 30, 1971, 94-55180-14. The author
last visited the church in the summer of 2019.

4. *Washington Post, Times Herald*, "The Harris Survey," May 6, 1971, A22; Letterhead Memo,
SA Jones to SA Bishop, June 8, 1971, 94-51060-209.

5. Richard Hack, *Puppetmaster: The Secret Life of J. Edgar Hoover* (Beverly Hills, CA: Phoenix
Books, 2007), 1–25; Paul Letersky and Gordon Dillow, *The Director: My Years Assisting J. Edgar
Hoover* (New York; London: Scribner, 2021), xi–xviii, 231–250.

6. Funeral Program, Services for the Honorable J. Edgar Hoover, Thursday, May 4, 1972, 11
O'clock, The National Presbyterian Church, Washington, DC, The Ervin N. Chapman Memo-
rial Archives, The William Smith Culbertson Memorial Library, The National Presbyterian
Church, Washington, DC; *Memorial Tributes to J. Edgar Hoover in the Congress of the United
States and Various Articles and Editorials Relating to His Life and Work*, 93rd Congress, 2nd Sess.,
Senate Document 93-68, Senate Concurrent Resolution 64 and House Joint Resolution 64
(Washington, DC: Government Printing Office, 1974); Hack, *Puppetmaster*, 1–25; US House of
Representatives, "Individuals Who Have Lain in State or Honor," https://history.house.gov
/Institution/Lie-In-State/Lie-In-State/, accessed June 23, 2020; Michal R. Belknap, "Secrets of
the Boss's Power: Two Views of J. Edgar Hoover," *Law and Social Inquiry* 14, no. 4 (Autumn
1989): 823–838; Letersky and Dillow, *The Director*, xi–xviii, 231–250.

7. Funeral Program, Services for the Honorable J. Edgar Hoover, Thursday, May 4, 1972, 11
O'clock, The National Presbyterian Church, Washington, DC, The Ervin N. Chapman Memo-
rial Archives, The William Smith Culbertson Memorial Library, The National Presbyterian
Church, Washington, DC; Hack, *Puppetmaster*, 1–25; US House of Representatives, "Individuals
Who Have Lain in State or Honor," https://history.house.gov/Institution/Lie-In-State/Lie-In
-State/, accessed June 23, 2020; Belknap, "Secrets of the Boss's Power," 823–838; Letersky and
Dillow, *The Director*, xi–xviii, 231–250.

8. Letersky and Dillow, *The Director*, xi–xviii, 231–250.

9. *Memorial Tributes to J. Edgar Hoover in the Congress of the United States and Various Articles
and Editorials Relating to His Life and Work*, 93rd Congress 2nd Sess., Senate Document 93-68,

Senate Concurrent Resolution 64 and House Joint Resolution 64 (Washington, DC: Government Printing Office, 1974); Hack, *Puppetmaster*, 7; Letersky and Dillow, *The Director*, xi–xviii, 231–250.

10. *Memorial Tributes to J. Edgar Hoover in the Congress of the United States and Various Articles and Editorials Relating to His Life and Work*, 93rd Congress 2nd Sess., Senate Document 93-68, Senate Concurrent Resolution 64 and House Joint Resolution 64 (Washington, D.C: Government Printing Office, 1974), emphasis mine. Hack, *Puppetmaster*, 7; Letersky and Dillow, *The Director*, xi–xviii, 231–250.

11. Funeral Program, Services for the Honorable J. Edgar Hoover, Thursday, May 4, 1972, 11 O'clock, The National Presbyterian Church, Washington, DC, The Ervin N. Chapman Memorial Archives, The William Smith Culbertson Memorial Library, The National Presbyterian Church, Washington, DC; *Memorial Tributes to J. Edgar Hoover in the Congress of the United States and Various Articles and Editorials Relating to His Life and Work*, 93rd Congress, 2nd Sess., Senate Document 93-68, Senate Concurrent Resolution 64 and House Joint Resolution 64 (Washington, DC: Government Printing Office, 1974); Letersky and Dillow, *The Director*, xi–xviii, 231–250.

12. *The Pentecostal Evangel*, May 26, 1972, 4; January 14, 1973.

13. *Christianity Today*, "Future of the FBI," May 26, 1972.

14. See Frank Church—Chairman United States Senate Select Committee to Study Governmental Operations with Respect to Intelligence Activities, *Final Report of the Senate Select Committee to Study Governmental Operations with Respect to Intelligence Activities, Supplementary Detailed Staff Reports on Intelligence Activities and the Rights of Americans, Book 3* (Washington, DC: US Government Printing Office, April 23, 1976).

15. On how the military's management of faith helped to shape and make America's modern religious landscape, see Ronit Stahl, *Enlisting Faith: How the Military Chaplaincy Shaped Religion and State in Modern America* (Cambridge, MA; London: Harvard University Press, 2017).

16. Father Daniel Berrigan, SJ, *America Is Hard to Find* (New York: Doubleday, 1972), 120–127.

17. FBI News, "Moving the Diversity Needle," February 26, 2021, https://www.fbi.gov/news/stories/fbis-first-chief-diversity-officer-a-tonya-odom-reflects-on-tenure-022621, accessed June 2, 2021. FBI News, "Celebrating Women Special Agents," July 17, 2012, https://www.fbi.gov/news/stories/celebrating-women-special-agents-part-2, accessed June 2021; FBI News, "Our History, Our Service: The First African-American Female Special Agent," March 28, 2019, https://www.fbi.gov/news/stories/our-history-our-service-sylvia-mathis-first-african-american-female-special-agent-032819, accessed November 8, 2021; Author Interview with Retired SA Linda Berry, October 11, 2017, Phone; "Former Black special agents say FBI's culture is 'not conducive to minorities,'" *CBS News*, https://www.cbsnews.com/news/fbi-culture-minorities-black-special-agent/, accessed December 21, 2021; Jim Mustian and Eric Tucker, "We mean it: FBI takes on sexual misconduct in its ranks," *PBS New Hour*, https://www.pbs.org/newshour/politics/we-mean-it-fbi-takes-on-sexual-misconduct-in-its-ranks, accessed December 21, 2021.

18. J. Michael Kenndy and William Overend, "FBI Discriminated Against Latino Agents, Judge Rules," *LA Times*, October 1, 1988, https://www.latimes.com/archives/la-xpm-1988-10

-01-mn-4259-story.html, accessed December 21, 2021; Eric Lichtblau, "FBI Settles Black Agent's Discrimination Lawsuit," *LA Times*, May 1, 2001, https://www.latimes.com/archives/la-xpm-2001-may-01-mn-57894-story.html, accessed December 21, 2021; FBI News, "Moving the Diversity Needle," February 26, 2021, https://www.fbi.gov/news/stories/fbis-first-chief-diversity-officer-a-tonya-odom-reflects-on-tenure-022621, accessed June 2, 2021; FBI News, "Celebrating Women Special Agents," July 17, 2012, https://www.fbi.gov/news/stories/celebrating-women-special-agents-part-2, accessed June 2021.

19. Janet Reitman, "I Helped Destroy People," *New York Times Magazine*, September 5, 2021. The Bureau has relaunched and rebranded its targeted HBCU recruitment efforts, "The Beacon Project." See *FBI News*, https://www.fbi.gov/video-repository/beacon-090721.mp4/view.

20. See FBI File, 94-HQ-46705; *NPR News*, "FBI Invited Controversial Church to Talk to FBI Agents," June 29, 2011, https://www.npr.org/2011/06/29/137454497/fbi-invited-controversial-church-to-talk-to-agents, accessed July 27, 2021.

21. *FBI News*, https://www.fbi.gov/about/community-outreach/dcla/2018/norfolk-dr-antipas-harris, accessed December 21, 2021.

22. Retired FBI Special Agent Frank Burton Jr., *From FBI Agent to an Apostle: Saga of a Spiritual Sniper* (Xulon Elite, 2015).

23. Ibid.

24. Trevor Aaronson, "Capitol Rioter Admits False Statements to FBI, But Prosecutors Haven't Charged Him with Felony," *The Intercept*, January 3, 2022; FBI Counterterrorism Division, FBI Intelligence Assessment: "Black Identity Extremists Likely Motivated to Target Law Enforcement Officers," August 3, 2017; "Among Those Who Marched into the Capitol on Jan. 6: An F.B.I. Informant," *New York Times*, September 29, 2021, https://www.nytimes.com/2021/09/25/us/politics/capitol-riot-fbi-informant.html, accessed October 6, 2021; The Council of Foreign Relations, *Terrorism by the Numbers*, https://world101.cfr.org/global-era-issues/terrorism/terrorism-numbers, accessed December 21, 2021; Janet Reitman, "US Law Enforcement Failed to See the Threat of White Nationalism . . ." *New York Times Magazine*, November 3, 2018, https://www.nytimes.com/2018/11/03/magazine/FBI-charlottesville-white-nationalism-far-right.html, accessed December 21, 2021.

25. "Tribute to the Honorable John Edgar Hoover by The Reverend Dr. Edward L. R. Elson, Chaplain of the US Senate, Dedication Ceremonies, The FBI Building Courtyard, Washington, DC, Saturday October 13, 1979," Record Group 253 Box 10, Folder 1, Reverend Edward L.R. Elson Papers, 1924-1988, Presbyterian Historical Society Archives, Philadelphia, PA.

Abridged Archival Sources

Archives of the Archdiocese of New York
Francis Cardinal Spellman Collection
Billy Graham Center Archives, Wheaton College, Wheaton, Illinois
    Records of the Billy Graham Evangelistic Association
Georgetown University Special Collections
    Woodstock Letters, Jesuit Archives Digital Collections and Resources, Woodstock College
        (Woodstock, Maryland)
    Special Collections, Woodstock Theological Library
    Archives of the Maryland Province of the Society of Jesus
    Stephen F. McNamee, SJ Papers
Congressman Kenneth B. Keating Collection, Department of Rare Books, Special Collections
    and Preservation, University of Rochester River Campus Libraries
The Ervin N. Chapman Memorial Archives, The William Smith Culbertson Memorial Library,
    The National Presbyterian Church, Washington, DC
Flower Pentecostal Heritage Center, Springfield, Missouri
FBI Files Obtained Under the Freedom of Information Act
Jack Willis Collection, Department of Special Collections, Washington University in Saint
    Louis Libraries
J. Edgar Hoover Personal Estate Collection, National Law Enforcement Museum, Washington, DC
Jesuit Archives and Research Center, St. Louis, Missouri
John F. Kennedy Presidential Library
Records of the Southern Christian Leadership Conference, King Library and Archive at the
    Martin Luther King, Jr. Center for Non-Violent Social Change in Atlanta, Georgia
LBJ Presidential Library
Loyola University Chicago Digital Special Collections
Monsignor W. Ronald Jameson Cathedral Archive, Cathedral of St. Matthew the Apostle, Wash-
    ington, DC
    Father John K. Cartwright Papers
The National Archives and Record Administration II, College Park, Maryland
Record Group 65 FBI Files
The National Archives of the United Kingdom (TNA) Kew, Richmond, England
Presbyterian Historical Society Archives, Philadelphia, Pennsylvania
Raynor Memorial Libraries Special Collections and University Archives, Marquette
    University

Kenneth O'Reilly Research Materials 1922–1991, Series 90, FBI Investigation and Surveillance
    Records
Rhoads Memorial Archives, Mount St. Mary's University, Emmitsburg, Maryland
Society of Former Special Agents of the FBI, Inc. Oral History Program

Author's Oral History Interviews

Ruth Dunham, Interview with Author, Quinn Chapel AME Church Chicago, Illinois, July 1,
    2016
Retired SA Allen (Al) Jordan, FBI Agent 1968–2000, October 17, 2017, telephone
Retired SA Henry Hoffman, February 1, 2018, telephone
Retired SA Charles "Charlie" Wiley, December 11, 2017, telephone
Retired SA Linda Berry, second Black woman through Quantico, October 11, 2017, telephone
Retired FBI Agent Alan Ouimet, June 22, 2020, telephone
Retired SA Jesse House, March 10, 2017, telephone; September 18, 2017, Atlanta, Georgia
Former FBI and CIA Director William Webster, May 25, 2016, telephone
Retired Special Agent in Charge Wayne Davis, October 6, 2015, telephone; November 4, 2016,
    Saint Louis, Missouri

Index

Page numbers in italics indicate illustrations.